DONNE'S AUGUSTINE

Donne's Augustine

Renaissance Cultures of Interpretation

KATRIN ETTENHUBER

OXFORD
UNIVERSITY PRESS

OXFORD
UNIVERSITY PRESS

Great Clarendon Street, Oxford OX2 6DP

Oxford University Press is a department of the University of Oxford.
It furthers the University's objective of excellence in research, scholarship,
and education by publishing worldwide in

Oxford New York

Auckland Cape Town Dar es Salaam Hong Kong Karachi
Kuala Lumpur Madrid Melbourne Mexico City Nairobi
New Delhi Shanghai Taipei Toronto

With offices in

Argentina Austria Brazil Chile Czech Republic France Greece
Guatemala Hungary Italy Japan Poland Portugal Singapore
South Korea Switzerland Thailand Turkey Ukraine Vietnam

Oxford is a registered trade mark of Oxford University Press
in the UK and in certain other countries

Published in the United States
by Oxford University Press Inc., New York

© Katrin Ettenhuber 2011

British Library Cataloguing in Publication Data

Data available

Library of Congress Cataloging in Publication Data

Data available

Typeset by SPI Publisher Services, Pondicherry, India
Printed in Great Britain
on acid-free paper by
MPG Books Group, Bodmin and King's Lynn

ISBN 978–0–19–960910–9

3 5 7 9 10 8 6 4 2

For my parents, and for my brother

Preface

This is a book about the poetics of charity, and in writing it I have incurred many debts to institutions and individuals. I am especially grateful to the Master and Fellows of Christ's College, Cambridge, for their financial and intellectual support. During the nine years I spent there, first as a student and, more recently, as a research fellow, I benefited greatly from the wisdom and example of Richard Axton, Malcolm Bowie, Kelvin Bowkett, Freya Johnston, John Rathmell, David Sedley, and Quentin Skinner. At Christ's, Gavin Alexander first introduced me to Donne, supervised the doctoral thesis which underpins this project, and helped me to become a better reader. Pembroke College, Cambridge, proved an extremely congenial environment in which to complete work on this project, and I am particularly indebted to Mark Wormald and Loraine Gelsthorpe for their kind encouragement when faith was occasionally failing. I have relied far too much on the patience of the staff at Pembroke Library, and especially on Pat Aske, who cheerfully wheeled out the multi-volume folio editions of Augustine's works in the midst of a very busy term.

A number of teachers, colleagues, and friends were kind enough to read and comment upon drafts of particular chapters and of the book as a whole: Colin Burrow, Brian Cummings, Lori Anne Ferrell, Kenneth Fincham, John Kerrigan, Peter McCullough, Anthony Milton, Janel Mueller, Emma Rhatigan, Jeanne Shami, Richard Todd, and Andrew Zurcher. They and others have saved me from many blunders: responsibility for any remaining errors of fact and judgement is of course my own. I would also like to thank the two anonymous readers for Oxford University Press for their immensely helpful advice, and all those involved in the production process. Among the latter, I am grateful to Andrew McNeillie, who first took an interest in this project, and especially to his successor, Jacqueline Baker, who has been extremely supportive in seeing it through to publication. I would also like to thank Ariane Petit, Brendan Mac Evilly, and my exemplary copy-editor Dorothy McCarthy.

Finally, my greatest debt of thanks is to my family, for their forbearance and their willingness to suspend disbelief: to my father, Peter; my brother, Christoph; to Linda and John; to David, without whom none of this could have been done, and, above all, to my mother, Ursula, whom I could not miss more.

Some portions of Chapter 5 appeared as '"Take heed what you heare": Re-reading Donne's Lincoln's Inn Sermons', *John Donne Journal*, 26 (2007), 127–57.

Contents

Note on Texts

For ease of reference, all Augustinian texts are cited from the *Patrologiae cursus completus... series latina*, ed. J.-P. Migne et al., 221 vols (Paris, 1844–1903). I refer to Augustine's works by book and chapter numbers (*Confessions* 11.3 corresponds to Book 11, chapter 3 of that text, for example) and cross-reference to the volume and column numbers of *Patrologia Latina* (*Confessions* 11.3 is referred to as *PL* 32.811). Migne's *Patrologia* is also available online to subscribing institutions, at http://pld.chadwyck.co.uk/.

Many of Migne's texts have been superseded by later scholarship; the best recent editions are published in two series: the *Corpus Scriptorum Ecclesiasticorum Latinorum* (CSEL) and the *Corpus Christianorum, Series Latina* (CC). Full details of Augustine's texts in these editions can be found in the bibliography; Migne's text has been amended where necessary. Readers of the *Confessions* may also wish to refer to James J. O'Donnell's three-volume text and commentary (Oxford, 1992; available as a searchable text online, at http://www.stoa.org/hippo/). The *Corpus Augustinianum Gissense* (CAG 2) is an electronic database which contains all known works by Augustine in the best and most recent editions; at the time of publication, the CAG 2 was only available on CD-ROM.

Donne's poems are cited from the *Complete English Poems*, ed. C. A. Patrides, 2nd edn. (London, 1994). The *Variorum Edition* (Bloomington, Ind., 1995–) will be the definitive text for Donne's poetry; but since the vast majority of the poems cited in this book have yet to appear in the *Variorum* series, and since my quotations are often brief and illustrative, I have used the most accessible edition. Patrides' text, based on the 1633 edition of Donne's *Poems*, is widely available in paperback: I have amended and annotated references as appropriate. My own quotations from the Bible (as opposed to those of my sources) are taken from the *Authorized King James Version*, ed. Robert Carroll and Stephen Prickett (Oxford, 1997).

In quoting from early modern printed books and manuscripts I have retained original spelling and punctuation, except in the case of long 's' and 'vv', which are silently modernized; I have silently lowered raised letters and expanded contractions and abbreviations. Dates are Old Style, except that the year is taken to begin on 1 January rather than on Lady Day, 25 March.

Translations from Augustine's works are my own, except for the *Confessions*, *De Doctrina Christiana*, and *City of God*. The *Confessions* are cited from Henry Chadwick's translation (Oxford, 1991; Oxford World's Classics paperback, 1992); *De Doctrina Christiana* from R. P. H. Green's *On Christian Teaching* (Oxford, 1997); and English references to *City of God* are taken from R. W. Dyson's translation (Cambridge, 1998). Augustine's complete works are being translated in a new series, *The Works of St. Augustine: A Translation for the*

21st Century, edited by John Rotelle, OSA (New York, 1990–). All other translations from ancient and foreign languages are my own, unless specified otherwise.

Brief introductions to Augustine's writings can be found in *Augustine through the Ages: An Encyclopedia*, gen. ed. Allan D. Fitzgerald (Grand Rapids, 1999). For Augustine's biography, see Peter Brown, *Augustine of Hippo* (Berkeley, 1967) and James J. O'Donnell, *Augustine, Sinner and Saint* (London, 2005). Augustine's reception history is the subject of a major research project based at the University of St Andrews and directed by Professor Karla Pollmann ('After Augustine: A Survey of his Reception from 430 to 2000'). The principal outcome of the project will be the multi-volume *Historical Guide to the Reception of Saint Augustine* (Oxford University Press).

Introduction

'I am loath to part from this father, and he is loath to be parted from.'

(Donne on Augustine)[1]

It is difficult to overemphasize the importance of Augustine's writing and influence, both in his own time and in the history of Western thought after it.[2] This influence can be measured in key concepts: we owe to Augustine the idea of original sin, the theory of 'just war', and, according to some scholars, even the invention of the modern self.[3] It can be measured in sheer volume: Augustine wrote nearly five million words during his lifetime, and the medieval theologian Isidore of Seville famously remarked that anyone claiming to have read all of Augustine's works must be a liar, since there was simply too much for a man to plough through in one lifetime.[4] And it can be measured in the sheer intensity of authorial presence constructed by Augustine's best-known text, the *Confessions*—an autobiographical narrative outlining his sinful youth and conversion to Christianity. Augustine invests his analysis of the moral self with a new sense of emotional depth and immediacy; he anatomizes his youthful indiscretions with painful precision, demonstrating a relentless appetite for exposing his own failings and flaws. An iconic episode from Book 2 of the *Confessions*, for instance, recounts the theft of some pears with 'a gang of naughty adolescents': a venial sin, at best, to the average reader, but to Augustine a potent symbol of the depravity of the godless soul. 'It was foul, and I loved it. I loved the self-destruction, I loved my fall, not the object for which I had fallen but my fall itself. My depraved soul leaped down from your firmament to ruin.'[5]

Augustine insists on the exceptional wickedness of his actions as he catalogues the perverse pleasure he derived from a seemingly senseless act: he makes a point

---

[1] *The Sermons of John Donne*, ed. George R. Potter and Evelyn M. Simpson, 10 vols. (Berkeley, 1953–62), 9.102. All subsequent citations from the sermons will be to volume and page number of this edition. Donne's sermons are currently being re-edited in 16 vols. for Oxford University Press under the general editorship of Peter McCullough; the new *Sermons* will provide full annotations on Donne's intellectual influences, including his patristic reading.

[2] Augustine was born at Thagaste in 354; he became Bishop of Hippo in 396 and died there in 430.

[3] See e.g. Phillip Cary, *Augustine's Invention of the Inner Self: The Legacy of a Christian Platonist* (Oxford, 2000).

[4] *Patrologia Latina*, vol. 83, col. 1109A: 'Mentitur, qui te totum legisse fatetur.' All subsequent references to the *Patrologia Latina* will be by volume and column number; all other references to Augustine's works will be by book and chapter numbers.

[5] Augustine *Confessions* 2.4 (*PL* 32.679).

of telling us that he did not consume any of the pears, but stole them 'merely to throw them to the pigs'. But even as he protests the extraordinary nature of his crime, and portrays his teenage self as the chief of sinners, another narrative pattern begins to obtrude itself on the reader's mind. Augustine's account of the theft is saturated with allusions to other texts: there are obvious resonances with the Genesis narrative, although Augustine prefers a different type of fruit, and he also references the Book of Psalms. But, above all, the pear episode is steeped in echoes and citations from Sallust's account of the Catiline conspiracy, the *Bellum Catilinae*. Augustine moves from allusion to citation to overt reference, and concludes his damning self-indictment with a direct comparison: 'not even Catiline himself loved his crimes; something else motivated him to commit them'.[6] He is no ordinary sinner—that much is clear—but instead of asserting rhetorical singularity, Augustine constantly seeks illumination through recourse to other writings: he imposes a pattern on his life by reading it through a series of intertexts. Once his soul is ready, in Book 8, a voice will tell him to 'Pick up and read' the Scriptures, and in the most exalted moments of spiritual communion, Augustine's narrative voice will give way entirely to a tissue of quotations from the Bible.[7] But from the moment he starts to tell his story, Augustine the writer is also Augustine the reader: he achieves understanding and, eventually, faith, through reading, misreading, and re-reading a series of core texts—Virgil, Cicero, Plato, Moses, David, and Paul.

This image of Augustine the reader was crucial to another voracious consumer of books: the poet, controversialist, and preacher John Donne (1572–1631). He too, of course, underwent a remarkable process of transformation: from the well-publicized indiscretion of his clandestine marriage, to a stellar career in the Church of England. Reflecting on the dynamics of sin and forgiveness in a sermon on Psalms 32:1–2 ('Blessed is he whose transgression is forgiven'), Donne invokes the example of Augustine's *Confessions*. Characteristically, he calls his audience's attention to the power of texts to effect spiritual change and regeneration:

> S. *Augustine* confesses, that the reading of *Cicero's Hortensius, Mutavit affectum meum,* began in him a Conversion from the world, *Et ad teipsum, Domine, mutavit preces meas,* That booke, sayes he, converted me to more fervent prayers to thee, my God; *Et surgere jam cœperam ut ad te redirem,* By that help I rose, and came towards thee.[8]

This is a book about how one early modern writer, John Donne, read, absorbed, and re-worked the writings of the most canonical of all Church Fathers, Saint Augustine. Donne was, at least according to his first biographer, uniquely equipped to take on the challenge of Augustine's massive *oeuvre*: Izaak Walton reports that Donne was in his late teens when he began 'seriously to survey and consider the Body of Divinity, as it was then controverted betwixt the Reformed and the *Roman*

---

[6] *Confessions* 2.4–5 (*PL* 32.679–80); on Augustine and Sallust, see James J. O'Donnell (ed.), *Confessions*, 3 vols. (Oxford, 1992), 3.126–34, and Pierre Courcelle, 'Le jeune Augustin, second Catilina', *Revue des Études Anciennes*, 73 (1971), 141–50.

[7] *Confessions* 8.12 (*PL* 32.762): '*Tolle, lege*'.

[8] *Sermons*, 9.253–4; *Confessions* 3.4 (*PL* 32.685).

Church.[9] In the period leading up to the publication of *Pseudo-martyr* in 1610, Donne immersed himself in the corpus of controversial writing surrounding the Oath of Allegiance debate, probably with the benefit of Bishop Morton's library;[10] another burst of scholarly activity is recorded by Walton for the years immediately preceding Donne's ordination in 1615, when 'he applied himself to an incessant study of Textual Divinity'.[11] These projects, and others, provoked endless encounters with Augustine, the most dominant textual presence in sixteenth- and seventeenth-century religious culture, at first hand and through a panoply of medieval and early modern intermediary sources.[12] Donne returned to Augustine's texts throughout his career with almost obsessive frequency: there are more than a thousand acknowledged references to Augustine in the prose works composed between 1607 and 1631, and Donne clocks up citations from sixty-one different Augustinian texts. In the sermons alone, Augustine outstrips any other non-scriptural source by, on average, three to one; of the 160 extant sermons, only five do not mention Augustine at all.[13]

METHODOLOGICAL CONTEXTS

This study is the first sustained account of Donne's reading habits: of the books he consulted in search of Augustinian material, and of the intellectual precepts and procedures that guided him in collecting, digesting, and re-presenting Augustine's texts in his own work. But it also aims to reach out into two fields that are closely related to these concerns: the history of readership and the history of religion. The history of reading practices has received a wealth of attention in recent decades, with the best work focusing either on material objects—libraries, book collecting, book ownership—or on the study of marginalia. Donne's library has mostly languished in the shadows since the compilation of Keynes's bibliography; and appearances of occasional pencil marks in Donne's books merely serve as a painful

---

[9] Izaak Walton, *The Lives of John Donne, Sir Henry Wotton, Richard Hooker, George Herbert and Robert Sanderson*, ed. G. Saintsbury (London, 1925), 25.

[10] On the nature and extent of the debate see R. C. Bald, *John Donne: A Life* (Oxford, 1970), 212–25; Peter Milward, *Religious Controversies of the Jacobean Age* (Lincoln, Nebr., 1978), 89–94; and Johann P. Sommerville, 'John Donne the Controversialist: The Poet as Political Thinker', in David Colclough (ed.), *John Donne's Professional Lives* (Cambridge, 2003), 73–96.

[11] Walton, *Lives*, 46. While Walton is generally acknowledged as a less than reliable source for factual information, Donne's sustained scholarly work is also evident from citations in the earliest sermons, *Pseudo-martyr*, and the *Essayes in Divinity*; see also, on Donne's reading of Bellarmine, Mary Hobbs, '"To a Most Dear Friend"—Donne's Bellarmine', *The Review of English Studies*, NS 32 (1981), 435–8.

[12] Citational practices in the early modern period are the subject of the AHRC project 'Patterns of Reference and Networks of Authority: Classical and Biblical Citations and the Production of a New Canon of Early Modern Culture 1500–1800'. See, for instance, Femke Molekamp, 'Using a Collection to Discover Reading Practices: The British Library Geneva Bibles and a History of their Early Modern Readers', Electronic British Library Journal (2006), art. 10, 1–13; http://www.bl.uk/collections/eblj/2006/pdfarticles/article10.pdf

[13] See *Sermons*, 10.347. For a more detailed breakdown of the statistical evidence, see below, pp. 27–8.

reminder of the copious evidence afforded by other writers, such as the notes and marginalia of Sir William Drake.[14] Donne's reading habits, then, must be inferred from internal evidence: from Augustinian quotations, in Latin and English, embedded in his writings. But since there are more than one thousand quotations to work with, this need not be a disadvantage, either in terms of evidence or approach. In fact, a study of embedded reading can help clarify some of the methodological difficulties that have emerged in the history of the book. We have yet to formulate a coherent framework for the ways in which notes and marginalia—material traces extraneous to the text—relate to the far more dynamic and complex act of reading, for instance: to annotate a book is not the same as to produce a reading of it. Citations, by contrast, are integrated in the target text, and thus allow us to reconstruct processes of selection and transformation more fully: by investigating the place of a reference in the source text, observing changes that occur at the point of extraction, and analysing its new contexts and applications as the quotation is transplanted. All these different stages give indications of a reader's priorities; in the case of religious reading, individual reading acts are also performed against a well-defined background of interpretive precepts and protocols, as we will see.

By positing a model of reading based on the incorporation of other texts, Donne's Augustinian negotiations invoke yet another disciplinary context: intertextuality. The writing that emerges through Donne's dialogue with Augustine is a 'mosaic of quotations', a multi-layered construction of different textual forms, subject to processes of contextual adaptation and transformation.[15] To read Donne's reading of Augustine is not merely to observe the influence of one writer upon another, or the simple transfer of textual authority from a patristic to an early modern text. Quotation in Donne's works is a highly complex and dynamic transaction, in which authority is constantly re-interpreted, re-assigned, retracted, and re-given. As they engage, contest, or impersonate Augustine's multiple voices, Donne's works defy any attempt to define clear textual boundaries. Foucault's description of intertextual exchange in *The Archaeology of Knowledge* provides a useful point of orientation here:

> The frontiers of the book are never clear-cut: beyond the title, the first lines and the last full stop, beyond its internal configuration and its autonomous form, it is caught up in a system of references to other books, other texts, other sentences: it is a node within a network. And this network of references is not the same in the case of a mathematical treatise, a textual commentary, a historical account[.] . . . The book is not simply the object that one holds in one's hands[;] . . . and its unity is variable and relative.[16]

Donne's Augustine is situated precisely within such a network of references, and we have to reconstruct a whole range of synchronic and diachronic intertexts to gauge

[14] Geoffrey Keynes, *A Bibliography of Dr. John Donne, Dean of Saint Paul's*, 4th edn. (Oxford, 1973). On Drake, see Kevin Sharpe's ground-breaking *Reading Revolutions: The Politics of Reading in Early Modern England* (New Haven, 2000).
[15] Julia Kristeva, 'Word, Dialog and Novel', in *The Kristeva Reader*, ed. Toril Moi (New York, 1986), 34–61 (37).
[16] Michel Foucault, *The Archaeology of Knowledge* (London, 1974), 23.

his influence and impact fully. Sometimes, Donne's use of patristic material seems to speak directly to the best recent trends in Augustine's reception history. Eric-Leland Saak, for instance, has advocated a more precise attention to the sources of Augustine's late-medieval heritage, a form of 'hard' intertextuality which focuses not on the study of doctrinal analogues and influences, but on specific and local Augustinian references: 'only by an analysis of the knowledge and use of Augustine's works evidenced in the texts and margins of late medieval manuscripts can we chart Augustine's influence more accurately and historically than by appeals to parallel doctrines'.[17] My study, likewise, does not concentrate on 'parallel doctrines' but on specific quotations, references in Donne's prose works which are explicitly marked as Augustinian, either in the text ('*Austin* saith' etc.) or through some form of annotation. I have endeavoured to establish, in each of the cases I discuss, the provenance and context of Donne's Augustinian quotations, at the point of composition, extraction, and redeployment. Quotation—wording, provenance, positioning—matters in this approach. In this sense, my definition of 'Augustinianism' is narrowly textual: it refers overwhelmingly to extracts from works which are designated by Donne as Augustinian.

Despite the apparent simplicity of this approach, the direct lines of descent described by Saak are relatively rare in Donne's writing. Alongside examples of exact quotation derived at first hand from Augustine's works, we encounter a whole spectrum of intertextual alternatives: the merging of references from different texts; the misremembered reference; the suppressed reference; the submerged reference; the disowned reference; the partially rewritten reference; the oblique reference; the recycled reference; the distorted reference, or the reference creatively transformed. These complications multiply when we delve further into Foucault's network of textual nodes. Each genre has its own protocols of intertextual citation; when texts traverse such generic frontiers, they must be re-framed and re-interpreted. While Donne, on occasion, seeks to replicate the precise setting of an Augustinian reference—as when his own preaching on St Paul's texts invokes iconic moments from Augustine's Pauline sermons—more commonly, quotations need to be re-contextualized, as they travel from polemic to homiletic, from solitary meditation to communal edification, and so on.

Furthermore, the 'structuration' of intertextual meaning takes place not simply in the direct exchange between Donne and Augustine, but through a vast number of mediating sources, which range from Augustine's first anthologist, the fifth-century writer Prosper of Aquitaine, via the main medieval exegetes of Augustine (Aquinas, Lombard, Lyra), to early seventeenth-century debates over the role of the Fathers in the Church of England.[18] Recovering these lines of textual mediation is important in order to establish an accurate picture of Donne's intertextual

---

[17] Eric-Leland Saak, 'The Reception of Augustine in the Later Middle Ages', in *The Reception of the Church Fathers in the West: From the Carolingians to the Maurists*, ed. Irena Backus, 2 vols. (Leiden, 1997), 1.367–404 (399).

[18] The term 'structuration' is Julia Kristeva's and emphasizes the processual nature of intertextual relations. See *Le Texte du Roman*, cited in *Language and Materialism: Developments in Semiology and the Theory of the Subject*, ed. Rosalind Coward and John Ellis (London, 1977), 52.

transactions; even more critically, however, excavating the material and intellectual contexts of these Augustinian intermediaries enables us to reconstruct Donne's own rhetorical strategies and purposes more accurately. Donne habitually 'disowns' Aquinas as a source for Augustinian references and allusions, for instance, preferring instead to present them as the fruits of his own reading; such acts of citational camouflage always have their own story to tell.

These 'soft' or mediated forms of intertextuality have not received a great deal of attention in studies of Renaissance literature and culture. But they have substantial implications for the ways in which we conceptualize religious writing and, beyond that, for our understanding of religious doctrine and ideology. Donne's reading of Augustine often takes place in layers, with texts being channelled through multiple levels of mediation. The end result of these processes has much to tell us about scholarly procedures, and gives us new tools for gauging how patristic knowledge was acquired, stored, and transmitted in the early modern period; how it was mediated, distilled, re-configured, and transformed. But if the study of such different intertextualities complicates our approach to the Renaissance archaeology of knowledge, it also has revisionary implications for our understanding of religious self-fashioning and display. In Donne's Augustinian transactions, the art of memory meets the art of forgetting: suppressing Aquinas is a gesture of doctrinal self-definition, wiping out any traces of 'the schoole' is to eradicate, symbolically, 1,000 years of Roman corruption.[19] By orchestrating direct encounters with Augustine's writings, Donne combines the humanist dream of textual integrity with the Protestant vision of a pure and primitive ecclesiology. These sustaining fictions undergird theological argument, give it rhetorical and moral traction.

The doctrinal and devotional discourses that emerge from Donne's Augustinian reading are neither transparent nor merely instrumental. They do not express and codify a set of pre-formed concepts, but shape ideology by aggregating, interpreting, and re-framing a vast multiplicity of sources and intertexts: Donne's reading is not linear, but involves secondary and tertiary forms of mediation—to trace the outlines of his patristic thought, we need a special kind of intertextual archaeology. The citational manoeuvres on display in Donne's texts offer new ways of conceptualizing the formation of religious doctrine and show us the scholar's mind in action, as he moves between different textual territories, crosses linguistic, historical, and confessional boundaries, and imports far-fetched ideas into current polemical and pastoral concerns. We need to pay the closest possible attention to these small-scale textual processes in order to understand the global ramifications of religious ideology. Such a method will demand a multi-pronged approach, combining the gritty detail of intensive source study with the conceptual tools of intertextual theory, and close scrutiny of the rhetorical and scholarly conventions used by Renaissance writers and readers.

In emphasizing the fluid and dynamic nature of religious discourse, this study takes inspiration from the best recent scholarship on early modern English culture.

---

[19] On the art of forgetting, see Harald Weinrich, *Lethe: Kunst und Kritik des Vergessens* (Munich, 1997).

Brian Cummings rightly insists, for instance, that as long as we continue to treat religious language as 'a transparently ideological construct', its cultural, social, and literary significances will continue to elude us.[20] The theological writing of the period cannot simply be distilled into timeless doctrinal visions; doctrine is itself embedded in complex practices of display, performance, and representation—inseparable from the rhetorical and material contexts that surround and articulate it. Kevin Sharpe has argued that religion 'was not just about doctrine, liturgy or ecclesiastical government; it was a language, an aesthetic, a structuring of meaning, an identity, a politics'.[21] If belief and dogma are mediated in this way, any study of religious writing must start with the textual, rhetorical, and material aspects of religious discourse. One way of achieving this, I would suggest, is through a more contextually differentiated approach to intertextuality: the detailed analysis of how one early modern religious writer, Donne, read, extracted, interpreted, and re-worked the theological structures of language and knowledge offered by Augustine. Tracking the transmission of an Augustinian quotation from its early Christian point of origin to its Renaissance reinventions means that we are able to highlight more precisely the modes of religious display and performance at work in cultural processes, and observe the 'structuring of meaning' in action. This involves attention to the contexts of reading and writing: the cultural, political, and literary circumstances that inflect Augustine's and Donne's religious language and are in turn shaped by it.[22] The Fathers, as a composite corpus of theological ideas, vocabularies, and identities, are ubiquitous presences in early modern culture. As John Milton notes with a nod to Tertullian in *The Doctrine and Discipline of Divorce*, 'He that thinks it the part of a well-learned man to have read diligently the ancient stories of the Church, and to be no stranger in the volumes of the Fathers, shall have all judicious men consenting with him.'[23] Our study of religious and political discourses in this period will be incomplete until we have a fuller

[20] Brian Cummings, *The Literary Culture of the Reformation: Grammar and Grace* (Oxford, 2002), 12.

[21] Kevin Sharpe, *Remapping Early Modern England: The Culture of Seventeenth-Century Politics* (Cambridge, 2000), 16. For an excellent summary of recent methodological developments in the study of religious ideology, see Ken Jackson and Arthur Marotti, 'The Turn to Religion in Early Modern English Studies', *Criticism*, 46 (2004), 167–91. For some masterful illustrations of how these principles can be applied in scholarly practice see, for instance, the work of Peter Lake, Anthony Milton, and Peter McCullough, cited below.

[22] In this, as in many other respects, I am indebted to recent historicist work on Donne's sermons, most notably Jeanne Shami, *John Donne and Conformity in Crisis in the Late Jacobean Pulpit* (Cambridge, 2003); Lori Anne Ferrell and Peter McCullough (eds.), *The English Sermon Revised: Religion, Literature and History, 1600–1750* (Manchester, 2000); Lori Anne Ferrell, *Government by Polemic: James I, the King's Preachers, and the Rhetorics of Conformity, 1603–25* (Stanford, 1998); and Peter McCullough, *Sermons at Court: Politics and Religion in Elizabethan and Jacobean Preaching* (Cambridge, 1998).

[23] Milton, *The Doctrine and Discipline of Divorce*, in *Collected Prose Works*, ed. Don M. Wolfe, 8 vols. (New Haven, 1953–82), 1.650. As Mark Vessey notes, the study of patristics can contribute to our broader understanding of Renaissance humanist culture: 'with the classical elements in any early modern "renaissance" of English letters must also be reckoned a *patristic* culture of a type only possible after the advent of humanism'. Mark Vessey, John Donne (1572–1631) in the Company of Augustine: Patristic Culture and Literary Profession in the English Renaissance', *Revue des Études Augustiniennes*, 39 (1993), 173–201 (174).

appreciation of the ways in which this patristic heritage was absorbed and adapted into the literary, controversial, and devotional writing of post-Reformation England.[24]

Augustine is by far the single most frequently cited authority in English writing of the early modern period and just as ubiquitous in Continental thought. Initial investigations of the Fathers' impact on English religious culture have yielded significant results at every turn: Anthony Milton, for instance, has recently studied the career of the scholar and bishop John Overall, 'a crucial developer (in some ways, indeed, an inventor) of what we might term an "Anglican" methodology . . . moderate, patristic, distrustful of speculative theology, drawn to a via *media*'.[25] Overall's pioneering project to 'reposition the Church of England' was defined to a significant extent by his 'insistence on the importance of patristic authority'.[26] John Williams, the Archbishop of York, reportedly observed that 'above all men that ever he heard, he [Overall] did most pertinently quote the fathers, both to the right sense of their phrase, which few did understand, and out of those their treatises, wherein especially they handled their cause, for which he appealed unto them'.[27] Williams's emphasis on Overall's patristic expertise—he has studied a broad range of works, knows them in depth, and cites accurately—is a commonplace of controversial rhetoric, as we will see, which invokes a humanist ideal while at the same time setting up a tactical play. Investigating the rhetorical strategies and citational practices employed by early modern readers of the Fathers, then, is absolutely crucial to understanding the parameters of religio-political discourse in the period.[28]

There is one final point of methodology which deserves closer scrutiny. The discipline of intertextuality emerged from a preoccupation with structuralist poetics: we are familiar (too familiar, perhaps) with shorthand accounts of Roland Barthes's formulations on the death of the author, and on the writer as orchestrator and textual *bricoleur*.[29] In Julia Kristeva's work, the perpetual echo-chamber of intertextuality is transformed into an infernal Babel, which turns every text into a 'living hell of hell on earth'.[30] Not much remains here of the author as originator or creator, and even less of the original author and of His transcendental signifier, the Word. Yet the assumption of authorship, and the idea of the Scriptures as an emanation of perfect, unified, and providential significance, are foundational to the ways in which religious

---

[24] See, on this, Eugene F. Rice, *Saint Jerome in the Renaissance* (Baltimore, 1985); and, more recently, Vessey, 'Company', and Hilmar M. Pabel, 'Reading Jerome in the Renaissance: Erasmus' Reception of the Adversus Jovinianum', *Renaissance Quarterly*, 55 (2002), 470–97.

[25] Anthony Milton, '"Anglicanism" by Stealth: The Career and Influence of John Overall', in *Religious Politics in Post-Reformation England*, ed. Peter Lake and Kenneth Fincham (Cambridge, 2006), 159–75 (160, 176).

[26] Ibid. 163.

[27] John Hacket, *Scrinia Reserata* (1693), 1.11.

[28] See, on this, Jean-Louis Quantin's important monograph, *The Church of England and Christian Antiquity: The Construction of a Confessional Identity in the 17th Century* (Oxford, 2009). Quantin's study appeared after the substance of this book had been completed.

[29] Roland Barthes, *S/Z* (London, 1974), 21.

[30] Julia Kristeva, *Desire in Language: A Semiotic Approach to Literature* (New York, 1980), 66.

texts speak to each other in the early modern period. In the structuralist model, the linguistic or intertextual system pre-exists individual writers, who can therefore only converse in the language of the 'already-written'.[31] But one of the principal aims of Donne's Augustinian recourse is to celebrate the original creator of meaning, and in that sense his intertextuality is about the apotheosis of God-as-author, not his death. While many of Donne's textual strategies are decidedly earth-bound and strategic, a powerful arsenal of Augustinian intertexts also, paradoxically, seeks to lift him out of the Babel of quotations, the 'living hell of hell on earth'.

For Augustine, as we will see, the chief aim of reading is to overcome it, and to return to a purer form of cognition, which originates in God but was lost in the act of original sin: the redeemed self enjoys unmediated and uninterrupted communion with the divine. In this vision of perfect understanding, we are no longer mired in a tissue of texts but perceive meaning intuitively; we are liberated from time and history, and from the historicity and temporality of reading—God sees everything at once and completely. Donne's writings construct Augustine as a conduit to this higher form of cognition; his texts are used as hermeneutic platforms, stepping-stones to a fuller comprehension of God's word in the world. A sermon preached at Whitehall on 2 April 1620 provides an example of this interpretive philosophy. Donne's text, Ecclesiastes 5:13–14, speaks of the vanity of riches, and his discussion takes him initially to some textual difficulties. He points out with reference to the *Retractations*, for instance, that Augustine's early readings were based on a flawed copy of the Scriptures: instead of '*vanitas vanitatum*', the vanity of vanities—or vain things—Augustine's text reads '*vanitas vanitantum*', the vanity of vain men. For ordinary readers, this would doubtless lead to serious problems and distortions, but Augustine is different. Instead of ploughing through the text sequentially, like most people, Augustine has a panoramic understanding of the Scriptures. He embodies the text's principles so completely that even when he produces a localized misreading, the end result is perfectly consonant with God's will and word:

> Saint *Augustin* . . . reads that, *vanitas vanitantum:* O the vanity of those men that delight in vanity[.] . . . And so certainly he might safely do; for though, as he saies, in his Retractations, his Copies misled him, yet that which he collected even by that errour, was true, they that trust in vain things are as vain, as the things themselves. If Saint *Augustin* had not his warrant to say so from *Solomon* here, yet he had it from his Father before, who did not stop at that, when he said *Man is like to vanity,* but proceeds farther; surely, . . . *every Man . . . is altogether vanity.*[32]

Donne sets up Augustine as the perfect reader by creating a perfect intertextual tableau for him: Augustine may have misconstrued the literal meaning of Ecclesiastes 1:2, but his interpretation is borne out by two other Scriptural passages, Psalms 144:4 ('*Man is like to vanity*') and Psalms 39:5 ('*surely, every Man is altogether vanity*'). Augustine, in other words, cannot misread Solomon because he knows David: all

---

[31] Barthes, *S/Z*, 21.
[32] *Sermons*, 3.49.

Scripture texts are available to him simultaneously, and in this timeless vision Augustine manifests a spirit of rectified reading that brings him closer to God.

Discovering such superior modes of interpretation is a key aspiration in Donne's Augustinian reading, but the process is never unproblematic. Platonic ascents towards God inevitably meet with the gravitational pull of fallen cognition; idealized reflection is balanced out by hard-headed polemical co-options of Augustine's authority. Yet in all his intertextual transactions, Donne is acutely aware of the temporality of reading and citation; this in turn has implications for any critical recuperation of his Augustinianism. Donne's textual strategies work across several competing timelines: he is embedded in the flow of human history, for instance, but yearns to be liberated from it, and to be re-incorporated into the eternal felicity of providential time. Intersecting with both these models are complex notions of institutional and political time: Donne the Protestant theologian, as we will see, seeks to bypass a thousand years of corrupt Roman tradition and re-insert himself into the purer doctrinal heritage of the primitive Church. The problem of time also confronts Donne at a more localized level: in 1629, for instance (as Chapter 6 shows), Donne finds himself wishing for an acceleration of human history, so that the political crises of the present can be folded back into God's timeless wisdom.

Donne's self-conscious temporalization of the reading act makes intellectual demands on his own readers. This book investigates, in the broadest sense, the influence of one author's philosophy of reading and interpretation upon another; it is a study, therefore, in the history of ideas. In classic accounts of the Anglo-American approach to this field, much depends on the contextualization of sources and concepts. Quentin Skinner, for instance, argues that the meaning of a concept can only be revealed by probing the intellectual and rhetorical conditions that gave rise to its formulation: what an author 'was *doing in* writing a work' is contingent upon 'the prevailing conventions governing the treatment of the issues or themes with which the text is concerned'.[33] Thought is embedded in the flow of historical time, bounded by the frontiers of contemporary knowledge. Donne's treatment of Augustine, however, subtly changes the parameters of this model, precisely because it operates with different notions of temporality, constructs events in literary and religious time rather than in the framework of secular history.[34] At the very least, we can say that one of the most radical forms of contextualization at work here is the defiance of history: Donne can imagine encounters with Moses and Augustine when he moves along these alternative timelines, because in the divine mode of interpretation, 1,500 years pass in the blink of an eye. Finally, it is worth reiterating

---

[33] Quentin Skinner, 'Motives, Intentions and Interpretation', in *Visions of Politics*, 3 vols. (Cambridge, 2002), 1.90–102 (101–2).

[34] The temporal dimension of historical concepts has received greater attention in German traditions of intellectual history, and especially in the work of Reinhart Koselleck (1923–2006). See, for an introduction to Koselleck's thought on historical time, chs. 5–7 in *The Practice of Conceptual History: Timing History, Spacing Concepts*, trans. Todd Samuel Presner et al. (Stanford, 2002), and 'Perspective and Temporality: A Contribution to the Historiographical Exposure of the Historical World', in *Futures Past: On the Semantics of Historical Time*, trans. Keith Tribe (Cambridge, Mass., 1985), 130–55. See further on Koselleck's approach, Melvin Richter, *The History of Political and Social Concepts: A Critical Introduction* (Oxford, 1995).

that in the case of Donne's Augustine, the available conventions emerge through complex forms of textual accretion; Augustine's works do not travel directly from fifth-century North Africa to seventeenth-century England, but undergo various stages of medieval and early modern redaction until they arrive at their destination.

WHICH AUGUSTINE?

'From one perspective, a century or more of turmoil in the Western Church from 1517 was a debate in the mind of long-dead Augustine.'[35]

'. . . it all depends on what you mean by "Augustinian."'[36]

From one perspective, argues Diarmaid MacCulloch, the vast narrative, chronological, and geographical sweep of Reformation history can be reduced to an account of Augustine's influence on the religious, political, and cultural landscape of Western Europe in the early modern period, a posthumous psychomachia fought out by competing interest groups. In the famous formulation of B. B. Warfield, whose views MacCulloch is summarizing here, 'the Reformation, inwardly considered, was just the ultimate triumph of Augustine's doctrine of grace over Augustine's doctrine of the Church'.[37] Augustine as *doctor gratia*, discovered by Luther in a finely crafted moment of conversion, is certainly also the most powerful version in any *outward* consideration of the history of sixteenth-century religious change: in the theological, institutional, and political consequences of a doctrine founded on individual grace and faith rather than on the works-based operations of a clerical hierarchy.[38] But, as MacCulloch observes, 'there is much more to Augustine than his soteriology'.[39] It is perhaps the greatest achievement of Augustine's most recent biographer, James J. O'Donnell, to remind us that 'there are many Augustines' and to reveal some less familiar incarnations of a figure whose shadow looms large over so many contested intellectual territories in Western thought. Even the most cursory glance at O'Donnell's chapter titles demonstrates a pervasive interest in the plurality of Augustinian constructs, both self-made and those imposed, contemporaneously and posthumously, by his exegetes. Chapter XI is entitled 'Augustine the Theologians', and chapter IV, 'Augustine Unvarnished', lists some of the least savoury parts inhabited by O'Donnell's subject both before and after his installation at Hippo, among them 'Augustine the Self-Promoter', 'Augustine the Social Climber', and 'Augustine the Troublemaker'.[40]

[35] Diarmaid MacCulloch, *Reformation: Europe's House Divided 1490–1700* (London, 2003), 111.
[36] David Steinmetz, *Luther and Staupitz: An Essay in the Intellectual Origins of the Protestant Reformation* (Durham, NC, 1980), 15.
[37] B. B. Warfield, *Calvin and Augustine* (Philadelphia, 1956), 332.
[38] On Luther and Augustine in their literary and theological contexts, see Cummings, *Literary Culture*, 57–87.
[39] MacCulloch, *Reformation*, 111.
[40] James J. O'Donnell, *Augustine: Sinner and Saint* (London, 2005), 5; see also two other excellent introductions to Augustine's biography and theology: Peter Brown, *Augustine of Hippo* (Berkeley, 1967) and Eugene TeSelle, *Augustine the Theologian* (New York, 1970).

But if O'Donnell's biography highlights Augustine's ability to reinvent himself in response to personal, professional, and political exigencies (with an eye to decorum entirely fitting for a man who had occupied the chair of rhetoric at Milan), it also recognizes that effective self-fashioning involves the opposite of such occasional responsiveness: a substratum of ideas, indeed ideals, which lends moral substance and rhetorical conviction to the shifting contextual tides of conflict and controversy. Augustine is rightly hailed, in retrospect, as the inventor of a Christian doctrine of love and can yet be accused, with equal justification, of turning the language of charity and peace into a polemical weapon when it suited his purposes. His Donatist opponent Petilianus puts the case against Augustine succinctly:

> in whatever veil of goodness you have hidden yourself ('velamine bonitatis obtexeris'), under whatever name of peace you wage war with kisses ('nomine pacis bellum osculis geras'), wherever you seduce the race of men with the word *unity*; you, who up to now deceive and beguile, truly you act as the son of the devil as you betray the father in your conduct.[41]

Petilianus's complaint attests to an awareness, Augustine's and his own, that words are weapons whose significance and polemical value are determined through acts of writing and interpretation: sudden unilateral re-definitions of meaning and desperate scrambles to regain the semantic high ground. Such awareness was, of course, equally acute among the preachers and controversialists of early modern England who laid claim to an Augustinian inheritance. Augustine's charity is his defining virtue for Donne, as we will see, but he also caricatures its polemical applications in *Biathanatos*. He responds to Augustine's terminological landgrabs as well as his most exalted idealism.

Augustine's first biographer, Possidius, fully absorbs this emphasis on the power of writing and textuality to shape historical image and legacy. His *Life* of Augustine uses both the brute power of the material word and the subtler craft of narrative structure to create a portrait of Augustine as founder and defender of the Catholic Church militant. The *indiculus* or bibliography of Augustine's works that accompanies the biography provides a material-textual frame which reinforces the priorities determined by this reading: the first nine sections are exclusively occupied by controversial and anti-heretical writings, thus cataloguing the struggle for institutional and political supremacy. The narrative itself constantly reinforces the notion that Augustine was born to champion the cause of the Catholic faith: of the thirty-one sections of the *Vita*, barely one devotes itself to the pre-conversion Augustine; the rest (as they say) is Church history. The tone of Possidius's biography is well captured by the chapter headings of an early twentieth-century English translation of the *Vita*. In chapter 9, Augustine 'contends with the Donatists'; chapter 10 sees our hero fight 'The Madness of the Circumcellions', followed by 'The Progress of the Church through Augustine' (chapter 11), a propitious escape from 'an

---

[41] *Epistula ad presbyteros et diaconos Donatistas adversus Catholicam*, quoted by Augustine in *Contra Litteras Petiliani* 2.17 (*PL* 43.270).

ambuscade laid for him' (chapter 12), and, in chapter 13, the 'Peace of the Church through Augustine'.[42] It is crucial to note, of course, that Possidius's hopes and desires for the peace of *his* Church had a significant part to play in the shaping of his Augustine: the *Vita Augustini* was designed to consolidate the position of the Catholic Church as much as to chronicle its history.

Possidius's fifth-century text marks an inaugural moment in the history of Augustine's reception, and it manifests the complex entanglement of textual and contextual concerns, of debt and self-interest, which has come to characterize so many forms of Augustinianism during the millennium-and-a-half or so following his death.[43] This book is an account of one episode in that reception, an analysis of how Donne read and re-worked Augustine's texts; how he responded to the many different personae that populate Augustine's own writings, and to the plethora of Augustinian constructions that were available to him, a Catholic-turned-Protestant clergyman, barely a century after the most ruptural moment of Augustinian re-invention—the Reformation. But it aims to reach out from this single case study and to enhance our understanding of seventeenth-century religious, textual, and political culture, in which Augustine's status was nothing less than totemic. The French Jansenist Pasquier Quernel (1634–1719), for instance, in formulating his views on grace and predestination, discovered a devastatingly simple method for disarming his enemies: 'You must burn Augustine if the statement is false.'[44] In England, the Puritan William Crompton and the Catholic John Brereley turned a global religio-political dispute over the nature of the one true Church into a scholarly disputation over the right reading of Augustine. Crompton's *Saint Austins Summes* (1624) was a direct reply to Brereley's *Sainct Austines Religion* (1620); both texts discuss questions of doctrine exclusively through the parsing of Augustinian quotations.[45] The 1611 Authorized Version of the Bible defends its scholarly methods against the 'cavils' of uncharitable readers by leaning heavily on the authority of Augustine's *De Doctrina Christiana*. And in the same year, Thomas Tuke's *A Very Christian, Learned, and briefe Discourse, concerning the true, ancient, and Catholicke Faith* applied Augustine as a panacea for '*all wicked and vp-start Heresies . . . Papists, Anabaptists, Arrians, Brownists, and all other Sectaries*'.

Some early modern versions of Augustine have already left their mark on biographical and critical studies of Donne's work. The most persistent of these first appears in Walton's biography, which reads Augustine's life as a model of experiential identification, arguing that Donne's spiritual reformation ushered in

---

[42] Possidius, *Sancti Augustini Vita*, ed. and trans. Herbert T. Weiskotten (Princeton, 1919).

[43] See, for the first systematic attempt to outline Augustine's reception history, the *Historical Guide to the Reception of Saint Augustine*, gen. eds. Karla Pollmann and Mark Vessey, Oxford University Press, forthcoming.

[44] Cited in Jean-Louis Quantin, 'The Fathers in Seventeenth Century Roman Catholic Theology', in Irena Backus (ed.), *The Reception of the Church Fathers in the West: From the Carolingians to the Maurists*, 2 vols. (Leiden, 1997), 2.982: 'Il faut brûler S. Augustin si la réflexion est fausse'.

[45] For a more detailed assessment of this debate, see Robert Dodaro OSA and Michael Questier, 'Strategies in Jacobean Polemic: The Use and Abuse of Augustine in English Theological Controversy', *Journal of Ecclesiastical History*, 44 (1993), 432–49.

the birth of 'a second St. *Austine*'.[46] It is easy to see why this idea may have appealed
to Donne during the tough process of re-defining his professional aspirations; the
rhetorical bifurcation of his literary personae into 'Jack' and 'Doctor Donne'
certainly suggests as much. In the wake of Walton's account, the dramatic narrative
of tortured subjectivity offered by the *Confessions* has appealed to many readers of
Donne's works, which everywhere tempt us with images of divided selfhood and
internal struggle, whether in the realm of secular love or religious devotion.[47]
However, as Gregory Kneidel has noted, Donne's sermons do not in fact display
'the normative Pauline-Augustinian narrative of conversion'.[48] Kneidel's reading
presents a Donne who, instead of looking inward, shapes a model of 'corporate
Christianity', 'an enduring, collective, public ethic of all believers'.[49] It is in this
context that we best appreciate the most methodologically sustained approach to
Donne's Augustinianism, Mark Vessey's 'John Donne (1572–1631) in the Company
of Augustine: Patristic Culture and Literary Profession in the English Renaissance'.
Vessey re-reads Walton's conversion narrative as a process of vocational reinvention;
his Augustine helps Donne shape a sense of corporate identity, of what it means to be
a professional divine.[50] From this perspective, Donne's Augustinianism sits comfortably alongside the best recent historical scholarship on Donne's Protestantism, which
stresses Donne's sense of priestly and pastoral vocation, and emphasizes his commitment to defending the mainstream Calvinist consensus of the Jacobean Church.[51]
Vessey's Augustinian Donne helps to explain the priestly self-fashioning of the Dean
of St Paul's in the very public sphere of religious politics.[52] However, as David
Colclough reminds us, Donne's intellectual work 'goes beyond the search for place

---

[46] Walton, *Lives*, 47–8: 'Now the *English Church* had gain'd a second St. *Austine*, for, I think, none
was so like him before his Conversion: none so like St. *Ambrose* after it: and if his youth had the
infirmities of the one, his age had the excellencies of the other; the learning and holiness of both.' It is
worth noting that Augustine is here alleged primarily as a cipher for conversion; Donne shared his
youthful indiscretions, but the processes and motives of spiritual reformation remain opaque. On
Walton's biographies, see Jessica Martin, *Walton's Lives: Conformist Commemorations and the Rise of
Biography* (Oxford, 2001).
[47] One of the elegies in the 1633 edition of Donne's poetry, 'To the deceased author' (attributed to
one Thomas Browne), proposes an Augustinian framework for reading Donne's secular works; it
appeals to the 'knowing eyes' of a sympathetic audience who will 'dare reade even thy *Wanton Story*,/As
thy *Confession*, not thy *Glory*' (ll. 13–14). See, on this poem as a template for reading the 1633
collection, Benjamin Saunders, 'Circumcising Donne: The 1633 Poems and Readerly Desire', *Journal
of Medieval and Early Modern Studies*, 30 (2000), 375–99.
[48] Gregory Kneidel, *Rethinking the Turn to Religion in Early Modern English Literature: The Poetics
of All Believers* (Basingstoke, 2008), 6.
[49] Ibid. 3.
[50] Vessey, 'Company', 200. For a detailed discussion of Vessey's methodology, see Chapter 1, and
for an evaluation of his findings in relation to the *Essayes in Divinity*, see Chapter 3.
[51] See above, n. 22, especially the work of Jeanne Shami.
[52] Mary Arshagouni Papazian, 'The Augustinian Donne: How a "Second S. Augustine"?', in
Papazian (ed.), *John Donne and the Protestant Reformation: New Perspectives* (Detroit, 2003), 66–89.
See also, on Donne's Augustinianism, William Halewood, *The Poetry of Grace* (New Haven, 1970);
Papazian, 'Literary "things indifferent": The shared Augustinianism of Donne's Devotions and
Bunyan's Grace Abounding', in *John Donne's Religious Imagination: Essays in Honour of John
T. Shawcross*, ed. Raymond-Jean Frontain and Frances M. Malpezzi (Conway, Ariz., 1995), 324–49;
Janel Mueller's excellent introduction to her edition of *Donne's Prebend Sermons* (Cambridge, Mass.,
1971); Robert L. Hickey, 'Donne's Art of Preaching', *Tennessee Studies in Literature*, 1 (1956), 65–74;

or status. Donne certainly sought advancement . . . [yet] he also wanted effectively to use and manipulate the structures of language and knowledge by which the debates he chose to enter proceeded.'[53] For Donne, Augustine's texts offered precisely this: a dynamic set of linguistic and rhetorical tools to be used and manipulated; a theological discourse which enabled interventions in complex processes of cultural transmission; and, not least, a structure of knowledge in its own right. Priestly vocation is only one of many Augustinian ideas in play in Donne's works.

In the course of this book, we will encounter a broad range of Augustinian personae and impersonations, those which Donne would have known and imagined, as well as those which he himself fabricated. It is one of my central contentions, however, that for Donne, the most important version of Augustine was not the saint, the convert, the theologian of grace, or the professional divine, but Augustine the reader and interpreter of texts. Donne used Augustine primarily as a model for exegesis and argument: Augustine's writings offered theories of reading and exemplary exegetical applications, which could in turn be mapped onto models of right moral action, spiritual self-construction, and eschatological self-realization. It is important to note that his focus on hermeneutics did not limit Donne's perspective on Augustine; in fact, it was a facilitating rhetorical strategy which enabled him to address a host of other cultural concerns: political, legal, doctrinal, polemical, epistemological, and ethical, among others. What holds these diverse preoccupations together, however, is a set of intellectual principles first articulated in Augustine's reflections on reading and interpretation. A brief survey of these ideas is needed before we move on to Donne's patristic transactions.

AUGUSTINE AND 'THE WEST'S FIRST DEVELOPED THEORY OF READING'

Brian Stock's magisterial *Augustine the Reader* anatomizes 'Augustine's attempt to lay the theoretical foundations for a reading culture'. Crucial to this endeavour is Stock's examination of the interplay between interpretation and other disciplinary contexts: issues of 'mental representations, memory, emotion, cognition, and the ethics of interpretation'. The 'subsequent union of philosophical, psychological, and literary insights', Stock contends, 'gave birth to the West's first developed

Dennis B. Quinn, 'Donne's Christian Eloquence', *English Literary History*, 27 (1960), 276–97; Quinn, 'John Donne's Principles of Biblical Exegesis', *Journal of English and Germanic Philology*, 61 (1962), 313–29; John S. Chamberlin, *Increase and Multiply: Arts-of-Discourse Procedure in the Preaching of John Donne* (Chapel Hill, NC, 1976); P. G. Stanwood and Heather Ross Asals (eds.), *John Donne and the Theology of Language* (Columbia, 1986); Gillian R. Evans, 'John Donne and the Augustinian Paradox of Sin', *The Review of English Studies*, NS 33 (1982), 1–22; Patrick Grant, 'Augustinian Spirituality and the Holy Sonnets of John Donne', *English Literary History*, 38 (1971), 542–61; Terry G. Sherwood, 'Reason, Faith, and Just Augustinian Lamentation in Donne's Elegy on Prince Henry', *Studies in English Literature, 1500–1900*, 13 (1973), 53–67; Tracy Ware, 'Donne and Augustine: A Qualification', *Notes and Queries*, 30.5 (1983), 425–7.

[53] David Colclough, 'Introduction', in Colclough (ed.), *John Donne's Professional Lives*, (Cambridge, 2003), 4.

theory of reading'.[54] Karla Pollmann has offered a ground-breaking analysis of the 'universalist' aspirations of Augustine's hermeneutic; she too situates Augustine's interpretive methodology in the context of his intellectual or 'disciplinary' heritage.[55] Pollmann stresses the 'theoretical comprehensiveness' of Augustine's approach: interpretation is not merely instrumental or reactive, but represents the master discipline for the Christian thinker, 'comprising all others and giving them perspective'.[56] What matters to Augustine, above all, is the ultimate goal and purpose of the reading: interpretation is always directed towards the achievement of eschatological (re)union with God. Augustine formulates pragmatic rules for moving through the scriptural landscape (he stipulates, for instance, that difficult places in the Bible can be unlocked by collating them with clear and easy passages); he imposes dogmatic restrictions (exegesis must conform to the rule of faith, as embodied in Church doctrine); and, above all, he embeds hermeneutics in a more global theory of ethics and philosophy, in which 'charity' functions as the dominant interpretive category.[57] Augustinian 'caritas', rightly deployed, allows the exegete to read with the eyes, and in the image, of a loving divinity: it focuses the gaze inwards and upwards, envisages communion with God and the contemplation of eternal truths. In this Platonic scheme, the human 'doctrina' of reading and interpretation has a merely temporary status; it is superseded by a higher mode of wisdom ('sapientia'), as the mediated, fallen modes of human knowledge transform into an intuitive apprehension of God. Augustine articulates this movement through the citation of key scriptural texts, principally 1 Corinthians 13:12 ('For now we see through a glass darkly, but then face to face; now I know in part, but then I shall know, even as also I am known') and Matthew 5:3–9.[58]

---

[54] Brian Stock, *Augustine the Reader: Meditation, Self-Knowledge, and the Ethics of Interpretation* (Cambridge, Mass., 1996), 1. Donne's engagement with Augustine's theory of memory has received detailed attention. See, for instance, Achsah Guibbory, 'John Donne and Memory as "the Art of Salvation"', *Huntington Library Quarterly*, 63 (1980), 261–74; Malcolm Guite, 'The Art of Memory and the Art of Salvation: The Centrality of Memory in the Sermons of John Donne and Lancelot Andrewes', *The Seventeenth Century*, 4 (1989), 1–17; Robert L. Hickey, 'Donne's Art of Memory', *Tennessee Studies in Literature*, 3 (1958), 29–36; for the case against Augustine and for the Thomistic–Aristotelian derivation of Donne's *ars memoria*, see Noralyn Masselink, 'Donne's Epistemology and the Appeal to Memory', *John Donne Journal*, 8 (1989), 57–88, and Masselink, 'Memory in John Donne's Sermons: "Readie"? Or Not?', *South Atlantic Review*, 63 (1998), 99–107; Donald M. Friedman, 'Memory and the Art of Salvation in Donne's Good Friday Poem', *English Literary Renaissance*, 3 (1973), 418–42; Helen B. Brooks, 'Donne's "Goodfriday" and Augustine's Psychology of Time', in *John Donne's Religious Imagination*, ed. Frontain and Malpezzi, 284–305. And see especially, for an account of Donne's theory of memory which makes the case for Augustine in the context of a broader theory of epistemology and psychology, Janel Mueller, *Donne's Prebend Sermons*, 30–5.

[55] Generally, the relationship between hermeneutics and exegesis is one of theory to practice (see Hans-Georg Gadamer, *Wahrheit und Methode*, 6th edn. (Tübingen, 1990), 169, where 'Hermeneutik' is defined as 'the art of comprehension'—'die Kunst des Verstehens'). In the early modern period, as we will see, the boundaries between these terms were less sharply defined.

[56] Karla Pollmann, 'Augustine's Hermeneutics as a Universal Discipline!?', in Pollmann and Mark Vessey (eds.), *Augustine and the Disciplines: From Cassiacum to Confessions* (Oxford, 2005), 206–31 (231); on the relation of hermeneutics and exegesis (see above), see ibid. 206.

[57] Ibid. 212–14.

[58] See Augustine, *De Sermone Domini in Monte* 1.3–1.4 (*PL* 34.1233–5; see Pollmann, 'Hermeneutics', 226); Chapter 7 discusses this movement from interpretation to intuition in more detail.

Augustine's interpretive procedures build on moral and spiritual principles which pre-exist both text and reader. The most important of these is charity, the defining property of a benign deity: God demonstrates his love through the actions of Christ, and human readers emulate this gesture through loving attention to his Word, the Scriptures. On the terms of this model, failure to produce an interpretation which shores up the love of God and neighbour is the failure to produce a correct or truthful reading, as Augustine makes clear in the first book of *De Doctrina Christiana*:

> So anyone who thinks that he has understood the divine scriptures or any part of them, but cannot by his understanding build up this double love of God and neighbour, has not yet succeeded in understanding them.[59]

Augustine offers an extreme version of a hermeneutic circle here: the truth of love is encoded in the text, but in order to solve the puzzle, the reader must already know the truth and live it. The 'regula dilectionis', or rule of charity, thus becomes the goal and the main criterion of interpretation: only a charitable reader can uncover God's message of love.[60]

Despite the eschatological orientation of Augustine's thought, it must be stated at once that his hermeneutic is no Platonist utopia. While it takes seriously the role of charitable interpretation in the construction and realization of Christian self-hood, Augustine's theory of reading is equally alive to the potent polemical force of its rhetorical tools. Augustine's hermeneutic repertory relies on a handful of key terms, of which charity and faith are the most prominent. These concepts are far from simple or morally mono-dimensional: they can accrue or divest themselves of polemical significance as the context requires, and can combine the heights of eschatological ascent with profoundly problematic acts of rhetorical aggression, in sometimes brutal collisions of idealism and opportunism. Recourse to the moral and spiritual implications of charity, for instance, can be an effective tactic in controversial debate, because it allows highly partisan interventions to be camouflaged as Christian altruism. There is no better way of illustrating this than to return, briefly, to Augustine's opponent Petilianus, for whom the language of charity and moderation is a mere 'veil of goodness', and 'the name of peace' and 'the word *unity*' just that—labels which usefully 'deceive and beguile' with rhetorical 'kisses', a cynically strategic invocation of Christian values designed to mask political hostility. The 'son of the devil' can cite Scripture *and* the language of charity.[61]

Donne adopts and adapts the foundational terms of Augustine's interpretive model, charity and faith, and turns them to a variety of polemical and aesthetic uses. 'The charitable man is the great Philosopher', Donne observes, and this dictum is embodied most fully in Augustine, that 'classique Father', 'that charitable

---

[59] Augustine, *De Doctrina Christiana* 1.36 (*PL* 34.34).
[60] *De Doctrina Christiana* 1.22 (*PL* 34.27).
[61] On the strategic and polemical uses of charity in seventeenth-century controversy, see Chapter 6. See also, on early modern responses to Augustine's anti-Donatist rhetoric of charity, Alexandra Walsham, *Charitable Hatred: Tolerance and Intolerance in England, 1500-1700* (Manchester, 2006), esp. 40–9.

Father'.[62] Augustine represents the 'discreet and charitable temper which becomes every man'; God's will is best expressed through the 'voyce of his blessed Servant, S. *Augustine*'.[63] On the other hand, Augustine also supplies material for some of the more obvious moments of flattery in Donne's sermons, as when he compares Lord Keeper Thomas Egerton to the Fathers and Doctors of the Church: 'A good father at home, is a S. *Augustin,* and a S. *Ambrose* in himself; and such a *Thomas* may have governed a family, as shall, by way of example, teach children, and childrens children more to this purpose, then any *Thomas Aquinas* can.'[64]

Donne's Augustinian applications variously suggest the desire for faithful emulation and the urge towards open intertextual confrontation; they draw on Augustine's timeless authority and update him for contemporary controversy. Donne's writings constantly speak to a conviction that rhetorical meaning is context-bound, and to an awareness that Augustine was more deeply immersed than most in the local circumstances of controversial debate—never more so, paradoxically, than when he fought battles over universal principles of faith. This has implications for the ways in which patristic documents are interpreted. In a St Paul's sermon preached on 21 June 1626, for instance, Donne explains why the Fathers must be read with a careful attention to context: they speak figuratively to 'stir up the affections of their auditory', so we must not take them literally; they palliate 'the sharpnesse and bitternesse' of some doctrinal truths to 'hold [their] auditory together' and spare 'weaker stomachs', so we must examine the place, audience, and circumstances of preaching. But, above all, they are professional polemicists who manipulate language in the service of a political and doctrinal agenda:

> So also, they confesse too, that *ex vehementia declinarunt*, In heat of disputation, and argument, and to make things straight, they bent them too much on the other hand, and to oppose one Heresie, they endangered the inducing of another, as in S. *Augustines* disputations against the Pelagians . . . and the Manicheans . . . we shall sometimes find occasions to doubt whether S. *Augustine* were constant in his owne opinion, and not transported sometimes with vehemency against his present adversary, whether Pelagian, or Manichean.[65]

Donne addresses a difficulty which Augustine's own writings consistently deflect or deny: that the process of terminological redefinition always involves an element of moral slippage, because doctrinal 'things' cannot exist apart from the polemical languages and rhetorics that embody them. If language is 'bent' too far, doctrine itself acquires a dangerous kind of pliability. In a Candlemas sermon of 1627 Donne discusses at length Augustine's desire to keep this process in check: in an epistle to Bishop Fortunatianus, 'he repents, and retracts his bitternesse' of tone, 'but his opinion, his doctrine . . . S. *Augustine* never retracted'.[66] Augustine insists, time and again, that doctrine, language, and context can be treated as distinct

---

[62] *Sermons*, 5.89, 4.208, 9.76.
[63] *Sermons*, 8.360, 9.241.
[64] *Sermons*, 8.96, (on Donne's relationship with Egerton, see Bald, 93–127).
[65] *Sermons*, 7.203.
[66] *Sermons*, 7.342. For a more detailed discussion of this sermon, see Chapter 7.

entities, even as the force of his own rhetorical interventions brings them into constant and uncomfortable contact. It is in the contested relationship between 'words' and 'things'—in the rhetorically enabling and morally problematic notion of meaning in context—that Donne's engagement with Augustine is most profound, complex, and interesting.

All the case studies in this book document Donne's close attention not only to Augustine's hermeneutic vocabulary, but to the moral and epistemological assumptions that underpin it: the motives, purposes, and cognitive conditions which govern ethically sustainable forms of Christian reading and textuality. Donne's focus on Augustine the reader is a way of mobilizing and re-framing a range of other versions: Augustine the theologian, Augustine the polemicist, Augustine the political opportunist, Augustine the Bishop, Augustine the philosopher, Augustine the rhetorician, Augustine the preacher of God's word. The cross-disciplinary Augustinian hermeneutic is one of the driving forces behind Donne's own 'multi-lingual' or 'multi-discursive' modes of argument and thought, which work across generic, professional, and controversial boundaries. This debt to Augustine remains constant and unchanging; it is especially apparent, in fact, at moments when his local engagement with an Augustinian text or idea is openly eristic or oppositional.

A study of Donne's Augustinianism gives us unprecedented access to his intellectual influences and textual sources; it also allows us, for the first time, to observe Donne the reader in action. But it also adds an important dimension to our understanding of Renaissance reading habits more generally. Scholars such as Anthony Grafton, Lisa Jardine, and William Sherman have investigated models of textual engagement that emerge from the secular humanist culture of the court. Grafton and Jardine's ground-breaking study of 'How Gabriel Harvey Read his Livy' focuses on 'the ways in which humanistically trained readers assimilated and responded to the classical heritage' and aims to 'reconstruct the social, professional and personal contexts in which reading takes place'.[67] Humanist scholarly reading is defined above all as a practical, 'active' endeavour, 'goal-orientated' and 'intended to give rise to something else': Henry Wotton, for example, recommends 'the drawing of the platform of battles' alongside the study of military histories. The text is conceived of as a repository of axiomatic wisdom, a collection of fragments that can be extracted and re-applied to suit the reader's purpose, with little or no attention given to authorial motive and intent.

One might contrast this model with discussions of Augustinian interpretation in the work of Terence Cave.[68] In 'The Mimesis of Reading in the Renaissance', Cave outlines an approach that is characterized by interpretive compliance, submission, and passivity: the reader, far from acting as 'a transformative force', emerges as a mere conduit for God's illuminating grace. The complex hermeneutic transactions

---

[67] Anthony Grafton and Lisa Jardine, '"Studied for Action": How Gabriel Harvey Read his Livy', *Past and Present*, 129 (1990), 30–78.
[68] Terence Cave, *The Cornucopian Text* (Oxford, 1979); 'The Mimesis of Reading in the Renaissance', in *Mimesis: From Mirror to Method, Augustine to Descartes*, ed. John D. Lyons and Stephen G. Nichols, Jr. (London, 1982), 149–65.

between text, context, and reader are replaced by the notion of epiphany: 'caritas' enables 'claritas', readerly charity leads to the revelation of divine truth. Cave argues that the sixteenth century saw a movement away from this Augustinian model and towards more active and creative forms of interpretation, which come to the fore in Montaigne's *Essais*. This shift coincides with a revolution in citational practice, a decline in the authoritative status of texts which manifests as 'a shift from the citing (*allégation*) of *auctoritates . . .* to free quotation'.[69] It is true, of course, that Augustine's hermeneutic privileges the intent of a divine author over the interests of the human reader. But this unproblematic transmission of grace always yields, in *De Doctrina Christiana*, to more complex reflections on textual communication (Cave himself is quick to recognize that he describes an ideal fiction rather than a viable set of practices). In Book 2 of that treatise, which dwells in detail on the theory and practice of interpretation, Augustine initially explains that the aim of 'readers is simply to find out the thoughts and wishes of those by whom the Bible was written down and, through them, the will of God, which we believe these men followed as they spoke'. But he acknowledges also that reading is difficult, that in some passages readers 'find no meaning at all that they can grasp' and that they encounter 'fog created by some obscure phrases'. 'I have no doubt', he concludes, 'that this is all divinely predetermined, so that pride may be subdued by hard work and intellects which tend to despise things that are easily discovered may be rescued from boredom and reinvigorated.'[70] Even Scripture is mediated by human authors and exists 'in various languages of translators'; direct revelation is a fiction which, in practice, is superseded by readerly labour and the prudent exercise of interpretive responsibilities. The initial act of faith in the cohesion of the text ('the will of God, which we believe these men followed') thus gives way to complex enquiries into authorial 'thoughts and wishes'. And although these processes ultimately function to reveal God's charity, the human articulation of that single truth is multiple, complex, and radically embedded in its local contexts.[71] Practising the principle of charity, as recent scholarship on Augustine's thought has recognized, 'is not the same as canonizing one's source'; there is 'no contradiction' between applying the rule of charity and being an active, 'critical judge of sources and texts'.[72]

Donne's Augustinianism allows us to make new kinds of enquiry and conclusion about reading as an intellectual method, spiritual discipline, or even a form of philosophy.[73] For Augustine, the only logical extension of autobiography is exegesis: having charted a path to conversion, the final books of the *Confessions* offer an

[69] Cave, 'Mimesis,' 155–6, citing Antoine Compagnon, *La Seconde Main, ou le travail de la citation* (Paris, 1979).
[70] Augustine, *De Doctrina Christiana* 2.6.7 (*PL* 34.38), trans. R. P. H. Green (Oxford, 1997). See Chapter 3, on the *Essayes in Divinity*, for Donne's use of the notion that scriptural difficulty is a test of faith.
[71] *De Doctrina Christiana* 2.5.6 (*PL* 34.38).
[72] Ineke Sluiter, 'Metatexts and the Principle of Charity', in *Metahistoriography: Theoretical and Methodological Aspects in the Historiography of Linguistics*, ed. Peter Schmitter and M. J. van der Wal (Münster, 1998), 11–27 (25, 26).
[73] Augustine's own exegetical methods have been described as the enactment of ascetic discipline: see Elizabeth A. Clark, *Reading Renunciation: Asceticism and Scripture in Early Christianity* (Princeton, 1999).

allegorical reading of Genesis—Augustine frames the future of his soul through an act of interpretation. Self, God, and creation are put in touch with each other through uncovering the spirit of the text, in a prayerful, meditative revelation of providential meaning. The philosophical assumptions of this model should encourage us to rethink key categories in the history of reading: there are different understandings of authorial intent at work here, and a different kind of scholarly ethos. Paying attention to the broader moral and spiritual purposes of a text, for instance, means that it cannot simply be approached as a storehouse of useful aphorisms and sentences; the aim, for Augustine's reader, is to see (with 1 Corinthians 13:12) not in parts but in wholes.[74] This mentality creates not a submissive collective of saintly readers, who merely imbibe Augustine's wisdom; nor does it give birth to a generation of 'wit-pyrates' who update or transform Augustine's texts to serve a contemporary agenda.[75] For Donne, the ultimate Augustinian reader, textual excerption, compilation, quotation, and re-contextualization are issues of ethical and even religious import, which require careful reflection and meditation. Donne's thinking about text, context, and authorial intent may on occasion manifest as the gratuitous violation of Augustine's hermeneutic principles, but this affirms rather than undermines the seriousness of his endeavour. Religious or patristic habits of reading, therefore, offer an important new insight into the ways in which a different type of Renaissance reader—the professional divine rather than the professional facilitator of knowledge—approached a world of texts. Donne the reader deserves our sustained attention, but his engagement with Augustinian theories and practices of interpretation also has much to tell us about the wider intellectual culture of Renaissance England. It uncovers a tradition of theological reading that has been obscured, to some extent, by the secular humanist emphasis on *praxis* and application, and reveals methods of argument, reading, and citation which are crucial to our understanding of early modern religio-political thought, and to the discourses of devotion, meditation, and spiritual reflection that sustain it.

ITINERARY

The opening chapters of this book aim to demonstrate the breadth and range of Donne's Augustinian reading: I look at how many (and which) of Augustine's works Donne cited; whether he consulted the original Augustinian texts or intermediary sources, and how he dealt with these different types of patristic recourse; which editions he used; what mechanics of quotation are deployed; and what underlying scholarly and philosophical principles inform Donne's citational procedures. I survey a broad spectrum of Augustinian texts and a panoply of textual intermediaries: from anthologies of the Fathers, via Scripture commentaries and

---

[74] Peter Mack has recently pointed out that dialectical models of reading also focus on the structural properties of entire texts rather than individual extracts. See his 'Rhetoric, Ethics and Reading in the Renaissance', *Renaissance Studies*, 19 (2005), 1–21.
[75] Donne, '*Upon Mr* Thomas Coryats Crudities', l. 65.

ecclesiastical histories, to patristics handbooks and controversial tracts; from the fifth-century disciple of Augustine, Prosper of Aquitaine, via Lombard, Aquinas, and the *Glossa Ordinaria*, to Bellarmine, Pererius, and Daillé. Chapters 1 and 2 constitute the first part of this book, which combines quantitative and empirical source study with a survey of Donne's citational methods and practices. The second part, Chapters 3 to 7, investigates particular sources and modes of recourse in depth, discovering a variety of applications for Donne's Augustinian hermeneutic. In the *Essayes in Divinity*, Augustine's approach to interpretation is formulated and analysed for the first time (Chapter 3). *Biathanatos* aggressively repudiates Augustine's philosophy of reading and problematizes the discourse of charity which sustains early modern casuistical thought (Chapter 4). In a set of Lincoln's Inn sermons preached in 1620, Augustinian charity is camouflaged as equity, and Donne uses both terms to debate the terms of prerogative justice (Chapter 5). A Whitsunday sermon preached in 1629 mobilizes Augustine's interpretation of Genesis 1:2 to reframe the repressive Laudian rhetoric of political acquiescence as a vision of transcendental peace (Chapter 6). And, finally, in a set of Easter and Candlemas sermons, Donne invokes Augustine's ideas of eternal beatitude to envisage the end of the hermeneutic journey begun in the *Essayes in Divinity*. He imagines a return to God which transforms mediated communication into direct, intuitive vision, and interpretation into unmediated communion (Chapter 7).

1

How Donne Read Augustine

Despite major developments in other areas of study, such as politics and religion, Donne scholarship has shown comparatively little interest in the history of reading. This applies both to the material aspects of book use—habits of annotation, excerption, and compilation—and to the literary relations that such use implies. While our knowledge of the polemical and pastoral contexts of Donne's preaching has been immeasurably advanced over the last three decades, the study of Donne's sources, intertexts, and analogues has been largely neglected.[1] The last sustained attempt to trace the textual heritage of Donne's works was Potter and Simpson's appendix to their ten-volume edition of the sermons, which endeavours to demonstrate Donne's debt to the Scriptures, the Fathers, and medieval and Renaissance commentators. Potter and Simpson pay particular attention to Donne's use of Augustine: they include a census of quotations and allusions for volumes three, six, and nine of their edition, an estimate of the total number of Augustinian references, and a list of identified citations from Augustine's writings. Augustine, Potter and Simpson conclude, 'is above all the Father to whom Donne turned most constantly', and Donne's references to him 'cover almost the whole field of Augustine's thought'.[2]

The sermons editors' effort to track Donne's patristic influences has recently come under attack, especially from scholars attuned to the subtler principles of source criticism. In a 1996 article on 'Donne's Reinvention of the Fathers', for instance, Paul Stanwood analyses Potter and Simpson's quantitative approach, and his assessment merits quoting in full:

> Perhaps students of Donne, influenced by the tendentious judgements of some earlier editors, have long supposed that the sermons reveal significant patristic influence simply because the Fathers so often appear in his texts. This may indeed be so; but

---

[1] There are some notable exceptions: see, for instance, Randall McLeod, 'Obliterature: Reading a Censored Text of Donne's "To his Mistress Going to Bed"', *English Manuscript Studies 1100–1700*, 12 (2005), 83–138; R. V. Young, 'Donne and Bellarmine', *John Donne Journal*, 19 (2000), 223–34; Anne Prescott, 'Donne's Rabelais', *John Donne Journal*, 16 (1997), 37–58; Mary Paton Ramsay, *Les Doctrines Médiévales chez Donne*, 2nd edn. (Oxford, 1924); Richard Wollman, '"The Press and the Fire": Print and Manuscript Culture in Donne's Circle', *Studies in English Literature, 1500–1900*, 33 (1993), 85–97; Thomas A. Festa, 'Donne's *Anniversaries* and his Anatomy of the Book', *John Donne Journal*, 17 (1998), 29–60; Winfried Schleiner, *The Imagery of Donne's Sermons* (Providence, RI, 1970). See also the work by Stanwood, Vessey, and Brown, cited below. The John Donne Society continues to attract outstanding work on all aspects of Donne's writing, but especially on the religio-political contexts of Donne's religious thought; see Introduction, above.

[2] *Sermons*, 10.346; 10.354.

I think we must look with care at a great many more quotations to see if Donne is not in fact wresting the Fathers out of their own texts. We should not be surprised to discover that 'influence' needs redefining and may even flow in two directions; for Donne's copious invention and powerful imagination create new terms in the midst of old works.[3]

Stanwood's principal point is that Potter and Simpson counted too much and weighed too little. His own research, aided in part by electronic, searchable editions of the Fathers' works, has evolved a more nuanced and refined approach to Donne's patristic heritage. This book follows Stanwood's important and timely call for a more thorough-going investigation of Donne's patristic references: it aims to 'look with care at a great many more quotations' than have hitherto been examined— those likely derived from Augustine's sources directly and those gleaned at second or third hand. However, in doing so, it also seeks a critical engagement with some of the findings and the underlying assumptions of more recent scholarship on Donne's patristics. Potter and Simpson may have been too easily persuaded by Walton's portrait of Donne as 'a second St. *Austine*',[4] nor can it be denied that their assessment of Augustine's influence is overdetermined by a strong sense of biographical parallel and analogy: '[Donne] recognized Augustine's warm humanity, and displayed an interest in his life and personality which he does not show for any other Father. He saw a parallel between the sins and failures of his own youth and those of Augustine as narrated by the Saint himself in his *Confessions*.'[5] But where Potter and Simpson's Donne is perhaps too eager to emulate Augustine's conversion narrative, Stanwood's version may pull us a little too far in the opposite direction. His observation that 'Donne's copious invention and powerful imagination create new terms in the midst of old works' rightly champions Donne's creative use of his sources, but it also runs the risk of committing too firmly to another powerful image of Donne: the original genius of Thomas Carew's elegy, commander of an 'imperious wit' and purger of 'The Muses garden', where 'The lazie seeds/ Of servile imitation' are 'throwne away;/And fresh invention planted'.[6] This Donne imposes a superior poetic energy and 'ingenuity' on 'old texts', sometimes mischievously, as when he reinvents Tertullian's ideas 'in elaborately misleading ways'; and sometimes rather more assertively, when he 'bends' patristic texts to 'recreate these sources in accord with his immediate rhetorical purpose'.[7] Just as in Carew's poem 'stubborne language bends' and submits to the demands of a 'Giant phansie', so the Fathers are remade in Donne's image.[8]

---

[3] P. G. Stanwood, 'Donne's Reinvention of the Fathers: Sacred Truths Suitably Expressed', in *Sacred and Profane: Secular and Devotional Interplay in Early Modern British Literature*, ed. Helen Wilcox, Richard Todd, and Alasdair MacDonald (Amsterdam, 1996), 195–201 (200).

[4] Izaak Walton, *The Lives of Dr. John Donne, Sir Henry Wotton, Mr. Richard Hooker, Mr. George Herbert* (London, 1670), 47–8.

[5] *Sermons*, 10.348.

[6] Thomas Carew, 'An Elegie upon the death of the Deane of Pauls, Dr John Donne', ll. 49, 26–8; cited from Donne, *Complete English Poems*, ed. C.A. Patrides, 2nd edn. (London, 1994).

[7] Stanwood, 'Reinvention', 199, 195.

[8] Carew, 'Elegie', ll. 50, 52.

The force of such creative energies is also reflected in Donne's textual practices. Stanwood suggests that in 'the composition of his sermons, John Donne seldom confers with his patristic sources directly, and then often quotes inaccurately and out of context'.[9] His method of quotation 'is not interested so much in what the original says, but in the manner of language and its ability for enhancing the argument'.[10] Stanwood further argues that Donne had compiled a set of common-place books filled with headings and sententiae extracted from patristic and later authors; when a reference was needed, he would consult these tools or simply work from memory.[11] This account of Donne's patristic recourse echoes Walton's discussion of his composition habits in the *Life*. After Donne had finished preaching a sermon, Walton reports, 'he never gave his eyes rest, till he had chosen out a new Text, and that night cast his Sermon into a form, and his Text into divisions; and the next day he betook himself to consult the Fathers'.[12]

Walton portrays the Fathers as an afterthought, a secondary source in more ways than one: what matters is Donne's unique take on the Scripture text. This sense of the Fathers as ancillary, marginal, and ornamental, survives even in the best recent scholarship on Donne's patristics. Stanwood concludes that Tertullian, on the whole, 'contributes very little to the substance of Donne's argument':[13] the quotations 'provide only a strange shimmer of patristic authority, a superficial yet amplifying ornament'.[14] Mark Vessey similarly contends that the majority of Donne's patristic citations can be 'reckoned stylistic ornaments or elements of rhetorical elocution'[15] and suggests that a 'careful sifting of his [Donne's] citations of the Fathers would lead . . . to the conclusion that much of what we have taken for erudition is more rightly considered a form of display'.[16] Stanwood's and Vessey's work has improved our understanding of Donne's patristic borrowings significantly, but there are aspects of these accounts that deserve elaboration and re-investigation. One central issue is the manner of Donne's recourse to the Fathers: I want to put pressure on the argument that Donne rarely consulted his sources directly. In doing so, it is not my intention to suggest that Donne's estimation of the Fathers, and especially Augustine, rivals the primacy of the Scriptures, or that he re-read the entire *Bibliotheca Patrum* every time he embarked upon the composition of a sermon. Donne, like all of his learned contemporaries, had been trained in the practices of annotation, excerption, and compilation; he knows how to take a short cut. Walton, for instance, famously reports that Donne 'left the resultance of 1400. Authors, most of them abridged and analysed in his own hand . . . So he did the

[9] P. G. Stanwood, 'Donne's Art of Preaching and the Reconstruction of Tertullian', *John Donne Journal*, 15 (1996), 163–9 (153).
[10] Stanwood, 'Reinvention', 197.
[11] Stanwood, 'Tertullian', 166.
[12] Walton, *Lives*, 67.
[13] Stanwood, 'Tertullian', 161.
[14] Ibid. 165.
[15] Mark Vessey, 'Consulting the Fathers: Invention and Meditation in Donne's Sermon on Psalm 51:7 ("Purge me with hyssope")', *John Donne Journal*, 11 (1992), 99–110 (104).
[16] Ibid. 107.

copies of divers Letters and cases of Conscience . . . and, divers other businesses of importance; all particularly and methodically digested by himself.'[17]

Evidence from Donne's library also shows that he made use of excerpt collections and other scholarly aids. As Piers Brown notes, in Donne's copy of the *Opera Omnia* of Aeneas Silvius Piccolomini (Keynes, L176) 'the most intensive annotation is reserved for the *gnomonologia*', the section of the work that catalogues quotable passages.[18] And in the note appended to the list of 'Authors cited' in *Biathanatos*, Donne reflects explicitly on his textual protocols: 'In citing these authors, for those which I produce only to ornament and illustration, I have trusted my owne old notes.'[19] Donne points out that in the case of some quotations, he did not 'refresh them with going to the Originall', but he is careful to emphasize that these excerpts served 'only' for 'ornament and illustration'.[20] It is difficult to know if we can take him entirely at his word here—the principal modern editor of *Biathanatos* suggests that these remarks should never have been printed[21]—but Donne's 'confession' allows us to glean three simple yet significant facts about his textual practices: that Donne made notes and kept commonplace books as a matter of habit; that he revisited the originals from which these notes had been excerpted to confirm readings; and that the manner of textual recourse depends on its matter or purpose—'old notes' and second-hand quotation will do for ornament and elaboration. Unsurprisingly, perhaps, for a writer so attuned to the subtleties of rhetorical decorum, Donne stresses the functionality of intertextual relations: how you quote and what you quote depends on the envisaged effect of a reference. But if this is the case, categories such as 'erudition', 'display', and 'fidelity' are of limited use in assessing Donne's approach to his sources. A. E. Malloch recognized this more than a half-century ago in his incisive analysis of *Biathanatos*:

> The authorities in *Biathanatos* are quoted for effect, and so it is more appropriate for us to ask what effect Donne is seeking in a given reference, and if this effect explains the inaccuracy of the reference, than to ask the sort of question which would suggest that Donne was at all concerned with accuracy *per se*.[22]

Taking as a starting-point this emphasis on functionality, purpose, and effect, my chief aim in Chapters 1 and 2 is to establish a more precise picture of what kinds of patristic material were available to Donne, how these sources were assessed in contemporary discourses of quotation, and how they were used in Donne's works.[23] This includes a survey of early modern editions of the Fathers, but also of the burgeoning industry of Augustinian epitomes, excerpt collections, and

---

[17] Walton, *Lives*, 67–8.

[18] Piers Brown, '"Hac ex consilio meo via progredieris": Courtly Reading and Secretarial Mediation in Donne's *The Courtier's Library*', *Renaissance Quarterly*, 61 (2008), 833–66 (855).

[19] John Donne, *Biathanatos*, ed. Ernest W. Sullivan (Newark, Del., 1984), 5.

[20] Ibid.

[21] Ibid., p. xxxvii.

[22] A. E. Malloch, 'The Definition of Sin in Donne's *Biathanatos*', *Modern Language Notes*, 72 (1957), 332–5 (334).

[23] Some of these questions are formulated by Vessey, 'Consulting the Fathers', which offers a five-point agenda for future research into Donne's patristics (106–7).

indices—the material and intellectual conditions, in short, that framed Donne's patristic recourse. It also involves a lot of counting and weighing: I want to examine how many of Augustine's works Donne references, and where he gets his quotations from. I am interested, therefore, in Donne's reading methods and scholarly procedures but, above all, in the different applications of his diverse patristic materials.

The extant evidence regarding Donne's reading habits is slim, but there are some clues to suggest that he encountered patristic texts directly, as well as drawing on anthologies, indices, and notes. Walton, as we have seen, highlights Donne's practice of compiling synopses of important texts ('the resultance of 1400. Authors'). He also notes that Donne bequeathed to a friend his copy of Bellarmine—'all the Cardinals works marked with many weighty observations under his own hand'; these are, perhaps, the kinds of notes that could have supplied Donne with material for 'ornament and illustration' in *Biathanatos*. The heavy annotation of Bellarmine's works seems to have been the exception rather than the norm, however. Other than his title-page inscriptions, Donne's marginalia are primarily in pencil and, rather than consisting of 'weighty observations', mark the text with vertical and diagonal lines and brackets, and, very occasionally, NBs, question marks, and underlining.[24] Some of the markings clearly specify material for later excerption, but in most cases Donne was working directly from the text, entering passages into a notebook or transferring quotations into a rough sermons draft. We might compare this with the reading techniques of John Jewel, Bishop of Salisbury: as John E. Booty notes, Jewel habitually marks passages with underlinings, in blue or black ink, and also brackets passages in red ink; he employs a system of symbols which helps to divide material into polemical themes and doctrinal topics, and he has a numbering system which cross-references with the commonplace book in which the passage is to be entered. In addition, Jewel occasionally writes short notes in his books, as in his 1637 copy of Erasmus's Jerome.[25]

While these physical indicators give us a preliminary impression of how Donne used his books, it is nevertheless the case that the nature and extent of Donne's patristic reading must primarily be inferred from his own works. This brings us to a first set of key questions: how many Augustinian texts did Donne refer to in his writings, how well did he know these works, how did he read them, and what are the modes of citation he employed when he imported Augustine's works into his own? The immediate starting-point for these questions, once again, is Potter and Simpson's edition of the sermons. In the selective census of volumes three, six, and nine compiled by Winifred Holtby, Augustine emerges as the leading patristic authority, clocking up a total of 226 references. From their knowledge of the remaining volumes, Simpson and Holtby estimate that Augustine is quoted or

---

[24] See Brown, 'Courtly Reading', 852.
[25] John E. Booty, *John Jewel as Apologist of the Church of England* (London, 1963), 113. Jewel, unlike Donne, had a fleet of research assistants charged with the task of transferring passages from the original texts to commonplace books. See on markings in early modern books more generally, William H. Sherman, *Used Books: Marking Readers in Early Modern England* (Philadelphia, 2008).

referred to about 700 times in the whole edition of Donne's sermons; they also
identify the textual sources for a total of 98 Augustinian references. In my own
research, I have taken Troy D. Reeves's *Index to the Sermons of John Donne* as a
point of departure.[26] In volume two, the Index to Proper Names, Reeves lists
approximately 1,000 references under Augustine's entry; *Biathanatos* and the
Essayes add another fifty between them. I have examined all of these citations,
supplementing missing references where necessary, and using the electronic
version of *Patrologia Latina* and modern scholarly editions of Augustine, as well
as the three principal sixteenth-century editions of Augustine's *Works*. Potter and
Simpson also draw some preliminary conclusions regarding Donne's favourite
Augustinian texts:

> [Donne's Augustinian references] are drawn for the most part (as far as we have been
> able to identify them) from the *Confessions, De Civitate Dei,* the *Sermons, Enarrationes*
> on the Psalms, *De Doctrina Christiana,* and the *Epistles,* with occasional references to
> *De Gen.*[esi] *con.*[tra] *Man.*[ichaeos], *De Moribus Ecclesiae* [Catholicae], *De Trinitate,*
> *De Vera Religione, Enchiridion, Quaest.*[ionum] *in Heptateuchum, Retractationes,* etc.[27]

In total, Potter and Simpson identify references to twenty-four Augustinian texts;
research for this book has yielded quotations from sixty-one different Augustinian
works (of which seven are now regarded as spurious).[28] The sermons editors are
correct in emphasizing the popularity of the *Confessions,* the *City of God,* the
sermons, the epistles, and the *Enarrations on the Psalms.* *De Doctrina Christiana* is
also a key text, but its influence tends to make itself felt not so much through direct
quotation as through broader allusions to exegetical and homiletic principles.[29]
A larger sample of Augustinian references 'upgrades' some of Potter and Simpson's
texts from 'occasional' to essential sources: *On the Values of the Catholic Church* (*De
Moribus Ecclesiae Catholicae*), *On the Trinity,* and Augustines various expositions of
Genesis are regular ports of call for Donne in the sermons, as are the treatises *On
Order* (*De Ordine*) and *Eighty-Three Various Questions* (*De Diversis Quaestionibus
Octoginta Tribus*). The most significant omission from Potter and Simpson's list,
however, is Augustine's principal attempt to explicate the Gospel of John, the
Homilies on the Gospel of John (*In Johannis Evangelium Tractatus*)—a work which
underpins Donne's approach to his favourite New Testament text. Augustine's
emphasis on divine love and charity deeply resonated with Donne's own view of
John's Gospel and shaped his thought on ethics and exegesis throughout his
preaching career.

---

[26] Troy D. Reeves, *Index to the Sermons of John Donne,* 3 vols. (Salzburg, 1980). As Jeanne Shami
rightly points out in her trenchant review of Reeves's work, the *Index* is uneven and at times unreliable.
(See *Renaissance and Reformation,* NS 8 (1984), 59–62.) Despite these shortcomings, however, the
Index is a useful tool for launching quantitative work on the sermons.

[27] *Sermons,* 10.354.

[28] For the purposes of this census, the sermons and letters are counted as single texts; a full list of
texts is included at the end of this book (Appendix: List of Augustine's works cited by Donne).

[29] See *John Donne and the Theology of Language,* ed. P. G. Stanwood and Heather Ross Asals
(Columbia, 1986).

Donne refers to sixty-one texts across his prose output, but less than a dozen of these were routine ports of call for him. As subsequent chapters will demonstrate, Donne only scrutinized half a dozen texts in detail, with the *Confessions* occupying a special position in his personal canon. It is crucial to note that this is a characteristic intellectual profile for professional divines in the period—especially in relation to sermons and Scripture commentaries—and that Donne was by no means alone in deploying his patristic knowledge with a mixture of efficiency, competence, and creativity. Anthony N. S. Lane's analysis of the sources in Calvin's Genesis commentary reveals that Calvin used only nine patristic works in the preparation of his text; that he frequently re–used material from his own earlier works such as the *Institutes*; and that he also cited texts he had consulted for previous projects. Lane concludes that one of Calvin's most remarkable skills was 'the ability to read little and then to make the maximum use of this material in producing a commentary of lucid brevity'.[30] The German theologian and Augustinian friar Johannes von Paltz (d. 1511) saturates his pastoral works with Augustinian quotations, but his detailed reading is limited to a corpus of texts that looks remarkably similar to Donne's: the *City of God*, the *Confessions*, the *Enarrations on the Psalms*, the *Homilies on the Gospel of John*, *On the Literal Interpretation of Genesis*, *On the Trinity*, *Eighty-Three Various Questions*, sermons and epistles.[31] And Johann von Staupitz (1460–1524), the Vicar-General of the Augustinian Order in Germany and one-time teacher of Luther, includes hundreds of references to Augustine in his sermons but has in-depth knowledge of no more than half a dozen works, including the *City of God*, the *Confessions*, *On the Trinity*, *The Literal Interpretation of Genesis*, and the *Enchiridion on Faith, Hope, and Charity*.[32] Closer to Donne's own intellectual milieu, John Hales of Eton, who was closely involved in the production of the Eton edition of Chrysostom and was described by Clarendon as 'one of the greatest scholars in Europe', was also clearly capable of operating at a remarkable level of efficiency.[33] His *Sermon [. . .] Concerning the Abuses of Obscure and Difficult Places of Holy Scripture* (Oxford, 1617), which will be discussed in detail in Chapter 3, cites at length from the *City of God*, *The Literal Interpretation of Genesis*, and the *Epistles*, but the references derive almost exclusively from the opening and closing sections of these texts. Hales's use of these quotations suggests in-depth familiarity with Augustine's thought, but it is clear that he was highly selective in his consultation and deployment of Augustine's texts, especially at the point of composition. Although his quotations are collected with great economy, and with careful attention to genre and context, Hales's grasp of Augustinian thought is

---

[30] Anthony N. S. Lane, *John Calvin: Student of the Church Fathers* (Edinburgh, 1999), 234.

[31] Bernd Hamm, *Frömmigkeitstheologie am Anfang des 16. Jahrhunderts: Studien zu Johannes von Paltz und seinem Umkreis* (Tübingen, 1982), 316.

[32] Richard Wetzel, 'Staupitz Augustinianus: An Account of the Reception of Augustine in the Tübingen Sermons', in *Via Augustini: Augustine in the Later Middle Ages, Renaissance, and Reformation: Essays in Honor of Damasus Trapp, O.S.A.*, ed. Heiko A. Oberman and Frank A. James, III, in co-operation with Eric Leland Saak (Leiden, 1991), 72–115 (101). Wetzel notes that Augustine is 'omnipresent' in Staupitz's work; in a sample of nine sermons, Staupitz introduces more than 30 passages from the *Enarrations on the Psalms*, a work he has only encountered at second hand.

[33] *The life of Edward, earl of Clarendon . . . written by himself*, new edn., 3 vols. (1827), 1.58–62.

nevertheless profound. Donne, as we will see, also quotes and re-reads selectively, and he had a similar talent for making his sources last.[34]

This chapter falls into two principal parts. I will begin by providing a survey of the patristic editions that were available to divines in the early modern period, focusing on the three sixteenth-century editions of Augustine's *Works*. The second part outlines what one might term Donne's philosophy of quotation, the ways in which his scholarly protocols were theorized and put to a variety of uses. My work on Donne's intertextual transactions continues in Chapter 2, a series of case studies illustrating Donne's approach to Augustine, both through first-hand consultation and through a range of medieval and early modern mediators of Augustine's works.

1. PATRISTIC EDITIONS

In 1556, hearing of the Zurich reformer Heinrich Bullinger's plans to translate the letters of Saint Ignatius, the English humanist John Cheke wrote from exile in Strasbourg to implore his friend to include the original Greek text:

> I request you now, my Bullinger, and implore you again and again, to take care that the Greek be printed together with the translation. For it is of very great importance to scholars to read the author himself in his own language, and especially when grave and controverted matters are to be considered. I have never read a translation without requiring the author himself as an interpreter of it. . . . Now translations are obtruded upon us, to the depreciation of the authors themselves, that here of necessity must arise that inconvenience which the papists object to us in the eucharist, namely, that we use the antitypes instead of the prototypes.[35]

By insisting that Bullinger 'read the author himself in his own language', Cheke's letter activates one of the most familiar topoi of humanist rhetoric. Unless we hear the writer's 'voice' in the original, the text's meaning cannot be revealed fully: the linguistic familiarity of translation always entails an estrangement from the author's true intent. Cheke's call for a close acquaintance with the original patristic text is rendered more acute by controversial pressure: without a firm textual basis, Cheke suggests, the Reformers could be in danger of succumbing to 'papist' objections. A quick glance at the state of patristic scholarship in the early modern period confirms that Cheke's fears were by no means unfounded. S. L. Greenslade notes, for instance, that 'historical and controversial theology in the Reformation was bedevilled by the ascription of spurious matter to the Fathers'.[36] Among the many examples cited by Greenslade, perhaps the most revealing is that taken from chapter 6 of John Fisher's reply to Luther's *Babylonian Captivity*: within a matter of

---

[34] It is clear that this evidence of early modern reading habits further complicates the concepts of 'erudition', 'use', and 'display'.

[35] Cheke to Bullinger, cited in Hastings Robinson (ed.), *Original Letters Relative to the English Reformation written during the Reigns of King Henry VIII, King Edward VI, and Queen Mary, Chiefly from the archives of Zurich*, 2 vols. (Cambridge, 1846–7), 1.146.

[36] S. L. Greenslade, *The English Reformers and the Fathers of the Church* (Oxford, 1960), 10.

paragraphs, Fisher, the Bishop of Rochester, introduces four spurious quotations and discredits his entire armoury of ante-Nicene Greek Fathers before his argument has properly begun.[37] It was clearly difficult to build a convincing polemical argument on such shaky textual foundations.

During the prolonged polemical exchanges between Bishop Jewel and the Catholic controversialist Thomas Harding, both sides accused each other of citing spurious proof-texts.[38] Jewel raised the rhetorical stakes early on in the debate when he denounced Harding for inventing and manufacturing authorities: 'let him no more imagine councils and canons that he never saw', Jewel fumed, 'let him no more bring us neither his Amphilochius nor his Abdias nor his Clemens nor his Leontius, nor any other childish forgeries, nor his guesses, nor his visions, nor his dreams, nor his fables'.[39] Although theologians on both sides were guilty of relying on inauthentic or corrupt works of the Fathers, it was 'popish' divines who were most frequently charged with fabricating or falsifying patristic texts.[40] Fifty years after Jewel's attack on Harding, Thomas James included with his *Treatise of the Corruption of Scripture* a special 'Appendix to the Reader', outlining the main elements of what was to become a staple of Protestant polemic—the patristic conspiracy theory:

> In the *Vatican Librarie*, there are certaine men maintained onely to transcribe Acts of the Councels and Copies of the Fathers Workes. These men, appointed for this busines, doe (as I am credibly informed) in transcribing bookes imitate the letter of the auncient copies, as neere as can be expressed. And it is to be feared, that in copying out of bookes, they doe adde, and take away, alter and change the words, according to the pleasure of their Lord the Pope.[41]

James's chief target was the Typographia Vaticana, an institution founded by Pope Sixtus V in 1588 'to restore the works of the holy fathers and to spread the Catholic faith over the entire world'.[42] Seen through the lens of James's controversial argument, the Typographia was simply a factory devoted to the mass production of patristic forgeries, fabricated documents that would delude 'the world with a shew of Antiquitie' and thus keep it permanently in the thrall of Roman doctrine; in the Pope's institution, the Fathers were '*daily depraued by this sinfull and deceitfull*

---

[37] Ibid. 16.

[38] On the Jewel–Harding controversy, see Peter Milward, *Religious Controversies of the Elizabethan Age: A Survey of Printed Sources* (Lincoln, Nebr., 1977), 1–6.

[39] John Jewel, *A Replie vnto M. Hardinges Answeare* (London, 1565), sig. ¶3v.

[40] Greenslade provides an apt summary of the effects of textual corruption on the overall quality of controversial debate: '[I]t must at the time have been most exasperating to have one's arguments countered from the utterly bogus writings of Abdias, Bishop of Babylon, planted there by the apostles, and Martial, Bishop of Bordeaux, sent thither by St. Peter, both of them held to have been among the seventy-two disciples of Jesus' (*English Reformers*, 18).

[41] Thomas James, *A Treatise of the Corruption of Scripture, Councels, and Fathers, by the Prelats, Pastors, and Pillars of the Church of Rome, for Maintenance of Popery and Irreligion* (London, 1611), sig. *8r.

[42] This was an inscription which adorned the entrance to the offices of the Typographia Vaticana; quoted in Pierre Petitmengin, 'A propos des éditions patristiques de la Contre-Réforme: le "saint Augustin" de la Typographie Vaticane', *Recherches Augustiniennes*, 4 (1966), 199–251 (206).

Romish brood'.[43] James, who was also Bodley's first librarian, made it his life's project to produce a complete corpus of patristic writings in England, with a view to making Protestant controversialists independent of the Catholic textual tradition. Between 1610 and his death in 1629, James vigorously lobbied for funding among prominent English divines in order to set up a research facility that could produce reliable editions of the Fathers, collated with the best manuscripts, and freed from Catholic errors and corruptions.[44] 'I am verelie perswaded', James reported, that

> if the *Fathers* works were once trulie let forth by the *Protestants*, with fit Censures and Annotations, and especiallie, if the times were preciselie set downe when euerie Treatise was written (as neerely as could be learned by pregnant circumstances), the greatest Controuersies of these times, would soone be determined, and haue a happy end: which, whiles they vrge one Edition, and wee another, they commending theirs, and we ours, both differing, is scarce to be hoped for.[45]

Once a proper edition of patristic writings was available, once the forgeries were exposed, the corruptions eliminated, and the texts restored by consulting the relevant manuscripts, the controversial debate would not only be put on a firmer scholarly footing, but the Fathers would speak firmly on the Protestant side. James's hopes, however, remained unfulfilled. After a promising beginning in 1610 with the publication of the collected manuscript variants of Gregory's *Pastoral Care*, the scheme soon ran into financial difficulties, and over the coming years met many 'promises but not performers'.[46]

The aim of this section is to provide a preliminary description of the principal patristic texts that were available to English divines between 1467 and Thomas James's death in 1629. The year 1467 was a watershed moment in the history of Augustine's texts: it saw the publication of the *editio princeps* of the *City of God*. While I intend to give a general overview of the patristic texts used by English preachers and controversialists, my particular focus will be on editions of Augustine's writings (including texts now known to be inauthentic, but which Donne would have regarded as Augustine's own), from the earliest editions printed in the second half of the fifteenth century to the principal patristic collections of the 1620s.

Although James's concerns regarding the quality of current patristic editions were clearly justified—in 1604, William Perkins could still devote the first forty pages of his treatise *Problema de Romanae Fidei* (nearly a fifth of the entire text) to a list of spurious works of the Fathers—there can be no doubt that the state of textual scholarship had seen a marked improvement since the first decades of patristic editing. Johann Amerbach's 1495 Basel edition of Augustine's sermons, for

---

[43] James, *Corruption*, sig. ¶3v.

[44] Initially, James's aim was simply to record textual variants; the decision to publish a complete edition was not made until the 1620s.

[45] James, *Corruption*, sig. B3v.

[46] G. W. Wheeler (ed.), *Letters of Sir Thomas Bodley to Thomas James* (Oxford, 1926), p. xv. See Paul Nelles, 'The Uses of Orthodoxy and Jacobean Erudition: Thomas James and the Bodleian Library', *History of Universities*, 22 (2007), 21–70.

instance, begins with the seventy-six sermons *ad fratres in eremo* ('To our hermit brothers'), of which only two are genuine and the rest from the fourteenth century. And the 1491 Strasbourg edition of Augustine's *opuscula* contains thirty-four alleged works of Augustine, of which only nine are authentic. In view of these statistics, one can only wonder, with Greenslade, 'what impression of Augustine, with his immense authority, can have been current'.[47]

One of the first things to note is that English readers of the Fathers were almost entirely dependent on Continental texts. As early as the 1490s, Continental printers included England as part of their market: Greenslade gives an account of the correspondence between the London stationer Andrew Ruwe and Johann Amerbach in 1495, in which Ruwe requests copies of several key works of Augustine (among them *On the Trinity*, *Enarrations on the Psalms*, *Letters*, the *City of God*, and *Homilies on the Gospel of John*), as well as texts by Ambrose, Jerome, and Gregory.[48] Personal relationships also played a significant part, with travelling scholars such as Erasmus and Peter Martyr introducing their English colleagues to new editions of patristic texts. When Martyr came to England on Cranmer's invitation with Bernardino Ochino in 1547, the total cost of their journey from Basel to London was around £126, of which over £43 was spent on books, including editions of Augustine, Cyprian, and Epiphanius for Martyr.[49]

In the sixteenth century, the sum total of English patristic scholarship consisted of three partial editions of Chrysostom's homilies in the Greek original, one by the Regius Professor of Greek at Cambridge, John Cheke (1543, also including a Latin translation), and two by Cheke's opposite number at Oxford, John Harmar (1586 and 1590; both based on manuscripts held at New College, Oxford).[50] The seventeenth century, by contrast, saw a flowering of patristic scholarship in England, although editorial efforts were focused on the ante-Nicene Fathers, and especially on the Greek Fathers and Byzantine writers. The most notable achievement in the early part of the seventeenth century was Thomas James's work on Gregory, mentioned above, as well as two major editions of Greek Fathers produced at Eton: Henry Savile's monumental eight-volume Chrysostom (1610–13) and Richard Montagu's edition of Gregory Nazianzen's two *Discourses against Julian* (1610).

Continental scholarship on the Fathers presents a considerably more complex picture. Here the journey initially takes us to Venice, where Aldus Manutius

[47] Greenslade, *English Reformers*, 10.
[48] Ibid.
[49] See William P. Haugaard, 'Renaissance Patristic Scholarship and Theology in Sixteenth-Century England', *Sixteenth Century Journal*, 10 (1979), 37–60 (50). On patristic holdings and sales in Oxford, see Guy Fitch Lytle, 'The Church Fathers and Oxford Professors in the Late Middle Ages, Renaissance, and Reformation', in *Acta Conventus Neo-Latini Bononiensis*, ed. Richard J. Schoeck (Binghamton, NY, 1985), 101–15.
[50] Cheke's edition contained only two homilies: *D. Ioannis Chrysostomi homiliae duae nunc primum in lucem aeditae* (London, 1543). Harmar started with six homilies in 1586 and followed up with another twenty-two homilies four years later: *D. Ioannis Chrysostomi Archiepiscopi Constantinopolitani Homiliae sex* (Oxford, 1586); *D. Joannis Chrysostomi . . . Homiliae ad populum Antiochenum . . . duæ et viginti* (London, 1590).

published the first significant editions of Origen: his *Homilies* on the five books of
Moses, and on the books of Joshua and Judges, appeared in 1503. The year 1506
saw the publication of Origen's commentary on *Romans*, also in Venice, and in
1514 Origen's *De Principiis* became available. As Irena Backus has noted, while
'Italian Renaissance scholars were interested in Origen because of his Platonism and
because of his moral qualities, their French counterparts took an interest in him
because of his mastery of allegorical exegesis of the Bible'.[51] Patristic publishing,
then, was clearly inflected by doctrinal emphases, controversial pressures, and
stylistic tastes. All of these factors contributed to the publication of most of
Origen's authentic works by the Paris theologian Jacques Merlin in 1514, for
instance. The most authoritative edition of Origen, however, was that of Erasmus,
which appeared in 1536.[52]

Erasmus was by far the most prolific contributor to patristic scholarship in the
sixteenth century. Working primarily with Froben's publishing house at Basel,
from the 1510s through to the end of the 1530s Erasmus was involved in editing
the writings of nearly a dozen Church Fathers. The most prominent of these efforts
include, in chronological order: (1) Jerome's *Operum Omnium*, nine volumes in
five (1516); (2) Athanasius, *Opera* (1519); (3) Cyprian, *Opera* (1520); (4) Arnobius, *Commentarii in Omnes Psalmos* (1522); (5) Hilary of Poitiers, *Opera/Lucu-
brationes*, two volumes (1523); (6) Irenaeus, *Opus in quinque libros digestum*
(1526); (7) Ambrose, *Omnia Opera*, four volumes (1527); (8) Augustine, *Omnium
Operum*, ten volumes (1528–9); (9) Chrysostom, *Opera*, five volumes (1530); (10)
Origen, *Opera*, two volumes (1536). Erasmus's work on the Fathers represented a
marked advance in philological and textual scholarship; his editions of the Latin
Fathers in particular were the first port of call for Protestant English divines in the
sixteenth and early seventeenth centuries.

Other prominent editors of patristic works included, on the Reformed side,
Johannes Oecolampadius, Conrad Pellicanus, and Wolfgang Musculus: Musculus
provided the first Greek text of Gregory Nazianzen and translated other Greek
Fathers—including Chrysostom and Basil—into Latin; Basil's *Opera*, published in
1540, marks the high point of his scholarly achievements. Pellicanus, having edited
the Amerbach edition of Augustine (see below), also laid the editorial groundwork
for Erasmus's Jerome, while Oecolampadius published, during the 1520s, Latin
versions of parts of the Greek Fathers, including works by Chrysostom, Gregory
Nazianzen, Cyril of Alexandria, and Theophylact. Among Catholic editors, besides
Erasmus, the names of Beatus Rhenanus and Sigismund Gelenius stand out. Beatus
Rhenanus produced an important edition of Tertullian's *Opera* in 1521 (he also
finished Erasmus's Origen in 1536), while Gelenius collaborated with Erasmus on
many of the key patristic editions published by the Basel printer and stationer
Johann Froben. Thus, by 1530, patristic texts from the late second, third, and

[51] Irena Backus, 'The Early Church in the Renaissance and Reformation', in *Early Christianity:
Origins and Evolution to AD 600: In Honour of W. H. C. Frend*, ed. Ian Hazlett (London, 1991),
291–303 (297).
[52] Ibid. 298.

fourth centuries could be studied more accurately, although Clement of Alexandria was not published until 1550; the principal works of the second-century apologists were published in the 1540s and 1550s (Tatian, Theophilus, Athenagoras). The Apostolic Fathers, by contrast, were little known.[53] By 1550, then, divines could draw on an exhaustive range of patristic writings, although a significant number of Greek Fathers were still only available in Latin translation. The main centres of patristic publication were Basel, Lyon, Paris, Venice, Leipzig, and Cologne.

In 1575, the French theologian Marguerin de la Bigne (c.1546–c.1595) published the first comprehensive collection of patristic texts. The Paris edition of the *Sacra Bibliotheca Sanctorum Patrum* initially appeared in nine volumes (eight plus index), and was expanded and revised numerous times over a period of 200 years. The Cologne edition of 1618, published as the *Magna Bibliotheca Veterum Patrum* in fourteen volumes by Antonius Hierat, introduced a crucial change of editorial principles by presenting the texts in chronological order. From the first edition of Bigne's patrology, the collection was characterized by strong polemical concerns. The strident tones of post-Tridentine controversial rhetoric permeate the preface, which aims to reclaim the Fathers for the Roman side: 'every single volume is a record and index of the achievements of our church over the centuries.'[54] Finally, between 1679 and 1700, the Benedictine monks of St Maur produced the first complete patrology, which remained the standard reference work until Migne's nineteenth-century *Patrologia Latina* and *Patrologia Graeca*.[55]

Next, we need to turn our attention to early modern editions of Augustine's works more particularly. The chief aim of this section is to analyse the three editions of Augustine's *Opera* before the Maurist patrology: Amerbach's eleven-volume Basel edition of 1506 (*Librorum diui Aurelii Augustini*); Erasmus's ten-volume *Operum Omnium* of 1528–9, printed by Froben at Basel; and the *Opera* in ten volumes edited by a team of theologians at the university of Louvain and printed by Christopher Plantin in Antwerp in 1576–7.

Amerbach

In the third volume of his pioneering *Patristique en Moyen Age* (1948), Joseph de Ghellinck presents a survey of the editions of Augustine's *Opera* before the Maurists. This includes accounts of the Amerbach, Erasmus, and Louvain editions, as well as a brief description of Pope Sixtus V's abortive plans for a definitive edition of Augustine by leading Vatican scholars in the late 1580s. Among these efforts, Amerbach's edition comes in for the harshest criticism: 'vague in its indications of provenance, mediocre in its textual criticism, and with a poor record as regards the

---

[53] See Greenslade, *English Reformers*, 13.

[54] Pierre Petitmengin, 'Les Patrologies avant Migne', in *Migne et le renouveau des études patristiques*, ed. A. Mandouze and J. Fouilheron (Paris, 1985), 15–38 (esp. 20–7, 'Les Controverses post-Tridentines et l'essor des *Bibliothecae Patrum*'; reference at 22).

[55] See Daniel-Odon Hurel, 'The Benedictines of St.-Maur and the Church Fathers', in *The Reception of the Church Fathers in the West: From the Carolingians to the Maurists*, ed. Irena Backus, 2 vols. (Leiden, 1997), 2.1009–38 (*passim*).

analysis of spurious texts—so bad as to be almost negligible'.[56] This may be an accurate judgement from the perspective of modern textual criticism; when viewed in its historical context, however, Amerbach's achievement is more easily appreciated. As Heiko Oberman observes, the simple fact of having Augustine's principal works collected in a single edition immeasurably facilitated scholarship on this most popular of Church Fathers: 'Amerbach's edition marked a watershed moment in the history of Augustine's reception, for the simple reason that theologians . . . could consult his works directly, with easy access to one comprehensive edition.'[57]

In fact, Amerbach's *Librorum diui Aurelii Augustini* of 1506 was the culmination of an Augustinian project begun almost two decades earlier.[58] In the late 1480s and 1490s, Amerbach had published six major single editions of Augustine's works: the *City of God* (1489); *On the Trinity* (1489); the *Expositio Evangelii Secundum Joannem* (=*Homilies on the Gospel of John*) tentatively dated to 1490/1; the *Explanatio Psalmorum* (=*Enarrations on the Psalms*), in three volumes (1489); the *Letters* (1493); and the *Sermons*, in seven volumes (1494–5). The first print run of Amerbach's edition amounted to a total of 2,200 copies.

When Amerbach embarked on the eleven-volume edition of Augustine's collected works, he charged the Friesian scholar Augustin Dodon with the task of examining and procuring manuscripts in Germany, France, and Italy; the bulk of the editorial work was carried out by the Franciscan monk Pellicanus, who later converted to Lutheranism.

One of the principal innovations of Amerbach's edition was the division of Augustine's texts into chapters and paragraphs; the Amerbach editors placed great emphasis on ease of textual navigation.[59] Amerbach prints Augustine's texts in two to four columns of relatively small type, and divides them into chapters and sections; texts are often preceded by corresponding passages from Augustine's *Retractations* (the work which summarizes, assesses, and often revises, Augustine's earlier written pronouncements on theology and politics); Amerbach also often supplies brief chapter summaries and synopses, and cross-references texts with Scripture passages and Augustine's other works. Some of Augustine's writings include additional tools for textual orientation: *Homilies on the Gospel of John* comes equipped with a handy 'Annotatio principalium sententiarum'—an index of noteworthy sentences to be gleaned from the main text; and from 1497 onwards, Amerbach's edition of *Enarrations on the Psalms* contains a topical index or *Tabula*, from which Donne almost certainly benefited. Some texts of the Amerbach edition, such as the *Confessions*, *De Doctrina Christiana*, and *Questions on the Gospels*, are

Joseph de Ghellinck, SJ, *Patristique en Moyen Age*, vol. 3 (Paris, 1948), 377. See also, for a briefer description of the edition, Berndt Hamm, *Frömmigkeitstheologie am Anfang des 16. Jarhunderts* (Tübingen, 1982), 320 n. 115.

[57] Heiko A. Oberman, *Werden und Wertung der Reformation*, 2nd edn. (Tübingen, 1979), 90; Oberman, 'Tuus sum, salvum me fac: Augustinréveil zwischen Renaissance und Reformation', in *Scientia Augustiniana: Studien über Augustin, den Augustinismus und den Augustinerorden*, ed. Cornelius Mayer and Willigis Eckermann (Würzburg, 1965), 350–94 (358).

[58] The full title is *Prima-Vndecima Pars Librorum Diui Augustini* (Basel: Amerbach, Froben, Petri, 1506).

[59] de Ghellinck, *Patristique*, 376.

accompanied by a marginal commentary by the Franciscan scholar Francis of Meyronnes.[60] As Richard Wetzel has shown in his work on Johann von Staupitz, early modern preachers were keen to put these scholarly aids to good use. Staupitz's sermon *De temptationibus tribulationibusque* (*On temptations and tribulations*) refers to three of Augustine's *Enarrations on the Psalms*: all of these quotations can be found in the *Tabula* under the key words 'temptari' or 'tribulari'.[61]

Erasmus

By the time Erasmus's edition of Augustine's collected works appeared in 1528–9, he already had more than half a dozen other patristic editions under his belt. However, judging by the tone of his letters, no other Church Father posed a comparable challenge to his patience, stamina, and scholarly expertise. When the project was first mooted in 1517, Erasmus baulked at the 'enormous magnitude of the undertaking'.[62] And the release of the first volume in 1522—an edition of the *City of God*, with a new commentary by the Spanish humanist Juan Luis Vives—marked a less than auspicious beginning. Vives's edition arrived with royal endorsement: a prefatory note by Henry VIII praised Vives for having brought Augustine, 'long time imperfect and obscure . . . from darknesse to light' and for restoring him 'to his ancient integrity, or all posterity, whom these your *Commentaries* shall infinitely profit'.[63] Still, sales were slow, and Vives's commentary was widely criticized. Erasmus's printer Johann Froben returned from the Frankfurt book fair in 1522 without having sold a single copy; Vives, meanwhile, came under fire for replacing the popular medieval annotations on the *City of God* by two English Dominican Friars, Nicholas Trevet and John Waleys.[64] As work on the *Omnium Operum* continued at an agonizingly slow pace (due at least in part to disappointing sales), the tone of Erasmus's correspondence became increasingly desperate. The edition 'is killing me', he complained, 'I have to keep seven presses going at a time'; '[d]uty drives me: otherwise I would not have taken all this trouble, not for 1000 Florins'.[65] And, on a final note of exasperation: 'I shall die of this; there are so many blunders, and the author is interminable.'[66] Pragmatic difficulties

[60] Francis of Meyronnes (1288–1328), author of a large body of tracts, sermons, and commentaries. He wrote a commentary on Lombard's *Sentences*, and also published *florilegia* of Augustine's *De Civitate Dei* and *De Genesi ad Litteram*. See further Bartholomäus Roth, 'Franz von Meyronnes und der Augustinismus seiner Zeit', *Franziskanische Studien*, 22 (1935), 44–75.

[61] Wetzel, 'Staupitz Augustinianus', 99.

[62] *Opus Epistolarum Des. Erasmi Roterodami*, ed. P. S. Allen, 12 vols. (Oxford, 1906–58), 5.118.

[63] I am quoting from the English translation of 1610, *St. Avgvstine, of the Citie of God: With the Learned Comments of Io. Lod. Vives, Englished by J.H.*, sig. A4r.

[64] See John C. Olin, 'Erasmus and the Church Fathers', in *Six Essays on Erasmus* (New York, 1979), 33–47 (39). On Trevet and Waleys, see Beryl Smalley, *English Friars and Antiquity in the Early Fourteenth Century* (Oxford, 1960), 58–65, 88–100, and esp. 121–32.

[65] Erasmus, ed. Allen, 7.471–2.

[66] Erasmus, ed. Allen, 7.493. See also P. S. Allen, *Erasmus: Lectures and Wayfaring Sketches* (Oxford, 1934), 52–3. As Allen notes, 1,000 Florins would have kept Erasmus in board and lodging for about five years; since the edition took more than eight years to complete, Erasmus was probably justified in feeling that he had made a bad bargain.

aside, Erasmus's lack of enthusiasm stemmed, at least in part, from his acute sense of Augustine's failings as a philologist and prose stylist. Unlike Jerome, Augustine struggled with Greek and Hebrew, and close scrutiny of his style left Erasmus less than impressed: 'long-winded and convoluted', 'tortuous syntax', 'in need of a reader willing to do tedious, hard work', he opined.[67]

Yet despite these numerous drawbacks, Erasmus's achievement in eliminating 'so many' textual 'blunders' was nevertheless considerable. Vives's edition of the *City of God*, as John Olin notes, had the relatively rare distinction up to that time of indicating the manuscripts used in preparing the published text: one was borrowed from the dean of St Donatian's cathedral at Bruges, another was lent by the Carmelites there, and a third was procured through Erasmus's connections at Cologne.[68] Arnoud Visser observes that Erasmus's philological expertise also played a major part in the elimination of spurious texts: his 'awareness of the historical development of Latin enabled him to make some solid judgements', as in the case of *De fide ad Petrum Diaconum* or *De vera et falsa poenitentia*.[69] At times, however, Erasmus's dislike of Augustine's style also led him astray: the authentic work *On the Good of Widowhood* is dismissed from the canon, for instance, because 'the remarkable ease and clarity of expression scream out that it is not by Augustine'.[70] In the Erasmus edition, Augustine's works were organized in ten volumes according to their general character, theme, or genre: letters, instructional treatises, polemical writings, sermons, and so on. Erasmus incorporated captions, occasional 'censurae' (or brief critical commentaries), and marginal notes providing a variety of information—scriptural and literary references, brief synopses, variant readings, transliterations, and etymologies.[71] However, the most significant advance on Amerbach's edition was the inclusion, in volume 1, of a detailed alphabetical index to Augustine's works. The importance of this index as a scholarly aid cannot be overemphasized: Erasmus does not simply offer a single-keyword index (e.g. 'baptism') but subdivides the list of alphabetical topics further (the entry under 'baptism', for instance, contains over fifty sub-topics) to allow for a much more precise identification of doctrinal and devotional material. Few of the available sixteenth- and seventeenth-century patristic anthologies could rival the detail, depth, and scope of Erasmus's Index, which allowed preachers and controversialists to spot Augustinian passages in a much more economical and target-orientated way. Erasmus's Index helpfully cross-references 'beatitudo' with 'felicitas', 'cognitio', and 'videre', for instance, reflecting Augustine's belief that 'beatitude' consists chiefly in the vision of God: the scholarly tools in Erasmus's edition offer doctrinal as well as thematic guidance.

---

[67] Erasmus, ed. Allen, 8.155. See Arnoud Visser, 'Reading Augustine through Erasmus' Eyes: Humanist Scholarship and Paratextual Guidance in the Wake of the Reformation', *Erasmus of Rotterdam Society Yearbook* (2008), 67–90 (77–8).

[68] Olin, 'Erasmus', 39.

[69] Visser, 'Reading Augustine', 80–1.

[70] *Operum Omnium*, 4.725: 'Mira dictionis facilitas et candor clamitat non esse Augustini.' (Cited in Visser, 81.)

[71] Olin, 'Erasmus', 40.

Erasmus's edition was completed after many setbacks in 1529, and dedicated to Archbishop Alfonso Fonseca of Toledo, the Primate of Spain; it included a eulogy of Fonseca which stressed his support of humanist studies.[72] Despite initial slow sales, Erasmus's Augustine was reprinted ten times in total, with additions and corrections: notably at Basel (1569; 1579), Paris (1552), Venice (1570), and Lyon (1561–96, in fifteen octavo volumes).[73] Erasmus's patristic editions became an indispensable tool for Protestant divines: John Jewel owned a copy of his Jerome, and the Erasmus edition of Augustine continued to be used well into the seventeenth century. To name just two examples, the anti-Puritan divine Egeon Askew refers to it in a sermon printed in 1605; and Daniel Tossanus's *Synopsis de Patribus* (1603; English 1635) observes that 'the workes of Saint *Austine* are distributed into ten Tomes', and draws his citations from Erasmus's editions of the Fathers throughout.[74]

The Theologians of Louvain

Neither the Amerbach nor the Erasmus editions of Augustine's *Opera* were blessed with commercial success. The edition prepared by the theologians of Louvain, and printed by Plantin in Antwerp in 1576–7, did not fare much better. Arguably, however, financial gain was not the principal motivating factor behind the enterprise. De Ghellinck delicately points to 'the air of suspicion which surrounded Erasmus's Basel edition';[75] in fact, these suspicions culminated in a ban on the entire edition in the first papal Index of Prohibited Books (1557). This wholesale ban was relaxed in favour of more localized and specific forms of censorship after the Council of Trent: the *Index Expurgatorius* compiled at the University of Louvain in 1571 contains a comprehensive list of passages which were to be excised from Erasmus's edition.[76] Nevertheless, it is clear that one of the aims of the Louvain Augustine—much like that of the Bigne patrology of the same decade— was to present the Fathers from a counter-Reformation perspective. The project was initiated by the Flemish theologian Gozaeus and completed after his death in 1571 by his Louvain colleague Johannes Molanus; both were aided in their editorial

---

[72] Erasmus to Lord Mountjoy, 8 September 1529, announcing that the work was ready for commercial distribution: 'Augustinus totus prodiit, qui me pene confecit.' (Cited by de Ghellinck, *Patristique*, 385.)

[73] See, on these editions, Pierre Petitmengin, 'Editions princeps et Opera omnia de saint Augustin', in *Augustinus in der Neuzeit*, ed. Kurt Flasch and Dominique de Courcelles (Turnhout, 1998), 33–51.

[74] Egeon Askew, *Brotherly reconcilement preached in Oxford for the vnion of some, and now published with larger meditations for the vnitie of all in this Church and common-wealth: with an apologie of the vse of fathers, and secular learning in sermons* (1605), 294: '*Aurelius Augustinus*, then which writer the world hath nought *vel magis aureum vel augustius*, saith *Erasmus*'. The marginal note is to '*Epist. Praefix. tom.* I. *August*'. Tossanus, *A Synopsis or Compendium of the Fathers* (1635; Latin edn. 1603) references Erasmus e.g. at 9, 16, 34, 47, 50, 55.

[75] Lucien Ceyssens, 'Le "Saint Augustin" du xviie siècle: l'édition de Louvain (1577)', *XVII Siècle*, 34 (1982), 103–20; see also de Ghellinck, *Patristique*, 387.

[76] See Visser, 'Reading Augustine', 85. See also Roland Crahay, 'Les censeurs louvanistes d'Érasme', in *Scrinium Erasmianum: mélanges historiques publiés sous le patronage de l'université de Louvain*, ed. Joseph Coppens (Leiden, 1969), 221–49.

work by a further sixteen scholars from the university.[77] The Louvain team added
a number of authentic letters and sermons to the extant store of Augustinian
texts, and a 1654 reprint of their edition published, for the first time, the *The
Incomplete work against Julian*. They also made significant advances on Erasmus's
textual work, collating over two hundred manuscripts and including a list of
manuscripts used for each of Augustine's writings.[78] In many other key aspects,
however, the Louvain scholars relied heavily (and usually without acknowledgement) on Erasmus's edition: they printed the texts in the same order and, like
Erasmus, in ten volumes, and incorporated much of his critical commentary and
marginal annotations. The Louvain edition was reprinted nine times in Donne's
lifetime, and a further seven times during the remainder of the seventeenth
century.[79]

Which Augustine (again)?

Jean-Louis Quantin has shown that in the Protestant territories, Erasmus was the
first port of call for readers wanting to access Augustine's complete works.[80] The
papal ban on the edition, which came into force nearly thirty years after its
publication, had little negative impact on sales in England; in fact, many Protestant
divines were reluctant to be associated with the counter-Reformation Augustine
from Louvain. One telling exception was Archbishop Laud, who owned a copy of
the first re-issue of the Louvain edition (Paris, 1586), now housed in the Bodleian
Library at Oxford. But there is also internal evidence to suggest that Donne made
use of Erasmus's Augustine. First of all, as subsequent chapters will show in detail,
Donne often consulted the Augustinian texts at first hand. Overwhelmingly, this
did not mean acquainting himself with the whole text in detail, but rather skim-
reading selected passages—usually from the beginnings and ends of chapters and
books—and establishing some basic contexts for citations and borrowings (see
Chapter 2). *Biathanatos* and the *Essayes in Divinity* show that this habit is well
established before Donne's ordination: both texts make frequent use of intermediaries, but close inspection of their Augustinian citations demonstrates that Donne
often verified his references by returning to some of the original texts, especially the
Confessions and parts of the *City of God* (see Chapters 3 and 4). This method applies
to a wide range of Augustinian works, including those Donne evidently read and
lesser-known texts he would have encountered mostly at second hand, suggesting
that he had access to part or all of a complete edition. The high degree of overlap

---

[77] de Ghellinck, *Patristique*, 393–4, speculates that the Louvain theologians worked by annotating
Erasmus's edition, either from the 1528–9 original or a 1569 reprint.

[78] Ceyssens, 'Louvain', 108.

[79] de Ghellinck, *Patristique*, 394, 402 (the principal places of publication are Venice, Lyon, Paris,
and Cologne).

[80] Jean-Louis Quantin, 'L'Augustin du xviie siècle? Questions de corpus et de canon', in *Augustin
au XVIIe Siècle*, ed. Laurence Devillairs (Florence, 2007), 3–77: 'Beaucoup, surtout en terre
protestante, continuèrent jusque là à lire Augustin dans l'édition d'Érasme... ou l'une de ses
nombreuses rééditions' (8).

between Donne's Augustinian quotations and the Index of Erasmus's edition overwhelmingly suggests that the *Operum Omnium* was Donne's main source. 'Overlap' here refers to the frequency with which citations listed under an Erasmian topic (i.e. in the alphabetical index) appear in Donne's texts, but also to the high degree of thematic and verbal overlap between formulations found in the Index and Donne's own language, especially in the sermons and the *Essayes*. This is true especially of briefer citations, references which occur as part of a list, and of quotations which serve as intertextual 'padding' rather than structural or thematic substance. Thus, in a sermon on Genesis 1:2, 'And the Spirit of God moved above the face of the waters', Donne provides a brief conspectus of opinions on the office of the Holy Ghost; a brief glance at Erasmus's Index under the heading 'spiritus Dei ferebatur super aquas' sends the reader straight to chapter 4 of Augustine's *Incomplete Commentary on Genesis* (in volume 3 of Erasmus's edition), which offers the precise wording of the passage cited by Donne (*Sermons*, 9.96; see also Chapter 6). A Christening sermon on Galatians 3:27 introduces a quotation from Augustine's *Contra Julianum* with the phrase 'Christ calls his *death a Baptisme*'; Erasmus's Index, under the heading 'Baptizari in morte Christi quid sit', directs us to the quotation Donne uses, '*Quod crux Christo, & Sepulchrum, id nobis Baptisma*' (*Sermons*, 5.165; *Against Julian* 1.6, in volume 7 of the Erasmus Augustine). Donne may also have used Erasmus's Index as a source of his own commonplace book (which may well have arranged and prioritized passages differently).

Two possible exceptions must be noted, however. Erasmus's Index contains relatively few references to the *Enarrations on the Psalms* and the *Sermons*. But these are two key texts for Donne in the sermons (though not in the pre-ordination prose), and here the internal evidence suggests that he used the indexed/tabulated single editions of the *Enarrations* and the *Sermons* published by Amerbach in 1489 and 1494–5 respectively. All three copies of the rare Amerbach *Sermons* in England are located in cathedral libraries (Hereford, Lincoln, York Minster); it is likely that Donne would have had access to a copy of the topical *Tabula* in the library of St Paul's cathedral. At the same time, it is important to stress that the majority of Donne's citations to the *Enarrations*, and to Augustine's exegetical writings more generally, are much more straightforward: Augustine proceeds chronologically through the Book of Psalms, verse by verse, through a form of homiletic commentary, and Donne usually simply finds the scriptural passage that interests him. The first sustained engagement with the *Enarrations* occurs in Donne's sermon series on Psalm 38, dated by Potter and Simpson to spring or summer 1618.[81] Donne drew heavily on Augustine's reading of this psalm in the *Enarrations*, following the development of Augustine's thought as his own discourse evolved. Another example of such intensive use is the sermon preached at the Churching of the Countess

---

[81] See Potter and Simpson, vol. 2, nos. 1–6; see Augustine, *Enarrationes in Psalmos* 37. Augustine's Latin text of the psalms follows the Septuagint, which for Psalms 9–147 is one behind the Hebrew enumeration used in modern Bibles: so Augustine's *Enarration* 37 refers to modern Psalm 38. See e.g. *Sermons*, 2.110, a close translation of Augustine's reading of Psalm 38:4 (*PL* 36.401, Section 8 of that *Enarration*).

of Bridgewater, which invokes *Enarrations on the Psalms* 34, 84, and 147, as well as *City of God* 10.7.[82] Two other favourite sources among Augustine's exegetical works are the *Questions on the Gospels* (especially on Luke) and *Consensus of the Evangelists* (usually Book 2, on Matthew).[83]

But Donne's debt to Erasmus is not only felt in specific textual transactions. The figure of Augustine, as it emerges from Donne's numerous writings, has recognizably Erasmian contours. In the prefatory material to the *Operum Omnium*, Erasmus carefully constructs a version of Augustine which reflects his reading of the fifth-century texts, but is also acutely responsive to more contemporary concerns. As Arnoud Visser has argued, the Augustine created by Erasmus through close philological scrutiny is above all the exemplary bishop endowed with exceptional pastoral talents.[84] Although Augustine takes a tough stance against heretics when he needs to, there is little sign in Erasmus's prefaces and annotations of the militant theologian of grace—from a positive or negative perspective. There can be little doubt that this emphasis on Augustine as bishop was strategically advantageous (the edition was, after all, dedicated to a major benefactor of Erasmus's project, Archbishop Alfonso of Toledo). But showcasing Augustine's episcopal virtues also made sense from the vantage point of Erasmus's broader theological programme: reviving the memory of the Bishop of Hippo could present 'an important ethical model in a time of crisis'.[85] What mattered to Erasmus, and to Donne, however, was not primarily Augustine's episcopal authority but the pastoral virtues associated with his office. Above all, Augustine is imbued with the defining gift of the Holy Spirit: charity. Erasmus's dedicatory epistle to Archbishop Alfonso begins with a brief narrative survey of the Fathers' achievements: Jerome is the supreme Scripturalist; Basil is praised for the 'pious melodiousness' of his style; Ambrose occupies the office of bishop with dignity, but only Augustine embodies its spirit. The Holy Ghost has blessed no Father with greater gifts than Augustine, Erasmus writes, as though he had wanted to present in a single model all the virtues of the ideal bishop.[86] In ᵗʰ ᵉ preface to volume 2 of his edition, Erasmus expands on this description, with further specification of the pastoral talents exemplified in his subject: 'piety, charity, clemency, politeness, care of the flock entrusted to him, love of unity and a passion for God's house'. Erasmus also compares Augustine to 'an evangelical hen, careful and concerned to protect and cherish her chicks under her wings'.[87]

---

[82] See Potter and Simpson, vol. 5, no. 10 (on Micah 2:10); see e.g. *Sermons*, 5.206–7 and 214–15.

[83] See e.g. *Sermons*, 6.148 (Matthew 3:17), *De Consensu Evangelistarum* 2.14 (*PL* 34.1093) and 6.230 (Matthew 19:17), *De Consensu Evangelistarum* 2.63 (*PL* 34.1136–7): this was clearly a favourite Augustinian text in 1624/5; and *Sermons*, 1.163, *Quaestiones Evangeliorum Libri Duo* 2.33 (on Luke 15:20; *PL* 35.1346).

[84] Visser, 'Reading Augustine', 89.

[85] Ibid.

[86] Erasmus, ed. Allen, 8.147: 'At non arbitror alium esse doctorem in quem opulentus ille iuxta ac benignus Spiritus dotes suas omnes largius effuderit quam in Augustinum; quasi voluerit in vna tabula viuidum quoddam exemplar episcopi representare.'

[87] *Operum Omnium*, vol. 2, sig. [a1v]. The translation is Arnoud Visser's (76).

Erasmus's epistle to Alfonso of Toledo never tires of extolling Augustine's charity: Augustine discovers human connections in the midst of heated controversy, and leads the community at Hippo with unswerving diligence and clemency.[88] In defining Augustine's achievement, Erasmus relies on a characteristic connection between knowledge and love, which is mobilized by way of a quotation from 1 Corinthians 8:1, 'Knowledge puffs up, but charity edifies.' Augustine was the consummate pastor because he understood that teaching was edification, and that edification could only emerge through a bond of charity between preacher and audience.[89] For Donne, as we will see, Augustine's knowing love was the defining characteristic of a complex theology; in a sermon on Genesis 1:2, for instance, the equation of truth and love—and the links between Augustinian charity and the Holy Spirit—are made explicit (see Chapter 6). And although Donne was very much conscious of the less than saintly applications of charity in Augustine's work (see especially Chapter 4), Erasmus's portrait of the Bishop of Hippo provided a vital point of orientation, a textual model upon which his own constructions of Augustine could be built.

2. DONNE'S PHILOSOPHY OF QUOTATION

Throughout his career, and across a broad range of poetic and prose writings, Donne demonstrated a sustained concern with the theological, moral, and philosophical discourses that surrounded practices of quotation in the early modern period. My principal aim in this section is to catalogue and evaluate Donne's prescriptive statements on textual scholarship, and to establish a preliminary picture of the complex interactions of intertextual theory and practice.

Contexts: Why Quotation Matters

Ralph Keen has observed that 'the Reformation in its simplest form is an example of the use of the past to correct the errors in the present'.[90] The 'past' Keen speaks of was above all the primitive Church, which preserved the earliest witnesses to apostolic forms of worship and Church governance. In post-Reformation controversy, the writings of the Fathers became one of the chief battlegrounds for debate between Roman and Protestant divines. Catholic theologians marshalled quotations from the Fathers in an attempt to demonstrate the value of institutional continuity and tradition; against this background, it was easy to portray Protestant

---

[88] Erasmus, ed. Allen, 8.152.

[89] Erasmus, ed. Allen, 8.153: 'Haec pietas, haec charitas, hic ardor pectoris facit vt omnia illius scripta non minus inflammant ad pios affectus quam doceant intellectum.... Sunt subtiliter doceant necessaria, sed non efficiunt vt quod intelligitur ametur.... Frustra intelligas, nisi diligas quod percepisti.'

[90] Ralph Keen, 'The Fathers in Counter-Reformation Theology in the Pre-Tridentine Period', in Backus (ed.), *Reception of the Church Fathers*, 2.701–44 (738).

doctrine as a recent innovation, a heretical fad whose adherents 'preached nothynge but newfangels'.[91]

Protestant divines used the patristic tradition differently. In citing the Fathers, their chief aim was to re-interpret the Catholic argument of continuity as a process of degeneration, corruption, and inexorable decline. By compiling catalogues of patristic citations, Protestant scholars promised the recuperation of a purer form of worship, of which the current model of Catholicism was merely a warped and outdated reflection. As the controversialist John White argued, 'Our Adversaries ... may, in some points possible, pretend antiquitie, but *Prioritie*, which is the first and best antiquitie, they cannot in any one thing wherein they refuse us.'[92]

The politics of quotation emerges against this background of fierce controversy: it encompasses both the pragmatics of day-to-day combat—the trading of references, disputes about citational accuracy, debates about textual provenance and authenticity—and more thoroughly theorized reflections on scholarly ethos and procedure. Reputations could be made through deft citational manoeuvres; conversely, a bad reference could haunt the quoter even beyond the grave. Daniel Featley's *Life* of the bishop and controversialist John Jewel illustrates the imbrication of such textual politics in more global religio-ethical concerns. After listing his subject's many virtues and professional accomplishments, and having dispatched him to the literary afterlife with a suitably godly death-scene, Featley ends his narrative not with a final encomiastic flourish or with an edifying exhortation to the audience, but with a tale of misquotation:

> He [Jewel] chanced, among multitude of arguments, to faile in one, by misconceiuing a text of Scripture, *Mark*. 13.37.... This escape was first reproued by *M. Harding*, after repeated by *M. Hart*, and in this vlcer hath lately *M. Parsons* pierced his sharpest naile.... [T]he ingenuitie of our renowmd [*sic*] Bishop appeareth ... in this, That he both acknowledged and corrected his errour. *If this will not satisfie the ranced affection of some, yet when it may be sayd, Who art thou that iudgest? and shewen that their owne Doctours are guiltie of the like escapes: it may be that they will iudge of him more charitably.*[93]

Even after Jewel's death, the memory of his citational blunder lives on in the writings of his opponents and causes serious concern among his allies. In view of Jewel's track record as a patristic polemicist, this is unsurprising: many a Roman divine would have queued up to stick a nail in his 'vlcer'. It was Jewel, in his famous

---

[91] John Scory, *Two bokes of the noble doctor and B.S. Augustine* (?Emden, 1556), fol. 3v. On Scory see Mark Vessey, 'English Translations of the Latin Fathers, 1517–1611', in Backus (ed.), *Reception of the Church Fathers*, 2.775–835. Donne uses Augustine's Letter to Dioroscurus (Epistle 118, *PL* 33.441; Secunda Classis) to make a similar point in a sermon on 2 Pet. 3:13: 'But *Perniciosissimus humano generi*, sayes *Saint Augustine*... When to all our sober preaching, and serious writing, a scornfull ignorant, shall thinke it enough to oppose that one question of contempt, *Where was your Church before Luther?*' (*Sermons*, 8.67).

[92] John White, *A Defense of the Way to the True Church* (1614), sig. **4v.

[93] *The Works of the Very Learned and Reuerend Father in God Iohn Iewell* (1609), sig. ¶¶6v. Featley also notes that Jewel, as a 'young reader ... being but a Batchelar ... sifted much of the flower of *S. Augustine* with diuine aphorisms' (sig. ¶¶¶1v).

'Challenge Sermon' of 1559, who had put the controversial spotlight firmly on the Fathers. Cataloguing the 'faults and abuses' of the Catholic mass, Jewel confidently claimed the patristic tradition for the Protestant side: 'the doctors and old catholic fathers . . . are yours: ye shall see the siege raised, ye shall see your adversaries discomfited and put to flight'.[94] And in the challenge that was to become eponymous with his performance, Jewel raised the rhetorical stakes even further: 'if any man alive were able to prove any of these articles by any one clear and plain clause or sentence, either of the scriptures, or of the old doctors, or of any old general council, or by any example of the primitive church . . . I am content to yield unto him, and to subscribe'.[95] Jewel's sermon had a significant impact on the tone, style, and method of patristic discourses in the sixteenth and early seventeenth centuries. It is no exaggeration to say that, after Jewel, the question of who represented the one true Church was irrevocably intertwined with the question of who owned the Fathers, and who could allege their authority most powerfully and efficiently. In light of these events, his enemies were understandably keen to keep alive the memory of his citational faux-pas, long after Jewel himself had slipped away.

Similar connections between citational and controversial politics can be detected in a letter from Donne to his friend Henry Goodyer. Sent from Donne's home in Mitcham, Surrey, it discusses the Oath of Allegiance debate to which Donne himself was to contribute, in the form of *Pseudo-martyr*, in 1610. The letter comments on a tract published by a member of the Protestant faction, and Donne is found worrying about a number of scholarly failings:

> But for this particular Author, I looked for more prudence, and humane wisdome in him, avoiding all miscitings, or mis-interpretings, because at this time, the watch is set, and every bodies hammer is upon that anvill; and to dare offend in that kinde now, is, for a theef to leave the covert, and meet a strong hue and cry in the teeth[.] . . . [T]he Book is full of falsifications in words, and in sense, and of falshoods in matter of fact, and of inconsequent and unscholarlike arguings . . . and of neglecting better and more obvious answers, and of letting slip some enormous advantages which the other gave, and he spies not.[96]

Donne's alarm is localized in 'miscitings, or mis-interpretings', breaches of academic protocol which endanger the broader polemical objective. '[F]alsifications', 'falshoods', and 'unscholarly arguings' are construed as the textual equivalent of

[94] John Jewel, 'The copie of a Sermon pronounced by the Byshop of Salisburie at Paules Crosse . . . shortly set forthe as nere as the authour could call it to remembraunce, without any alteration or addition', in John Ayre (ed.), *The Works of John Jewel*, 4 vols. (Cambridge, 1845–50), 1.2–25 (7, 22). The sermon was preached by Jewel as bishop-elect of Salisbury at Paul's Cross on 26 November 1559, repeated at court on 17 March, and again at Paul's Cross on 31 March 1560; it initiated one of the most significant, prolonged, and textually prolific controversies of Elizabeth's reign. On this, see Peter Milward, *Religious Controversies of the Elizabethan Age: A Survey of Printed Sources* (London, 1977), 1–8. Jewel's main opponent on the Catholic side was the Thomas Harding mentioned in Featley's text (formerly Regius Professor of Hebrew and Warden-Elect of New College, Oxford). Harding had retracted his Protestantism under Mary, and had received a benefice in the Diocese of Salisbury, only to be ejected by the new bishop, John Jewel (ibid. 3).
[95] Jewel, 'Paules Crosse', 21.
[96] John Donne, *Letters to Severall Persons of Honour* (London, 1651), 161, 163.

breaking cover, a tactical error which introduces an element of vulnerability and forces the Protestant side to play defence when a better citational positioning could have enabled them to attack confidently.

Donne's engagement with the controversial debates of the period may have been less intense and prolonged than Jewel's (he produced only one work of professional polemic, *Pseudo-martyr*), but his interest in the ethics and politics of quotation is sustained and profound none the less.[97] In order to consolidate this argument, we need to investigate in more detail Donne's views on the theory and practice of quotation in a wide range of texts: the prose and verse letters, the sermons, *Biathanatos*, *Pseudo-martyr*, the satires (*Metempsychosis*, Satire 2, 'Coryats Crudities'), *The Courtier's Library*, and the *Essayes in Divinity*.

Textual Digests and Textual Digestion

A survey of Donne's philosophy of quotation takes us, initially, to a set of broader questions. What were the principles that guided the processes of knowledge acquisition through reading? What kinds of material should be used: was recourse to scholarly aids such as abridgements and excerpt collections permissible, or should readers strive for a direct encounter with the author's voice? And how could the information gleaned from various reading regimes be adapted and transmuted, and put to work in the reader's own spheres of intellectual activity? The answers to all these questions are, for Donne, highly context-dependent; nevertheless, there are a number of core ideas about reading and knowledge use that recur throughout his writing. The fact that these pronouncements are mostly found in his satirical works may in itself speak to the difficulty of mapping precept on to practice, but it is worth attending to Donne's textual reflections in detail before testing them against specific examples and applications.

The Courtier's Library, Donne's satirical account of one particular group of readers, certainly takes a firm view on the value of scholarly cribs, props, and mediators. The central conceit of the work takes intellectual minimalism to an extreme. Donne's courtiers have a dual aim: they want to 'avoid both the shame of ignorance and the bother of reading [*legendi fastidium*]'. One way of achieving this is to ignore the original texts and consult one of the many shortcuts available to early modern readers: 'epitomes, paradoxes, and the stings of extravagant wits . . . [by] Ramon Lull, Gemma Frisius, Raimond Sebond, Sextus Empiricus, and Abbot Trithemius, Henry Cornelius Agrippa, Erasmus, Peter Ramus, and heretical writers'.[98] But for Donne's courtier, even the smaller labour of mediated and filtered study proves too burdensome, and so he relies on a more ingenious solution

---

[97] But see Bawcutt and Kelliher, whose account of the 1626 Convocation notes that Donne was hailed, by other members, as an effective polemicist of the Church of England: Nigel Bawcutt and Hilton Kelliher, 'Donne through Contemporary Eyes: New Light on his Participation in the Convocation of 1626', *Notes & Queries*, NS 42 (1995), 441–4 (442).

[98] The translation is Piers Brown's, appended to the article cited above in n. 18 (859).

still: an entirely fictional library, whose contents cannot be tested or contested in conversation, and is therefore perfectly suited to effortless displays of learning.

Reading as a form of mindless consumption and display is also the focus of Satire 2, which targets another community of readers well known for their love of abridgements and cribs—the lawyers:

> But hee is worst, who (beggarly) doth chaw
> Others wits fruits, and in his ravenous maw
> Rankly digested, those things out-spue,
> As his owne things; and they are his owne, 'tis true,
> For if one eate my meate, though it be knowne
> The meate was mine, th'excrement is his owne.[99]

Like those who snatch up the discarded remains of others' food, Donne's beggarly reader in Satire 2 feeds on 'Others wits fruits'. The main problem, however, lies in the digestive tract: it is not simply that the nourishment is poor in the first place, but that it is insufficiently assimilated and absorbed. The end result, unsurprisingly, reflects all of these flawed processes; the regurgitation of poorly digested fragments inevitably produces intellectual 'excrement'.[100] Thomas Nashe's *Anatomie of Absurditie* (1589) develops a similar critique of mediated knowledge when he discusses 'the excrements of arts . . . bought at second hand'.[101]

Biathanatos freely acknowledges that it is not entirely the fruit of its author's own learning. Donne has taken 'light from others' throughout his treatise, but takes pains to showcase his intellectual debts:

> Euery branch, which is excerpted from other Authors and engrafted here, is not written for the Readers faith, but for illustration, and Comparison. Because I vndertooke the declaration of such a proposition, as was controverted by many, and therefore was drawne to the citation of many Authorityes, I was willing to go all the way with Company, and to take light from others, as well in the iourney, as at the iourneys end. If therefore in multiplicity of not necessary citations, there appeare vanity, or Ostentation, or digression, my honesty must make my excuse, and compensation who acknowledge as . . . *Plinie* doth, *That to chuse rather to be taken in a theft, then to giue euery man his due, is obnoxij animi, et infelicis ingenij.*[102]

Once again, the threat of consumerist reading looms large in Donne's textual rhetoric. *Biathanatos*, not least through its pointed opposition to 'scholastique' forms of argument, encourages more active habits of interpretation in its audience. Quotations are 'not written for the Readers faith, but for illustration, and

---

[99] Satire 2, 'Sir; though (I thanke God for it) I do hate', ll. 25–30.

[100] Donne here inverts one of the stock images of early modern discourses of imitation, derived from Seneca's Epistle 84. In Seneca, imitation is a transformative activity: the bees gather material from the flowers and create a new product through a process of their own. See, on this and other models of imitation, G. W. Pigman III, 'Versions of Imitation in the Renaissance', *Renaissance Quarterly*, 33 (1980), 1–32.

[101] Thomas Nashe, *The Anatomie of Absurditie*, in *Works*, ed. R. B. McKerrow, rev. F. P. Wilson, 5 vols. (Oxford, 1958), 1.20; cited in Robin Robbins's commentary on Satire 2 in *The Complete Poems of John Donne* (Harlow, 2010), 379.

[102] *Biathanatos*, 32.

Comparison'; they need to be scrutinized and their authority tested. An excerpt collection or a patchwork of 'beggarly' fragments can only be taken on faith or be rejected outright, but Donne's text wants to be argued with. This emphasis on judgement and discretion culminates in Donne's definition of his ideal audience: 'Siues' who will sift through the evidence, track references through their sources, and 'retayne the best onely'.[103] The 'best', as we will see in Chapter 4, is a highly complex category, but *Biathanatos* is unequivocal in its commitment to active, contextualized, engaged reading, and in its distrust of blind citational authority.

The scatological rhetoric of textual digestion in Satire 2 is taken to a more extreme level in Donne's poem '*Upon Mr* Thomas Coryats Crudities'. An account of Coryate's five-month walking tour in Europe in 1608, the *Crudities* is now chiefly remembered for the 107 pages of mock-panegyric verses composed by some of the most prominent literary figures of the time, including Donne, Ben Jonson, John Harington, and John Hoskins. The main conceit of Donne's mock encomium, however, derives from the analogies between textual composition and bodily digestion, which are triggered by the title of Coryate's book: *Coryats crudities hastily gobled vp in five moneths . . . newly digested in the hungry aire of Odcombe in the county of Somerset, & now dispersed to the nourishment of the trauelling members of this kingdome*. Coryate's title is cited in the *OED* as an example of a figurative use of the word 'crudity': 'the state of being imperfectly digested, or the quality of being indigestible . . . also, in old physiology, imperfect "concoction" of the humours'.[104] Donne's poem works off the fundamental assumption that Coryate has failed to assimilate and digest the information accumulated during his travels: his text is an imperfect and toxic concoction of fragmented experiences, which any reader will want to expel as soon as possible. Coryate's idiosyncratic method of composition is matched, in Donne's account, by an equally unique process of publication and dissemination. Because Coryate has failed to assimilate his sources properly, Donne imagines his text as lacking coherence in the literal as well as the figurative sense: the *Crudities* not only have a looser texture than most other works, but possess an active drive towards self-fragmentation. Thus, the elements of Coryate's crude narrative will find their way back to the foreign lands from which they originated, leaving the text in pieces:

> The bravest Heroes, for publike good
> Scatter'd in divers lands, their lims and bloud.
> Worst malefactors, to whom men are prize,
> Do publike good cut in Anatomies.
> So will thy booke in peeces: for a Lord
> Which casts at Portescues, and all the board,
> Provide whole bookes; each leafe enough will be
> For friends to passe time, and keepe companie.
> . . . .
> Nor shall wit-pyrates hope to finde thee lye
> All in one bottome, in one Librarie.

---

[103] *Biathanatos*, 32.   [104] *OED*, 'crudity', 2.

> Some leaves may paste strings there in order bookes,
> And so one may, which on another lookes,
> Pilfer, alas, a little wit from you,
> But hardly much; and yet I think this true;
> As *Sybils* was, your booke is mysticall,
> For every peece is as much worth as all.[105]

At one level, Donne's account of the *Crudities* is simply a material analogy for flawed writing: a metaphor for the imperfect assimilation of sources and the failure to transmute raw substance into a coherent textual whole. But there is also a gleeful (if mildly disturbing) note of triumph in the notion that, because of its drive towards self-dismemberment, Coryate's text has managed to escape the greedy grasp of the 'wit-pyrates'; that it need not worry about being excerpted, exploited, and torn to pieces by others because it has already destroyed itself. At the same time, and in a further paradoxical modulation, Coryate's text acquires authenticity and authority through its fragmentary nature—oracular like Sybil's leaves.

Despite their satirical and scatological refractions, Donne's verses on Coryate's *Crudities* offer an important perspective on his theory of textuality. If nothing else, they lead us to search for a remedy or tonic with which the intellectual dyspepsia of Satire 2 and the *Crudities* can be addressed. Some of Donne's texts offer a deceptively simple cure: *Pseudo-martyr*, for instance, tries to breed healthy readers willing to commit to a serious and demanding course of study. While intellectual magpies will only pick out 'the Heads and Grounds handled in this Booke',[106] Donne recommends a more sustained form of intellectual engagement. To mount a credible critique of his argument in *Pseudo-martyr*, the consumer of texts must first transform himself into a reader, and no one can 'well and properly be called a Reader, till he were come to the end of the Booke'.[107]

Polemic and Textuality: Rags and Bones

Although, as we will see, Donne stopped emphatically short of a categorical dismissal of mediated knowledge and frequently drew on sentence collections and other scholarly aids in his own citational practice, it is clear that the idea of a return to the sources of patristic authority held considerable *polemical* promise for him. While Donne evidently regarded recourse to the original text as a broader principle of citational ethics (he points out in *Biathanatos* that there are only a 'few' places that he has 'not seene in the bookes themselues'—although it must be re-stated that having 'seene' them is not the same as having read the entire work),[108] he was also doubtless aware of its value for controversial debate. If the English Church was to prove itself as the true heir to the primitive tradition, it needed to revisit the first

---

[105] '*Upon Mr* Thomas Coryats Crudities', 51–5, 65–72.
[106] *Pseudo-Martyr*, ed. Anthony Raspa (Montreal, 1993), 8. All subsequent quotations from the text are from this edition.
[107] Ibid.
[108] *Biathanatos*, 5

witnesses to its practices: the Fathers. And unless these patristic sources could be studied closely, and in their most authentic and authoritative versions, the Protestant case for 'priority' stood little chance of success. A sermon on Psalms 6:8–10, probably delivered in the spring of 1623, forcefully conveys this classic Protestant equation of doctrinal and textual reformation; as scholarly tools and methods evolve, Donne argues, the Fathers will speak clearly in support of the Protestant Church:

> at the beginning of the Reformation . . . because most of those men who laboured in that Reformation, came out of the Romane Church, and there had never read the body of the Fathers at large; but only such ragges and fragments of those Fathers, as were patcht together in their Decretat's, and Decretals, and other such Common placers, for their purpose, and to serve their turne, therefore they were loath at first to come to that issue, to try controversies by the Fathers. But as soon as our men that imbraced the Reformation, had had time to reade the Fathers, they were ready enough to joyne with the Adversarie in that issue[.] . . . [A]nd howsoever at the beginning some men were a little ombrageous, and startling at the name of the Fathers, yet since the Fathers have been well studied, for more then threescore yeares.[109]

Donne's damning indictment of 'the Romane Church' finds a ready target in specific reading procedures—the use of 'Common placers' rather than the original sources—but also encompasses broader questions of scholarly decorum and ethics. Rome's controversialists have no interest in the true meaning of the Fathers, only in the fragments that can be patched together 'for their purpose, and to serve their turne'. Donne frequently draws on the humanist rhetoric of textual integrity in his attacks on Catholic textual practice. An early sermon preached on Luke 23:4 at Whitehall (20 February 1618) also mobilizes the caricature of Rome as a patchwork religion:

> It is not for man to insert, to inlay other words into the word of God. It is a gross piece of *Mosaick* work, to insert whole Apocryphal books into the Scriptures. . . . It is a counterfeit piece of *Mosaick* work, when having made up a body of their Canon-Law, of the raggs and fragments torne from the body of the Fathers, they attribute to every particular sentence in the book, not that authority which that sentence had in that Father from whom it is taken, but that authority which the Canonization (as they call it) of that sentence gives it; by which Canonization, and placing it in that book, it is made equal to the word of God.[110]

Donne illustrates these mechanisms with an example, the *Thesaurus Catholicus*, compiled by Jodocus Coccius and published in Cologne in 1600. This 'counterfeit piece of *Mosaick* work' emerges in two stages: excerption, as 'raggs and fragments [are] torne from the body of the Fathers' and, once the dismemberment is complete, a reconstitution of the pieces in light of Roman doctrine. The result of this textual metamorphosis bears little resemblance to the patristic original: excerption implies decontextualization, strips the text of authorial meaning and (in a near-sacrilegious act) remakes it in the image of a human tradition. In the

---

[109] *Sermons*, 6.56.   [110] Ibid. 1.252–3.

monstrous new 'body' of the 'Canon-Law', for instance, the Fathers speak not with 'that authority which that sentence had in that Father from whom it is taken, but that authority which the Canonization . . . of that sentence gives it'. This dual dynamic of fragmentation and corruption is also a prominent trope in Thomas James's *Treatise of the Corrvption of Scripture*, which argues that Catholic divines 'raze' their texts, 'and pare them, and blurre them, els they cannot uphold their irreligion'.[111] Daniel Tossanus, in his *Synopsis de Patribus*, weighs in with a similar accusation: '*they dare not stand to the decision of the sacred Scriptures, nor of the Fathers themselves, except they bee mutilated, and altred according to their will, and deformed with many supposititious books*'.[112]

To find out more about the guiding principles of Donne's own citational philosophy, we need to subject his critique of Catholic textuality to closer examination. The questions which underpin this critique could not be more ambitious: Donne addresses ideas which are fundamental to Protestant views on the status of human tradition and the progress of history. But in order to grasp these big ideas precisely, we need to analyse an apparently small-scale phenomenon: the language of textual rags and fragments. Detaching a small piece of writing from its context, without regard for occasion, place, and audience, is for Donne a defining characteristic of Rome's textual mentality: he routinely accuses Roman controversialists of using 'raggs and fragments torne from the body of the Fathers',[113] as we have seen, but rumination on fragmented reading and re-composition is not confined to the sermons and controversial writings alone.

A letter to Henry Goodyer sent in 1614 applies the rhetoric of fragmentation to Donne's own writing. Having resolved to enter the Church, Donne tells Goodyer that he must undertake a final poetic project, 'a valediction to the world before I take Orders': 'I am brought to a necessity of printing my Poems, and addressing them to my L[ord] Chamberlain [Robert Ker, Earl of Somerset]. . . . By this occasion I am made a Rhapsoder of mine own rags, and that cost me more diligence to seek them, then it did to make them.'[114] This parallels almost exactly a disparaging comment in *Pseudo-martyr* four years earlier, on 'these Rhapsoders, and fragmentary compilers of [church] Canons'. 'Rhapsoder' is Donne's (almost unique) version of the word 'rhapsodist', 'a collector of literary pieces'.[115] Both these uses of the word also seem to play on its etymology, from the Greek verb 'to stitch together', and both imply (although in the case of *Pseudo-martyr* in a rather more aggressively negative sense) a suspicion that the end-result of the process may be less than perfectly formed. The third meaning of the word 'rhapsodist', 'one who rhapsodizes . . . with implication of want of argument or fact', is also present in Donne's lexical negotiations. The canonists of *Pseudo-martyr* show a distinct lack of textual understanding, both at the point of extraction and at the stage of reconstitution, when fragments are converted into a new text. The same charge is levelled at

[111] James, *Corrvption*, sig. ¶3v.
[112] Daniel Tossanus, *A Synopsis or Compendium of the Fathers* (1635), sig. A8r.
[113] *Sermons*, 1.253.   [114] *Letters*, 196–7.   [115] *OED*, 'Rhapsoder', 1.

compilers of Scripture commentaries such as Peter Lombard, whom Donne describes, in *Biathanatos*, as the original patristic '*Rhapsoder*'.[116]

The most trenchant critique of this textual combinatorics is mounted in the sermon on Psalm 6, discussed above, and especially in Donne's claim that the Catholics admit as evidence 'only such ragges and fragments of those Fathers, as were patcht together in their Decretat's, and Decretals, and other such Common placers'.[117] Donne is similarly dismissive of other composite texts: in *Pseudo-martyr*, '*the body of the Canon law*' is described as 'a *Satyr*, and *Miscellany* of divers and ill digested Ingredients'.[118] His distrust of artificially reconstituted texts also surfaces in the use of macaronic verse, the ultimate patchwork genre: as the high point of his satirical deconstruction at the end of '*Upon Mr* Thomas Coryats Crudities', or as the verbal manifestation of Coscus's corruption in Satire 2.

Finally, we return to Donne's less than flattering review of Protestant scholarship in the letter to Goodyer. Having glanced at a number of printed contributions to the Oath of Allegiance controversy, Donne turns down Goodyer's request for a more detailed comment on the polemical exchange: '[it] were no service to you', Donne argues, 'to send you my notes upon the Book, because they are sandy, and incoherent ragges, for my memory, not for your judgement'.[119] Unlike some of his colleagues, Donne refuses to lay himself open to charges of 'miscitings' and 'falshoods': his own records must undergo a further process of review, digestion, and fact-checking; they need to be dusted off and put into their proper order to produce a text that can withstand scrutiny. Time and again, Donne's approach is characterized by this complex combination of scholarly principles and polemical reflexes. Textual authorities, whether consulted at first hand or encountered through a mediating source, must be absorbed and re-worked with care. Through-out his works, Donne adopts a series of shifting and complex perspectives on the issue of textual fidelity. Although the appearance of direct textual recourse is strategically valuable, just as important to Donne is the use of a source through multi-layered processes of interpretive absorption and reincorporation.[120]

'Ragges . . . patcht together' is one of the small textual details which Donne habitually invests with more universal doctrinal significance. The Roman approach to patristic sources encapsulates more global failings; habits of quotation illustrate the different value assigned by Protestants and Catholics to human tradition, for

---

[116] *Biathanatos*, 31. On Lombard, see more below (Chapter 2).

[117] *Sermons*, 6.56.

[118] *Pseudo-martyr*, 191.

[119] *Letters* (1651), 162.

[120] Once again, there are parallels here with descriptions of imitation in core texts such as Seneca's Epistle 84. The metaphors used by compilers of patristic anthologies to describe their work are strikingly similar to those used by compilers of secular anthologies and manuals of imitation: the most common one, according to Anthony Lane, is that of 'the bee travelling from flower to flower; the bee is an example of industry but also of prudent selectivity, gathering that which is best for the beehive'; the result of such labours can be compared to a storehouse, to which one can turn for apt quotations, but it is also a transitional stage in textual 'digestion' and further literary production. Anthony N. S. Lane, 'Justification in Sixteenth-Century Patristic Anthologies', in *Auctoritas Patrum: Zur Rezeption der Kirchenväter im 15. und 16. Jh.*, ed. Leif Grane et al. (Mainz, 1993), 69–93 (93).

instance. In his sermon on Luke 23:40, as we have seen, Donne objects to the 'Canonization' of patristic opinion, which makes human writing 'equal to the word of God'.[121] For Donne, the limitations of a work such as the *Thesaurus Catholicus* reveal themselves, above all, in its flawed view of human history: by patching together an apostolic Father and a twelfth-century theologian, Roman divines wilfully ignore the seams and stitches which characterize any chronological narrative. Tradition and authority, in this model, speak with a timeless, unified voice: this is why texts can be gutted and reconfigured at will, and without detriment to doctrinal cohesion. It is precisely this notion of history and textuality that comes under attack in Donne's sermons and *Pseudo-martyr*, often through the systematic exposure of anachronism and tonal dissonance. *Pseudo-martyr* asks, for instance, how the Old Testament prophet Samuel could possibly be invoked as an authority on papal supremacy:

> upon what place of Scripture may they not build this supremacy, and this obedience to it, after a Pope, who is heire to an *Active* and *Passive infallibility*, and can neither deceive nor be deceived, hath extorted from *Samuel*, so long before the *Apostolique* Sea was established, a testimony, *That not to obey the Apostolique Sea, was the sinne of Idolatrie, teste Samuele*[.][122]

Donne insists that an author cannot simply be isolated from historical circumstance and transplanted into a controversy whose premises would have been completely alien to him. *Pseudo-martyr* abounds with case studies which illustrate this problem: examples of 'any litle rag torn or fallen off' from a text, 'casually and incidentally fallen into a letter of another purpose', which—by a process which seems at once byzantine and random—eventually passes into canon law and 'binde[s] the whole Church, *De fide*'.[123] In Donne's (highly partial) account, such processes are frequently seen to yield absurd results, as in the case of the *Corpus Iuris Canonici*, the main collection of canon law precepts originally compiled by the twelfth-century jurist Gratian. Guided by the imperative to produce orthodox readings, Gratian's official commentators often stop glossing altogether, and correct their source instead: 'for the *glosse* doth sometimes (when no reconciliation can serve him) depart from *Gratian* with some disdaine'.[124]

Donne's approach to contextual reading is itself subject to variations in context, and often he is found using precisely the strategies of excerption and compilation he excoriates in his Roman rivals (especially in controversial debate; see further the section 'Principles and Practice' on p. 59). On the whole, however, he is mindful of the local situatedness of the texts he cites. In a sermon preached at St Paul's on 21 June 1626 (on 1 Corinthians 15:29), for instance, Donne advises caution in dismissing controversial patristic doctrine too quickly. In framing their ideas, the Fathers were precisely attuned to the demands of rhetorical decorum—the nature of their audience, and the time and place of delivery. This has implications for patristic reception and interpretation; a sermon will seek to engage its audience

---

[121] *Sermons*, 1.253.   [122] *Pseudo-martyr*, 76.
[123] Ibid. 198–9.   [124] Ibid. 195.

emotionally as well as intellectually, and we ignore the linguistic markers of these strategies to our own detriment: 'The Fathers often applyed themselves in figurative, and Hyperbolicall speeches, to exalt the devotions, and stir up the affections of their auditory, and therefore must not be called to too severe, and literall an account, for all that they uttered in that manner.'[125] In compiling his patristic references, as Chapter 2 will demonstrate, Donne attends in detail to developments and changes in Augustine's thought, both in order to display his expertise and to gauge the tonalities of Augustine's texts more precisely.

For better or worse, human readers and writers must negotiate the complex, composite, and frequently dissonant narrative of history; only the resurrection will reunite and resolve all the different voices into a perfect harmony. Fragmented understanding is a fact of fallen existence; we cannot read from the perspective of eternal providence, only through plodding contextual reconstruction. Paradoxically, Donne's commitment to this model is clearest when he imagines himself outside of time, as in a late sermon on Matthew 6:21, which envisages the resurrection as a grand reunion of theologians through the ages. In heaven, Donne says expectantly, 'I shall finde the Fathers of the first Age, dead five thousand years before me; and they shall not be able to say they were a minute before me.'[126] Suspension from the flow of time is a recurring feature of Donne's hermeneutic thought: it means perfect cognition, and unmediated communion with voices that have ceased to be audible across the chasm of history—the Patriarchs, 'dead five thousand years', the Fathers, and above all Augustine. We will see different elements of this vision at work in the *Essayes in Divinity* (Chapter 3), and in Donne's Easter sermons (Chapter 7), which anticipate the glories of hermeneutic 'Redintegration' in heaven.[127] In both cases, liberation from the contexts of reading is figured as a radical shift in perspective. While on earth, we proceed along the horizontal axis of history, embedded in events as they occur; Donne's ultimate aspiration, however, is a more elevated viewpoint: the panoramic breadth and accuracy of quasi-divine vision in heaven. From the vantage point of the resurrected souls, historical differences are levelled out and Donne can encounter Augustine face to face. There are counterfeit versions of this cognitive perfection, however: chief among them the Roman fiction of a flawless '*Mosaick*' of witnesses, of course, and the timeless conversation of authorities engineered in canon law and other sources.

Lest we despair at the idea of a patchwork universe, Donne reminds us that even God himself does not work in entirely seamless ways; in the Scriptures, the Holy Ghost's own efforts are presented as composite:

> As the Tabernacle of God was, so the Scriptures of God are of this *Mosaick* work: The body of the Scriptures hath in it limbs taken from other bodies; and in the word of God, are the words of other men, other authors, inlaid and inserted. But, this work is onely where the Holy Ghost is the Workman: It is not for man to insert, to inlay other words into the word of God.[128]

---

[125] *Sermons*, 7.203.   [126] Ibid. 9.188.   [127] Ibid.   [128] Ibid. 1.252.

This is one of the many ways in which the Holy Spirit connects God with humankind, and thus provides comforting glimpses of a superior pattern in the apparent chaos and disorder of life on earth. In his sermons and prose tracts, Donne puts in the work required to move along the horizontal axis of human interpretation: sifting evidence, assimilating information, contextualizing sources. This is why he is so receptive to rhetorical occasion, why he reads audiences, places of preaching, and religio-political circumstances so carefully. But there is also another driving force behind Donne's hermeneutic transactions: one that moves along the vertical axis, upward and downward. It operates through timeless Augustinian categories like charity and faith, which allow Donne to read beyond the surface meaning and to recover a deeper sense; in the words of a favourite Scripture text, 1 Timothy 1:5, 'the end of the commandment is charity'. Such interpretations seek to realize the spirit of the text, articulate the animating principle behind all the Scriptures: God's providential love for humanity. But they are rarely simple: Chapters 5 and 6 give two different examples of the textual calisthenics required to graduate to this higher, and deeper, level of interpretation. Donne, then, relies on two interrelated assumptions: that the texts we produce are anchored in local contexts; and that while we are enjoined to read diligently, full understanding must be deferred until the next life. Both of these assumptions have implications for Donne's theory of quotation.

The first implication is that Donne rejects overly fastidious methods of textual scrutiny, which easily shade into distrust, suspicion, and malicious curiosity. In the sermons, he caricatures the 'supercilious, and fastidious delicacy' of so-called 'Text men' and deplores the

> impertinent curiosity [of those], who though the sense be never so well observed, call every thing a falsification, if the place be not rightly cyphard, or the word exactly cited; and magnifie one another for great Text men, though they understand no Text, because they cite Book, and Chapter, and Verse, and Words aright. [129]

Hermeneutic curiosity is also a key issue in Donne's scriptural meditations in the *Essayes in Divinity*, as Chapter 3 will demonstrate. And *Pseudo-martyr* addresses 'the curious malice of those men, who in this sickly decay, and declining of their cause, can spy out falsifyings in every citation: as in a jealous, and obnoxious state, a Decipherer can pick out Plots, and Treason, in any familiar letter which is intercepted'. [130] The Roman approach to quotation, paradoxically, is at once irresponsible and excessively fastidious; the large-scale fabrication of evidence happily coexists with paranoid scrutiny of sources and witnesses. To *Pseudo-martyr* we also owe an almost unique glance into the realities of scholarly work, albeit with a familiar polemical inflection. There Donne explains that in citing sources, 'I doe not alwayes precisely and superstitiously binde my selfe to the words of the Authors;

---

[129] *Sermons*, 9.205–6.
[130] *Pseudo-martyr*, 10. See also Item 9 in Donne's *Catalogus*: 'What you please out of what you please [Quidlibet ex quolibet]; *Or the art of deciphering and finding some treason in any intercepted letter*, by Philips' (Piers Brown's translation).

which was impossible to me ... because sometimes I collect their sense, and
expresse their Arguments or their opinions ... in two or three lines'. As arguments
are summarized and digested, the reader gains distance from the source text; this
centrifugal momentum is multiplied, for Donne, in the case of 'Catholique
Authors' being cited 'out of their owne fellowes, who had used the same fashion
of collecting their sense, without precise binding themselves to All'.[131]

Donne's sermons frequently present examples of inexact quotation. Preaching at
St Paul's on Easter Day 1630, for instance, he observes that the angel who reported
Christ's departure from the tomb (Matthew 28:6) did not quote Christ precisely:
'[I]n this place, the Angel referres the women to Christs words, and yet if we
compare the places, (that where Christ speaks the words, and that where the Angell
repeats them) though the sense be intirely the same, yet the words are not altogether
so [Matthew 17:22 and Luke 24:6].'[132] In another sermon, Donne notes that
'neither Christ in his preaching, nor the holy Ghost in penning the Scriptures of
the new Testament, were so curious as our times, in citing Chapters and Verses, or
such distinctions, no nor in citing the very, very words of the places'.[133] The Holy
Ghost, unsurprisingly, puts more emphasis on the spirit than the letter, and Donne
follows suit; he has no wish to copy the example of his 'Text men', who 'understand
no text', even though 'they cite Book, and Chapter, and Verse, and Words aright'.[134]

Further confirmation of this approach is provided by a brief glance at Donne's
position on Scripture translation. Here, as in his citational philosophy, Donne's
reflections focus on the relationship between letter and spirit:

> We must doe in this last [part], as we have done in our former two parts, crack a shell,
> to tast the kernell, cleare the words, to gaine the Doctrine. I am ever willing to assist
> that observation, That the books of Scripture are the eloquentest books in the world,
> that every word in them hath his waight and value, his tast and verdure. And therefore
> must not blame those Translators, nor those Expositors, who have, with a particular
> elegancy, varied the words in this last clause of the Text, *my witnesse,* and *my record.* The
> oldest Latine Translation received this variation, and the last Latine, even *Tremellius*
> himselfe, (as close as he sticks to the Hebrew) retaines this variation[.] ... But other
> places of Scripture will more advance that observation of the elegancy thereof[.][135]

---

[131] *Pseudo-martyr*, 10.
[132] *Sermons*, 9.206.
[133] Ibid. 5.44, the example is from Isaiah: '[I]f we consider that one place in the prophet *Esay,*
[6:10] ... and consider the same place, as it is cited six severall times in the new Testament, we shall
see, that they stood not upon such exact quotations, and citing of the very words.' This was a
commonplace of Protestant exegesis and controversy, designed to expose the unthinking literalism of
the Roman (and Jewish) opposition. Protestant controversialists, by contrast, often portrayed their
faction as reading for the sense and the spirit. See, for instance, Thomas Wilson, *Theologicall Rules to
Gvide Vs in the Vnderstanding and Practise of holy Scriptures* (1615), Rule 36, pp. 37–8: 'In sundry
places out of the old testament cited by Christ and his Apostles, the sense is kept, but not the same
words alwaies ... and often elsewhere Christ and his Apostles follow the translation of the *Septuagint* in
Greek, which rendreth the sense, and not the words. Also this is done to shew that Scripture is
considered by the meaning, and not by letters and syllables. Lastly, God dealeth as an interpreter,
therefore addeth or changeth words, for the better keeping of the sense. This rule puts to silence
cauilling aduersaries of Gods blessed word.'
[134] *Sermons*, 9.205–6.   [135] Ibid. 226–7.

Donne, once again, draws on the rhetoric of surface and depth here, while also demonstrating the requisite sensitivity to philological detail. It is precisely because of the elegant craftsmanship of the Scriptures that the translator must at times be allowed to vary and modify; to cleave ploddingly to the 'very, very words' would destroy the spirit of the text, its 'tast and verdure'. It is absolutely crucial to note, however, that these liberties in translation are hedged about with strict provisions: any reading that departs from the letter must be collated with other authoritative translations and Scripture places. In Donne's sermons, the Vulgate version of the Bible is often cited as an example of such regulated liberty; he notes of the Vulgate rendering of Psalm 2:12, for instance, that 'if we consider the very words only, [it] is far from the Originall, but if we regard the sense, it is most proper'.[136] And in a sermon on 1 Corinthians 16:22, he observes that the Vulgate's departures from the letter are not only sanctioned by other translators and confirmed by the broader scriptural context; their main use and purpose is audience edification:[137]

> there is mortification enough, (and mortification is vivification, and ædification) in this obvious consideration [Job 19:26]; *skinne and body*, beauty and substance must be destroy'd; And, *Destroyed by wormes,* which is another descent in this humiliation, and exinanition of man, in death; *After my skinne, wormes shall destroy this body.* I will not insist long upon this, because it is not in the Originall; In the Originall there is no mention of *wormes.* But because in other places of *Iob* there is, [i.e. Job 21:26 and 24:20] . . . and because the word *Destroying* is presented in that form and number, *Contriverint,* when *they* shall destroy, *they* and no other persons, no other creatures named; both our later translations, (for indeed, our first translation hath no mention of *wormes*) and so very many others, even *Tremellius* that adheres most to the letter of the Hebrew, have filled up this place, with that addition, *Destroyed by worms.* It makes the destruction the more contemptible.[138]

Donne justifies his deviation from the literal sense through recourse to the sermon's broader homiletic purpose: the preacher's intent to mortify and, ultimately, edify his audience. Edification, sustained by the key Augustinian virtue of charity, is the hermeneutic principle which allows Donne to gauge just how much exegetical latitude a given text permits. In all of his texts—but especially in *Biathanatos* and the Lincoln's Inn sermons, as we will see—Donne examines the porous boundaries between readerly liberty and licence, and re-negotiates the complex relationship between universal hermeneutic categories and local contexts.

We have heard a lot about the value of citation in controversy, and about the close links between textual philosophy and polemical practice. Before we move on to investigate if Donne conforms to his own citational principles, it is worth reflecting briefly on the general outlines of his patristic approach. Donne's doctrinal

---

[136] *Sermons,* 3.115.
[137] It is equally crucial to note, however, Donne's numerous and stringent critiques of the Vulgate's mistranslations and textual additions: see e.g. a sermon preached at Whitehall, 18 April 1626, on John 14:2 (ibid 7.118–40).
[138] *Sermons,* 3.106. See, on this sermon, Dennis Quinn, 'Donne's Principles of Exegesis', *Journal of English and Germanic Philology,* 61 (1962), 313–29.

pronouncements on the Fathers strongly echo the patristics manuals published by moderate Protestants on the Continent at the beginning of the seventeenth century, especially those of Abraham Scultetus and André Rivet, and, to a lesser extent, Daniel Tossanus's *Synopsis de Patribus* (see Chapter 2 for discussion of these texts). He rejects two extreme contemporary positions on patristic scholarship: hardline Scripturalism on the one hand, and comprehensive emulation of patristic doctrine on the other. At one end of the spectrum, the physician and card-carrying 'anti-pater' John Bastwick argued, for instance, that 'there is not the poorest Minister, that is called a Puritan, but upon a weeks deliberation, will make a Sermon, that shall have more true learning and matter of edification in it, then all the Fathers homilies together'.[139] At the other end, leading anti-Calvinist divines such as Lancelot Andrewes, John Overall, and Richard Montagu 'were moving beyond invoking patristic authorities simply as a polemical strategy . . . and were more emphatically provoking the strict imitation of patristic doctrine and practice as normative for the present church of England'.[140] The evidence of Donne's sermons suggests a qualified endorsement of patristic authority; he is closest to the mainstream Calvinist position on the Fathers, as notably summarized by John Jewel:

> But what say we of the fathers, Augustine, Hierome, Cyprian, etc.? What shall we think of them, or what account may we make of them? They be interpreters of the word of God. They were learned men, and learned fathers; the instruments of the mercy of God, and vessels full of grace. We despise them not, we read them, we reverence them, and give thanks unto God for them. They were witnesses unto the truth, they were worthy pillars and ornaments in the church of God. Yet they may not be compared with the word of God. . . . They are our fathers, but not fathers unto God; they are stars, fair and beautiful and bright; yet they are not the sun: they bear witness of the light, they are not the light.[141]

Donne's pronouncements on the Fathers are entirely consonant with Jewel's. He eschews the reformist zeal of Puritans and anti-Calvinists alike, opting instead for a pragmatic approach to patristic testimony which is tempered by a sense of historical and geographical context. The Fathers are firmly subordinated to the Scriptures in terms of chronological and doctrinal priority, and Donne is unequivocal in asserting the supremacy of God's word over human tradition: 'It is the text that saves; the interlineary glosses, and the marginal notes, and the *variae lectiones*, controversies and perplexities, undo us.'[142] In the same sermon, preached at Whitehall in February 1621, Donne follows up with a swipe at Trent and 'the Idolaters of that Council', clarifying his views on the doctrine of patristic infallibility:

---

[139] John Bastwick, *The Vanity and Mischeife of the Old Letany* (1637), 22.
[140] Milton, *Catholic and Reformed*, 275. On Andrewes's patristic influences, see Nicholas Lossky, *Lancelot Andrewes the Preacher (1555–1626): The Origins of the Mystical Theology of the Church of England*, trans. Andrew Louth (Oxford, 1991), and the annotations in Peter McCullough (ed.), *Lancelot Andrewes: Selected Sermons and Lectures* (Oxford, 2005).
[141] *The Works of John Jewel*, ed. John Ayre, 4 vols. (Cambridge, 1845–50), 4.1173–4.
[142] *Sermons*, 3.208.

The Gospel was delivered all together, and not by Postscripts. Thus it is, If we go to the Record, to the Scripture: and thus it is, if we aske a Judge (I do not say, The Judge, but A Judge) for, the Fathers are a Judge; a Judge is a Judge, though there lie an appeal from him.[143]

As so often for Donne, the difference between idolatry and true devotion lies in minute linguistic detail. By choosing the indefinite article, Donne puts the Fathers firmly in their place: they are the best that the human tradition has to offer, and may sit in judgement on key matters of doctrine, but they will always be overruled in the supreme court of divine authority. With the insistence that patristic testimony is part of a fractured human narrative comes the recognition that the Fathers' pronouncements are essentially context-bound. Careful study of their linguistic usage and polemical concerns, of audience and occasion, reveals not a timeless, stable doctrinal consensus, but a complex and shifting set of rhetorical priorities and exigencies. A sermon preached on the conversion of St Paul in 1629 reiterates Donne's qualified endorsement of patristic authority: 'Let us follow the Fathers as Guides, not as Lords over our understandings, as Counsellors, not Commanders. It is too much to say of any Father that which *Nicephorus* sayes of S. *Chrysostome* . . . I am as safe in *Chrysostomes* words, as in the words of God; That is too much. . . . God knows, if it be modestly done, and with the reverence, in many respects, due to them, it is no fault to say the Fathers fell into some faults.'[144] Within this patristic canon, as we will see, Augustine is accorded special status and authority: he is quoted more frequently and accurately than any other Donnean source, and his opinion is often cited as a general shorthand for patristic authority.

Principles and Practice

In *Pseudo-martyr*, Donne's attack on the scholarly failures of Rome's controversialists is one of the main planks of his polemical offensive. The clearest illustrations of this approach can be found in Chapter 10, which presents Donne's case from the perspective of canon law, and aims to discredit the canons both as a work of scholarship and as a witness to the traditions of the early Church. Starting with Gratian's *Decretum* (subsequent sections target the glosses and the decretals, later additions to Gratian's canons), Donne recounts the critique of that text by Augustinus, the Archbishop of Tarragona, in the aftermath of the Council of Trent:

he [Augustinus] sayes, *He* [Gratian] *did not onely never Judge and waigh, but never see the Councels nor the Registers of Popes, nor the workes of the Fathers:* And therefore sayes

---

[143] *Sermons*, 3.209. Augustine was especially useful to Protestant polemicists because he frequently downplayed his own authority in relation to Scripture, as in this letter to Jerome: 'I cannot believe that you want your books to be read as books of a prophet or apostle, whose infallibility it would be wicked to doubt.' Cited in S. L. Greenslade, 'The Authority of the Tradition of the Early Church in Early Anglican Thought', *Oecumenica*, 3 (1971–2), 9–33 (17).

[144] *Sermons*, 9.160–1. On the Fathers and the Church of England in the seventeenth century, see the magisterial account by Jean-Louis Quantin, *The Church of England and Christian Antiquity: The Construction of a Confessional Identity in the Seventeenth Century* (Oxford, 2009).

hee, *There is onely one remedy left, which is, Una litura.* And in another place, *That there can bee no use at all made of this Collection, but that a better must be attended, out of the Originals.*[145]

Gratian, according to Donne, never approached the criteria for readerly excellence set out in *Biathanatos*: he never judged, weighed, and sifted—in other words, he does not qualify for the sieve-category reserved for the best interpreters.[146] Just as pernicious, however, is the indictment that Gratian never encountered at first hand the texts from which he compiled his collection. The remedy proposed by Archbishop Augustinus is to delete and start again, this time taking references '*out of the Originals*'. Donne's principal claim, that the polemical force of an argument could be compromised by reliance on scholarly aids and mediators, was by no means an unfamiliar one in controversial discourse. In the preface to John Jewel's 1583 sermons, his literary executor John Garbrand makes a point of highlighting Jewel's textual integrity. Garbrand notes that the controversial pressures of the 1560s encouraged Jewel to reconsider his approach to patristic and biblical scholarship. When preparing to do battle against the Catholic controversialist Harding, Jewel discarded his cribs, intermediaries, and notes, and returned to the patristic texts themselves:

> he had purpose to set downe the aucthorities out of the Fathers, and the quotations, truely and playnely: whereas in times before, hee had gathered sundrie bookes of common places out of the Greeke, and Latine, and later writers, he did peruse afresh the authors themselues, and made euery where in them speciall markes, for the difference of such places whereof hee made choyce.[147]

Half a century later, Richard Montagu launched his controversial tract *Appello Caesarem* in similar terms, insisting that

> [t]he course of my studies was never addressed to moderne Epitomizers; but from my first entrance to the studie of Divinity, I balked the ordinarie and accustomed by-paths of BASTINGIUS'S Catechisme, FENNERS Divinitie, BUCANUS Common places, TRELCA-TIUS, POLANUS, and such like; and betooke my selfe to *Scripture* the *Rule of Faith*, interpreted by *Antiquity*, the best *Expositor of Faith*, and applyer of that *Rule.*[148]

Lest we be too quick to confer sainthoods on Jewel, Montagu, and Donne for their citational probity, however, it is worth pausing briefly to reflect on the complex relationship between textual principles and practice. Jewel, as we will see in Chapter 4, despite his express commitments to thorough scholarly investigation and a return

---

[145] *Pseudo-martyr*, 192.
[146] The preface to *Biathanatos* distinguishes between four types of readers: 'Spunges which attract all without distinguishing; Howre-glasses which receive and power out as faste; Bagges which retaine only the dregges of the Spices and let the Wine escape; And Sives which retaine the best onely.' Donne, as we have seen, favours readers in the last category. John Donne, *Biathanatos*, ed. Ernest W. Sullivan II (Newark, Del., 1984), 32.
[147] John Jewel, *Certaine sermons preached before the Queenes Maiestie, and at Paules crosse* (1583), sigs. qiiv–iiir.
[148] Richard Montagu, *Appello Caesarem. A iust appeale from two vniust informers* (London, 1625), sig. C2r.

ad fontes, was not above ignoring inconvenient evidence when it suited his purposes. Donne himself, as Anthony Raspa's edition demonstrates, suppresses obvious flaws in Archbishop Augustinus's refutation of Gratian and fails to verify
dubious references which could have served to exculpate his opponent.[149]
Donne, as I discuss in detail in Chapter 2, also routinely cites a variety of mediating
sources, including some of the ill-digested works of Roman scholarship he excoriates in *Pseudo-martyr*. And *Biathanatos*, as we will see in Chapter 4, presents a
radically distorted version of Augustine's position on suicide.

The humanist trope of textual integrity emerges as a polemical tool well before
the advent of Reformation controversy. Petrarch, for instance, paid a rather back-
handed compliment to the compiler of the anthology *Milleloquium Sancti Augustini*, Bartholomew of Urbino, when he remarked that the volume 'will have pleased
Clement the Roman Pope, a most literate but very busy man and for this reason
most eager for this compendium'—with a cattiness that would have pleased the
author of *The Courtier's Library*.[150] Anthologies, Petrarch implies, are for lazy
readers, more intent on display than on serious study. The clarion call to textual
fidelity proves especially useful in a polemical text such as the *Invective contra
Medicum*, where Petrarch's addressee comes under constant fire for failing to read
properly. 'Read, you pitiful wretch', Petrarch thunders, 'and reread that passage
from Aristotle—from the third book of the *Rhetoric*—from where you take your
badly constructed syllogism; and be sure to take out not just this word or that,
without understanding anything, so that you might seem to read Aristotle, but
examine the whole passage.'[151] Petrarch insists that proper scholarship is grounded
in a practice of contextualized reading; authorial intent should be examined
through careful study of 'whole' arguments. This strategy is contrasted with two
types of short cut: a quick skim of a passage, followed by the extraction of textual
excerpts that suit *the reader's* purpose; or, worse, using an anthology of quotations.
Petrarch, however, frequently failed to put his own textual principles into practice.
As Carol Quillen shows in an extended analysis of his Augustinian quotations,
Petrarch's interpretation of a given passage is often 'shaped by the exigencies of his
own argument' rather than by the author's intent; he uses anthologies and often
excerpts passages with little regard to context: to put it charitably, Petrarch 'did not
always follow the advice he gave to others'.[152]

At the height of Reformation debates about the nature of the one true faith,
Philip Melanchthon—author of the patristic anthology *Sententiae veterum aliquot
scriptorum* (1530)—still found time to denigrate the efforts of an influential

[149] *Pseudo-martyr*, Introduction, p. xli.

[150] *Familiares*, 8.6.2, in Francesco Petrarca, *Le familiari [Familiarium Rerum Libri]*, ed. V. Rossi
and U. Bosco, 4 vols. (Florence, 1933–42); translation from *Letters on Familiar Matters*, ed. Aldo
S. Bernardo (Baltimore, 1985), 158.

[151] Francesco Petrarca, *Invective Contra Medicum*, ed. P. G. Ricci (Rome, 1950), 3.63; cited (with
translation) in Carol Everhart Quillen, *Rereading the Renaissance: Petrarch, Augustine, and the Language
of Humanism* (Ann Arbor, 1998), 73.

[152] Ibid. 89.

medieval predecessor, Peter Lombard.[153] Surveying the citations from the Fathers
on the topic of 'natura hominis' in Lombard's vastly influential Scripture commentary, the *Sentences*, Melanchthon describes his scholarship as the febrile hallucina-
tions of a madman; Lombard is the 'magisterculus', a small mind with oversized
pretensions. This frenzied rhetorical attack of one patristic anthologist upon
another should remind us that the use and compilation of intermediaries could
encompass a wide range of practices, and cuts across tidy boundaries between
primary and secondary sources. Melanchthon's argument builds on the distinction
between reading and understanding: his patristic compilation stems from thorough
first-hand study of the Fathers, properly contextualized and digested; Lombard's,
on the other hand, is a mere patchwork of textual fragments which, much like the
author's mind, is coming apart at the seams. The dichotomous configuration of
'reading' and 'understanding', as Petrarch's text shows, had obvious polemical
ramifications, but it is nevertheless a key category for understanding the uses of
patristic material in the Renaissance. Although Donne, like Petrarch, did not always
take his own medicine, he took seriously the idea of 'digesting' and 'understanding'
his sources: his most violent invectives, as we have seen, are reserved for writers and
readers who deal in textual 'rags'. It is crucial to deconstruct the binary relation
between readers and magpies, between the complete patristic work and the parasit-
ical excerpt collection that polemical rhetoric presents. Patristic anthologies could
act as suppliers of quotations, but they also acted as guides to the original source
text, where readers could consider quotations in context and assign them places in a
commonplace book. Secondary recourse, as we will see, involves complex mechanisms of discrimination and judgement, even though these processes do not always
correlate with modern notions of fidelity to the source text.

The diversity and complexity of patristic mediators is nowhere illustrated more
clearly than in early modern handbooks on note-taking, which give advice on how
to excerpt quotations, and on how they should be stored and arranged in commonplace books. The Jesuit Jeremias Drexel, author of the influential manual *The Mine
of All Arts and Sciences, or the Habit of Excerpting*, stresses the difficulty of this task
throughout his work. Books are mines of precious material, and the reader must
excavate choice passages through dedicated labour.[154] But note-taking is not just
the province of hard grafters: readers must proceed not simply 'assidue' (diligently),
but 'cum iudicio', with judgement and discrimination: 'you will call yours what you
have excerpted with judgement in your activity'.[155] Tossanus's *Synopsis de Patribus*
draws a similar contrast between such prudent note-takers and

---

[153] On Melanchthon and the Fathers, see Pierre Fraenkel, *Testimonia Patrum: The Function of
Patristic Argument in the Theology of Philip Melanchthon* (Geneva, 1961).
[154] Jeremias Drexel, *Aurifodina artium et scientiarum omnium: Excerpendi sollertia, omnibus
litterarum amantibus monstrata* (Antwerp, 1638); my citations are to the Bratislava edition of 1659.
See, on Drexel and other theorists of note-taking, Ann Blair, 'Note-Taking as an Art of Transmission',
Critical Inquiry, 31 (2004), 81–107. For a prominent English example, see Vernon F. Snow, 'Francis
Bacon's Advice to Fulke Greville on Research Techniques', *Huntington Library Quarterly*, 23 (1960),
369–78.
[155] Drexel, *Aurifodina*, 119; see Blair, 'Note-Taking', 103 (Blair's translation).

those wretched Summularies or Florists [who] *are the Very Bane of Learning, who in stead of culling out the choice flowres doe indeed, nothing but weed Authours: They leave the pure wine behinde and give their thirstie Readers the unsavoury Lees to drinke. Beleeve mee, the Fountaines themselves are farre sweeter.*[156]

Unsurprisingly, advice on note-taking generated some highly formulaic precepts. Most manuals distinguish between two basic forms of excerption, for instance: the epitome or abridgement, which proceeds chronologically through a text; and commonplacing, which selects passages of interest and arranges them under thematic or topical headings.[157] But overall one comes away from these handbooks with a keen sense of the diversity of note-taking habits. Drexel explains at length that readers excerpt for different reasons ('diversis rationibus'), in a variety of contexts, and for a number of purposes. He devotes entire chapters to specific professions and procedures: historians sift and catalogue their material differently from physicians; preachers cannot work along the same lines as controversial theologians. Time and again, Drexel stresses that good note-taking is preceded by copious reading. In the first part of his treatise, a survey of core reading for all the major professions, Drexel recommends that in the realm of religious writing, the diligent reader should consult Augustine first of all. Drexel acknowledges that this might be a difficult job; he remarks, rather dryly, that 'Augustine wrote quite a lot', but urges the reader to persevere: Augustine is definitely worth the effort.[158] Part III of the treatise is entitled 'Of the Different Uses of Note-Taking' and distinguishes carefully between 'sacred' and 'profane' genres, 'jocular' and 'serious uses'. Most importantly of all, however, Drexel shows that there are various types of notes which are tailored to specific uses and effects, and therefore imply different types of citational decorum. Drexel discusses a class of notes called 'historia' or 'exempla', brief anecdotes that can be used for illustration and ornament. Such passages may be 'noted briefly or described in their entirety', but Drexel makes no distinction between such paraphrase and exact quotation.[159] As Ann Blair notes, the early modern 'habit of citing inaccurately but as if with precision may be explained by this way of combining quotations with paraphrases in one's notes without signaling the difference'.[160] Yet Drexel's advice is also entirely consonant with his general emphasis on the contexts and circumstances of quotation, which we also find in Donne's *Biathanatos* (as in his admission that in the case of references for 'ornament and illustration', he has 'trusted . . . old notes').[161] Drexel's work sheds further light on Donne's treatise in its discussion of another type of note, the lemmata. These are the briefest type of note: a simple record, under various topical headings, of bibliographical information (author, title, place of publication), without actual quotation from the text. These lemmata would have provided plentiful material

---

[156] Tossanus, sigs. A3v–A4r.
[157] See Blair, 'Note-Taking', 86–7.
[158] Drexel, *Aurifodina*, 56–7. As a starting-point, Drexel recommends Book 5 of the *City of God*.
[159] See ibid. 185; historical exempla are discussed in Part II, chs. 8 and 9 of Drexel's treatise.
[160] Blair, 'Note-Taking', 100.
[161] *Biathanatos*, 5.

for Donne's notes in *Biathanatos*, which list multiple references but do not, on the whole, incorporate quotations.[162]

Early modern handbooks on the Fathers also comment on the intellectual benefits of the commonplace method. Wolfgang Musculus's *Common places of Christian religion* (1578) takes on some of the most popular objections to topic-based arguments: that they are fragmented, incoherent, and lacking in depth. By contrast, Musculus insists that commonplaces instil forms of lateral and connective thought which allow for a deeper understanding of the Scriptures. Because of this, he wants to see topical analysis extended from reading to preaching; commonplaces enable a fuller and more integrated exposition than a tiny sliver of the Bible:

> what a lacke it is to the Church that many Preachers doe verie selde apply themselues to open and expounde to the people any one Common place of doctrine in Religion, but take it to be sufficient for them, if they handle some text or peece of Scripture to declare it pistellike, as they terme it.[163]

There is evidence to suggest that Renaissance divines were all too aware of the 'diligence' and 'much reading' required to build up a viable store of patristic expertise; while they expected to learn and borrow from each other, theologians and scholars also clearly had some sense of intellectual property. S. L. Greenslade reports the case of a notorious magpie, the Roman theologian Stephen Gardiner, who freely borrowed from the patristic quotations which another divine 'had with great travail gathered, and stole his thanks and glory like unto Esop's chough, which plumed himself with other birds' feathers'.[164]

We now have a sense of the patristic editions that were available to early modern readers, and of the precepts that guided Donne's approach to citation. We are prepared, therefore, to observe his quotations in practice and get a firmer grasp on the primary and secondary sources Donne used in order to acquire, store, and apply his patristic material. This is the subject of the next chapter.

---

[162] On lemmata, see Drexel, *Aurifodina*, Part II, chs. 4 and 5 and Blair, 'Note-Taking', 98; on Drexel's third type of note, adversaria, see Part II, chs. 6 and 7 and Blair, 'Note-Taking', 99.

[163] Wolfgang Musculus, *Common places of Christian religion, gathered by Wolfgangus Musculus, for the vse of such as desire the knowledge of godly truth. Translated out of Latine into English, by Iohn Man of Merton Colledge in Oxforde* (1578), sig. Biv.

[164] See Greenslade, *English Reformers*, 14.

2
Augustinian Case Studies

This chapter will outline some of the most characteristic ways in which Donne absorbs, digests, and (re-)presents Augustine's texts. It falls into two halves: the first part focuses on citations likely gleaned from Augustine's works directly, while the second devotes itself to the medieval and early modern mediators available to Donne. Methodologically, this marks a transition from theory to practice: having outlined Donne's philosophy of interpretation in the first chapter, I now turn to citation in action. It should be acknowledged from the outset that this section of the book makes certain demands upon the reader. To reconstruct Donne's reading is to encounter a whole spectrum of texts that rarely make an appearance outside specialist commentaries on Renaissance theology. My analysis of patristic mediators in particular relies on a corpus of scholarly tools—the *florilegium*, the *catena*—whose significance is now largely lost to us, but which would have been indispensable to preachers and controversialists in the seventeenth century. The principal aim of this chapter is to demonstrate the sheer chronological and methodological range of Donne's Augustinian recourse, while subsequent portions of the book concentrate on five in-depth case studies from the prose tracts, sermons, and poems. Depth will be preceded by breadth, then, in an effort to retrace Donne's intellectual habits and strategies. This has implications for the presentation of material: in the first half of the chapter, I summarize the evidence for Donne's first-hand knowledge of Augustine's texts and present examples designed to showcase his Augustinian expertise in different ways. The second half, on second- and third-hand references, is organized according to textual genre and category: here I survey patristic handbooks, Scripture commentaries, and various types of excerpt collections, among others, to track the sources and mediating channels of Donne's Augustinian citations.

1. DONNE'S AUGUSTINIAN QUOTATIONS: PRIMARY SOURCES

The first thing we need to note is that the term 'primary recourse' covers a broad spectrum of practices. In some cases, as with the *Confessions*, for instance, the evidence suggests in-depth familiarity with an Augustinian text which has been studied and re-worked at some length.[1] In others, as with many of Augustine's

---

[1] See further on this, Chapters 3 and 6 especially.

anti-heretical tracts, it simply means that Donne has chased up a reference which originates in a mediator and therefore knows only a fraction of Augustine's work.[2] In a third scenario, a familiar text is revisited selectively, to recover quotations either dimly remembered or partially excerpted in a personal commonplace book. When this happens, Donne often follows one of his favourite strategies: culling quotations either from the beginning or the end of a text (this applies to books, chapters, subdivisions, and even entire works—*Confessions* 1.1 and *City of God* 22.30 are two prominent examples of this last phenomenon). This habit applies to texts that Donne knew in detail, to those he knew only in part but used frequently, but also to those which he usually encountered through a mediator, or through indices such as Erasmus's and Amerbach's. Donne's browsing routine is especially useful for works that come in multiple parts: Augustine's letters, sermons, and the *Enarrations on the Psalms*.

At one level, of course, this habit of excerpting from the beginnings and ends of texts is a matter of economy and efficiency. Yet we should be wary of assuming that such intellectual routines are merely strategic, or that they necessarily indicate ignorance. As my discussion of the *Essayes in Divinity* shows (Chapter 3), Donne was not alone in using this technique: John Hales, for instance, the notable Oxford scholar of Augustine and contributor to the Eton Chrysostom, follows the same pattern in distilling his citations, even in the case of well-known works such as the *Confessions* and *On the Literal Interpretation of Genesis*. More importantly, however, Donne's referencing system acknowledges the philosophical significance of inaugural and closural moments in Augustine's work. The exposition of Genesis looms large in Augustine's thought: he made five major attempts to explicate the creation narrative, and returned to this subject in countless sermons and letters (see Chapter 6). The beginning of the world mattered to Augustine not least because of his belief that in these events God had encoded his entire providential plan: the words of creation foreshadow the Word incarnate, and with it man's ultimate salvation and return to God. Donne clearly recognized the importance of reading ends into beginnings: two of his most substantial engagements with Augustine— the *Essayes in Divinity* and a sermon on Genesis 1:2—dwell in detail on the creation, and on the ways in which that story spells the 'end' of the world, in the multiple senses of purpose, motive, and destination.[3]

Donne, by his own admission, did not always 'binde' himself 'precisely and superstitiously' 'to the words' of his source texts.[4] In many cases, the reasons for this are simply philological: Donne is accustomed to thinking in Latin, and adapts cases when he transfers Augustine's language into English. But there are other motivations. *Pseudo-martyr*, as we have seen, gains rhetorical and polemical traction by insisting on the historical complexities of intertextual relations and by satirizing

---

[2] See e.g. Chapters 3 and 4.

[3] See, on this dynamic, e.g. *Sermons*, 9.47–67. Donne preached at court in April 1629, on Genesis 1:26; his performance starts with a reference to Genesis 1:1 and ends with a whole series of quotations from Revelation.

[4] *Pseudo-martyr*, preface, 10.

Rome's fiction of citational fidelity. The conviction that texts cannot traverse historical boundaries unproblematically is foundational to Donne's textual philosophy. This realization can be a painful one, as we will see, especially in moments when he seeks the comfort of timeless communion or direct revelation. But it also impacts on his reading in more constructive ways. In presenting their Augustinian sources, Donne's texts tend to display an awareness of their contextual situatedness; we witness frequent attempts to reconstruct at least some of the historical or doctrinal background against which Augustine's arguments are developed and played out. Donne is also concerned to demonstrate his familiarity with, and detailed knowledge of, a number of Augustinian works. This desire to highlight his Augustinian expertise, as Chapter 7 shows, can itself be deployed in the service of display and performance; it does not map easily onto actual proofs of erudition and fidelity. However, even in these cases Donne's intertextual negotiations are never simple, and his citational displays overwhelmingly functional and deliberate. The composition of a sermon rarely occasions detailed (re-)reading of an entire Augustinian work, but neither does it offer excuses for the careless recycling of second-hand quotations. It is the broad spectrum of textual transactions connecting these two extremes which offers the most valuable lessons as to the nature and scope of Donne's Augustinianism.

Demonstrations of Textual Knowledge

There are obvious indicators to suggest that Donne consulted a number of his sources at first hand. Subsequent chapters will give evidence of sustained engagement with individual texts; here, I am concerned to demonstrate that a substantial number of quotations cannot simply be traced back to excerpt collections and other cribs. One important clue in this regard is Donne's habit of citing adjacent passages from the same Augustinian text: since the majority of excerpt collections are thematic, one would not usually find whole sequences of citations from the same work. The following quotation from a Whitsunday sermon on John 16:8–11 starts by introducing a quotation from *Confessions* 1.13 ('*Quid miserius*' etc.) and moves on to present an excerpt from the previous chapter, 1.12 ('*Iussisti Domine*' etc.):

> For the first . . . we condole first the misery of this Ignorance, for, *Quid miserius misero, non miserante seipsum?* What misery can be so great, as to be ignorant, insensible of our owne misery? Every act done in such an ignorance as we might overcome, is a new sin; And it is not onely a new practise from the Devill, but it is a new punishment from God; *Iussisti Domine, & sic est, ut pœna sit sibi omnis inordinatus animus,* Every sinner is an Executioner upon himselfe; and he is so by Gods appointment, who punishes former sins with future.[5]

A more complex example can be found in a sermon on Genesis 1:2 (see also Chapter 6): there, once again, Donne has clearly visited the original source, in this

---

[5] *Sermons*, 7.216. Augustine: 'Quid enim miserius misero non miserante seipsum' (*PL* 32.670); 'Jussisti enim, et sic est, ut poena sua sibi sit omnis inordinatus animus' (*PL* 32.670).

case Book 1 of Augustine's *Literal Interpretation of Genesis*. In the concluding section of his sermon, Donne introduces the notion of God's 'supereminent' love, a key idea in Augustine's exegesis:

> *Non amor ita egenus & indigus, ut rebus quas diligit subjiciatur,* sayes S. *Augustine*
> excellently: The love of God to us is not so poore a love, as our love to one another; that
> his love to us should make him subject to us, as ours does to them whom we love; but
> *Superfertur,* sayes that Father, and our Text, he moves above us[.][6]

Donne starts by selecting a specific quotation and follows up with a paraphrase of the rest of the chapter: both references can be traced back to *Literal Interpretation of Genesis* 1.7.[7] But Donne draws further ammunition from Augustine's text. In Augustine's exposition, the expression of 'supereminent' love is followed by an affirmation of God's abiding care for his creatures: the notion that his solicitude does not simply manifest itself in the act of creation, but unfolds throughout history. Augustine argues that 'there are two purposes in God's love of His creation: first, that it may exist, and secondly, that it may abide'.[8] Donne uses this idea at an earlier moment in the sermon: 'for God had two purposes in the creation, *Vt sint, ut maneant,* That the creature should be, and should be still; That it should exist at first, and subsist after; Be made, and made permanent.'[9] Once again, the practice of quoting two neighbouring passages suggests direct acquaintance with the Augustinian source: Donne examines a substantial portion of the original work, establishes some rudimentary context, and assigns the two passages prominent places in the *dispositio* of his sermon. This is a characteristic way of proceeding.

Donne's sermons contain approximately sixty references to Augustine's biography. These tend to focus on Augustine's personal, intellectual, and spiritual development, and on familial and professional relationships. Donne characteristically draws on the texts that are most revealing of these aspects of Augustine's life: the *Confessions*, the *Retractations*, and the letters. For Donne, Augustine's journey towards God is associated with significant textual events: reading Cicero's *Hortensius*, discovering the divine artistry of the Scriptures, communing with Paul, experiencing a visionary encounter with Jerome, or hearing Ambrose preach at Milan. I will discuss some of these scenes in detail in later chapters. For now, I simply want to highlight one significant purpose of these biographical vignettes: that they seek to demonstrate Donne's familiarity with Augustinian modes of thought and rhetorical self-presentation. Two episodes which illustrate Augustine's relationship with his mother are particularly revealing in this regard: Monica's

---

[6] *Sermons*, 9.103.

[7] *De Genesi ad Litteram* 1.7.13. '[P]rius dicente Scriptura, *Terra autem erat invisibilis et incomposita, et tenebrae erant super abyssum*; ac deinde inferente, *Et Spiritus Dei superferebatur super aquam*? An quoniam egenus atque indigus amor ita diligit, ut rebus quas diligit, subjiciatur; propterea cum commemoraretur Spiritus Dei, in quo sancta ejus benevolentia dilectioque intelligitur, superferri dictus est, ne facienda opera sua per indigentiae necessitatem potius quam per abundantiam beneficentiae Deus amare putaretur?' (*PL* 34.251).

[8] Ibid. 1.8.14: 'Duo quippe sunt propter quae amat Deus creaturam suam; ut sit, et ut maneat' (*PL* 34.251).

[9] *Sermons*, 9.99.

prayers for the salvation of her son's soul in the years before his conversion (*Confessions* 3.12, discussed at *Sermons*, 4.343, 5.224, and 10.72), and Augustine's response to his mother's death, which leads Donne to reflect on the legitimacy of praying for the dead (*Sermons*, 4.332, 7.179, 8.153, and 9.200). Donne is keen, of course, to express his disagreement with Augustine's position on purgatory—even Augustine will not persuade him to enter doctrinal limbo. More interesting, however, is the fact that Donne explicitly addresses the emotional complexity of the situation: in a sermon on John 11:35 ('Jesus Wept'), for instance, Donne notes that Augustine's prayers for Monica were evidence of 'a humane and pious officiousnesse, in a devotion perchance indigested'. And in his Easter Day sermon of 1630, Donne exhorts his audience to a 'charitable interpretation' of Augustine's actions.[10]

In the third book of the *Confessions*, Augustine recounts his mother's early efforts to convert him to Christianity. Monica tries to convince the local bishop to advise her wayward son; he refuses, but reassures Monica that her prayers for Augustine are bound to have an effect eventually: 'as you live, it cannot be that the son of these tears should perish'.[11] In a Candlemas sermon on Matthew 9:2, Donne recounts this episode as a laudable example of faith and maternal devotion. At this point in Augustine's life, Donne suggests, there were no signs that he would become 'the son of predestination'—he was simply the feckless offspring of a pious mother: 'When Saint *Augustines* Mother lamented the ill courses that her sonne tooke in his youth, still that Priest, to whom she imparted her sorrowes, said, *Filius istarum lacrymarum, non potest perire;* That Son, for whom so good a Mother hath shed so many teares, cannot perish.'[12] Donne makes adjustments to create a syntactical parallelism between the English and Latin versions, but he clearly reproduces the basic sentiment of Augustine's words.

Donne's sermon on John 11:35 deploys the same episode from the *Confessions*, but readjusts some of its emphases to bring out parallels with its Scripture text, 'Jesus Wept':

> To end all, to weep for sin is not a damp of melancholy, to sigh for sin, is not a vapour of the spleene, but as *Monicaes* Confessor said still unto her, in the behalfe of her Son S. *Augustine, filius istarum lachrymarum,* the son of these teares cannot perish; . . . not I, but the spirit of God himself is thy Confessor, and he absolves thee, *filius istarum lachrymarum,* the soule bathed in these teares cannot perish.[13]

The fundamental point of the passage remains intact: Monica's tears represent an exemplary act of maternal love and Christian charity. But Donne also uses the priest's words to launch a meditation on the redemptive effect of Christ's tears; Monica's son and the son of God are brought into close devotional proximity. This is a typical rhetorical manoeuvre in the sermons: Donne establishes the contextual

---

[10] *Sermons*, 4.332 (Whitehall, Lent 1622/3); 9.200 (St Paul's, Easter Day 1630).
[11] *Confessions* 3.12: 'ita vivas: fieri non potest ut filius istarum lacrymarum pereat' (PL 32.693).
[12] *Sermons*, 10.72 (preached on Candlemas Day, undated).
[13] Ibid. 4.343.

outlines of a quotation, but once this is accomplished, he feels free to amplify it in ways which conform to the spirit rather than the letter of the text.

Donne's third approach to *Confessions* 3.12 constitutes a marked deviation from Augustine's text. In a sermon on Esther 4:16, Donne once again notes that '[i]t was a great confidence in that Priest that comforted Saint *Augustines* Mother, *Fieri non potest, ut filius istarum lachrymarum pereat,* It is impossible that the son, for whom so good a mother hath poured out so devout tears, should perish at last'.[14] The lesson he extracts from this quotation, however, seems to depart significantly from Augustine's meaning: 'it was a confidence which no man may take to himself, to go to Heaven by that water, the tears of other men'.[15] The loving commitment of others, Donne argues, does not absolve us from our own responsibilities: Augustine must find his own way to heaven.

At first glance, this looks like an example of intertextual wresting or bending. On closer inspection, however, we find that Donne is in fact far from ignoring Augustine's intent and goes to some length to justify his citational deviation. The 'mis-use' of the *Confessions* is counterbalanced by a second Augustinian quotation, taken from a sermon on Philippians 3:3–16. Donne uses this extract to demonstrate that his reading of *Confessions* 3.12 can be defended when placed in the broader context of Augustine's thought: the loving prayers of family and friends may play a part in our spiritual welfare, but only as a complement to our own religious commitment. This is exactly the sentiment expressed in Augustine's sermon, as referenced by Donne: '*Qui fecit sine te, non salvabit te sine te,* is a saying of Saint *Augustine,* never too often repeated; . . . I am bound to trust to my making sure of my salvation, by that which I do my self, rather then by that which I procure others to do for me.'[16] This is a more complex type of textual fidelity: although Donne's reading has not emerged naturally from the *Confessions*, it nevertheless stays true to the broader outlines of Augustine's thought. Just as Donne seeks to justify interpretations of Scripture texts by collecting and comparing different parts of the Bible, so his exegesis of Augustine builds on a method of collating and conflating excerpts from a vast and diverse body of texts. In this example, Donne's citational strategy also practises what it preaches: rather than following the lead of one authority, he uses textual initiative to plot his own way through Augustine's devotional writings. It is important to note the register and tone of Donne's argument here, however: the two Augustine quotations are introduced in the context of general moral exhortation, and this means that they are subject to a less rigorous form of contextual scrutiny than explicitly doctrinal statements. If Augustine's text is treated like a 'seamless garment' here, this is justified by the pastoral emphasis of Donne's rhetoric.[17]

---

[14] *Sermons*, 5.224 (preached at Middle Temple, undated).
[15] Ibid. 5.225.
[16] Ibid. 5.224. Compare Augustine, *Sermo* 169 (De Scripturis), chapter 11 (*PL* 38.923): 'Qui ergo fecit te sine te, non te justificat sine te. Ergo fecit nescientem, justificat volentem.' (Donne's change from 'justificat' to 'salvabit' removes the soteriological sting.)
[17] In his context-bound treatment of patristic texts, Donne follows classic Protestant prescriptions for dealing with the Fathers. These are usefully summarized by Milton, *Catholic and Reformed*,

Donne's demonstrations of Augustinian expertise also emerge in his frequent and self-conscious alignment of quotation and occasion. Thus, a sermon preached on the Conversion of St Paul (27 January 1628, on Acts 20:25) builds its reflections on Christian suffering and death on a series of quotations from Augustine's sermon on the apostle's conversion.[18] This emphasis on *decorum*, the idea of accommodating a sermon to place, time, and audience, is itself a quintessentially Augustinian topos, as Donne's discussion of Augustine's preaching shows.[19] Donne's use of Augustine is subtly attuned to different tonalities, rhetorical styles, and methods of exposition and elucidation. For instance, Donne clearly distinguishes between three different registers in Augustine's Christology: the doctrinal (questions regarding the hypostatic union and predestination, for instance); moral (Christ as an embodiment of love and charity); and 'patheticall'/meditative. Each of these categories is associated with a particular homiletic style, and Donne often calibrates his own presentational strategy with Augustine's. In practice, this means that Donne tends to set a 'doctrinal' discussion alongside an Augustinian text which is primarily doctrinal or controversial in nature: in the case of the hypostatic union, for instance, an exposition from the anti-Pelagian tract *On the Predestination of the Saints*.[20]

Conversely, the choice of Augustinian texts on a given topic can be revealing of Donne's own homiletic priorities: his meditations on death draw on Augustinian treatments of original sin (*On Admonition and Grace* is a favourite source text here), but even in the early part of Donne's preaching career, references to Augustine's sermons predominate.[21] Death viewed through an Augustinian lens is—perhaps surprisingly—a subject of pastoral instruction and edification for Donne, and often offers an opportunity to inspire repentance and hope.

Tracking Key Texts

Donne also asserts his patristic expertise through detailed attention to changes and developments in Augustine's thought. There are numerous examples in the sermons which show Donne tracing a particular idea through the various phases of Augustine's career. On the question whether 'the soule of man is a part of the Essence of God', for instance, Donne notes that while he was a Manichean disciple, Augustine adhered to a dualistic model of metaphysics: 'Saint *Augustine* at first

---

273–4: 'It was insisted that...their writings were fallible, often rhetorical, regularly prone to overemphasize certain doctrines at the expense of others as the polemical context required. They should only be treated as authoritative on matters where they spoke with one voice, and when they wrote consciously in absolute doctrinal terms.' See, on patristic polemic in context, Donne, *Sermons*, 7.203 (discussed above); and on doctrinal pronouncements, 9.344: 'where the Fathers speak unanimously, dogmatically, in matters of faith, we are content to be tried by the Fathers'.

[18] Augustine, *Sermo* 279 (De Sanctis), chapter 1 (*PL* 38.1278): 'si potest vivi, tolerabile est: si non potest vivi, migrare hinc facit. Non exstinguit, sed accelerat. Quid accelerat? Ipsum praemium, ipsam dulcedinem; quae cum venerit, sine fine erit. Opus cum fine, merces sine fine.' Compare Donne, *Sermons*, 8.168–9.

[19] See e.g. 4.109–14; see also 7.330 ('we must preach in the Mountaine, and preach in the plaine too; preach to the learned, and preach to the simple too').

[20] *De Praedestinatione Sanctorum*, chapter 15 (*PL* 44.981–3); see *Sermons*, 4.290.

[21] *De Correptione et Gratia, PL* 44.

thought so: *Putabam te Deus, Corpus Lucidum, & me frustum de illo Corpore;* I took thee, ô God, (says that Father) to be a Globe of fire, and my soule a sparke of that fire'. But in the later stages of his career, Donne observes, 'Saint *Augustine* does not onely retract that in himselfe, but dispute against it, in the Manichees.'[22] The reference to the 'Globe of fire' is to *Confessions* 4.16, a text which charts Augustine's conversion from Manicheism and which Donne knew in detail, as we will see. Augustine also 'disputes' his original hypothesis in *On Genesis against the Manichees*, 1.17.

So far, I have stressed Donne's familiarity with his primary sources: his careful attention to the rules of decorum (place, occasion, and audience) and his concern to establish some sense of context for the excerpts he chooses. No less suggestive, however, are instances of citation that show little sign of such contextualization. Augustinian maxims, aphorisms, and taglines occur frequently in Donne's sermons, and can be deployed as the homiletic situation requires. Such stock quotations always look as though they might be easy to track down, but they rarely are; as Damasus Trapp notes of his investigations of medieval 'happy quoters', the pithier a tagline, the greater the chances of its being 'vague or incorrect [in its] connotations'.[23] Many of Donne's Augustinian axioms centre on the nature of evil and the consequences of sin. 'Unde malum' ('What are the origins of evil?'), for example, is a question frequently asked in the early sermons. Throughout his preaching career, Donne uses Augustinian maxims like these to dwell on the nature and effects of original sin: its hereditary nature ('omnium voluntates in Adam'; 'the wills of all are in Adam'), the moral and spiritual impotence resulting from it ('perdidimus possibilitatem boni'; 'we have lost the capacity for goodness'), and the significance of free will in Adam's act—that he was created with the ability not to die had he remained free from sin ('posse non mori').

The idea that we lost all capacity for good in original sin ('perdidimus possibilitatem boni') is a staple of Augustine's soteriology, and Donne uses it on a number of occasions throughout his preaching career. It derives from *On the Grace of Christ and Original Sin*.[24] Donne applies this maxim to almost every aspect of his theology of sin and salvation: sin as death (as in a Christmas sermon conjecturally assigned to 1629, on John 10:10); the punishment or wages of sin (Lincoln's Inn, on Psalms 38:2); the effects of sin on the soul and natural faculties (Easter 1626, on 1 Corinthians 15:29); the character of human sin (Whitsunday ?1624, on 1 Corinthians 12:3); and Christ's mercy in saving us from sin and restoring us to grace (Whitehall, 12 April 1618, on Genesis 32:10).[25]

Another popular Augustinian maxim, the claim that Adam was created with the 'ability not to die' ('posse non mori'), offers an intriguing insight into Donne's approach to patristic emulation. Adam, Augustine argues, originally had the

---

[22] *Sermons*, 9.79–80.
[23] Damasus Trapp, OSA, 'Hiltalinger's Augustinian Quotations', *Augustiniana*, 4 (1954), 412–49 (434).
[24] *De Gratia Christi et de Peccato Originali* 1.4 (*PL* 44.362–3).
[25] See *Sermons*, 2.49–71, 7.94–117, 6.114–31, 1.268–84.

capacity to resist sin: in this sense, he was immortal. The formulation 'posse non mori' occurs four times in Augustine's works: *City of God* 22.30; *On Admonition and Grace* 12.33; *The Incomplete Work against Julian* 6.24; and *On the Literal Interpretation of Genesis* 6.25.[26] This is a well-known example of Augustine's penchant for textual recycling and self-quotation; he frequently modifies key ideas and accommodates them to a variety of audiences and rhetorical occasions. The final chapter of the *City of God*, for instance, focuses on the contrast between two types of immortality: the possibility of withstanding sin bestowed on Adam in the act of creation, and the eternal freedom from sin and death in the resurrection. Here, 'posse non mori' becomes transformed into 'non posse mori': Adam was created 'able not to die'; in heaven, he will 'not be able to die'. This emphasis on the second form of immortality in the resurrection is invoked by Donne in a sermon preached at the marriage of Lord Bridgewater's daughter, 19 November 1627, on Matthew 22:30:

> *Adams* first immortality was but this, *Posse non mori*, that he needed not to have died, he should not have died; The Angels immortality, and ours, when we shall be like them, in the Resurrection, is, *Non posse mori*, that we cannot die[.][27]

In the anti-Pelagian tract *On Admonition and Grace*, Augustine re-addresses the issue of sin and death. There the focus is, unsurprisingly, on the relationship between free will and divine grace: Augustine uses the phrase 'posse non mori' to downplay the role of human volition. In Donne's earliest extant sermon (preached on 30 April 1615, on Isaiah 52:3), we find the axiom 'posse non mori' deployed in a related context, as a thumping dismissal of free will:

> *Adams* first Immortality was, *posse non mori* he needed not to have died: It was in his own power whether he would keep a free-will, or no, and he spent that stock, he lost that free-will. . . . *Adam,* spent his utterly: he spent it so, that he and we have no freewill at all left.[28]

A third incarnation of the phrase 'posse non mori' can be found in Augustine's *Incomplete Work against Julian*, the sequel to his first attack on the Pelagian writer Julian of Eclanum. Once again, the occasion is a controversial one, as Augustine is called upon to defend his vision of divine justice. Death, Augustine argues, is the consequence of sin, and just punishment for it: without sin, Adam would not have died. A third sermon by Donne, drawing further support from Ambrose, makes the same point:

> [F]or, that was mans first immortality, *Posse non mori*, That he needed not have dyed. When man killed himselfe, and threw upon all his posterity the *morte morieris*, that we must dye, and that *Death* is *Stipendium peccati*, *The wages of sin*, and that *Anima quæ peccaverit, ipsa morietur*, that *That soule, and onely that soule that sins, shall dye*[.][29]

---

[26] *De Civitate Dei, PL* 41; *Contra Julianum Opus Imperfectum*, ed. Ernst Kalinka and Michaela Zelzer, CSEL 85 (Vienna, 1974); *De Correptione et Gratia, PL* 44; *De Genesi ad Litteram, PL* 34.

[27] *Sermons*, 8.107.

[28] Ibid. 1.162.

[29] Ibid. 7.218, Whitsunday ?1626, on John 16:8–11. Ambrose, *De Excessu Fratris Sui Satyri Libri Duo*, 2.36 (*PL* 16.1324D).

Far from bending Augustine's meaning, Donne's approach suggests meticulous attention to the modulations of Augustine's thought. Having identified a central Augustinian axiom, Donne investigates its various occasional incarnations before grafting Augustine's words onto his own discourse. In all these cases, Donne not only quotes accurately but also replicates some of Augustine's intellectual methods, taking his cue from Augustine's local recycling and adaptation of core ideas. However, it is impossible to establish exactly how far Donne was prepared to go in tracking down these Augustinian texts. The fact that the second (incomplete) treatise *Against Julian* was not available as a printed text during Donne's lifetime suggests that he initially discovered the extract by cross-referencing the phrase 'posse non mori' with a patristic index or anthology.[30] But once again, Donne's demonstrable effort to contextualize Augustine's excerpts attests to a careful and self-conscious 'digestion' of his sources.

As these examples demonstrate, a number of Augustine's texts were sufficiently resonant to stay with Donne throughout his preaching career. To argue that these cases are more than a convenient recycling of stock quotations is not to deny that Donne could be efficient with his material when he needed to be; as we will see, his store of citations includes a number of Augustinian taglines (or, as Donne calls them, '*Aphorisms*') which can be applied to almost any topic, with little regard for context or audience. Just as significant, however, are references that are re-deployed functionally, to establish a link between two sermons or to reinforce a particular doctrinal, polemical, or pastoral point. One such case is an excerpt from *On the Values of the Catholic Church*, which is used by Donne on two highly charged occasions: first on 3 April 1625, in the first sermon preached to the new king, Charles I, at St James's Palace; and then again three and a half weeks later, on 26 April, at Denmark House, 'some few days before the body of King James, was removed from thence, to his buriall'.[31]

The first sermon before King Charles includes a long excursus on the foundations of Church authority which is largely indebted to Augustine. Donne begins with five quotations from *On the Unity of the Church* 19.50,[32] and then introduces the crucial Augustinian testimony, from *On the Values of the Catholic Church*:

> *Nihil in Ecclesia catholica salubrius fit, quam ut Rationem præcedat Autoritas:* Nothing is safer for the finding of the *Catholique* Church, then to preferre *Authoritie* before my *Reason*, to submit and captivate my *Reason* to *Authoritie*. This the *Romane Church* pretends to embrace; but *Apishly;* like an *Ape*, it kills with embracing, for it evacuates the right *Authoritie;* The *Authority* that they obtrude, is the *Decretals* of their owne *Bishops*, The *authoritie*, which *Saint Augustine* literally and expressly declares himselfe to meane, is the *authoritie* of the *Scriptures*.[33]

---

[30] *The Incomplete Work against Julian* was not made available to readers in print until the 1654 re-issue of the Louvain edition of Augustine's *Opera*.

[31] *De Moribus Ecclesiae Catholicae* 1.25 (PL 32.1331).

[32] This text is now attributed to Cyprian; see *De Unitate Ecclesiae*, ed. E. H. Blakeney (London, 1928).

[33] *Sermons*, 6.252.

Less than a month later—preaching at another royal venue—we find a closely related passage on the links between institutional and scriptural authority, which draws support from the same Augustinian text:

> That which the *Scripture* says, *God* sayes, (says St. *Augustine*) for the Scripture is his word; and that which the *Church* says, the *Scriptures* say, for she is their word, they speak *in her*, they authorize her, and she explicates them; The *Spirit* of God *inanimates* the Scriptures, and makes them *his* Scriptures, the *Church actuates* the Scriptures, and makes them *our Scriptures*: *Nihil salubrius*, says the same Father, There is not so wholsome a thing, no soule can live in so good an aire, and in so good a diet, *Quam ut Rationem præcedat authoritas*, Then still to submit a mans own particular reason, to the authority of the Church expressed in the Scriptures.[34]

In both sermons, Donne uses Augustine to launch a classic Protestant argument: that the doctrines and customs of the early Church are superior to later Roman traditions ('*Bishops*' and '*Decretals*'), and that the Church of England is the only legitimate heir to these primitive witnesses. Augustine's vision of the Church is closer to 'That which... *God* says' precisely because it locates ecclesiastical authority not primarily in human institutions, but in scriptural edict and precedent. Even more suggestive for our present purposes, however, are the political implications of Donne's Augustinian citations. During a period of transition and instability, Donne's Augustinian quotations construct a unified Protestant Church and offer a model of continuity which can support the body politic, lest—as the text of Donne's first sermon darkly hints—'the foundations be destroyed' (Psalms 11:3). At a time of pressing uncertainty, Donne's quotations from *On the Unity of the Church* and *On the Values of the Catholic Church* assert the value of a Protestant consensus, 'the authority of the Church expressed in the Scriptures'.

Some of Donne's Augustinian negotiations operate at a level of sophistication that would have been difficult to appreciate for anyone except the most initiated listeners. At times, these subtle patristic borrowings actively seem to project a sense of intimate, personal communion between Donne, Augustine, and their God. A Whitsunday sermon on John 16:8–11, for instance, deploys a string of references from Augustine's *On Order* to figure forth the relationship between God's providential plan—eternal, invisible, and ineffable—and the external and visible decrees instituted by the Church.[35] Donne argues that

> *Gods work is perfect*... This is Perfection, That he hath established an order, a judgement.... Nothing can be contrary to that order; He [Augustine] is in a holy rapture transported with that consideration, That even disorders are within Gods order; There is in the order and judgement of his providence an admission, a permission of disorders: This unsearchable proceeding of God, carries him to that passionate exclamation, *O si possem dicere quod vellem!* O that I were able to expresse my self.[36]

---

[34] *Sermons*, 6.282.   [35] *De Ordine, PL* 32.   [36] *Sermons*, 7.231.

The early dialogue *On Order* focuses on the problem of evil and injustice, and is strongly inflected by Platonic thought. Augustine's defence of God centres on issues of cognition and perception. Human vision, he argues, is only capable of seeing events in isolation: if we could apprehend God's providential plan in its entirety, we would realize that evil is a mere appearance. God's transcendental order exists beyond the material world, in the intelligible realm; education, Augustine argues, can enable us to ascend from sense perception to a superior form of cognition, which offers brief glimpses of the true harmony and unity of God's 'intelligible' universe.

Donne's sermon exploits this interplay of the material and intangible realms. His meditation on Augustine's *On Order* starts with a quotation from Book 1, chapter 10, followed by extracts from chapters 9 and 6; it concludes with three quotations from Book 1, chapter 6, presented in the exact order in which they appear in Augustine's text. Thus, disorder gives way to order and sequence as Donne moves from fragmented quotation to the larger unity and coherence revealed by the final tableaux of references.[37] Since none of these extracts are identified—Donne only attributes them to 'S. *Augustine*', without specifying text or passage—this textual order would certainly have been 'invisible' to most of the audience. Donne's citational display thus presents the exact equivalent of Augustine's argument in *On Order*: if we could see or hear the extracts identified, everything would make perfect sense. But Donne keeps us in the dark, in a place that remains unsearchable—which is, of course, precisely the point of the citational philosophy unfolded here. In Donne's intertextual universe, this particular corner of the intelligible realm must remain hard to reach: Augustine's work is a figure for the mind of God—perfectly at one with itself, but completely opaque to all but the most initiated (perhaps even, in this example, to all but Donne himself). Our desire to see the bigger picture, to witness the divine order which puts evil in its place, will have to be deferred until the resurrection.

Misquotation and Mistranslation

As these Augustinian references demonstrate, Donne approached his source texts with creativity and imagination, but also with considerable scholarly care and sensitivity. He is concerned with accuracy of quotation; with acknowledging intellectual debt; and with establishing a rudimentary sense of citational context: in some cases, this desire to contextualize Augustinian quotations can even lead to linguistic corrections. This is by no means to suggest, however, that Donne was immune to minor slips or graver mistakes; nor is it the case that his reference protocol was applied evenly, or with complete consistency.

Donne was also certainly not alone in getting things quite wrong on occasion. The lawyer John Selden, for instance, reports the case of the 'Wicked Bible' where a thousand Bibles were printed in England with 'the Text thus (Thou shalt committ

---

[37] *De Ordine* 1.6–10 (*PL* 32.985–92).

adultery) The word (not) left out'.[38] This is simply misquotation by human error, and it happens a lot in early modern texts. A great many examples of imprecise quotation, however, are not failures of memory or slips of hand, but creative and deliberate re-workings of the source text. The Renaissance education system encouraged free adaptation of classical poetry and prose; as Julie Maxwell has suggested, 'Renaissance writers were taught to misquote creatively'.[39] T. W. Baldwin points out that '[t]he standard Renaissance justification for contextual misquotation was that the misquoter might make "better use", morally, of the author's "sentences (such as point towards any good matter)" than they could themselves'.[40] This early modern discourse of misquotation also intersects with theories of imitation, and in both cases imaginative approaches are valued more highly than slavish reproductions. Philip Sidney, for instance, formulates a critique of literal-minded imitation in the *Defence of Poesy*, which derides 'diligent imitators' and their 'Nizolian paper-books of . . . figures and phrases'; a superior approach would instead 'by attentive translation (as it were) devour them whole, and make them wholly theirs'.[41]

The issue of creative appropriation presents more complex challenges in the sphere of religious writing and quotation, where questions of textual authority and authorial intent occupy a position of infinitely greater significance. Nevertheless, this brief excursus into the secular rhetoric of intertextuality reveals that misquotation or mistranslation is not necessarily an indication of ignorance or a transgressive moment of defiance. It also reminds us that the function and importance of a quotation cannot solely, or even primarily, be gauged by its degree of accuracy or fidelity. All the major case studies in this book illustrate how crucial these imaginative adaptations of a source could be: many of Donne's re-workings take calculated liberties with the Augustinian works they seize on, but his texts also offer highly complex perspectives on what it might mean to make Augustine 'wholly theirs'. Before moving on to more elaborated instances of Augustinian imitation, however, we need to take a glance at some briefer examples of functional mistranslation. This takes us, first of all, to a truly eye-watering case found in the opening section of a Whitehall sermon preached in 1623, on John 11:35, 'Jesus Wept':[42]

---

[38] John Selden, *The Table Talk of John Selden*, ed. Frederick Pollock (London, 1927), 12; cited in Julie Maxwell, 'How the Renaissance (Mis)Used Sources: The Art of Misquotation', in *How to Do Things with Shakespeare: New Approaches, New Essays*, ed. Laurie Maguire (Oxford, 2008), 54–76 (58).

[39] Ibid. 58. Ascham suggests in *The Scholemaster*, for instance, that students should adapt and transform borrowed 'matter', and gives guidance on how 'sentences' and 'words' can be altered 'wittelie' for present purposes. Roger Ascham, *The Scholemaster* (1570), 47–8.

[40] T. W. Baldwin, *William Shakespere's Small Latine and Lesse Greeke*, 2 vols. (Urbana, 1944), 1.707, cited in Maxwell, '(Mis)Used Sources', 60. On the Renaissance practice of adapting and re-contextualizing commonplaces, see, principally, Ann Moss, *Printed Commonplace-Books and the Structuring of Renaissance Thought* (Oxford, 1996); Mary Thomas Crane, *Framing Authority: Sayings, Self, and Society in Sixteenth-Century England* (Princeton, 1993).

[41] Philip Sidney, *The Defence of Poesy*, ed. Gavin Alexander, in *Sidney's 'The Defence of Poesy' and Selected Renaissance Literary Criticism* (London, 2004), 49. Alexander (355) points out that 'Nizolian' refers to Marius Nizolius's anthology *Thesaurus Ciceronianus* (1535).

[42] This sermon is discussed in Peter McCullough, 'Donne as Preacher', in *The Cambridge Companion to John Donne*, ed. Achsah Guibbory (Cambridge, 2006), 167–81 (177–80).

I am now but upon the Compassion of Christ. There is much difference betweene his Compassion and his Passion, as much as between the men that are to handle them here. But *Lacryma passionis Christi est vicaria:* A great personage may speake of his Passion, of his blood; My vicarage is to speake of his Compassion and his teares . . . [B]e willing to heare him, that seeks not your acclamation to himselfe, but your humiliation to his and your God; not to make you praise with them that praise, but to make you weepe with them that weepe, *And Iesus wept.*[43]

The Latin quotation, '*Lacryma passionis Christi est vicaria*', is taken from a sermon 'On Tears, Compunction, and Penitence'.[44] The literal translation would be 'the tear is a substitute for (or representative of) Christ's passion', but Donne's sermon transforms Augustine's text through a series of surprising lexical choices: 'My vicarage is to speake of his Compassion and his teares.' 'Vicarius' turns into 'vicarage', cited by the *OED* as the earliest use of this word in the sense of 'position, office, or duties of a vicar or representative'.[45] This 'mistranslation' may initially seem painfully literal-minded, but it is in fact an entirely fitting representation of Donne's rhetorical strategy.

Preaching on the first Friday in Lent, Donne assumes a fitting posture of humility and contrition: while a 'great personage' in the ecclesiastical hierarchy may tackle the 'great' topic of Christ's passion on Easter Sunday, Donne will dedicate himself to Christ's compassion, seeking 'not your acclamation to himselfe, but your humiliation to his and your God'. Throughout the sermon, references from Augustine's sermons and letters advocate a stance of humble forbearance: Donne invokes, among other texts, Augustine's epistle to Augustinus Armentarius and his wife Paulina, which exhorts the couple 'to despise the world' ('ut mundum contemnant'), and Monica's plea to Augustine to abandon his worldly desires and submit himself to God's will.[46] While articulating the need for humility, however, the translation of the word 'vicarius' as 'vicarage' and its 'translation' from Christ's tears (*Lacryma . . . vicaria*) to Donne's office ('*My* vicarage') firmly realigns pastoral priorities. Christ's vicarious suffering may not inspire the rhetorical flights of 'the Passion', but it is the foundational gesture of love upon which all subsequent chapters of the salvation narrative are built. By insisting, through the process of mistranslation, on his 'vicarage', his status as Christ's representative in the pulpit, Donne asserts his pastoral authority at the very moment that he appears to deny it most sincerely. Humility, in the shape of the Christian paradox that suited Donne's mentality best of all, turns out to be the most exalted of virtues, and Donne achieves this insight by riding on Augustine's coat-tails.

---

[43] *Sermons,* 4.324.

[44] *Sermo* 11 (Ad Fratres in Eremo), now recognized as spurious: 'O lacryma . . . quae passionis Christi es vicaria' (*PL* 40.1254).

[45] *OED,* 'vicarage', 5.

[46] See *Sermons,* 4.340–1, 343 (Epistle 127, *PL* 33.483; Classis Tertia). This letter is routinely cited under entries such as 'laus humana' in patristic anthologies. See, for example, the 1555 edition of Bartholomew of Urbino, *Milleloquium Sancti Augustini* (1345, numerous sixteenth-century reprints), col. 1214 (discussed in further detail below). See also my discussion of Monica's intervention, above.

A characteristic feature of Donne's Augustinian recourse is his skill in deploying the same material in radically different textual circumstances. The same quotation can function as a brief nod towards Augustine's authority, without any contextual anchoring, only to re-emerge as a major plank of Donne's argument in another text. To illustrate these contextual variations, we need look no further than Book 10 of *On the Trinity*, the source text for one of Donne's favourite Augustinian maxims: 'we cannot love something unless we know it' ('amari nisi nota non posse').[47] Donne's method of introducing this quotation often indicates recourse to a secondary source, as in a sermon on Psalm 32:1–2, which suggests that 'we lay hold vpon *S. Augustins* Aphorisme, *Amare nisi nota non possumus*'. The term 'aphorism' points to a printed commonplace book or sentence collection, as does Donne's habit of confining the reference to a single line. However, we would be wrong to assume that this mode of recourse points to a lack of familiarity with *On the Trinity*: as later chapters will show, the Augustinian connection between knowing and loving is foundational to Donne's epistemology and ethics.[48]

Free Imitation

In contrast to most of the examples given thus far, a significant number of references in the sermons show no visible attempt to work with the context of the quotation they draw on. This happens, for instance, in the sermon preached to Queen Anne at Denmark House, on 14 December 1617, on Proverbs 8:17, 'I love them that love me, and they that seek me early shall find me'. Donne invokes multiple moments from the *Confessions*, but the key reference for my purposes is a passage from Book 10, which concludes his peroration:[49]

> Therefore shall every one that is godlie make his Prayer unto thee O God, in a time when thou may'st be found: we acknowledg this to be that time, and we come to thee now early with the confession of thy servant *Augustine, sero te amavi pulchritudo tam antiqua, tam nova;* O glorious beauty, infinitely reverend, infinitely fresh and young, we come late to thy love, if we consider the past daies of our lives, but early if thou beest pleased to reckon with us from this houre of the shining of thy grace upon us . . . grant that this day, this day of thy visitation, we fall into no sin, neither run into any kind of danger . . . as may separate us from thee, or frustrate us of our hopes in that eternall kingdom which thy Sonne our Saviour Christ Jesus hath purchased for us[.][50]

This is Augustinian *imitatio* in the loosest sense: although Donne's performance is clearly in keeping with the gist of the text—confession, prayer, praise—he makes no attempt to connect with the specific concerns of *Confessions* 10.27, an intensely

---

[47] This is quoted, for instance, at *Sermons*, 1.250, 4.121, 8.222, 8.236, 9.128, 9.251. See Augustine *De Trinitate* 10.1.2: 'et propterea miramur cur amet, quoniam firmissime novimus amari nisi nota non posse' (*PL* 42.973).

[48] See Janel M. Mueller (ed.), *Donne's Prebend Sermons* (Cambridge, Mass., 1971), 30–2.

[49] *Confessions* 10.27 (*PL* 32.795). This sermon is discussed in Peter McCullough, *Sermons at Court: Politics and Religion in Elizabethan and Jacobean Preaching* (Cambridge, 1998), 117–25.

[50] *Sermons*, 1.250–1.

introspective analysis of Augustine's past sins and anxious meditation on the prospect of future peace in God. Donne has picked up on the lyrical tone of Augustine's meditation, but is otherwise content to treat the reference as a launching pad for his own conclusion, which is concerned with audience edification rather than autobiographical meditation.[51]

Although many of Donne's Augustinian references suggest direct consultation of the source text, it is clear that he also made frequent recourse to commonplace books and patristic excerpt collections. In some cases, the clues that point towards the use of such auxiliary tools are fairly obvious. Donne's sermon for the dedication of Lincoln's Inn chapel, for instance, casts a passing glance at Augustine's *Homilies on the Gospel of John*: '*Saint Augustine* sayes that in his time, *Si quis nova tunica indueretur, Encæniare diceretur. If any man put on a new garment, hee called it by that name, Encænia sua.*'[52] Since the quotation mentions the key idea of Donne's sermon, 'Encaenia' or 'Dedication', it is likely that he discovered it by browsing a topical or alphabetical index of Augustinian quotations during the preparatory stages of composition.

The traces of such scholarly aids are most commonly found in passages of moral exhortation, where Donne's habit is to cite a whole range of Augustinian proof texts, using the Latin excerpts as a skeletal structure which can be fleshed out through rhetorical amplification. These are also the cases in which Donne most frequently misquotes. Sometimes, this is simply a mistake, but more frequently the adjustments are strategic: Donne's method is to distil a quotation into an aphorism upon which his argument can be built—in the process, antitheses emerge, wordplay is intensified, and structural features are brought into sharper focus. The following extract from Donne's third prebend sermon (on Psalms 64:10, 5 November 1626) is typical of this cumulative and dilatory procedure. We join him as he discusses the dangers of undervaluing human opinion (all sections in italic are quotations from Augustine):

> And so sayes that . . . Father, They that rest in the testimony of their owne consciences, and contemne the opinion of other men, *Imprudenter agunt, & crudeliter,* They deale weakly, and improvidently for themselves, in that they assist not their consciences, with more witnesses, And they deale cruelly towards others, in that they provide not for their edification, by the knowledge and manifestation of their good works. For, (as he adds well there) *Qui à criminibus vitam custodit, bene facit,* He that is innocent in his owne heart, does well for himselfe, but *Qui famam custodit, & in alios misericors est,* He that is known to live well, he that hath the praise of good men, to bee a good man, is mercifull, in an exemplary life, to others, and promoves their salvation. For, when that

---

[51] Donne's reliance on Augustine's conversion narrative, and his reminder that some believers 'came late' to God's love ('sero te amavi'), may be part of a broader rhetorical strategy. Peter McCullough has argued that Donne's sermon for a Catholic queen was designed to encourage conformity with the Church of England, if not conversion to its practices. The references to the *Confessions* shore up this reading: 'Preaching to a Court Papist? Donne's Sermon Before Queen Anne', *John Donne Journal*, 14 (1995), 59–82.

[52] Donne, *Sermons*, 4.378; Augustine, *In Johannis Evangelium Tractatus*—the reference is to *Homily* 48.2 (*PL* 35.1741).

Father gives a measure, how much praise a man may receive, and a rule, how he may receive it, when he hath first said, *Nec totum, nec nihil accipiatur,* Receive not all, but yet refuse not all praise, he adds this, That that which is to be received, is not to be received for our owne sakes, *sed propter illos, quibus consulere non potest, si nimia dejectione vilescat,* but for their sakes, who would undervalue goodnesse it selfe, if good men did too much undervalue themselves, or thought themselves never the better for their goodnesse.... S. *Augustine* found this love of praise in himselfe, and could forbid it no man, *Laudari à bene viventibus, si dicam nolo, mentior,* If I should say, that I desired not the praise of good men, I should belie my selfe.[53]

Donne starts with three quotations from Augustine's *On the Good of Widowhood,* segues into an extract from a letter entitled 'On the desire for praise', from which he distils two references, and concludes with an excerpt from Augustine's first ordination sermon.[54] Donne skilfully weaves an intertextual fabric which helps him frame his exhortation to the audience. His references could easily have been discovered in an index or commonplace book, under headings such as 'contemptus mundi' or 'laus humana': Donne's synthetic, collational approach strongly suggests as much.[55] Characteristically, Donne clinches his case with a biographical vignette and thus adds a human dimension to his saintly reflections. Augustine himself confessed to a love of praise on the day of his ordination: 'If I should say, that I desired not the praise of good men, I should belie my selfe.'

A significant number of Donne's textual borrowings in the sermons point to the use of a biblical concordance. In preparation for preaching on Psalm 38:2, 'For thine arrows stick fast in me', for instance, Donne clearly compiled a list of significant scriptural references focusing on the word 'arrows', among them half a dozen psalms. There is some evidence to suggest that this meditation on psalmic arrows led Donne to consult Augustine, one of the most famous expositors of David's book:

There is a *probatum est* in S. *Augustine, Sagittaveras cor meum,* Thou hast shot at my heart; and how wrought that? To the withdrawing of his tongue, *a nundinis loquaci-tatis,* from that market in which I sold myself, (for S. *Augustine* at that time taught *Rhetorique*) to turn the stream of his eloquence, and all his other good parts, upon the service of God in his Church.[56]

The Augustine reference is to the opening sentence of *Confessions* 9.2.3 ('sagittaveras tu cor nostrum'), and this quotation offers us an intriguing glimpse into the workings of Donne's mind. Psalm 11:2, also cited in the sermon, mentions arrows, as do Psalm 120 and Augustine's *Enarration* on that Psalm, which are all quoted at *Confessions* 9.2.2. If psalms, and Augustine's *Enarrations,* were on Donne's mind, he could well have been sent to *Confessions* 9.2.2, and from there to the next chapter, 9.2.3, where he discovered the reference that most suited his purpose for the sermon on Psalm 38.

---

[53] *Sermons,* 7.250.
[54] *De Bono Viduitatis,* ch. 27 (*PL* 40.448); Epistle 22, To Aurelius, Bishop of Carthage (*PL* 33.93; Classis Prima); *Sermo* 339 (De Sanctis), ch. 1 (*PL* 38.1480).
[55] Once again, the *Milleloquium* provides, under 'laus humana', cols. 1214–18.
[56] *Sermons,* 2.68.

2. MEDIATORS OF AUGUSTINIAN KNOWLEDGE

Early modern preachers like Donne also encountered the Fathers through a range of secondary or mediating sources: handbooks of patristic theology, polemical tracts, Scripture commentaries, ecclesiastical histories, and excerpt collections. I will look at these five categories in turn and then attend to some key patristic mediators in more detail (Gratian, Lombard, Aquinas). It is worth noting from the start that Donne's treatment of Augustine seems to be unique among his management of patristic material. While quotations from other Church Fathers can often be traced back quite easily to the most popular mediators—the *Glossa Ordinaria* or Lyra in the case of comprehensive Scripture commentaries, Bellarmine and Pererius for individual texts such as the Psalms or Genesis—Augustinian references are not usually found in the most obvious places. This is by no means to say that Augustine was always consulted in the original. But it does suggest a different type of recourse, and a more sophisticated awareness of the kinds of helps that were available to readers of Augustine's works. Donne's Augustinian quotations more frequently overlap with more specialist scholarly aids, as subsequent chapters will show: printed commonplace books, indices, and epitomes, among others. There are fewer misattributions for Augustinian quotations than for those from other Church Fathers, and Donne is signally more reluctant to acknowledge the use of a mediator: he wants to be seen to be quoting his favourite source directly. Augustine occupied a special place in Donne's heart and also, it seems, on his library shelves.

Before turning to the synopsis of patristic mediators, I want to illustrate the uses of second-hand reference through an in-depth analysis of a single source: Aquinas's *Summa Theologiae* (1265–74). This appears in Donne's second prebend sermon, preached at St Paul's on 29 January 1626, on Psalms 63:7: 'Because thou hast been my helpe, therefore in the shadow of thy wings will I rejoyce' (*Sermons*, 7.51–71). Donne's exegetical principles are defined in the second part of his *divisio*, in an extended excursus on the significance of divine 'ideas'. The importance of such 'ideas' is introduced through a patristic quotation, which Donne attributes to Augustine, but which is in fact taken from Aquinas. By analysing Donne's treatment of Aquinas's text, and by placing it alongside other key quotations in this sermon, I will explore the implications of Donne's citational camouflage and elucidate the scholarly practices that underpin his approach to patristic learning in this sermon. Mediators of the Fathers undoubtedly offered Renaissance divines more convenient modes of access and highly economic methods for gathering material during periods of intense professional pressure. But they also enable us to get a much more precise grasp of Donne's intertextual transactions. Discovering that Donne used a mediator rarely diminishes the richness and complexity of his patristic manoeuvres. In fact, closer inspection of Donne's recourse to these secondary sources reveals that they are often deployed alongside the original texts rather than replacing them entirely, and that they tend to open up a dialogue with the patristic source text rather than simplifying or distorting it, thus enabling creative re-workings of doctrinal and stylistic concepts.

Case Study: Aquinas on Divine Ideas

In her edition of the prebend sermons, Janel Mueller rightly emphasizes the 'poise and mastery of image and idea' which characterizes Donne's sermon on Psalms 63:7.[57] Even by the exacting standards of a typical Donnean *divisio*, the structural patterning of this sermon is remarkable for its depth, coherence, and rhetorical elaboration. This is a piece that deals in solid master tropes rather than loose connections and light analogies. In constructing his sermon, Donne relies on two interrelated conceits: first, the relations between God's eternal ideas and their historical incarnations; and, secondly, the challenge of extrapolating from past examples of God's actions to future expectations. This overt 'troping' is far from accidental. Donne's sermon is concerned above all with patterns, ideas, and examples, and with the ways in which God's providential plan can be mapped onto individual Christian lives: 'God does nothing, man does nothing well, without these Idea's, these retrospects, this recourse to pre-conceptions, pre-deliberations' (7.61). The dual preoccupation with universals and particulars, past and future events, is built into the central biblical figure of Donne's exposition: David 'was not onely a cleare Prophet of Christ himselfe, but a Prophet of every particular Christian' (7.51); he is able to reaffirm his faith in the face of tribulation and future uncertainty as soon as 'he takes knowledge of . . . Gods former proceedings towards him, Because God had been his helpe' (7.63). Indeed, the psalm text itself serves as a template for the sermon's two principal tropes: Donne remarks of the Psalms that they 'minister instruction to every man, in every emergency and occasion' (7.51), and ultimately represent 'the whole Compasse of Time, Past, Present, and Future' (7.52).

The importance of divine ideas to God's providential design and human action emerges in the second part of Donne's *divisio*, which—true to its own rules of replicating structural 'pre-conceptions'—proceeds from universals to particulars. Donne begins by explicating the concept of ideas at a general level, suggesting that 'it behoves us, in all our purposes, and actions, to propose ourselves a copy to write by, a patterne to worke by' (7.60). The best copy is the 'observation of Gods former wayes and proceedings upon us' (7.60), and this insight leads Donne to think in more detail about the origin and purpose of divine ideas:

> Of God himselfe, it is safely resolved in the Schoole, that he never did any thing in any part of time, of which he had not an eternall pre-conception, and eternall Idea, in himselfe before. Of which Ideaes, that is, pre-conceptions, predeterminations . . . S. *Augustine* pronounces, *Tanta vis in Ideis constituitur,* There is so much truth, and so much power in these Ideaes, as that without acknowledging them, no man can acknowledge God, for he does not allow God Counsaile, and Wisdome, and deliberation in his Actions, but sets God on worke, before he have thought what he will doe. (7.60)

Donne launches his discussion with a reference to 'the Schoole', but the substance of the argument is attributed to 'S. *Augustine*'. The *locus classicus* for Augustinian notions of divine ideas is Question 46 of his *Eighty-Three Various Questions*, a work

---

[57] Mueller (ed.), *Donne's Prebend Sermons*, 49.

composed in the early years of his conversion, between 388 and 396, which originated in conversations with friends.[58] However, the precise wording of Donne's quotation, '*Tanta vis in Ideis constituitur*' is found not in Augustine's text, but in Part I, Question 15 (Article 1) of Aquinas's *Summa Theologiae*, which in turn cites Augustine's definition of ideas: 'quod dicit Augustinus, in libro Octoginta trium quaest.: Tanta vis in ideis constituitur, ut, nisi his intellectis, sapiens esse nemo possit.'[59] Aquinas's debt to Augustine is acknowledged openly, but he also introduces some significant modifications to Augustine's definition of ideas; these changes are crucial to the shaping of Donne's own discourse.

In light of these Thomistic borrowings, it would be tempting to assume that Donne—for reasons of economy or convenience—was constructing the sermon primarily or exclusively from secondary sources. However, a more detailed examination of his references complicates this picture considerably. Donne's definition of divine ideas sets up a framework for the exegesis of two scriptural texts: John 1:3–4 and Hebrews 11:3. As Mueller shows, the interpretation of the passage from St John's Gospel probably derives from Augustine's *Homilies on the Gospel of John* (1.16), but could also have been taken from Aquinas's *Catena* (or exposition) on John, which cites Augustine's homily on John and alleges, as a further proof text, his *Enarration* on Psalm 63.[60] The sermon as a whole is replete with Augustinian references, and Mueller's annotations make a persuasive case for attributing them to Augustine's own texts rather than medieval or early modern mediators. Among these, citations from Augustine's *Enarration* on Psalm 62 and from his sermons are of particular relevance.[61] Donne's exposition of Hebrews 11:3, on the other hand, is indebted to Aquinas's *Commentary on Hebrews* (on which see more below). It is clear, then, that Donne was not simply taking short cuts here, and that he saw Augustine and Aquinas as mutually complementary sources upon which further productive elaborations could be built.

This still leaves us with the question of why Donne passed off his Aquinas quotation as Augustine in the first place. Donne's antipathy towards 'the Schoole', and Aquinas more particularly, almost certainly played a part in his decision; as we will see, Donne rarely associates himself with Thomistic thought and doctrine explicitly, even when he is patently indebted to the scholastic tradition. Furthermore, Donne rarely passes up an opportunity to showcase his Augustinian expertise; if he can suppress a mediator, he will—unless it serves his purpose to do otherwise. A more compelling reason, however, can be found in the rhetorical and thematic structure of the second prebend sermon itself. Donne's sermon explains the theological foundations of God's ideas, but he also seeks to embody these templates in human examples. The 'little great Philosopher *Epictetus*', for instance, 'would undertake no action, but he would first propose to himselfe, what *Socrates*,

---

[58] *De Diversis Quaestionibus Octoginta Tribus* (*PL* 40.29).
[59] Aquinas, *Summa Theologiae*, Blackfriars edition, 60 vols. (London, 1964), 1.15.1.
[60] Mueller (ed.), *Donne's Prebend Sermons*, 233. On the *Catena*, see more below.
[61] See Mueller (ed.), *Donne's Prebend Sermons*, 233, 235, 243.

or *Plato*, what a wise man would do in that case, and according to that, he would proceed' (7.60). Even the classical philosophers, then, conform to the divine archetype, God's 'patterne . . . to work after patterns' (7.61). At the level of Scripture narrative, David is a type of Christ, who will in turn perfect the art of divine mimesis, but he is also an example to all Christians. Finally, Donne's sermon finds its own exemplar and 'copie' in Augustine, whose views on creation, election, and redemption are invoked at every key stage in the discourse. Donne's sophisticated intertextual 'game' with *On Order* in the Whitsunday sermon on John 16:8–11 invokes the ineffable through its invisible Augustinian references. There, the Augustinian excursus allows us to imagine Augustine's text as a figure or map for the divine mind itself. In the prebend sermon, the idea of emulating Augustine and writing after his 'patterne'—even as Donne draws direct inspiration from Aquinas—similarly enables him to create a convincing 'copy' of God's own 'power', 'Counsaile, and Wisdome'.

Donne continues his discussion of ideas in the second part of the sermon. Following God's own habit of working 'after patterns', Donne's encourages his congregation to search for signs of God's design and purpose, for examples of his 'former proceedings' (7.63). But Donne does not simply sow the seeds of this idea; he also demands that we live by it. Once again, this movement is mimetic, based on God's own pattern of pre-deliberation and subsequent 'Action':

> And therefore let him be our patterne for that, to work after patternes[.] . . . If I aske God, by what Idea he made me, God produces his *Faciamus hominem ad Imaginem nostram*, That there was a concurrence of the whole Trinity, to make me in *Adam*, according to that Image, . . . that idea, which they had pre-determined. If I pretend to serve God, and he aske me for my Idea, How I meane to serve him, shall I bee able to produce none? . . . [I]f I come to pray or preach without this kind of Idea, if I come to extemporall prayer . . . I shall come to an extemporall faith, and extemporall religion; and then I must looke for an extemporall Heaven . . . for to that Heaven which belongs to the Catholique Church, I shall never come, except I go by the way of the Catholique Church, by former Idea's, former examples, former patterns, To beleeve according to ancient beliefes[.] (7.61)

Donne's reading of Genesis 1:26 ('*Faciamus hominem ad Imaginem nostram*') reveals the ultimate purpose of divine ideas: the creation narrative itself. God is presented as the 'patterne' or archetype; divine form re-creates itself in humanity, the 'image and likeness' of its originating principle. This also has ramifications for the history of the English Church: Donne uses the doctrine of ideas to reinforce a familiar polemical point regarding the superiority of the true 'Catholique Church' to its Roman counterpart. The Protestant consensus, in reviving the traditions of the Early Church, comes closest to 'ancient beliefes' and 'former Idea's'; it is, therefore, a truer likeness of God's mind.

Donne's philosophy of divine mimesis also undergirds his theology of grace and creation in the sermon (see 7.62–4). A substantial part of this argument derives from Aquinas's *Commentary on Hebrews*. Explicating Hebrews 11:3, Aquinas observes that 'visible things were produced from invisible ideal reasons in the Word of God, by Whom all things were made. . . . We understand through faith, as before, that the world was framed, i.e. suited and corresponded to the Word, that from invisible things visible things might be made.'[62] This corresponds exactly to Donne's reading of Hebrews 11:3, which suggests that

> *Things formerly invisible were made visible;* that is, we see them not till now, till they are made, but they had an invisible being, in that Idea, in that pre-notion, in that purpose of God before, for ever before. Of all things in Heaven, and earth, but of himselfe, God had an idea, a patterne in himselfe, before he made it. (7.61)

Aquinas also supplies Donne with a quotation from Boethius and the vital link between Hebrews 11:3 and Genesis 1:26.

The idea of human participation in God's likeness is the cornerstone of Donne's argument in the second prebend sermon. It is God's imitative relation to the creature—the idea of divine mimesis—which shores up faith in God's providential plan; as Hebrews 11:3 suggests, 'Through faith we understand that the worlds were framed by the word of God, so that things which are seen were not made of things which do appear.' This notion, crucially, is derived from Aquinas rather than Augustine, whose discussion of ideas in the *Eighty-Three Various Questions* concentrates on a different theological issue: the sinful soul's desire to connect with divine forms and ideas. Aquinas, by contrast, focuses explicitly on notions of imitation, creation, and providence. This emerges most clearly in the passage which provides Donne's original definition of ideas, *Summa Theologiae* 1.15: there, Aquinas argues that God's essence is 'imitable by the creature'; it can be known

> Not only as it exists in itself, but also insofar as it can be participated in by creatures according to one or another mode of likeness. . . . Each creature has its own proper essence insofar as it participates in some way in a likeness of God's essence. So, then, insofar as God knows His own essence as imitable in this way by such a creature, He knows it as a proper conception and idea of this creature.[63]

Donne's sermon embodies the essence of Aquinas's thought, and fleshes out the ideas presented in the *Summa Theologiae*. It is this mediating source, not the Augustinian original, which provides the substance of Donne's argument and enables its astonishing processes of rhetorical elaboration and application. Aquinas and Augustine, then, as the combined references from the *Summa* and the *Commentary on Hebrews*, from the *Homilies*, sermons, and the *Enarrations on the Psalms* show, work alongside each other in Donne's sermon discourse. Its underlying and sustaining conceit, however, emerges only through a closer scrutiny of intertextual relations: of the sources which are overtly acknowledged, those which are implied or submerged, and—finally—those which are actively disowned by the author. We ignore the mediators of Augustine's ideas at our own peril.

---

[62] Aquinas, *Commentary on the Epistle to the Hebrews*, trans. Chrysostom Baer, preface by Ralph McInerny (South Bend, Ind., 2006), 124.
[63] Aquinas, *Summa Theologiae*, 1.15.1.

Patristic Mediators: A Survey of Donne's Sources

I now turn to the mediating sources which supplied Donne with quotations from the Fathers. There are five main categories of text to be considered here: handbooks of patristic theology, polemical tracts, Scripture commentaries, ecclesiastical histories, and excerpt collections. Having surveyed these in turn, I conclude the chapter with a brief discussion of three medieval sources that played a major part in the early modern reception of patristic thought: Gratian, Lombard, and Aquinas. My main purpose is to illustrate the range of options available to Donne in collecting and gleaning his quotations; in-depth analysis of individual texts is reserved for later chapters. Most of the sources I draw on are now little known, and only a handful of them have been edited or translated. Titles, exceptionally, are cited in the original Latin throughout; I have tried to elucidate key terms (such as the *catena*) where necessary.

Patristics Handbooks

The patrological handbooks fulfilled a variety of purposes, providing summaries of key doctrines, textual commentary, choice passages for polemical combat, and prescriptive advice on how the Fathers were to be used. The first decades of the seventeenth century saw an increase in both output and sophistication, with key texts including, on the Catholic side, Robert Bellarmine's *Liber de Scriptoribus Ecclesiasticis* (1613). Among Protestant publications, André Rivet's *Critici Sacri Specimen* (1612) was marked by a strong emphasis on textual scholarship, while Abraham Scultetus's *Medullae Theologiae Patrum* (four parts, 1598–1613) concentrated on the polemical uses of patristic doctrine.[64] By 1607, Donne had read at least one of these handbooks: *Biathanatos* includes a reference to Irenaeus that derives from volume 1 of Scultetus's *Medullae*, as evidenced by Donne's marginal note to 'Pars 1 in Liber 4' of that text.[65] Another handbook referenced by Donne is Melchior Cano's *De Locis Theologicis* (1563), a highly systematic and innovative treatise focusing on theological method, and hailed by the editors of Donne's sermons as having inaugurated 'a new epoch in the history of theology'.[66] One of Cano's chief aims was to combine Catholic polemic with advanced patristic scholarship: to restore patristic texts, re-evaluate the Fathers' authority, and redefine the relationship between the Fathers and later witnesses. *Pseudo-martyr* picks up on this question of the patristic canon, which features in Book 11 of Cano's

---

[64] See Irena Backus, 'The Fathers and Calvinist Orthodoxy: Patristic Scholarship. The Bible and the Fathers According to Abraham Scultetus (1566–1624) and André Rivet (1571/3–1651). The Case of Basil of Caesarea', in Backus (ed.), *The Reception of the Church Fathers in the West: From the Carolingians to the Maurists*, 2 vols. (Leiden, 1997), 2.839–65 (856–8).

[65] *Biathanatos*, 133; 234; see *Medullae Theologiae Patrum* [Part 1] (Hamburg, 1603), sig. M3r. At *Sermons*, 7.129, Donne also mentions Johann Gerhard (1582–1637), the author of another influential Protestant patristic handbook, the *Patrologia* (published 1653, but composed significantly earlier).

[66] *Sermons*, 10.391.

treatise.[67] Most of these texts also acknowledge a debt to the first patristics handbook, the fifth-century *Commonitorium* by Vincent of Lérins. As Mark Vessey notes, Vincent's *Commonitorium* was appropriated by early modern controversialists on both sides, as 'evidence of a theory and practice of patristic argument deriving from the Fathers themselves'.[68] Donne references Vincent's *Commonitorium* most frequently in an attempt to position the English Church in a direct line of decent from these earliest traditions of Christian thought.[69]

Controversial Theology

Works of controversial theology also offered rich opportunities for gleaning and excerpting patristic quotations. Donne's own intervention in the polemical battles of the early seventeenth century, *Pseudo-martyr*, draws on a broad spectrum of controversial texts, and his library provides further evidence of his professional interest in the doctrinal disputes of the period. Among Catholic controversialists, Cardinal Robert Bellarmine is a frequent focus of patristic debate, both in Donne's sermons and in *Pseudo-martyr*. Chapter 3 of Donne's polemical treatise, for instance, takes issue with Bellarmine's reading of Jerome's commentary on Psalm 31 in the *Breviarum in Psalmos*, and shows close familiarity with the *Index Rerum* appended to each of the three volumes of Bellarmine's *De Controversiis*—a storehouse of references to the Fathers and later commentators used on both sides of the religious divide.[70] *Pseudo-martyr* also quotes from Bovosius's *Dispvtationes Catholicae* (1607), a popular handbook of early modern controversy which included many of the classic patristic proof-texts.

Scripture Commentaries: Medieval and Early Modern

Among medieval scriptural commentaries, three sources deserve special attention and emphasis: Nicholas of Lyra's *Postilla Litteralis Super Totam Bibliam* (1322–31) and the twelfth-century *Glossa Ordinaria* provided the most popular mode of access to the Fathers, and were routinely included with printed Bibles from 1495 onwards. Aquinas's *Catena Aurea* did not explicate the whole Bible but glossed only the Gospels, in the form of a sequential commentary compiled from the

---

[67] *Pseudo-martyr*, 92–3. The reference is to Book 11, chapter 6, entitled 'Qui sint probatae fidei auctores, qui contra non sint'. Donne refers approvingly to Cano at *Sermons*, 4.217, 7.123, and 8.135. The anti-Jesuit Cano (?1509–1560) was Professor of Theology at Salamanca between 1546 and 1552.

[68] Mark Vessey, 'English Translations of the Latin Fathers, 1517–1611', in Backus (ed.), *Reception of the Church Fathers*, 2.775–835 (820). The *Commonitorium* was published under the pseudonym Peregrinus as *Pro Catholicae Fidei Antiquitate et Universitate*.

[69] See, for example, *Sermons*, 2.280; and, for further significant and acknowledged references, *Sermons*, 8.117 and 8.145.

[70] *Pseudo-martyr*, 91 (Raspa notes Donne's disagreement with Bellarmine). *Disputationes Roberto Bellarmini Politiani, Societatis Iesu, De Controversiis Christianae Fidei, adversus huius temporis haereticos*, 3 vols. (Ingolstadt, 1586–93). Hobbs, '"To a Most Dear Friend"—Donne's Bellarmine', *The Review of English Studies*, NS 32 (1981), 435–8, argues that Donne used the 1603 edition of Bellarmine, which includes the *Index Rerum*.

opinions of the Fathers. Donne refers to all of these sources: *Biathanatos* quotes the *Catena* twice, drawing from it an interpretation of the Gospel of John, chapter 21 and, more importantly for our purposes, also using it as a way of mediating Origen's exegesis of Matthew 27:3.[71] As Chapter 7 shows, Aquinas's *Catena* also supplied Augustinian material for Donne's interpretation of Matthew 5:8.

Lyra is invoked in all of Donne's prose works: a copy of Lyra's commentary on the Vulgate Bible, in six volumes with the *Glossa Ordinaria*, was presented by Donne to the library of Lincoln's Inn in 1622. In the *Essayes in Divinity*, for instance, Lyra is used to convey Augustine's theory of 'res' and 'verba' (see *De Doctrina Christiana* 3.10.14): 'And as *Lyra* notes, being perchance too Allegorical and Typick in this, it [Scripture] hath this in common with all other books, that the *words* signifie *things;* but hath this in particular, that all the *things* signifie *other things*.'[72] Evidence from *Biathanatos* and the *Essayes in Divinity* suggests that Donne used a copy of the Bible which included not only Lyra's commentary, but also the Spanish divine Paul of Burgos's often-critical additions to Lyra's *Postilla*, as well as a defence of Lyra by the German theologian Matthew Doring of Thuringia.[73] Donne also frequently draws on the *Glossa Ordinaria* as a source for patristic quotations. A sermon preached at The Hague on Matthew 4:18–20 (19 December 1619; revised 1630) references Augustine in its definition of the good Christian life, for instance: '*Perfecta obedientia est sua imperfecta relinquere*, Not to be too diligent towards the world, is the diligence that God requires.'[74] A closer look at Donne's Latin quotation, however, reveals a different source—the *Glossa* on Matthew 4:20.[75] The reference to '*Perfecta obedientia*' does not, to the best of my knowledge, occur anywhere in Augustine's works, but the point is that it *sounds* distinctly Augustinian. The *Glossa Ordinaria* dwells in detail on the nature of charity, 'diligence', and properly directed love ('proprietate amore'), and it is easy to see how Donne may have made the connection with key ideas from the *Confessions* or *De Doctrina Christiana*.[76]

Renaissance Scripture commentaries reveal an even more complex intertextual picture. Here the reader needs to be attentive not simply to secondary sources: often, a tertiary reference is used to mediate secondary quotations which provide

---

[71] *Biathanatos*, 130, referencing *Catena Aurea in Quatuor Evangelia*; see the two-volume edition, ed. Angelico Guarienti (Turin, 1953), 2.592; and at *Biathanatos*, 140, a reference to 1.401–2 (both noted by Sullivan II).

[72] *Essayes*, 10. Although, as Mark Vessey rightly notes ('Company', 198), Donne's perspective on 'res' and 'verba' differs from both Lyra's and Augustine's. The reference to Augustine is unacknowledged in Donne; he is content to invoke Lyra.

[73] For Doring, see *Essayes*, 39 (erroneously referred to as Lyra's 'Apologist *Dornike*'—Raspa, 151, is right to correct this). For Paul of Burgos, see *Biathanatos*, 5, 26, 27, 138, 143. The 1603 edition of the *Postilla* includes Doring's and Burgos's commentary.

[74] *Sermons*, 2.284.

[75] See the *Glossa* on Matthew 4:20: 'Perfecta obedientia est sua imperfecta relinquere. Relictis retibus: quia et si postea resumunt, non cupiditate et proprietatis amore' (*PL* 114.87D).

[76] In his use of the word 'diligence', Donne frequently draws on its Latin—and Augustinian—etymology; see, for instance, *Confessions* 13.24.36, 'dilectio dei et proximi' ('the love of God and neighbour'). 'Diligence' in Donne carries implications of loving attention and charitable care.

access to the primary patristic source.[77] Sometimes, this process is made explicit, as in the closing pages of the *Essayes in Divinity*. There Donne alleges '*Calvin*, citing Saint *Hierome*', but his marginal note refers us neither to Calvin nor to Jerome, but to Augustin Marlorate's *Expositio Ecclesiastica, In Acta Apostolorum* (1561), which in turn cites Calvin. More commonly, though, the tertiary source is unacknowledged: *Biathanatos* uses an Index to the works of Aquinas, the *Tabula Aurea*, compiled by the Dominican Peter of Bergamo (1473) to mediate the Fathers' texts.[78] Two other important tertiary sources for patristic references are Johann Coppenstein's epitome of Aquinas's *Catena Aurea*, the *Dispositiones ex D. Thomae de Aquino Commentariis in Matthaeum et Ioann.[em]* (Mainz, 1616), of which Donne owned a copy (Keynes, L50); and Dominic de Soto's commentary on Peter Lombard's *Sentences*, the *Commentariorum . . . in Quatrum Sententiarum* (1555–60), cited in *Pseudo-martyr* (91).

Five key authors of Scripture commentaries deserve special attention in connection with Donne's patrological researches. The Protestant theologian Wolfgang Musculus, author of the influential anthology *Loci communes sacrae theologiae* (1564), is referenced by Donne in the sermons; Donne also quotes his commentary on the Gospel of John, *In Divi Ioannis Evangelium . . . Commentarii* (Basel, 1580), in the *Essayes*.[79] Balthasar Paez's *Commentarii in Epistolam B. Iacobi Apostoli* (Lyon, 1617) provides ammunition for Donne's exposition of the Epistle of St James, especially in the later years of his preaching career. In a 1628 sermon on James 2:12, for instance, Donne culls half a dozen patristic authorities from Paez's account: this debt usually emerges in small verbal changes which can be found in Donne and Paez, but not in the original source.[80] Seventeenth-century commentators like Paez also pay careful attention to textual provenance ('Ambrose says in his twelfth sermon on Psalm 118' etc.), and thus enable instant displays of learning with minimal effort. The Spanish Jesuit Benedict Pererius was an important port of call for Donne at least since 1607: his commentaries on Genesis and Exodus are cited in *Biathanatos*. Pererius's Genesis commentary is also one of the main sources of Donne's exegesis in the *Essayes in Divinity*, and makes frequent appearances in the sermons.[81] In Donne's first sermon on Genesis 1:26, for instance, he refers—in

---

[77] *Essayes*, 103.

[78] See A. E. Malloch, 'The Definition of Sin in Donne's *Biathanatos*', *Modern Language Notes*, 72 (1957), 332–5 (333). Such complicated textual negotiations were by no means uncommon. Richard Wetzel has excavated many examples of citational regress in Staupitz's sermons (e.g. an Augustinian self-quotation in the *Retractations* from *De Libero Arbitrio*, mediated via Lombard, via St Bonaventure; see Wetzel, 'Staupitz Augustinianus', 112).

[79] 'Transfiguratio specimen appositissimum resurrectionis' (*Sermons*, 3.118); *Essayes*, 56.

[80] See e.g. Donne, *Sermons*, 8.342, citing Ambrose: '*Ne quod luxuriat in flore, attenuetur & hebetetur in fructu;* lest that tree that blew early and plentifully, blast before it knit'. Paez, sig. 2Q3v: 'ne quod luxuriat, tenuetur & hebetetur in fructu, sicut dixit Ambr. Ser. 12 in Ps. 118.' Ambrose, *Expositio in Psalmum CXVIII, Sermo Duodecimus*, 8 (*PL* 15.1363B): 'Quod luxuriat in flore sermonibus, tenuetur et hebebetur in fructu'. Donne and Paez both add 'ne'.

[81] See *Biathanatos*, 35, 135, 137; *Essayes*, 9, 22, 59; *Sermons*, see Potter and Simpson, vol. X, under 'Pererius'. *Commentariorvm et Dispvtationvm in Genesim*, 4 vols. (Lyon, 1599); *Dispvtationvm in Sacram Scriptvram, Continens super libro Exodi Centum Triginta Septem Dispvtationes* (Lyon, 1607). Raspa convincingly argues that Donne used the 1606 edn. of the *Commentariorvm . . . in Genesim* when working on the *Essayes* (117).

the space of eight lines—first to Gregory the Great on Job and then to the medieval theologian Rupertus's *Commentariorum in Genesim*.[82] Both these authorities appear on the same page in Pererius's exposition of Genesis 1:26. Since it is unlikely that Donne would have consulted Gregory's discussion of Job in an attempt to elucidate the book of Genesis, Pererius seems like the most plausible mediator of both commentators.[83] In Donne's second sermon on this text, Pererius is also used to mediate the School; in these cases, the debt is especially obvious, since Donne tends not only to borrow Pererius's arguments, but usually takes over phrases wholesale.[84]

Donne also frequently draws on the—highly polemical—Scripture commentaries of another Jesuit divine, Maldonatus, or Juan Maldonato (1533–83). Maldonatus is a favourite target for Donne's anti-Jesuit diatribes; these attacks centre on the treatment of the Fathers whom, Donne claims, Maldonatus misrepresents, misinterprets, and denigrates (he is accused of describing the Fathers as heretics at *Sermons*, 9.159, for instance). Despite being characterized as 'an ill Intelligencer' (*Sermons*, 4.277) and a plagiarist, however—Donne notes at *Sermons*, 7.160 that Maldonatus has a habit of 'oftentimes making his use of whole Sentences of Calvins'—his New Testament commentaries are an important source for Donne's patristic citations: Donne quotes Maldonatus's work on the Gospels of Matthew and John, and on Acts, Revelation, and the first letter to the Corinthians. In the context of these references, Donne acknowledges his debt to patristic citations by Augustine, Chrysostom, and Theophylact.[85] In the sermons, there are no references to specific works by title; intriguingly, the only detailed mention of Maldonatus's texts is found in *Biathanatos*, and it points not to a primary source, but to an epitome of Maldonatus compiled by Martin Condognat, the *Summula* of 1604.[86] Once again, with regard to patristic *mediators*, Donne's emphasis is on scholarly efficiency and expediency. He is content to draw on Roman works of theology and controversy when it suits his purpose—as Raspa's magisterial annotations to *Pseudo-Martyr* and the *Essayes* show, his reading is at once comprehensive and eclectic—but this in no way diminishes the ferocity of his polemical attacks. A similar pattern emerges from closer examination of Bellarmine's commentaries.

[82] On Donne and Rupertus, see Arnold Williams, 'Commentaries on Genesis as a Basis of Hexaemeral Material in the Literature of the Late Renaissance', *Studies in Philology*, 34 (1937), 191–208.

[83] Donne, *Sermons*, 9.58. See Pererius, vol. 2, sig. Y1v. Rupertus, *Commentariorum in Genesim*, 10 vols., Book 2, chapter 1 (*PL* 167.247C).

[84] e.g. *Sermons*, 9.79: 'as we say in the Schoole, *Arguitivè*, and *Significativè*'; compare Pererius, *Commentariorvm in Genesim*, vol. 1, sig. 2B3ʳ: 'sicut in scholis loquutur Theologi, arguitiuè & significatiuè'.

[85] See e.g. *Sermons*, 3.176 (Maldonatus on Matthew 18:7); 5.255 (Matthew 28); 6.272 (Apocalypse 22:7); 7.122 (John 6:35); 7.158 (Matthew 18:12); 7.160 (Matthew 21:31); 7.205 (1 Cor. 15:29).

[86] See *Biathanatos*, 92: the reference is to Question 14, Article 6 of the *Summula* (Lyon, 1604). Another crucial source of mediated patristic knowledge, although not one—it seems—used to any significant degree by Donne himself, is Erasmus's *Paraphrases*. On the significance of Erasmus's biblical commentaries in the sixteenth and seventeenth centuries, see Hilmar M. Pabel and Mark Vessey (eds.), *Holy Scripture Speaks: The Production and Reception of Erasmus' Paraphrases on the New Testament* (Toronto, 2002), esp. ch. 8; see also J. W. Binns, *Intellectual Culture in Elizabethan and Jacobean England: The Latin Writings of the Age* (Leeds, 1990), chs. 6, 13, and 17.

A sermon preached to the king at Whitehall, on Psalms 6:6–7, makes use of Bellarmine's *Explanatio in Psalmos* and yet criticizes the same work at some length. In parsing his text, Donne includes reflections on the different versions of the Scriptures. More particularly, he attempts 'to speake neerest to the Originall [Hebrew], *Erosus est oculus, Mine eye is eaten out with Indignation*' (*Sermons*, 9.204). This is an almost exact reference to Bellarmine's reading of Psalm 6, which points out that the Hebrew version is most accurately translated as 'caligauit, seu corrosus est oculus meus' ('my eye is eaten out/gnawed away').[87] But only a hundred lines later, having consulted Bellarmine on the Hebrew Scriptures, Donne attacks his position on that text: '*Bellarmine* will needs think, that the Hebrew, the Originall, is falsified and corrupted' (*Sermons*, 9.207).

Histories of the Church

Ecclesiastical histories supplied further material for Donne's patristic quotations. Accounts of the growth and development of the Church had included patristic testimony from Eusebius onwards, but during the Reformation the battle over the past acquired a new sense of urgency. As Enrico Norelli has argued, the rebirth of ecclesiastical history as a type of apologetic can be seen 'as a by-product of the Reformation', as the Fathers and Doctors of the Church were variously invoked to defend Roman doctrine or legitimize the new Protestant Church.[88] On the Reformed side, this renewed polemical potential of Church history is demonstrated most clearly by the so-called *Centuries of Magdeburg*. Printed in Basel between 1559 and 1574 in seven volumes, and compiled under the guidance of the theologian and rhetorician Matthias Flacius Illyricus, this work covers the history of the Church from its origins until the end of the thirteenth century. Within the basic chronological framework, the structure is by theological topics, which are populated with quotations from the Fathers; the polemical concerns of the project are apparent throughout. As Flacius states, 'in this work, it can be clearly demonstrated on the sole basis of ancient documents that the first doctrine or religion of the Church was not the pope's but ours and that, subsequently, the errors now abounding in the papacy began to creep in immediately after the time of the Apostles'.[89] Upon its publication, the *Centuries* sparked off a prolonged controversial debate, led on the Catholic side by Caesar Baronius—one of Donne's main polemical targets in *Biathanatos*, *Pseudo-martyr*, and the sermons. Preaching on the anniversary of the Conversion of St Paul in 1629, Donne refers explicitly to the controversy surrounding the *Centuries*: a work which the Catholic opposition—and chiefly among them Baronius—has attempted 'to discredit, and blast, and annihilate'.[90] For Donne, Baronius epitomizes the inconsistency and incompetence that

[87] Robert Bellarmine, *Explanatio in Psalmos* (Lyon, 1611), sig. C4v.
[88] See Enrico Norelli, 'The Authority Attributed to the Early Church in the *Centuries of Magdeburg* and the *Ecclesiastical Annals* of Caesar Baronius', in Backus (ed.), *Reception of the Church Fathers*, 2.745–74 (772).
[89] Cited ibid. 747.
[90] *Sermons*, 9.158.

characterizes the Roman attitude towards the Fathers more generally: '[n]ever any in the Reformation hath spoken so lightly, nay, so heavily; so negligently, nay, so diligently, so studiously in diminution of the Fathers, as they have done.... The Fathers differ not from the Heretiques, concurre with the Heretiques. Who in the Reformation hath charged the Fathers so farr? And yet *Baronius* hath.'[91] Later in the same sermon, Donne sums up Baronius's controversial method as 'mischievously, and seditiously, and treacherously, and trayterously, and (in one comprehensive word) Papistically argued'.[92] Donne also engages with Baronius's work in *Biathanatos* and *Pseudo-martyr*. The latter work cites Baronius's massive twelve-volume *Annales Ecclesiastici* (Rome, 1588–1607) and Schultingius's *Thesaurus Antiquitatem Ecclesiasticarum* (Cologne, 1601), an epitome of the first seven books of Baronius's history.[93] *Biathanatos* cites Baronius out of Schultingius's epitome and acknowledges the debt.[94]

The records in Keynes's bibliography show that Donne owned at least one other text related to the Baronius controversy, Nicolas Vignier's *Concerning the Excommunication of the Venetians. A Discourse against Caesar Baronius, Cardinall of the Church of Rome* (London, 1607; Keynes, L187). Other ecclesiastical histories with special relevance to Donne's patrological studies are, in *Pseudo-martyr*, Eusebius (completed *c*.325, and probably mediated to Donne through the works of the sixteenth-century Dutch scholar Joseph Scaliger) and—among early modern examples—Pedro de Ribadeneira's *Historia Ecclesiastica* (1588–94).[95] In Donne's library we further find Matthew Parker's *De Antiquitate Britanniae Ecclesiae* (Hanover, 1605; Keynes, L137) and, of particular interest for its Augustinian associations, Massonus's account of the controversies between the Catholics and the Donatists, the *Gesta Collationis Chartageni Habitae Honorii Caesaris Iussu inter Catholicos et Donatistas* (Paris, 1588; Keynes, L118).

Excerpt Collections

The patristic excerpt collection is the most diverse and complex category of mediating sources. This genre originated, perhaps unsurprisingly, in an attempt to record and preserve the teachings of Augustine: the first patristic anthology, the *Liber Sententiarum Sancti Augustini*, is attributed to Prosper of Aquitaine (*c*.390–463), a correspondent of Augustine's and ardent defender of his teachings on grace, predestination, and free will; this focus on soteriology continues in the sixteenth-century anthologies. In his Easter Day sermon of 1629, Donne refers to Prosper's work: 'For, this is excellently said, to be the working of our election, by *Prosper,* the Disciple of S. *Augustines* Doctrines, and the Eccho of his words, *Vt fiat*

---

[91] *Sermons*, 9.159.
[92] Ibid. 164.
[93] *Pseudo-martyr*, 14, 50–1.
[94] *Biathanatos*, 60. In the body of the text, Donne introduces a quotation with the phrase '*Baronius* sayth', but the corresponding note ('g') references Schultingius.
[95] *Pseudo-martyr*, 34, 102. On Scaliger, see Anthony Grafton's ground-breaking *Joseph Scaliger: A Study in the History of Classical Scholarship*, 2 vols. (Oxford, 1983–93).

permanendi voluntaria, fœlixque necessitas, That our assurance of salvation by perseverance, is necessary, and yet voluntary.'[96]

This category of patristic mediators includes a vast spectrum of textual forms and practices: from the sustained exegetical and conceptual engagement of Peter Lombard's *Sentences*,[97] to anthologies compiled for specific polemical occasions,[98] to so-called *florilegia*—collections of quotations with little or no connecting argument or narrative, often organized alphabetically. Among the large group of anthologies organized by doctrinal topics, three early sixteenth-century compilations (or 'chrestomathies') proved particularly fruitful resources for preachers and controversialists in our period: Hermann Bodius's *Unio Dissidentium* (1527); Johann Piscator's three-volume *Omnium Operum Divi Augustini Epitome* (1537); and Andreas Musculus's *Enchiridion Sententiarum* of 1528.[99] Such material from the anthologies, alongside patristic information gleaned from handbooks, Scripture commentaries, and theological tracts, was often condensed further and copied into a preacher's personal commonplace book.[100] Donne likely worked with a combination of printed (and manuscript) mediators, his own commonplace books, and the scholarly helps offered by the Amerbach and Erasmus editions of Augustine's *Opera*, through an intertextual grid that offered both effective modes of recourse and comprehensive coverage of material.[101]

In the doctrinal debates of the sixteenth and seventeenth centuries, these various modes of accessing the Fathers were invested with different kinds of polemical weight and potential. A useful example of this process is the exchange between the Puritan Thomas Cartwright and the then Master of Trinity College, Cambridge, John Whitgift, in the 1570s.[102] Cartwright's acknowledgement of his debt to an influential patristic *catena*—Flacius Illyricus's *Catalogus Testium Veritatis* (1562)—was quickly converted into a sign of bumbling incompetence by his Protestant adversary, who took him to task for 'having scarcely read any one of the authors that

[96] *Sermons*, 8.370. The quotation is actually taken from *De Vita Contemplativa Libri Tres* by the fifth-century writer Julianus Pomerius, which was commonly ascribed to Prosper; see *De Vita Contemplativa*, 1.3 (*PL* 59.421A).

[97] Lombard, *Sententiarum Libri IV* (completed Paris, 1163). For an introduction to this massively influential work, see Philipp W. Rosemann, *Peter Lombard* (Oxford, 2004).

[98] See e.g. Cuthbert Tunstall's *De Veritate* of 1551, a *catena* of patristic citations on the Eucharist.

[99] See Anthony N. S. Lane, 'Justification in Sixteenth-Century Patristic Anthologies', in *Auctoritas Patrum: Zur Rezeption der Kirchenväter im 15. und 16. Jahrhundert*, ed. Leif Grane, Alfred Schindler, and Markus Wriedt (Mainz, 1993), 69–93.

[100] It should be noted that a considerable number of the most influential early-modern patristic *florilegia* were dedicated to Augustine alone; and that even in the excerpt collections which cover a broader range of Fathers, Augustine is the leading author by some distance (see Lane, 'Justification', 85: 'It will come as no surprise to any reformation scholar to discover that Augustine is by a long way the most frequently quoted Father, with nearly two thirds of the total number of passages').

[101] Although we do not have Donne's commonplace books, keeping such notes of reading was standard practice among theologians of the period. All other sources and methods are amply documented by the case studies in this book.

[102] This exchange was part of the so-called Admonition Controversy; see Peter Milward, *Religious Controversies of the Elizabethan Age: A Survey of Printed Sources* (London, 1977), 29–33.

you have alleged'.[103] Despite the strategic usefulness of such arguments, however, we should be wary of assuming that a patristic reference derived from a secondary source is necessarily a sign of ignorance or incompetence, or that the uses of the reference—doctrinal, literary, or otherwise—were less significant for being some way removed from the original text. Lombard's *Sentences* offer a sobering lesson in this respect. Augustine is the leading patristic authority in the *Sentences*, with a total of 680 citations; Ambrose comes in second, at some distance, with 66 references. Of the 680 Augustinian quotations, 310—nearly half—have been gleaned from *On the Trinity*. Astonishingly, however, none of these 310 quotations seems to have been taken from the Augustinian original: Lombard relied exclusively on a ninth-century mediator, Florus of Lyon, apparently without notable distortions or misrepresentations of Augustine's text.[104] Moreover, there is evidence to suggest that early modern preachers saw primary and secondary sources as complementary, rather than as mutually exclusive alternatives. Donne was frequently encouraged by his mediating sources to revisit a passage in the original, as we will see; conversely, close study of a primary text could send preachers to patristic anthologies and commonplace books, where topical indices offered corroborating evidence from other patrological sources; this kind of lateral thinking, as we saw in Chapter 1, could open up intellectual possibilities as well as offering convenient short cuts. Finally, a study that focuses on the reception of the Fathers must carefully negotiate the complex relations of textual fidelity and rhetorical significance. Whilst not necessarily offering a faithful representation of a Father's position in its original textual and cultural setting, the mediating sources—precisely through their varying degrees of de- and re-contextualization—offer rich and diverse opportunities for reinventing and re-articulating patristic ideas and forms of argument, especially in the literary sphere. By re-focusing our attention on the uses to which the Fathers were put, we can better understand the multiple relationships constructed by preachers between these different types of patristic access, and appreciate the interplay between primary and secondary sources as a profoundly enabling rhetorical process, rather than as a corruption of the source text.

Donne's references to these patristic *florilegia* span almost an entire millennium, and range from redactions of Oecumenius's works (late sixth and early seventh century), to later medieval sources such as Lombard's *Sentences* (1163), and to early modern collections such as D'Averoultius's *Catechismus Historicus* (1614).

Among medieval collections, the works of Oecumenius, a theologian active in Asia Minor in the sixth and seventh century, are a rich source of patristic testimony for Donne.[105] Oecumenius produced commentaries on several New Testament texts; his exposition of St Paul's epistles (which Donne chiefly draws on) is a

[103] William P. Haugaard, 'Renaissance Patristic Scholarship and Theology in Sixteenth-Century England', *Sixteenth Century Journal*, 10 (1979), 37–60 (54), citing Whitgift, *Works*, ed. John Ayre, 3 vols. (Cambridge, 1851), 1.448–9.

[104] Jacques-Guy Bougerol, 'The Church Fathers and the *Sentences* of Peter Lombard', in Backus (ed.), *Reception of the Church Fathers*, 1.113–64 (122).

[105] Donne clearly assumed that his works could be attributed to a single historical figure, but recent research suggests that 'Oecumenius', like the *Glossa Ordinaria*, is the result of a collective scholarly effort.

combination of commentary and excerpt collection. Oecumenius was most readily accessible through Latin epitomes; the most popular of these was Johannes Felicianus's *Catena Explanationum Veterum Sanctorum Patrum, ab Oecumenio ex Diversis Commentariis Collecta* (Venice, 1545, 1556; Basel, 1552). Donne's Easter sermon of 1628 illustrates his characteristic mode of recourse to Oecumenius: he is invoked at a crucial stage in the interpretation of 1 Corinthians 13:12, and serves to introduce key exegetical material from Chrysostom and Augustine: 'as S. *Chrysostome,* and the rest of the Fathers, whom *Oecumenius* hath compacted, interpret it [1 Cor. 13:12], *Cognoscam practice, id est, accurrendo,* I shall know him, that is, imbrace him, adhere to him. *Qualis sine fine festivitas!* what a Holy-day shall this be, which no working day shall ever follow!'[106] Donne assigns special significance to Oecumenius's interpretive authority as a mediator of the early Church; it is notable, for instance, that Oecumenius rarely forms part of a list of authorities or commentators. He often stands alone because, as Donne remarks in a sermon preached on 20 February 1629 at Whitehall, he 'is no single witness, nor speaks not alone, but compiles the former Fathers' (8.350; on James 2:12). This view is further corroborated by a sermon conjecturally assigned by Potter and Simpson to Christmas of the same year, on John 10:10: 'and *Oecumenius* is no single Father, but *Pater patratus,* a manifold Father, a complicated father, a Father that collected Fathers' (9.139).[107]

Donne also works with prominent medieval commonplace books, such as the *Liber in Distinctionibus Dictionum Theologicalium* by Alain de Lille (Alanus de Insulis, *c.*1128–1202), an alphabetical index of theological terms derived in large part from the Fathers. In a sermon on Psalms 6:2–3, for instance, Donne references a passage from Augustine on the process of creation: 'S. *Augustin* cannot conceive any interim, any distance, between the creating of the soule, and the infusing of the soule into the body, but eases himselfe upon that, *Creando infundit,* and *infundendo creat,* The Creation is the Infusion, and the Infusion is the Creation' (5.349). Although the idea of creation by infusion is a staple of Augustine's Genesis commentary, the precise wording occurs in the *Liber in Distinctionibus,* in the entry under 'cor'.[108] Donne also uses the *Libri Deflorationum . . . Patrum* by the twelfth-century divine Werner of St Blasius (see, for example, *Sermons,* 5.128).[109]

---

[106] *Sermons,* 8.235. The Augustine reference ('*Qualis sine fine festivitas*') is to chapter 27 of *Meditationum Liber Unus,* whose authenticity Donne rightly suspects (see Chapter 7 for further discussion of this text).

[107] According to Book 1 of Livy's *History of Rome,* the *pater patratus* was the representative of the Roman senate charged with declaring war on other states if Rome's interests were deemed to have been injured.

[108] See *PL* 210.751B.

[109] See Donne, *Sermons,* 5.128: 'S. *Augustines* words, *Accedat verbum, & fiat Sacramentum*'; compare Werner, '(AUGUSTINUS) . . . accedat verbum ad elementum, ut sit sacramentum' (*PL* 157.999A). See Augustine, *Homilies on the Gospel of John,* Homily 80: 'Accedit verbum ad elementum, et fit Sacramentum.' Augustine is commenting on John 15:1–3, while Werner's reference clearly speaks to Donne's concerns with baptism: the chapter from which Donne extracted the Augustinian reference is entitled 'What is Baptism?'

It is difficult to establish precisely Donne's debt to the many Renaissance redactions of the Fathers. He refers to several prominent authors of patristic *florilegia* in the sermons. One of the principal figures of interest here is Johann Piscator, whose three-volume *Omnium operum divi Augustini epitome* (1537) was not only one of the key sources for early modern preachers and controversialists, but also constitutes the model for many later Augustinian sentence collections in the period.[110] The arrangement is by doctrinal topics; within these doctrinal headings, Piscator's collection contains more than a hundred Augustinian quotations also found in Donne. It is hard to say anything more precise about provenance, since Renaissance excerpt collections tend to draw on each other and replicate a large percentage of their quotations. Moreover, in cases where Donne seems to have drawn on these collections, his quotations are usually brief and concise, which complicates the task of attribution through verbal overlaps or modifications. Neither the sermons nor the prose tracts mention any of the major Augustinian *florilegia*, but Donne refers to several divines who authored such collections: Hermann Bodius, compiler of the *Unio Dissidentium* (1527), is mentioned at *Sermons*, 4.141; Donne's library contains a work by the compiler of the well-known *Augustini et Chrysostomi theologia in communes locos digesta* (1539), Antonius Corvinus.[111] Among Donne's books we also find Joannes Drusius's *Miscellanea Locutionum Sacrarum* (Franeker, 1586; Keynes, L63), and Theodorus Petreus's *Confessio Tertulliana et Cypriana in Quatuor Digesta Libros* (Paris, 1603; Keynes, L142).[112] All the early modern anthologies are indebted to the *Milleloquium Sancti Augustini*, 'unquestionably the high point of Augustine scholarship before the Amerbach edition'.[113] The *Milleloquium* was compiled by Bartholomew of Urbino and completed by 1345. It consists of approximately 15,000 passages from Augustine's works, arranged alphabetically in 1,081 entries. Bartholomew only presents passages he claims to have checked himself, gives precise quotations, and flags up references where he is doubtful of precise wording. He also verifies the authenticity of Augustine's works with reference to his *Retractationes* and at times offers variant readings or expresses doubts about the authenticity

---

[110] See Lane, 'Justification', 77. Two key difficulties emerge, leaving aside the dearth of evidence from Donne's annotations: (1) the anthologies freely draw on each other (Lane shows that the majority of sixteenth-century compilers are dependent on Musculus, Piscator, and Bodius (see above)); (2) they are frequently reprinted, with minor modifications and revisions, but with re-attributions of authorship; Piscator is revised by Pesselius in 1539, which was reprinted three times in ten years; in 1565 the Genevan printer Jean Crespin reprinted the *Epitome* as the first volume of his own *Bibliotheca Studii Theologici*.

[111] *Contra Bogermann* (1614); see Keynes, L51.

[112] See also Johannes Filesacus, *De Sacra Episcoporum Auctoritate Comment* (Paris, 1606; Keynes, L73). And also, as a handbook for dealing with scholastic theologians such as Lombard or Aquinas, Paulus Ferrius's *Scholastici Orthodoxi Specimen Hoc est Salutis nostrae Methodus Analytica* (Gotstad, 1616; Keynes, L72). And, for bibliographical enquiries about Jesuit authors, Sommervogel's popular *Bibliothèque de la Compagnie de Jésus*, mentioned in *Pseudo-martyr*. The many handbooks of heresiology in Donne's library could also come under the category of auxiliary sources, as could Sayr's *Thesaurus* of cases of conscience (see Index to *Biathanatos*).

[113] Eric-Leland Saak, 'The Reception of Augustine in the Later Middle Ages', in Backus (ed.), *Reception of the Church Fathers*, 1.367–404 (381).

of certain works. He is credited, finally, with having discovered Augustine's *De Musica*. The *Milleloquium*, then, is 'not a mere collection of *dicta*, but a critical piece of scholarship by the leading Augustine scholar of his day'.[114]

Many of the entries Donne found in Erasmus's Index also appear in the *Milleloquium*, such as the quotation from *Sermons*, 5.165 which describes baptism as a kind of death ('*Quod crux Christo, & Sepulcrum, id nobis Baptisma*' (*Contra Julianum*, Book 1, chapter 6)).[115] Piscator's work, finally, receives approving comments in Donne's sermons: he is placed among the first rank of 'moderne expositors' (*Sermons*, 3.101); 'esteemed in his Division [i.e. the Reformed Church], a learned and narrow searcher into the literall sense of Scripture' (*Sermons*, 7.207); possessed of 'a holy ingenuity, and inclination to truth' (he sides with a Lutheran interpretation, even though 'he be very far from communion (in opinion) with them', *Sermons*, 7.207). Most importantly, he is a precise and faithful mediator of patristic learning: Donne observes in a sermon on Job 16:17–19 that the 'light, which S. *Chrysostome* gave to this place, shined not out' until Piscator, Calvin, and Tremellius—three key exegetes of 'the Reformation'—attended properly to the Father's texts.[116]

Gratian

Gratian's *Decretum* has already been mentioned, and it provided Donne with a broad range of patristic references in the early part of his career, especially in *Biathanatos*. The compilation, originally known as the *Concordia Discordantium Canonum (Concord of Discordant Canons)*, attempted to reconcile seemingly contradictory canons from previous centuries. Gratian quoted a broad range of authorities, including the Bible, papal and conciliar legislation, patristic sources, and secular law. The vulgate version of Gratian's collection was completed around 1150 (and at any rate after 1139, since it quotes from the Second Lateran Council, held in that year). Gratian, and the multiple and extensive additions to his work known by the sixteenth century as the *Corpus Iuris Canonici*, are referenced more than twenty-five times in *Biathanatos*; this is hardly surprising, since one of Donne's

---

[114] Saak, 382.

[115] Under the heading 'Baptismus', cols. 239–53: the wording is the same in Donne, Erasmus, and the *Milleloquium*. The 1555 copy of the *Milleloquium* in St John's College, Cambridge, was donated by Donne's former employer, Bishop Thomas Morton (on whom see also Chapter 4).

[116] *Sermons*, 9.222 (Preached to the King, 20 April 1630 [?]). Two other important sixteenth-century anthologies should be mentioned here: Ioannes Gastius's *D. Aurelii Augustini . . . tam in vetus quam in novum testamentum commentarii* (Basel, 1542), and Johann Hofmeister, *Loci communes rerum theologicarum* (Ingolstadt, 1550). On the anthologies, see Lane, 'Justification'; Eligius Dekkers, 'Quelques notes sur les florilèges augustiniens anciens et médiévaux', *Augustiniana*, 40 (1990), 27–44; Olivier Fatio, 'Un florilège augustinien du XVIe siècle: l'*Omnium operum Divi Augustini Epitome* de Johannes Piscatorius (1537)', *Revue des Études Augustiniennes*, 18 (1972), 194–202; and Joseph T. Lienhard, 'The Earliest Florilegia of Augustine', *Augustinian Studies*, 8 (1977), 21–31. Some of the anthologies simply list excerpts under a thematic heading, others provide brief synopses and explanatory glosses. A compiler's explanation can help to track a reference to its mediating source; however, I have not been able to identify any instances of overlap between an anthologist's gloss and Donne's patristic formulations.

tasks in this treatise is to examine the question of suicide from the perspective of canon law. *Pseudo-martyr* is also heavily indebted to 'this great body of the *Canon* law', and the glosses of Gratian, as Anthony Raspa observes in his introduction to the work, 'haunt Donne's marginalia' throughout.[117] While *Pseudo-martyr* heaps opprobrium on Gratian, his glossators, and five centuries of decretals, however, the sermons reserve their rhetorical venom for later incarnations of the canon law. Donne the preacher is keen to distinguish between Gratian's original *Decretum* and subsequent additions and accretions. In a sermon preached at Whitehall in April 1627, Donne presents Gratian as the only true canonist—the lone representative of a tradition that has retained a genuine connection with the Early Church. In contrast to the *Decretum*, later canonists daily invent 'a new *Decretall*, a new *Extravagant*'; as a consequence, we 'must contract a new, or enlarge, or restrain . . . old beleef'. In Donne's portrait of Church law, the later canonists sacrifice tradition to political expediency—a law is binding only 'till they fall out with some State, with whom they are friends yet'—to the point where Gratian's original corpus is supplanted by an ever-changing body of occasional decretals and dispensations:

> It is not the *Divine*, that is the Minister of salvation, but the *Canonist*. I must not determine my beleef in the *Apostles* Creed, nor in *Athanasius*, nor in that of the *Nicen* Fathers; not onely not the Scriptures, but not the Councels, nor Fathers must give the Materials, and Elements of my faith, but the *Canon law*; for so they rule it: *Gratian* that hath collected the sentences of Fathers and Councels, and digested them into heads of Divinity, he is no rule of our beleef, because, say they, he is no part of the body of the Canon law.[118]

References to Gratian in *Biathanatos* show that, on the whole, Donne seems to have consulted the *Decretum* at first hand, and that he found it a fertile—if frequently unreliable—repository of Augustinian quotations. Often, Donne seems to work with both Gratian and Augustine by his side. One likely example of this method comes in Part 2 of Donne's treatise, where he cites Augustine twice out of Gratian, while at the same time clearly demonstrating his familiarity with the Augustinian source text itself.[119] Donne begins by alleging 'an Epistle of S' Aug: to *Donatus* the *heretique*', which the accompanying note traces to chapter 23, Question 5 of Gratian. Having announced his intention to cite the views on suicide compiled in Gratian's text, Donne then digresses to 'speak alitle of S' Aug: in generall, because from him are deriued allmost all the reasons of the others, he writing purposely thereof, from the 17 to the 27 Chap: of his first Booke *De Ciuitate Dei*'—a text, as evidence from all the prose writings shows, that Donne knew well.[120] Donne's disquisition then circles back to Gratian chapter 23, which is used to introduce a quotation from the first book of *City of God*; he concludes by returning to the original source, however, and

---

[117] *Pseudo-martyr*, 196–7 (in a passage where Donne traces the development of 'this fat law' from Gratian to the present day); Raspa, Introduction, p. xxxiii.

[118] *Sermons*, 7.402.

[119] The precise reference to *Biathanatos* is to 'Part 2, Distinction 4, Section 1' (pp. 76–7).

[120] *Biathanatos*, 76–7.

closes with a much more detailed quotation-cum-paraphrase from the final sentence of *City of God*, Book 1, chapter 26, which is not in Gratian:

> And so, as *S' Aug:*, we with as much earnestnesse say *Hoc asserimus, hoc dicimus, hoc omnibus modis approbamus, That neither to auoyd temporall troubles, nor to remoue from others occasion of Sinne, nor to punish our owne past Sinnes, nor to preuent future, nor in a desire of the next Life* (where these considerations are onely or principally) *it cannot be Lawfull for any man to kill himselfe.*[121]

By going back to the original source, then, Donne is able to verify quotations, establish context, and collect further references with which to bolster his case. Collectively, Donne's recourse to Gratian in *Biathanatos*, *Pseudo-martyr*, and the sermons attests to the thoroughly situational character of his citational philosophy: Gratian offers a series of useful pointers in *Biathanatos*, serves to prop up (somewhat paradoxically) the case for a return *ad fontes* in the Whitehall sermon of 1627, and is utterly demolished as an authority in the anti-Roman polemic of *Pseudo-martyr* (as Donne notes sarcastically, even Bellarmine realized that '*Gratian was deceived by trusting a false copie of Saint Augustines workes*').[122] In the sermons, Gratian plays a much less prominent part as a mediator of the Fathers, but can function as a useful tool in passages of controversial argument.

Lombard

There are surprisingly few acknowledged references to Peter Lombard's work in Donne's writing—about two dozen altogether—and it is difficult to gauge the extent of his unacknowledged debt. In his preaching Donne introduces Lombard either as 'The Master of the Sentences' or as a representative of 'the Schoole'.[123] Donne's treatment of scholastic theology is rarely complimentary, and Lombard is no exception in this regard: at *Sermons*, 5.63, Donne describes one of Lombard's expositions as 'suspiciously, and . . . dangerously said'. Of the seven references to Lombard in *Biathanatos* and the *Essayes*, five are used to mediate Augustine.[124] Donne's comments and citational practices in these works confirm the impression that he was somewhat distrustful of Lombard's authority. In Part I of *Biathanatos*— a crucial part of the treatise where Donne evolves his definition of sin—he takes Lombard to task on two counts, for taking an intellectual short cut and for misrepresenting his Augustinian source:

---

[121] *Biathanatos*, 77; see *De Civitate Dei* 1.26: 'Hoc dicimus, hoc asserimus, hoc modis omnibus approbamus, neminem spontaneam mortem sibi inferre debere, velut fugiendo molestias temporales, ne incidat in perpetuas: neminem propter aliena peccata, ne hoc ipse incipiat habere gravissimum proprium, quem non polluebat alienum: neminem propter sua peccata praeterita, propter quae magis hac vita opus est, ut possint poenitendo sanari: neminem velut desiderio vitae melioris, quae post mortem speratur; quia reos suae mortis melior post mortem vita non suscipit.'

[122] *Pseudo-martyr*, 195.

[123] See *Sermons*, 4.332, 8.363.

[124] See *Biathanatos*, 23, 38, 125; *Essayes*, 42, 71.

Of all those definitions of Sinne, which the first *Rhapsoder Pet: Lombard* hath presented out of ancient learning, as well the *Summists*, as Casuists do most insist vppon that, which he brings from *Sᵗ Augustine;* as commonly where that Father serues theyr turnes they neuer go further. This Definition is, that Sinne is *Dictum, Factum, Concupientum, contra æternam Legem Dei.* This they stick to, because this Definition (if it be one) best beares theyr descant: and is the easiest conveyance, and cariadge, and vent, for theyr acceptions; and applying rules of Diuinity to particular cases; by which they haue made all our Actions perplex'd and litigious[.] . . . But for this vse this Definition can not bee thought to be applyable to Sinne onely, since it limits it to the externall Law of God. (Which word, though *Lombard* haue not, *Sayr,* and all the rest retayne.)[125]

The reference is to Lombard, Book 2, Distinction 35, quoting from Augustine's *Against Faustus the Manichee.* The word which Lombard is accused of having omitted in the *Sentences* is 'aeternam', and it is crucial to Donne's rejection of Augustine's definition of sin. Despite quoting from an intermediary source, Donne has taken the trouble to check Lombard's quotation, and delivers a withering indictment of his citational politics.[126]

The *Essayes in Divinity* offer a similar case: there, Donne's disquisition on God's mercy includes a reference to Book 4, Distinction 46 of the *Sentences,* 'ex August.', taken from the *Enchiridion.* However, as Raspa shows, Donne verified this account by consulting the Augustinian text directly—further proof, perhaps, of Donne's distrust of Lombard.[127]

Aquinas

Aquinas's *Summa Theologiae* (1265–74) occupies a special place among the many mediating sources that Donne drew upon. Even a cursory glance at Donne's comments on Aquinas indicates that he had no special affection for the Angelic Doctor. The *Essayes in Divinity* pay him a rather back-handed compliment: Donne appears to applaud Aquinas's intellectual zeal—nothing is 'too mineral nor centric for the search and reach of his wit'—but this praise pales in comparison with the assessment of Augustine which immediately precedes it. Augustine, clearly, is not just a thinking machine, but an inspired witness to God's love and providence, 'whom thou hast filled with faith, desire, reason and understanding'.[128]

In the sermons, Donne's references to Aquinas are usually slighting or dismissive. He is not above contemplating, with some glee, the prospect of 'offending a great

---

[125] *Biathanatos*, Part I, Distinction 1, Section 5 (p. 38).

[126] The difference between Lombard's and Augustine's quotations is pointed out by Sullivan II, 191. Lombard's definition reads as follows: 'Peccatum est, ut ait August., omne dictum, vel factum, vel concupitum, quid fit contra legem Dei.' *Sententiarum*, 4 vols., volume 2, distinctio 35 (*PL* 192.734). Compare Augustine's opening sentence to *Contra Faustum* 22.27 (*PL* 42.418): 'Ergo peccatum est, factum vel dictum vel concupitum aliquid contra aeternam legem. Lex vero aeterna est, ratio divina vel voluntas Dei, ordinem naturalem conservari jubens, perturbari vetans.'

[127] *Essayes*, 71; Raspa's note at 173–4 (the argument centres on the use of the word 'intervalla' in Donne's account, which is found in Erasmus's edition of the *Enchiridion*, but not in Lombard's *Sentences*).

[128] *Essayes in Divinity*, 19.

part in the Schoole' (*Sermons*, 8.231); another passage mockingly invites Aquinas to 'present his argument to the contrary' (*Sermons*, 10.83), only to mount a comprehensive refutation of his position a few moments later. Above all, Donne is keen to assert the superiority of the Fathers over the Doctors of the Church: 'To come lower, and to a lower rank of witnesses, from the Fathers to the Schoole, *Aquinas* hath another sense' (*Sermons*, 7.200). The contrast with Augustine is especially pronounced: at *Sermons*, 8.155, a quotation from Aquinas is introduced with a simple '*Aquinas* sayes'; the next quotation, three lines later, is from Augustine, and deemed to be 'excellently said by that excellent Father'. Aquinas bears the brunt of Donne's contempt for scholastic theology, with which he is often equated. Many references to 'the Schoole' are accompanied by detailed marginal notes to the *Summa Theologiae*; sometimes, the identification is spelled out even more clearly, as when Donne cites 'the Schoole in the mouth of Aquinas' (*Sermons*, 4.330). Characteristically, however, Donne's dislike of Aquinas does not prevent him from drawing freely on his patristic learning, both explicitly and implicitly. A passage on the sin of the angels openly acknowledges the debt: '*Illud quaesiverunt, ad quod pervenissent, si stetissent*, sayes *Aquinas* out of S. *Augustine*.'[129] Aquinas is also used to mediate other Fathers, such as Chrysostom, Jerome, Athanasius, and Gregory Nazianzen.[130] The *Summa Theologiae* mainly serves as a source for brief, aphoristic quotations, but as the case study on divine ideas has shown, Aquinas also supplies references of broader argumentative and structural import. Another example appears in a sermon preached at St Dunstan's on 1 Thessalonians 5:16 ('Rejoice evermore'), which argues for the need to rejoice even in the face of sorrow and death. In building his case, Donne draws on the combined support of Aquinas and Augustine:

> Can this sorrow and this joy consist together? very well. The School in the mouth of *Aquinas* gives instances; If an innocent man be condemned, *Simul placet ejus justitia, & displicet afflictio*, I congratulate his innocency, and I condole his death both at once. So *Displicet mihi quod peccavi, & placet quod displicet;* I am very sorry that I have sinned, but yet I am glad that I am sorry. So that, *Ipsa tristitia materia gaudii;* Some sorrow is so far from excluding joy, as that naturally it produces it. S. *Augustine* hath sealed it with this advice, *Semper doleat pœnitens,* Let him who hath sinned always lament; But then where is the *Gaudete semper?* he tels us too, *Semper gaudeat de dolore,* Let him always rejoyce, that God hath opened him a way to mercy, by sorrow.[131]

What Donne does not tell us here is that Aquinas also cites the passages from Augustine ('*Semper doleat pœnitens*') that conclude his peroration: once again, camouflaging the debt to Aquinas clearly seemed like the best option here.[132]

As a final example, we might cite Donne's definition of evil as privation in a sermon preached at Whitehall on 4 March 1625 (Matthew 19:17). Here, Donne's global reference to 'the Schoole' masks his debt to Questions 48 and 49 of the first

---

[129] *Sermons*, 7.230.   [130] See ibid. 4.195; 8.360.   [131] Ibid. 10.223.
[132] See Aquinas, *Summa*, 3.84.9: 'Unde nihil prohibet hominem simul gaudere et tristari, puta, si videamus iustum affligi, simul placet nobis eius iustitia, et displicet afflictio. . . . Unde et Augustinus dicit, in libro de poenitentia, *semper doleat poenitens, et de dolore gaudeat*.'

part of the *Summa Theologiae*, which are in turn indebted, respectively, to Augustine's *Enchiridion* and *Against Julian*.[133] While Donne's citations from Aquinas in the sermons are, on the whole, marked by accuracy and precision, *Biathanatos* (and, to a certain extent, the *Essayes*) present a different picture. Ernest W. Sullivan II's annotations to *Biathanatos* reveal a host of misquotations: the concluding paragraph to a discussion in Part I of Donne's treatise, for instance, introduces an accurate reference to *Summa*, Part I, Question 105, Article 6 (which in turn cites a passage from Augustine's *Against Faustus*, Book 26, chapter 3—the next quotation in Donne's text), but then follows up with four extracts from Aquinas whose sources are either imprecisely referenced or simply wrong.[134] The correct reference to the *Summa Theologiae* recurs in the *Essayes in Divinity* (including the quotation from Augustine's *Against Faustus*); this suggests, perhaps, that Donne had recorded it in writing, while quoting the other four from memory.[135] At any rate, he had learned to quote more accurately from Aquinas by the time he started composing his sermons. Citations in the *Essayes* show a greater degree of accuracy; however, as Raspa notes, the overall strategy here is to paraphrase authorities rather than to produce exact quotations from the source text.[136] There is also some evidence to demonstrate that Donne used 'tertiary' sources to help navigate the difficult terrain of Aquinas's text: *Biathanatos* includes two references to the *Summa Theologiae* which derive from Thomas Cajetan's epitome-cum-commentary of that work, the *Secunda Secundae Partis Summae Sacrosanctae Theologiae Sancti Thomae Aquinatis* (Lyon, 1562).[137]

What has emerged from this survey of patristic material? Donne discovers his quotations through multiple types of recourse: direct consultation, with detailed perusal of the source text; more selective reading or re-reading of a text, prompted either by memory, by a commonplace book, by one of a variety of patristic mediators, or by a patristic index. This last tool, the index, in some ways blurs the lines between primary and secondary modes of access: alongside Amerbach's *Tabulae* to the *Enarrations on the Psalms* and the *Sermons*, Erasmus's index offered a vital means of visual and intellectual orientation for Donne, and supplied a host of material and conceptual aids, which could be used as mines of information in themselves and as opportunities to re-establish contact with Augustine's works. Thus, throughout Donne's writings, immediate recourse to Augustine's texts merges with various forms of mediation, which open up new avenues for creative exploration. Early Christian, medieval, and early modern mediators provided

---

[133] This example was first noted by Potter and Simpson; see *Sermons*, 6.238 and 6.20 (editorial introduction). Augustine, *Enchiridion*, *PL* 40; *Contra Julianum*, *PL* 44.

[134] *Contra Faustum Manichaeum* (*PL* 42.481). The exact reference to *Biathanatos* is Part I, Distinction 1, Section 7 (p. 41).

[135] *Biathanatos*, 41 (and see Sullivan's notes at 192); see *Essayes*, 89 (Raspa notes that the Augustine quotation derives from Aquinas).

[136] *Essayes*, 177. Raspa's notes (*Essayes*, 22) also reveal that Donne uses Augustine, and more specifically the *City of God*, as a source for quotations of texts that are now lost—e.g. the epistle of Alexander the Great to his mother, referenced at *City of God* 12.10. This certainly suggests familiarity with Augustine's texts.

[137] See *Biathanatos*, 40–1.

quotations (either from unfamiliar texts or from those that Donne had originally read), but they also frequently acted as guides which lead Donne back to the Augustinian texts themselves, and their importance is profound. Donne can deploy the same Augustinian text in mediated and direct form in close textual proximity; it is also clear that Donne's modes of access and use depend both on his rhetorical purposes and on the availability of texts—again, this holds true both for the Augustinian works themselves and for intermediary sources. Donne's use of Gratian, for instance, varies widely between *Biathanatos*, *Pseudo-martyr*, and the sermons. Augustine's own sermons and the *Enarrations* appear in Donne's texts only after his ordination, when he had regular access to a cathedral library—the kind of environment where Amerbach's single editions of Augustine were most commonly held.[138] Finally, Donne's passionate invectives against Catholic mediators of the Fathers, in the sermons and in *Pseudo-martyr*, did not stop him from using these texts when it suited his objectives; sometimes such works are re-appropriated for Protestant purposes, but more frequently they are used as straightforward sources of patristic knowledge. Donne's use of the Fathers ranges from well-worn maxims to extended and subtle thematic references, from brief nods and patristic 'padding' to cases of profound conceptual and structural significance. Donne probably had in-depth knowledge of no more than about seven or eight Augustinian texts, among them the *Confessions*, the *City of God*, the *Enchiridion*, *On the Trinity*, *On the Literal Interpretation of Genesis*, the *Enarrations on the Psalms*, and *On the Values of the Catholic Church*. In this he was far from unusual: other Renaissance divines such as Calvin, Staupitz, and Hales, as we have seen, operated within comparable intertextual territory in sermons and commentaries, if not in their controversial writings. Donne and his contemporaries moved through the textual landscape with singular economy of reference, and with a degree of imagination and resourcefulness which forces us to reinvestigate critical binaries such as citational 'fidelity' and 'licence', 'erudition' and 'display'.

After this initial survey of the principal modes of Augustinian access, recourse, and presentation, I now move on to the first in-depth case study: Donne's reworking of the *Confessions* in the *Essayes in Divinity*.

---

[138] Copies of the Amerbach edition of the *Enarrations* (under the title *Explanatio [Libri] Psalmorum*) survive in the cathedral libraries of Durham, Exeter, Hereford, Lincoln, and Peterborough; copies of the sermons can be found in Hereford, Lincoln, and York Minster.

3

'Ascending Humility'

Augustinian Hermeneutics in the *Essayes in Divinity*

The *Essayes in Divinity* mark the transition to the second part of this book, which presents five case studies designed to illustrate different modes of Augustinian reference and recourse in Donne's work. Armed with a sense of how Donne accessed and reinvented the writings of his favourite Church Father, we can now turn to the main focus of the argument: Donne's use of Augustine's hermeneutic philosophy. And although, chronologically speaking, the *Essayes* are not Donne's first substantial engagement with Augustine's works (this takes place in *Biathanatos*, the subject of the next chapter), they constitute an important inaugural moment of spiritual orientation and interpretive self-definition. Donne's *Essayes* are best described as a series of prose meditations on the Scriptures, but they have a curiously narrow textual scope: he concentrates his analysis on the first verse of Genesis and Exodus, respectively. The *Essayes* were probably composed in or around 1614, the year before Donne entered into the priesthood, although they were not published until 1651.[1] They are, then, a liminal text—not unlike Herbert's 'The Church-porch'—which places Donne 'at the threshold' of God's word.[2] But in contrast to *The Temple*, which charts a full procession through the rhythms and rituals of the English Church, Donne's text homes in on a single aspect of churchmanship: scriptural interpretation. It is exegesis which provides the key to Donne's self-understanding as a Christian and future preacher, much as it did for Augustine, who crowns his autobiographical account in the *Confessions* with an extended interpretation of Genesis. In the thoroughly integrated, hard-won, and self-conscious

---

[1] Donne was ordained on 23 January 1615 in the Bishop of London's palace chapel (Bald, *Life*, 203). Positive evidence for dating the *Essayes* is thin on the ground. In his edition of the *Essayes*, Anthony Raspa argues that 'the influence of the King James Bible upon [the treatise's] citations and quotations, and the pagination of the 1614 edition of Buxtorf's *Synagoga Judaica* in Donne's marginalia towards the end of the *Essayes* confirm that he completed the work in that year [1614]'; see Raspa, pp. xxxix–xl (full details below at note 2). Buxtorf first published the work in German in 1603 and then in Latin in the following year. Raspa deduces from the pagination of Buxtorf's marginalia that Donne was working with the second Latin edition of 1614. Donne's text contains no explicit references to works published after 1614, so this date offers a plausible, if not watertight, *terminus ad quem* for the *Essayes*.

[2] John Donne, *Essayes in Divinity*, ed. Anthony Raspa (Montreal, 2001), 7. All references to the *Essayes* are to this edition and will be presented parenthetically in the text.

hermeneutic initiation of the *Essayes*, Donne discovers the beginnings of a new vocation, but also finds his Augustinian voice.

There are other, more pragmatic, reasons for starting an investigation of Donne's Augustinianism with the *Essayes in Divinity*. Because the text presents a limited number of explicit references to Augustine—twenty-three in total—and offers relatively straightforward ways of determining the provenance of these quotations and paraphrases, the *Essayes* can be used as a controlled sample of sorts. In the introduction to his edition of the *Essayes*, Anthony Raspa reminds us of the importance of medieval and early modern commentaries on Genesis and Exodus, the two scriptural texts whose opening verses Donne expounds in the *Essayes*. These range from orthodox Calvinist works in English, such as Andrew Willett's *Hexapla in Genesin* (1605) and *Hexapla in Exodum* (1608), to compendious Latin commentaries like the *Commentariorvm et Dispvtationvm in Genesim* (1591–9) by the Spanish Jesuit Benedictus Pererius. Despite radical differences in doctrinal conviction and methodological emphasis, most of the Scripture commentaries cited by Donne share a reliance on Augustine as a doctrinal and exegetical authority—an authority, however, which is mediated by a complex reception history spanning more than eleven centuries. This is the broadest sense in which the term 'Augustinian' applies to the *Essayes*; it is also the most elusive one to trace and delineate.

My discussion in this chapter is less concerned with Augustinianism in this broad sense; by contrast, it will concentrate on references that Donne consciously recognized and marked as Augustinian. These are either taken directly from Augustine's texts, as in the case of the *Confessions* and the *City of God*, or derive from mediators and secondary sources: this applies to the *Sermons*, *Against Adversaries of the Law and the Prophets*,[3] the *Enchiridion to Laurentius*, *De Doctrina Christiana*, *On the Good of Marriage*,[4] *On Nature and Grace*,[5] and *Against Faustus the Manichee*.[6] A rough taxonomy of Donne's Augustinian references allows us to distinguish between five different modes of intertextual recourse: (1) cases in which the length and detail of the quotation suggests direct acquaintance with the primary text (*Confessions* and *City of God*); (2) acknowledged references to a medieval or Renaissance mediator of Augustine, which lead Donne to consult the original text;[7] (3) acknowledged quotations from such intermediaries which give no indication of having led Donne back to the Augustinian text itself;[8] (4) references to Augustine's works which, on closer inspection, turn out to be indebted to an unacknowledged

---

[3] *Contra Adversarium Legis et Prophetarum*, PL 42.
[4] *De Bono Conjugali*, PL 40.
[5] *De Natura et Gratia*, PL 44.
[6] *Contra Faustum Manichaeum*, PL 42.
[7] See e.g. *Essayes*, 70, where Donne quotes from Lombard's *Sentences*, Book 4, Distinction 46, 'ex August'. Raspa (173–4) notes that Donne's use of the word 'intervalla' in this passage suggests consultation of the original: the word is found in Erasmus's edition of Augustine's *Enchiridion* in the 1531 edition of the *Opera*, but not in Lombard, who first points Donne towards the reference.
[8] See e.g. *Essayes*, 38, where a brief Augustinian vignette is reported through a reference to the cabalist Franciscus Georgius's *De Harmonia Mundi* (1545).

mediator (often Aquinas);[9] and (5) looser allusions to well-known Augustinian topoi, often found in the vicinity of an early modern source which draws extensively on Augustine's own texts.[10]

At the time of composing the *Essayes*, Donne probably knew only two of Augustine's texts at first hand, the *Confessions* and the *City of God*.[11] But these two texts shaped his thinking about the ministry—as a profession, and as a spiritual and intellectual disposition and discipline—in a profound and lasting way. I will argue more particularly that the *Confessions* inform Donne's sense of religious vocation in its institutional and public dimensions; more importantly, however, Augustine's text embodies an inward spiritual conviction which is founded on the notion of an 'ontological' or 'universal' hermeneutics. Augustine prescribes specific rules of exegesis, but also emphasizes the centrality of devotional conditioning: inward faith preconditions outward interpretation; reading is a spiritual discipline as well as an exercise of the intellect.

The *Essayes* draw on the *Confessions* more than a dozen times, in passages of doctrinal argument, moral exhortation, and, most crucially, in the context of building an interpretive philosophy on Augustine's example. Three sets of quotations are of especial relevance in this regard: first, an extract from *Confessions* 7.9.14 in the opening paragraphs of the *Essayes*, which establishes 'ascending humility' as the primary characteristic of the Christian interpreter; secondly, an extended translation from *Confessions* 11.3.5, which initiates Donne's exegetical efforts on Genesis 1:1 ('In the beginning'), articulates the principle of hermeneutic faith, and pushes him across the biblical threshold, into the company of 'professed divines'; and, finally, a passage from *Confessions* 11.12.14, which concludes Donne's reading of Genesis 1:1 and defines the boundaries between licit and illicit enquiry. In modelling his education on a reading of Augustine, Donne follows one of the master tropes of the *Confessions*, which discovers its own template for spiritual regeneration through a reading of St Paul. Donne's desire for spiritual emulation creates an intertextual relationship with Augustine which blurs the line between faithful and eristic imitation: in his re-articulation of Augustine's Pauline paradigm, Donne's meticulous fidelity to the details of his source text both invokes the authority of Augustine's example and seeks to surpass it.

[9] e.g. *Essayes*, 33, where a quotation from *Contra Adversarium Legis et Prophetarum* draws on Aquinas, *Summa*, Book 1, Quaestio 45, articles 1 and 2 ('De Modo Emanationis Rerum a Primo Principio'; see Raspa, 144).

[10] See, for instance, Donne's description of darkness and evil as 'privation' and 'nothing'—an Augustinian commonplace derived from Book 7 of the *Confessions* (*Essayes*, 33; see *Confessions*, 7.12–16). Raspa suggests that Donne's account of the relative powers of will and grace (*Essayes*, 87–8) echoes Augustine's *De Natura et Gratia*, possibly mediated through Azpilcueta of Navarre (Donne acknowledges neither).

[11] Donne's use of the *City of God* will be discussed at greater length in the next chapter, on *Biathanatos*, a text which pre-dates the *Essayes* by more than half a decade. See also Vessey, 'Donne in the Company of Augustine', 193–8; I agree with Vessey's observation that, while Donne had 'carefully meditated' the *Confessions* by the time he wrote the *Essayes* (195), he did not have 'a first-hand acquaintance' with *De Doctrina Christiana* (198).

This chapter begins by examining the three passages from the *Confessions* in detail, placing them in the context of Augustine's work and of the *Essayes* as a whole. *Confessions* 11.3.5, in particular, is a key text to which Donne returned throughout his career, at moments of acute spiritual and hermeneutic pressure. The final section will chart its re-emergence in the sermons and the *Devotions*. Throughout, I will argue for Donne's profound and consistent engagement with Augustinian principles of Scripture interpretation, both through direct recourse to the *Confessions* and through the absorption and re-working of these principles in early modern devotional writing. Donne's exegetical initiation at the hands of Augustine (and his seventeenth-century readers) establishes modes of thought, interpretation, and argument that are foundational to his career as a writer and preacher after 1615—even though the sermons will not replicate the density of sources or the conceptual complexity offered by the *Essayes*. As subsequent chapters demonstrate, the future applications of Donne's interpretive vocabulary will be acutely occasion-centred and polemical, intersecting with (among others) the politics of conscience, the politics of the law, and the politics of peace and charity. The *Essayes*, by contrast, are remarkable for their efforts to sidestep such local and polemical concerns: there, textual conversation and communion with Augustine is part of a larger project of interpretive self-realization, a transformation of self actuated through participation in a timeless community of readers and exegetes. This project is not without its problems, as the text recognizes; it is not easily reconciled, for instance, with Donne's insistence—in *Pseudo-martyr* and elsewhere—on the difference of the past and the historical specificity of Scripture interpretation. Despite these difficulties, however, the *Essayes* work hard to think themselves beyond the boundaries of controversial debate and doctrinal conflict; their aim is to stand (however fleetingly) 'outside of time', to carve out a place where the fiction of absolute truth and authority can be authenticated through Augustine's example. Donne's treatment of humility, which models itself on an episode from Book 7 of the *Confessions*, outlines the beginnings of a kind of interpretive method, to be fleshed out more fully in the rest of Donne's treatise. The excursus on interpretive faith, by contrast, illuminates the inward spiritual disposition needed to put these exegetical rules into practice; this too relies on *Confessions*, situating itself alongside a moment of hermeneutic and devotional crisis in Augustine's own text. Donne's strategy is to force the gaze inwards and backwards; the imagined return to Augustine—the iconic representative of a superior institutional tradition—symbolizes a fresh start for Donne, as he turns his attention towards 'professional Divinity'.

The hermeneutic approaches adumbrated by the *Essayes* are themselves implicated in two distinct but related strands of Augustine's Renaissance reception history. Sixteenth- and seventeenth-century manuals of Bible reading supply the foundation for the pragmatic aspects of exegesis. Here, John Hales's *Sermon . . . Concerning the Abuses of Obscure and Difficult Places of Holy Scripture* (1617) and Thomas Wilson's *Theologicall Rules for Guiding Us in the Understanding and Practise of Holy Scripture* (1615) will provide a measure for gauging the orthodoxy of Donne's Protestant reading framework: an expressly articulated desire to define, and show conformity to, a corpus of interpretive fundamentals, which serves as a further means of spiritual, doctrinal, and professional validation. While these manuals and guides freely reference and exploit Augustinian precepts of interpretation, however, they do not fully absorb the larger moral and ontological ramification of his hermeneutic. To contextualize these elements of Augustine's intellectual heritage, we need to turn to early modern treatises of meditation: it is in handbooks such as Joseph Hall's *The Arte of Divine Meditation* (1606) and Richard Greenham's *Grave Counsels and Godly Observations* (*Workes*, 1599), and in the burgeoning market of pseudo-Augustinian works of devotion, that the wider spiritual applications of Augustine's hermeneutic model are fully realized. The generic complexities of Donne's *Essayes*, I will suggest, are fully appreciated (and partly resolved) when we view the text as a form of private scriptural meditation in the Augustinian tradition. This means situating the activity of interpretation in a broader salvific scheme: the *Confessions* develop a hermeneutic which is embedded in a topographical and geographical model of religious conversion and self-realization. Faith and humility are the foundational virtues of the Christian reader, which enable access to difficult and obscure scriptural places, and ultimately plot a hermeneutic path back to the creator of the Word itself. This return to God is imagined as a revised version of the Platonic ascent through contemplation: it replaces the self-centred early quest for knowledge and worldly acclaim with Christian wisdom. As Augustine abandons Plato for Paul in Book 7 of the *Confessions*, so Donne's *Essayes* convert his 'Hydroptique, immoderate desire of humane learning' into a form of Christian learning and scholarship.[12] The habits of reading and interpretation that support this mentality force the gaze inward and encourage spiritual introspection. Without such commitment to hermeneutic meditation, Donne will remain an 'Interloper', outside 'the commission of Expositors of the Scriptures' (38). In the *Essayes*, as we will see, professional self-fashioning and inward contemplation are inextricably linked.[13]

CONFESSIONS 7.9.14 AND INTERPRETIVE HUMILITY

Donne's pre-ordination experiments with 'Unvocall preaching' (47) represent a conscious act of interpretive initiation: in the *Essayes*, he meditates on the conditions of textual production which contributed to the creation of the Scriptures and distils from them a set of interpretive rules which allows him to enter 'Gods fairest

---

[12] John Donne, *Letters to Severall Persons of Honour* (London, 1651), 51.

[13] I agree, therefore, with Jeffrey Johnson's sense that the *Essayes* are concerned with establishing Donne's 'hermeneutic principles'; but while Johnson locates these in the mathematics of infinity, my argument is that Donne's hermeneutic is fundamentally theological and Augustinian. See Jeffrey Johnson, '"One, four, and infinite": John Donne, Thomas Harriot, and *Essayes in Divinity*', *John Donne Journal*, 22 (2003), 109–43 (esp. 126–34; citation at 132). Kate Narveson situates the *Essayes* 'in the context of devotional writing by other lay gentlemen'; Donne's text certainly offers parallels with such writings, but I would question Narveson's claim that '[o]rdination within the Church of England is not the issue' in the *Essayes* (Kate Narveson, 'Donne the Layman Essaying Divinity', *John Donne Journal*, 28 (2009), 1–30 (3–4)).

Temple, his Word' (47). However, exegesis in the *Essayes* also serves as a metaphor for a broader gesture of doctrinal and spiritual accreditation: it is only by honing a rectified hermeneutic disposition that Donne will be able to claim the authority of the Word. '[I]nward humility', the *Essayes* argue, underpins and justifies the 'outward interpretations' of Scripture communicated by the Church (9). It is no accident, therefore, that Donne's *Essayes* draw on three formative moments of hermeneutic re-orientation in Augustine's text. *Confessions* 7.9 discovers the limitations of the '*libri Platonici*'—the books of Platonic philosophy which had fascinated Augustine in the early stages of his life—through an acknowledgement of Christ's sacrifice; this in turn initiates the reading of Paul that will lead to Augustine's conversion. The eleventh book of the *Confessions* (on which Donne draws most consistently in the *Essayes*) represents an important turning-point in Augustine's own spiritual and hermeneutic narrative: it marks the transition from the autobiographical part of the *Confessions*—with the climactic relation of his conversion experience in Book 9—to the concluding meditations on Genesis in Books 11–13. This hermeneutic and epistemological turn in the *Confessions* finds its counterpart in Donne's 'Entrance' into the Bible through the *Essayes in Divinity*. Book 11 of the *Confessions* serves, primarily, as a way of revealing the mental and spiritual disposition of its interpreter; it is an exemplary act of exegesis which sets up the moral and doctrinal principles informing Augustine's own sense of religious vocation. *Confessions* 11.3.5 articulates the need for interpretive faith through an imaginary colloquy with the author of Genesis, while 11.12.14 warns of the dangers of interpretive curiosity. Together, these three passages form a discursive and moral frame for Donne's own—curiously selective—reflections on the Bible in the *Essayes in Divinity*. Donne's focus on a single verse from Genesis and Exodus suggests that his exegesis is designed to be representative rather than comprehensive; furthermore, his explications invariably proceed from, and return to, discussions of more universal principles of interpretation. Hermeneutics, in the *Confessions* and in the *Essayes*, is deeply implicated in a broader ontology of revelation and spiritual rectification.

In order to grasp Donne's approach to interpretation, then, we must first attend to a set of key terms he evolves through intense engagement with Augustine's texts: 'humility', 'curiosity', and 'faith'. Donne's hermeneutic methodology is based on an injunction from the Gospel of John: '*Search the Scriptures, because in them ye hope to have eternall life*' (John 5:39; *Essayes* 8). In the *Essayes*, the story of the fallen interpreter's search becomes a journey of exploration, an existential quest. At the same time, Donne is keen to move beyond the Augustinian commonplace of the 'homo viator', or pilgrim man, whose life is defined as a constant attempt to find a way back to God. In the *Essayes*, the idea of the journey is re-conceived in textual terms, as 'that best way of expounding Scriptures by comparing one place with another' (64). Donne imagines himself as travelling between different scriptural 'loci' or places, and his ability to gain accreditation as a Christian reader and thinker depends on his ability to navigate through a complex biblical topography.

Donne's interpretive approach is framed by his status as a lay exegete seeking access to the company of professional Scripture readers. The biblical text is envisaged as a 'Castle': 'he that will enter, must stoop and humble himselfe' (7).

To 'reverend Divines, who by an ordinary calling are Officers and Commissioners from God, the great Doors are open'. Donne, by contrast, will 'with *Lazarus* lie at the threshold, and beg their crums' (7). Imagined physical posture props up Donne's rhetorical positioning here; while professional divines walk tall, Donne is lying low and keeps his ear—in more ways than one—close to the ground. This attitude prepares for the portrait of decorous Christian enquiry which follows, and which in turn draws on the etymological roots of the term 'humility', as it locates the quest for human knowledge on the vertical axis between heaven and earth ('humus'), immanence and transcendence:

> *Discite à me*, says our blessed Saviour, *Learn of me*, as Saint *Augustine* enlarges it well, not to do Miracles, nor works exceeding humanity; but *quia mitis sum*; learn to be humble. His humility, to be like us, was a Dejection; but ours, to be like him, is our chiefest exaltation; and yet none other is required at our hands. Where this humility is, *ibi Sapientia*. Therefore it is not such a groveling, frozen, and stupid Humility, as should quench the activity of our understanding, or make us neglect the Search of those Secrets of God, which are accessible. . . . It is then humility to study God, and a strange miraculous one; for it is an ascending humility, which the Divel . . . hath corrupted in us by a pride, as much against reason; for he hath fill'd us with a descending pride, to forsake God, or the study and love of things worse then our selves. (7–8)

Donne's opening quotation from Matthew 11:29—'Discite a me, quia mitis sum'—is the scriptural *locus classicus* for Augustine's definition of humility; the terms 'humilitas' and 'humilis' are used on more than 2,400 occasions in Augustine's works.[14] The link between humility and a personal quest for wisdom and knowledge is made most explicitly at *Confessions* 7.9.14, which records a kind of interpretive conversion; in this passage, Augustine realizes the failure of the Platonic books to account for the most significant events in human history—the incarnation and the Passion:

> But that 'he took on himself the form of a servant and emptied himself, was made in the likeness of men . . . and humbled himself being made obedient to death' [Philippians 2:6-8] that these books [of the Platonists] do not have. . . . [T]hose who, like actors, wear the high boots of supposedly more sublime teaching do not hear him who says 'Learn of me, that I am meek and humble in heart, and you shall find rest for your souls.' [Matthew 11:29][15]

The '*libri Platonici*', Augustine now admits, cannot teach the humility of the *logos*; because of this, his search will lead him, by the end of Book 7, to a different kind of text—Saint Paul's account of the Passion. This intellectual conversion from secular

[14] Cornelius Mayer, 'Humilitas', in *Augustinus-Lexikon*, ed. Cornelius Mayer et al., 5 vols. (Basel, 1986–), 3.443–56 (438, 450). On humility in Augustine, see Robert Dodaro, 'The Secret Justice of God and the Gift of Humility', *Augustinian Studies*, 34 (2003), 83–96; Michele Pellegrino, 'Via Christus Humilis (S. Agostino, Sermone 142.2)', *Studium*, 55 (1960), 126–30; Otto Schaffner, *Christliche Demut. Des hl. Augustinus Lehre von der Humilitas* (Würzburg, 1959); Adolar Zumkeller, 'Die Tugend der Demut nach der geistlichen Lehre des hl. Augustinus', *Cor Unum*, 40 (1982), 115–23.

[15] *Confessions* 7.9.14.

to sacred reading is inseparable, however, from a more comprehensive process of moral re-evaluation. The 'supposedly more sublime teaching' that Augustine rejects in this passage is motivated by pride and selfish love; as Augustine argues in his sermons, pride is the greatest evil, humility the greatest virtue ('superbia magnum malum, humilitas magnum bonum').[16] What Augustine recognizes in Christ's humility is the very opposite of proud self-elevation: a relational definition of identity and the voluntary abdication of self-determined action. Christian wisdom subverts the notion of human autonomy, and puts learning and knowledge into the service of God.

For Augustine, humility is not simply a religious virtue; it constitutes a more universal category which intersects with his views on anthropology and ontology. Humility is a defining element of Augustine's 'doctrina christiana', which helps us to locate man's place in a geographic model of salvation and providential history. In the *City of God* Augustine develops the paradoxical dynamic of humiliation and exaltation:

> For it is good to lift up your hearts; not to self, however, which is pride, but to the Lord. This is obedience, which can belong only to the humble. In a remarkable way, therefore, there is in humility something which exalts the mind, and something in exaltation which abases it. It may indeed seem paradoxical to say that exaltation abases and humility exalts. Godly humility, however, makes the mind subject to what is superior to it. But nothing is superior to God; and that is why humility exalts the mind by making it subject to God.[17]

Humility is, then, a key stage in the return and ascent to God: voluntary self-abasement, in the image of Christ, marks out the path to exaltation. This is Augustine's version of the maxim 'reculer pour mieux sauter' ('take a step back so that you can take a big leap forward'), and Donne replicates this movement by stepping back in Church history to prepare for his spiritual future. From the start of his scriptural meditations, Donne embeds questions of interpretive enquiry in broader devotional and ethical concerns. At the very moment that he rhetorically fashions his own conversion from 'humane learning', the Augustinian philosophy of humble searching provides a vital point of orientation. The opening of the *Essayes* emulates the language and conceptual topography of Augustinian humility: Christ's voluntary condescension is contrasted with the 'descending pride' of misdirected desire; only deliberate 'Dejection' can offer the prospect of true wisdom and genuine 'exaltation': this is what it means to practise 'an ascending humility'. Ascent and return to God, exaltation and eternal rest—these are the ultimate goals of Donne's hermeneutic journey. 'Saint *Augustine* enlarges it well' in his exposition of Matthew 11:29: Christ's humility, 'to be like us, was a Dejection; but ours, to be like him, is our chiefest exaltation; and yet none other is required at our hands.

---

[16] *Sermo* 354 (De Diversis), ch. 9 (*PL* 39.1568).
[17] *City of God* 14.13 (*PL* 41.421). In *Sermo* 115 (De Scripturis), ch. 2. Augustine spells out the terms of his spiritual topography more succinctly when he argues that 'those who exalt themselves, will be humiliated, and those who humiliate themselves, will be exalted' ('quia omnis qui se exaltat, humiliabitur; et qui se humiliat, exaltabitur', *PL* 38.656).

Where this humility is, *ibi Sapientia'* (7). Thus, the humility which underpins Donne's search of God's works and his Word is inspired by Augustine's interpretive conversion; the turn from secular reading to the Scriptures—from 'the study and love of things worse than our selves' to the 'study [of] God'—involves a wholesale redirection of focus. Augustine's hermeneutic calisthenics in the *Confessions* will ultimately enable Donne to attempt his own leap of faith.

HUMILITY AS A SAFEGUARD AGAINST INTERPRETIVE APATHY

In the concept of humility, Donne has discovered a safeguard against intellectual over-extension. At the same time, however, he is also keen to guard against another danger: that of interpretive apathy or stasis. As Donne argues in the opening section of the *Essayes*, humility does not 'quench the activity of our understanding, or make us neglect the Search of those Secrets of God, which are accessible' (7).[18] His text constantly re-affirms the priority of sustained and thorough hermeneutic enquiry; this applies to God's creation as well as his Word. Of the former, Donne notes that '[t]he Meditation upon Gods works is infinite' (45) and that 'there is enough to make us inexcusable, if we search not further' (10). The Bible—'his will in his words' (45)—requires an equally strong commitment to difficult mental labour, and both the sermons and the *Essayes* frequently allege Augustine in support of this precept. Preaching at St Paul's in 1622 on John 1:8, for instance, Donne draws on Augustine's authority to explain scriptural complexity: variations in tone, register, and rhetoric are necessary, '*ne semel lectas fastidiremus,* lest we should think we had done when we had read [the Scriptures] once'.[19] Earlier that year, preaching before the members of Lincoln's Inn on Ascension Day, Donne makes a similar point with a legal inflection, demanding that the lawyers search the Scriptures with 'a *Melius Inquirendum* . . . a thorough Inquisition (which is not easie for any man who makes it not his whole study and profession)'.[20] As a model of good exegetical practice, the *Essayes*, too, work towards the realization that 'a stupid and lazy inconsideration . . . (as Saint *Austin* says) is the worst of all affections' (15). Once again, Donne wants to replace 'inconsideration' with humility, not least because it guards against the danger of overvaluing human reason (and thereby devaluing the Scriptures). Donne's assertion that 'he which requires reason believes himselfe, and his own approbation and allowance of the reason' (10) is illuminating in this regard, and reminds us of the principle of relationality which circumscribes any and all interpretive activity. Explicating the Bible is a form of service to God, rather than an end in itself. In practice, disregard of this fundamental doctrine manifests itself

---

[18] See also Donne, *Sermons*, 1.316, where we find a further development of this notion through recourse to *Enarrationes in Psalmos* 77.3 (*PL* 36.984). In this Whitehall sermon of April 1618 (on 1 Timothy 1:15), Donne remarks that an 'undiscerning stupidity is not humility, for humility it self implies and requires discretion, for humiliation is not precipitation'.

[19] *Sermons*, 4.220.

[20] Ibid., 4.143–4.

in two contrasting but related exegetical failures: searching too far, or not searching far enough. The second of these issues, hermeneutic apathy, is frequently associated with the vice of self-love. Here it is instructive to draw on the testimony of early seventeenth-century guides to reading the Scriptures, both as a means of gauging the influence of Augustinian thought on Donne's interpretive philosophy and to establish the orthodoxy of his exegetical taxonomy.

John Hales's *Sermon [. . .] Concerning the Abuses of Obscure and Difficult Places of Holy Scripture* (Oxford, 1618), takes 2 Peter 3:16 as a textual platform from which to launch a crusade against readers who '*wrest* [the Scriptures] *vnto their owne destruction*'.[21] Hales launches his critique of faulty interpretation with a quotation from Augustine:

> They deale with Scripture as Chimickes deale with naturall bodies, torturing them to extract that out of them which God and nature never put in them. . . . [W]hen wee wade in Scripture, *non pro sententia divinarum Scripturarum,* as S[t] Austine speakes, *sed pro nostra ita dimicantes vt tam velimus Scripturarum esse quae nostra est:* When we striue to giue vnto it, and not to receaue from it the sense: when wee factiously contend to fasten our conceits vpon God: and like the Harlot in the booke of Kings, take our dead and putrified fancies, and lay them in the bosome of Scripture as of a mother, then are we guiltie of this great sinne of wresting of Scripture.[22]

Invoking Augustine's *Literal Interpretation of Genesis* (Book 1, chapter 18),[23] Hales traces a worrying inversion of interpretive order: instead of receiving the providential message recorded in the Scriptures, we impart and 'giue vnto it . . . the sense'. These poisonous grafts, however, ultimately harm the exegete rather than damaging the text itself. Nevertheless, bad readers will persist in looking for their 'owne shape and picture . . . in divers parts of Scripture where these men walke, they will easily perswade themselues that they see the image of their owne conceits'.[24] Thomas Wilson, the author of a mainstream Calvinist manual of Bible reading, *Theologicall Rules for Guiding Us in the Understanding and Practise of Holy Scripture* (1615), concurs: 'Wee must not bring a sense of our owne vnto the scripture, but meekely receiue that which the scripture giueth of it selfe. . . . It is the ready and high way to all error to interpret scripture by preiudice, in fauour of some opinion of our owne.'[25]

Donne's *Essayes* both reflect and implement the exegetical advice dispensed by guides such as Hales's and Wilson's. When interpretive negotiations fail, for

---

[21] Hales (1584–1656), a notable scholar of the Greek Fathers, was part of a network of patristic scholarship at Merton College, Oxford, and collaborated with Henry Savile (Warden of Merton and Provost of Eton, 1585–95) on the Eton Chrysostom (1610–12).

[22] Hales, *Sermon,* 4–5.

[23] *PL* 34.260.

[24] Hales, 7.

[25] Wilson, *Theologicall* Rules, 42–3. The idea that interpreters 'receiue' an interpretation from the Bible may strike the modern reader as a naive over-simplification, especially in the cold light of early modern religious and political controversy. In practice, early modern Scripture manuals acknowledge, through detailed analysis of reading habits and interpretive precepts, the active role played by both professional and lay readers. They are also aware, however, of the need for sustaining moral 'fictions' to channel and control the interpretive energies of their audiences.

instance, the *Essayes* often locate the roots of misunderstanding in 'our prejudices and foreconceived opinions', which 'blinde our Eyes' to the truth of God's word (46). Abortive exegesis reveals self-love because it inevitably involves hermeneutic short cuts: selfish readers quickly discover their 'owne shape and picture' and extrapolate from this projection to the whole. Donne contrasts these exegetical 'conceits' with the integrity of the Scriptures: 'So they demolish Gods fairest Temple, his Word, which pick out such stones, and deface the integrity of it, so much, as neither that which they take, nor that which they leave, is the word of God' (47). Scriptural unity is also threatened by the desire to align religious and secular forms of knowledge: 'since our merciful God hath afforded us the whole and intire book, why should wee tear it into rags, or rent the seamless garment? Since the intention of God, through *Moses*, in this, was, that it might be to the Jews a *Book of the generation of Adam* . . . to put him [Moses] in a wine-presse, and squeeze out Philosophy and particular Christianitie, is a degree of that injustice, which all laws forbid, to torture a man, *sine iudiciis aut sine probationibus*' (16–17). Once again, the parallels with Hales's account of interpretive 'torture' are revealing:

> [A] wrested proofe is like vnto a suborn'd witnesse. It never doth helpe so much whilest it is presumed to bee strong, as it doth harme when it is discouered to bee weake. St *Austine* in his bookes *de Genesi ad litteram* sharply reproues some Christians, who out of some places of Scripture misvnderstood, fram'd vnto themselues a kinde of knowledge in Astronomie and Physiologie, quite contrary vnto some parts of heathen learning in this kinde, which were true and evident vnto sense.[26]

The shared legal language of Hales's and Donne's extracts reinforces their insistence on due interpretive process; while the truth of Scripture is taken for granted, its outlines must be determined with methodological transparency and precision, through a reasoned heuristic approach. This requires, above all, a rigorous attention to the capacious category of 'context', which enables the recovery of meaning by embedding a scriptural place in its historical, linguistic, and narrative environment. In order to assess a passage in context, readers must collate it against other Scripture places, in yet another variation on the topographical model of reading. Hales, as we will see, frames interpretive conflict over difficult, rich, and polysemous Scripture places as a territorial dispute of competing doctrinal factions. A competent reader, on the terms of this geographical model, takes the long and difficult road towards God by comparing—or traversing—the widest possible spectrum of biblical locations. In the course of this journey, the interpreter is also destined to encounter contradictory or 'warring' places. In his examination of 'Number' in the Exodus section, for instance, Donne gets stuck on the question of how many Israelites had originally come into Egypt. He collates Genesis 46:27 with Deuteronomy 10:22, thus arriving at the number 70. However, on further searching, a different possibility emerges: 'And yet *Gen.* 46. 26. the Number is said to be but 66' (64). Because of the basic axiom that 'it is not enough that one place justify it self to say true, but

---

[26] Hales, 27–8; the Augustinian reference is to Book 1, chapter 19 of *De Genesi ad Litteram* (*PL* 34.260–1).

all other places produced as handling the same matter, must be of the same opinion, and of one harmony' (63), Donne proceeds to explore the immediate textual vicinity for additional evidence. In doing this, he uses a crucial interpretive tool which is frequently recommended in contemporary hermeneutic manuals. Wilson's exegetical credo, 'the context clears it',[27] is more fully articulated by Donne in his concluding disquisition on the theme of judgement:

> Judgement in the *Second* acceptation serves for practice, and is almost synonimous with Discretion; when we consider not so much the thing which we then do, as the whole machine and frame of the businesse, as it is complexioned and circumstanced with time, and place, and beholders. (98)[28]

Throughout the *Essayes*, Donne implements the rule for reading articulated in his discussion of biblical 'Number': 'that best way of expounding Scriptures, by comparing one place with another' (64). This call for contextualization, as we have seen, is a recurring feature of Donne's hermeneutic rhetoric, and also provides the key to most exegetical quandaries in the *Essayes*. A quick glance at Wilson's manual confirms the orthodoxy of this procedure. Wilson, like Donne, maintains that '[i]t is the best and surest way of interpreting scriptures, to expound one place of scripture by another', and later explains the importance of context to the resolution of conflicting places—tellingly, with another reference to Augustine:

> Such places as haue shew of repugnancy, are easily reconciled by an intelligent reader, *August[ine]* As, where it is written 1. *Tim.* 2. 3. *God will haue all to be saued*, yet *Rom.* 9. it is said, he will not haue mercy on all, a man of vnderstanding can see that one place speaks of one kinde of will, the other of another. . . . Thus by the thing before going, or comming after, and by the matter in hand, all seeming contrarieties may be reconciled[.][29]

Wilson concludes, in a summation of good hermeneutic practice which resonates with Donne's own, that '[t]he true cause why men erre in expounding scripture is for that they . . . do not vse by plainer places of scripture to seeke light for those which bee more difficult, and obscure; else because they come with preiudice imposing a sense from themselues in fauour of their owne false opinion, or bring not humble hearts and holy affections, desirous to know the truth that they may obey it'.[30] Donne's *Essayes* similarly insist on the connection between interpretive disposition and exegetical method: humility drives the continued search of God's word and is embodied in the pragmatic strategy of scriptural collation. The devotional value of this commitment is consolidated, paradoxically, through the very recognition of its *heuristic* futility. While God deliberately writes complexity into the Bible—Donne argues that He 'withdrawes it from present apprehension, and obviousness . . . [t]o make men sharpe and industrious in the inquisition of

[27] Wilson, *Theologicall Rules*, 56.
[28] The term 'discretion' has been important in revisionist readings of Donne's sermon politics. See, for instance, Jeanne Shami, 'Donne on Discretion', *English Literary History*, 47 (1980), 48–66.
[29] Wilson, *Theologicall Rules*, 40, 47–8.
[30] Ibid. 53–4.

truth' (63)[31]—human readers must live with the constant deferral of hermeneutic resolution: 'God will be glorified both in our searching these Mysteries, because it testifies our liveliness towards him, and in our not finding them' (32).[32] It is in this infinite meditation on the Scriptures that divine authority coalesces with meaningful human endeavour.

THE PROBLEM OF CURIOSITY

So far, this chapter has focused on remedies against hermeneutic apathy and paralysis. Continued hermeneutic enquiry should be undertaken in a spirit of humility, as the opening paragraphs of the *Essayes* make clear. Interpretive humility does not only guard against selfish ignorance, however; it is also an effective antidote to an exegetical vice located at the opposite end of the reading spectrum: curiosity. Donne's definition of proper scriptural searching argues that 'Humility, and Studiousnesse' are 'opposed to curiosity' (7); and his disquisition 'On Moses' ends by warning against satanic 'firebrands of Contention, and curiosity' (16). However, the most significant excursus on curiosity in the *Essayes* comes at the end of Donne's first exegetical set-piece—his reading of the phrase 'In the beginning'— with a translation of an extract from *Confessions* 11.12. Once again, Augustine offers a crucial opportunity for methodological self-legitimation, as Donne elaborates on a classic formulation of early modern interpretive theory.[33] It is worth, however, exploring Augustine's text in some detail before we move on to its seventeenth-century reception history.

Confessions 11.12 imagines a dialogue between Augustine and an inquisitive interlocutor who quizzes him about the origins of creation:

> This is my reply to anyone who asks: 'What was God doing before he made heaven and earth?' My reply is not that which someone is said to have given as a joke to evade the force of the question. He said: 'He was preparing hells for people who enquire into profundities' ['Alta, inquit, scrutantibus gehennas parabat']. It is one thing to laugh, another to see the point at issue, and this reply I reject. I would have preferred him to answer 'I am ignorant of what I do not know' rather than reply so as to ridicule someone who has asked a deep question and to win approval for an answer which is a mistake.[34]

---

[31] Wilson also argues that scriptural difficulty is designed 'to stirre vs vp to more search' (*Theologicall Rules*, 59).

[32] On this paradoxical hermeneutic dynamic, see Michael L. Hall, 'Searching and Not Finding: The Experience of Donne's *Essayes in Divinity*', *Genre*, 14 (1981), 423–40. Hall attributes the interpretive open-endedness of the *Essayes* to the essay form.

[33] Ignorance and curiosity often appear as related vices in Donne's sermons. At 3.328–9, for instance, Donne links the two in a discussion of sins against the second person of the Trinity: 'That then which we consider principally in the Son, is Wisdome. . . . And therefore sins against the second Person, are sins against Wisdome, in either extreame, either in affected and grosse ignorance, or in over-refined and sublimed curiosity. As we place this Ignorance in Practicall things of this world, so it is Stupidity; and as we place it in Doctrinall things, of the next world, so Ignorance is Implicite Beliefe: And Curiosity, as we place it upon Practical things, is Craft, and upon Doctrinal things, Subtilty[.]'

[34] Augustine, *Confessions* 11.12.14 (*PL* 32.815).

As Edward Peters notes, the key question of this passage—what was God doing before creation—'constitutes something of a leitmotif of Book 11, important in itself and also as an example of the wrong way to approach scripture, this one question standing as synecdoche for all wrong questions'.[35] At the end of Book 11, Augustine defines the boundary between licit ('quaerere') and illicit ('curiositas') forms of hermeneutic enquiry. The phrase 'alta . . . scrutantibus gehennas parabat' ('he was preparing hells for people who enquire into high/profound things') resumes the topographical emphasis in Augustine's hermeneutic; Peters observes that the word 'altus' in Augustine is regularly used as an attribute of God or to describe an improper object of human attention.[36]

Donne's citation of *Confessions* 11.12 comes at the end of a long imaginary dialogue with a number of 'busie inquirers'. After a protracted discussion about the beginning of the world, which features contributions from '*Alexander the Great*', the '*Caldeans*', the '*Egyptians*', and the '*Chineses*', Donne declares the question of '*When* . . . this Beginning *was*' (18) a moot point, and chooses instead to concentrate on the devotional implications of the creation narrative:

> yet since the world in her first infancy did not speak to us at all (by any Authors;) and when she began to speak by *Moses*, she spake not plain, but diversly to divers understandings; we must return again to our strong hold, *faith*, and end with this, *That this Beginning was, and before it, Nothing.* (23)

It is at this point, in the closing lines of the first part of his meditation on Genesis 1:1, that Donne introduces Augustine's text:

> And therefore Saint Augustin says religiously and exemplarily, *If one ask me what God did before this beginning, I will not answer, as another did merrily, He made Hell for such busie inquirers: But I will sooner say, I know not, when I know not, then answer that, by which he shall be deluded which asked too high a Mystery, and he be praysed, which answered a lie.* (23)[37]

Donne replicates the dialogic setting of *Confessions* 11.12, as well as Augustine's attempt to imbue this moment with exemplary value; his own critique of curiosity shores up authority through a faithful and humble act of Augustinian imitation. A passage from a St Dunstan's sermon, preached on New Year's Day 1624/5, on Genesis 17:24, helps to get a firmer grasp on the hermeneutic principles outlined in this extract. There, Donne argues that

[35] Edward Peters, 'What Was God Doing Before He Created the Heavens and the Earth?', *Augustiniana*, 34 (1984), 53–74 (55).

[36] Ibid. 73. See *Contra Faustum Manichaeum* 21.3 (*PL* 42.390): 'Occultum est, altum est, inaccessibili secreto ab humana cogitatione seclusum est, quemadmodum Deus et damnet impium et justificet impium.' See also Sirach, 3:22, 'altiora ne quaesieris', and Romans 11:20, 'noli altum sapere'. On the cultural history of Romans 11:20 in the early modern period, see Carlo Ginzburg, 'High and Low: The Theme of Forbidden Knowledge in the Sixteenth and Seventeenth Centuries', *Past and Present*, 73 (1976), 28–41.

[37] Donne, unlike Augustine's early modern and twentieth-century translators, renders 'alta interrogavit' as 'asked too *high*' rather than '*deep*' a mystery; this reinforces the topographical emphasis of his reading model.

It is a Dangerous and Infectious *Monosillable, How or Why* . . . So if that *infectious inquisition,* that *Quare, (Why* should God command this or this particular?) be entred into me, all my *Humilitie* is presently infected, and I shall look for a reason, why God made a world, or why he made a world no sooner then 6000. yeares agoe[.] . . . Saint *Augustine* saies justly, *Qui rationem quærit voluntatis Dei, aliquid majus Deo quærit,* He that seekes a reason of the will of God, seekes for something greater then God. It was the Devill that opened our eies in Paradise, it is our parts to shut them so farre, as not to gaze upon Gods secret purposes.[38]

The humble reader, then, will do well to avoid 'that *Quare'* or similarly poisonous parts of speech. This brief excursus into the necessities and dangers of humility also enables us to appreciate more fully the complexity of Donne's hermeneutic position. The 'shutting' of eyes is not simply an expression of fideism, but the end result of a sustained enquiry which acknowledges two related types of faith-bound limitation: doctrinal fundamentals and religious mysteries. In practice, the *Essayes* will only call off the textual search once all processes of reasoned enquiry have been exhausted; the sermons, in adhering to pastoral priorities and obligations, are often more rigorous in their attempts to contain the subversive energies of 'Dangerous and Infectious' monosyllables.[39]

The risks of hermeneutic curiosity are analysed at length in guides to scriptural interpretation; in counselling their audiences against intellectual overambitiousness, the authors of these sermons and manuals frequently quote from, or allude to, *Confessions* 11.12. Wilson, alleging Augustine, observes that the 'Profundity and depth of God's counsels and iudgements are not too narrowly and curiously to bee searched, but to be wondred at with astonishment, *Aug. De vocat. Gent. Lib. I. Cap. 4.* After the example of Paul, Rom. 11.33, *O the depth,* &c. . . . Such things as wee cannot know them, so it were not our profit to know them, as what day the Angels were made, and what God did before the world[.]'[40] Seven years later, in *A Checke to Cvriositie*—a sermon preached at Whitehall on 5 May 1622—John Denison also cites *Confessions* 11.12.14, adding that 'it is verie just that those, who in sacred things will sore beyond their pitch, haue the eies of their vnderstanding dazled'.[41] In John Hales's sermon, this image of a perverted ascent ('sore beyond

---

[38] *Sermons,* 6.188–9.
[39] The intensity, detail, and scope of Donne's exegetical investigations varies with audience and occasion, of course. On the relationship between reason and faith in Donne's works more generally see Terry G. Sherwood, *Fulfilling the Circle: A Study of Donne's Thought* (Toronto and London, 1984). Sherwood does not discuss the *Essayes* in detail.
[40] Wilson, *Theologicall Rules,* 56–7.
[41] John Denison, *The Sinners Acqvittance. A Checke to Cvriositie. The Safest Seruice* (1624), 88–9. Denison misquotes the text of the *Confessions,* claiming that Augustine *did* 'make hell' for curious enquirers. This is not uncommon in the hermeneutic manuals of the period, and does not necessarily suggest a lack of familiarity with Augustine's text. It seems that early modern preachers found the misquotation a more effective deterrent against curiosity. For a reading of Denison's sermon in the context of the 1622 *Directions,* emphasizing the connections between curiosity, religious factionalism, and political unrest, see Shami, *Conformity,* 70. It is characteristic of the irenic character of the *Essayes* that—unlike most of his contemporaries—Donne generally shies away from associating hermeneutic vices with the broader doctrinal misprisions of Catholicism. (Note, however, the connections between curiosity and schism at *Essayes,* 46–8.)

their pitch') is re-embedded in the topographical model of interpretation he has previously established. He also highlights the gravity of hermeneutic transgressions by associating them with the 'disease that my first Parents in Paradise had, a desire to know more then I need', and highlights the scriptural riddles and temptations ('*anachronismes, metachronismes*, and the like') which lure ambitious readers into exotic scriptural locations:[42]

> The texts of Scripture which are especially subiect to this abuse, are those that are of ambiguous and doubtfull meaning. For as *Thucydides* obserues of the fat and fertile places of Greece, that they were evermore the occasions of stirres and seditions, the neighbouring nations every one striuing to make it selfe Lord of them: so is it with these places that are so fertile, as it were, of interpretation, and yeeld a multiplicity of sense: they are the *Palastra* for good wits to proue masteries in, where every one desires to bee Lord and absolute.[43]

Hales emphasizes the divisive potential of risky exegetical expeditions: curiosity can cause ruptures at a textual, doctrinal, and institutional level. But he is also keen to stress the personal implications of interpretive excess, citing examples of a reader who 'not willing to loose the reputation of wit, chose rather to resigne his place in the Church, &, as I verily thinke, his part in heauen'.[44] This is another striking parallel between textual and spiritual topographies: readers who intrude on a secret place in God's book may well forfeit a place at God's side in the afterlife. Donne's Augustinian definition of curiosity in an Ascension Day sermon preached at Lincoln's Inn in 1622 characteristically draws out the moral issues alluded to in Hales's portrait of hermeneutic supremacy:

> What is curiosity? *Qui scire vult ut sciat*, He that desires knowledge only that he may know, or be known by others to know; he who makes not the end of his knowledge the glory of God, he offends in curiosity, says that Father; But that is only in the end. But in the way to knowledge there is curiosity too; In seeking such things as man hath no faculty to compass, unrevealed mysteries[.][45]

Donne's hermeneutic keeps the ways, means, and ends of interpretation firmly in view: by holding on to Augustine's authority, he is able to 'compass' the paradoxes which frame the boundless yet tightly circumscribed search of God's word.

[42] Hales, *Sermon*, 36–7.
[43] Ibid. 7–8.
[44] Ibid. 12.
[45] *Sermons*, 4.142–3. The *Augustinus-Lexikon* describes 'curiositas' as 'the most insidious' of the three great temptations of Augustine's spiritual life (the other two being carnal desire—'concupiscentia carnis'—and 'secular ambition'). One of the defining features of curiosity is 'le désir sacrilège d'accéder aux secrets de la divinité en opposition avec la "temperantia"'—the sacrilegious desire to access God's secrets, in defiance of religious temperance. See André Labhardt, 'Curiositas', in *Augustinus-Lexikon*, 1.188–96 (190). On curiosity in Augustine, see Hans Blumenberg, 'Augustins Anteil an der Geschichte des Begriffs der theoretischen Neugierde', *Revue des Études Augustiniennes*, 7 (1961), 35–70; Gunther Bös, *Curiositas. Die Rezeption eines antiken Begriffs durch christliche Autoren bis Thomas von Aquin* (Paderborn, 1995); E. P. Meijering, *Calvin wider die Neugierde. Ein Beitrag zum Vergleich zwischen reformatorischem und patristischem Denken* (Nieuwkoop, 1980); Hans Joachim Mette, 'Curiositas', in *Festschrift Bruno Snell zum 60. Geburtstag... von Freunden und Schülern überreicht* (Munich, 1956), 227–35.

In moments of acute exegetical complication, Donne argues, when 'to unentangle our selvs in this perplexity, is more labour then profit, or perchance possibility', it is imperative to rein in readerly curiosity:

> Therefore, as in violent tempests, when a ship dares bear no main sayl, and to lie stil at hull, obeying the uncertain wind and tyde, puts them much out of their way, and altogether out of their account, it is best to put forth such a small ragg of sail, as may keep the barke upright, and make her continue neer one place, though she proceed not[.] (15)

Hales, strikingly, activates a similar metaphor when he advises that '*In places of ambiguous and doubtfull, or darke and intricate meaning*', exegetes should focus on their 'inward furniture and worth, which should as it were ballance the minde and keep it vpright against all outward occurrents whatsoever'.[46] In these cases, he suggests, '*it is sufficient if we religiously admire and acknowledge and confesse: vsing that moderation of Austine . . .* To vnderstand belongs to Christ the author of our faith to vs is sufficient the glory of beleeuing.'[47]

CONFESSIONS 11.3.5 AND THE IMPERATIVE OF HERMENEUTIC FAITH

Donne's reliance on Augustine is most evident at the start of the *Essayes*, at the moment when he steps 'upon the *threshold*' (15) of interpretation and begins to explicate the opening three words of Genesis 1:1, 'In the beginning'. Donne's inaugural act of exegesis takes the form of a prayer which loosely paraphrases passages from *Confessions* 1.3 and 11.7, and *City of God* 12.14, before settling on an extended close translation of *Confessions* 11.3.5 (represented in italic in the quotation below). The first two extracts from the *Confessions* reflect on the divine transcendence of space and time, while the reference to *City of God* 12.14 prepares for the programmatic definition and performance of faith which follows:

> [H]aving decreed from all eternity, to do thy great work of Mercy, our Redemption in the fulnesse of time, didst now create *time* it selfe to conduce to it . . . though thy glorious work of Creation were first, thy mercifull work of Redemption was greatest [*City of God* 12.14]. Let me in thy beloved Servant *Augustine's* own words, when with an humble boldnesse he begg'd the understanding of this passage, say, *Moses writ this, but is gon from me to thee; if he were here, I would hold him, and beseech him for thy sake, to tell me what he meant. If he spake Hebrew, he would frustrate my hope; but if Latine, I should comprehend him. But from whence should I know that he said true? Or when I knew it, came that knowledge from him? No, for within me, there is a truth, not Hebrew, nor Greek, nor Latin, nor barbarous; which without organs, without noyse of Syllables, tels me true, and would enable me to say confidently to Moses, Thou say'st true*

---

[46] Hales, *Sermon*, 23.
[47] Ibid. 38. The reference is to *City of God* 18.52 (*PL* 41.619–20).

[*Confessions* 11.3.5]. Thus did he, whom thou hadst filled with faith, desire reason and understanding[.] (19)[48]

Donne presents two perspectives on the relationship between 'eternity' and 'time', transcendence and immanence. Human history is a major problem in this passage, because it puts Donne at a distance from the most reliable witnesses to God's providential plan: Moses and Augustine. But if this is the case, how can man ever hope to repair the rift between God and creature opened up by original sin? Donne's answer centres on 'thy mercifull work of Redemption', unfolded in human history through the incarnate Word. As Donne insists again and again in the *Essayes*, 'Salvation was ever from a faith in the promise of the *Messias*' (42). Donne's translation of Augustine's imagined colloquy with Moses focuses on a problem of exegesis, but the ultimate outcome of this abortive dialogue is a more universal validation of the '*truth . . . within*' ('*intus veritas*'), Christ. What is required, on Donne's part, is an affirmation of faith; and in the absence of the proper institutional and spiritual accreditation, Augustine serves as a conduit for his devotion. Once again, this gesture is implicated in a complex pattern of imitation and emulation. Donne's avowal of faith in the 'truth within' is rehearsed in much greater detail in the *Confessions*, as Robert Cushman explains in his classic account of that text's historical consciousness:

> It is *fides*, which alone apprehends the eternal within the historical, that is the correction of man's perversity. Man can be extricated from his unholy marriage to the creatures by God's appearance in the midst of the creatures. . . . Time and change become, by the Incarnation, the vehicle of the Eternal.[49]

Faith in Christ transmutes fallen history into hope, 'the vehicle of the Eternal'. Donne rehearses this movement through his own avowal of faith in Augustine. But before the search for illumination can turn inward, the limits of human knowledge must be exposed. At the beginning of the *Essayes*, Donne catches Augustine gazing into the chasm of history that separates him from God's word. Like the author of the *Essayes*, Augustine knows that the way to the divine will leads through Moses: '*If ye believed Moses, ye would believe me, for he writ of me.*' But Moses is not present; in Donne's translation, he is '*gon from me to thee*'. If, on the other hand, Moses '*were here*', Augustine could '*hold him, and beseech him . . . to tell me what he meant*'.[50] At this point in the *Confessions*, Augustine associates writing with absence; if Moses

---

[48] *Confessions* 11.3.5 (*PL* 32.811): 'Scripsit hoc Moyses, scripsit et abiit, transiit hinc a te ad te; neque nunc ante me est. Nam si esset, tenerem eum, et rogarem eum, et per te obsecrarem ut mihi ista panderet; et praeberem aures corporis mei sonis erumpentibus ex ore ejus. Et si hebraea voce loqueretur, frustra pulsaret sensum meum, nec inde mentem meam quidquam tangeret; si autem latine, scirem quid diceret. Sed unde scirem an verum diceret? Quod si et hoc scirem, num ab illo scirem? Intus utique mihi, intus in domicilio cogitationis, nec hebraea, nec graeca, nec latina, nec barbara veritas, sine oris et linguae organis, sine strepitu syllabarum diceret . . . Verum dicis.'

[49] Robert Cushman, 'Faith and Reason', in *A Companion to the Study of St. Augustine*, ed. Roy W. Battenhouse (Oxford, 1955), 287–314 (306–7).

[50] Augustine's phrase 'tenerem eum et rogarem' ('I would hold him and ask him what he meant') perhaps casts a sideways glance at Proteus, the sea-god who changes shape to avoid foretelling the future; the desire to 'hold' Moses may express a similar desire to reveal a providential design.

were physically present, in body and voice, Augustine could touch him, listen to him, plead with him: '*if he were here, I would hold him and beseech him for thy sake, to tell me what he meant*'. But this fiction of hope is quickly dashed, as Augustine's frustration is compounded by his own linguistic shortcomings: clearly an answer in Hebrew will not solve his problem. James O'Donnell also notes the significance of the word 'syllables' as a marker 'of the transience and imperfection of human speech' more generally.[51] This turns Augustine's linguistic challenge into a full-blown epistemological crisis, which is reflected in a series of anguished questions: '*But from whence should I know that he said true?*', Augustine asks. At this climactic point of his meditation, the pace suddenly changes. Augustine's emphatic '*No*' marks a dramatic shift from anxious interpretive probing to calm assurance: '[*F*]*or within me, there is a truth . . . which without organs, without noyse of Syllables, tels me true, and would enable me to say confidently to Moses, Thou say'st true.*' This comes as an answer to an internal dialogue, an unspoken conflict of hermeneutic registers: Augustine realizes that he has been asking the wrong questions in the wrong way. The problem is not philological, but devotional, and Augustine leaps to this conclusion without warning, without transition, and without reason. By putting his faith in Moses, Augustine achieves a far more profound insight into divine intentions, a direct, non-verbal communication with God which fills him with an assurance of scriptural truth.

For Donne, the stakes are even higher. The project of turning himself into a competent reader of the Bible is made doubly difficult by the fact that both Moses, the inspired scribe, and Augustine have '*gon from me to thee*'. Donne, like Augustine, is aware of the vast historical, hermeneutic, and spiritual distance that divides him from the divine origins of his text. In order to overcome this gulf, Donne falls back on the most efficient of Christian survival strategies, the concept of mediation. His key to successful conversion and interpretive initiation is Augustine: by trying to turn himself into Augustine's ideal reader, and finally into Augustine himself, he is hoping to tap into the source of his spiritual strength. In the context of Donne's desire for interpretive inspiration, the question '*from whence should I know that he said true?*' (19) takes on a double resonance. As Donne attempts a faithful translation of Augustine's text, struggling with a language that is not quite his own, his rhetoric implies that it is not just Moses', but Augustine's own reliability as a witness that has come under scrutiny here: how should Donne know that Augustine was telling the truth when he asserted the truth of Moses' claims? Donne, in other words, has stepped into Augustine's sandals by replicating his moment of spiritual crisis: like him, Donne has hit a stalemate and finds his linguistic tools wanting.

Donne's solution to the dilemma is designed to match Augustine's hermeneutic coping strategies as closely as possible. Like Augustine, Donne anxiously searches for a rational explanation but ends up abandoning analysis and argument for a display of interpretive faith. Tellingly, Donne makes no attempt to explicate or comment on the *Confessions*, but follows its authority unquestioningly and

---

[51] Augustine, *Confessions*, ed. James J. O'Donnell, 3 vols. (Oxford, 1992), 3.264.

unconditionally. His act of faithful repetition and quotation parallels Augustine's own leap of faith at the end of *Confessions* 11.3; Donne's answer to the question *'from whence should I know'* thus approximates Augustine's dictum *'crede, ut intellegas'*—'believe so that you will understand'. By invoking Augustine's own words at a moment of hermeneutic doubt and despair, Donne emulates his avowal of faith in Moses' truth in the *Confessions*.[52] Inward illumination is provoked through an almost ritualistic act of re-enunciation, faith in action, yet another inward turn with outward symbolic significance. Interpretation gives way to a hermeneutics of quotation. As James O'Donnell notes, Augustine's exegesis of Genesis 1 in Book 11 of the *Confessions* 'is certainly, and deliberately, exemplary. We see how the mind of the exegete works, and we work through his text with him.'[53] This involves seeing Augustine's interpretive principles operate in practice, but also focuses our attention on the spiritual qualities which inform those methods, chief among them faith and charity. Donne's own text presents the interpretive procedures of *Confessions* 11.3.5 as exemplary in more senses than one when he portrays Augustine as the ideal exegete, 'filled with faith, desire reason and understanding' (19). In the programmatic exposition of interpretive precepts which precedes this first exegetical attempt, Donne has framed rectified hermeneutic 'desire', 'reason', and 'understanding' in Augustinian terms. There, he asserts the primacy of readerly faith, 'that reverent, and pious, and reasonable credulity' (15) and then proceeds to put his principles into practice. After glossing *Confessions* 11.3.5 with a brief reference to Aquinas's *Summa* 1.46.2, Donne submits himself to 'the Spirituall, and peacable Tyranny, and easie yoke of sudden and present Faith' (19): the persistent presence of paradox here and throughout the *Essayes* (such as the 'easie yoke' of Matthew 11:30) is itself a reminder of the need for hermeneutic faith. Inspired with Augustine's 'humble boldnesse' (19), and armed with a solution to his philological shortcomings in the hermeneutics of quotation, Donne's search for scriptural meaning can begin.

Donne's Augustinian invocation can be captured more accurately when we attend to its rhetorical roots, and recognize it as an example of the figure of *prosopopoeia*: Donne explicates Augustine's hermeneutic vocabulary but he also performs it. Henry Peacham's *Garden of Eloquence* defines *prosopopoeia* as 'the faining of a person ... sometime he [the Orator] raiseth againe as it were the dead to life, and bringeth them forth complaining or witnessing what they

---

[52] Vessey notes of this passage: 'Augustine's imaginary interview with Moses, itself a dramatic illustration both of the importance of human *praedicatio* and of its dependence on divine illumination, here becomes the occasion for a secondary encounter between Donne and Augustine which ... serves in similar fashion to accredit a new *praedicator* ('Donne in the Company of Augustine', 194). Vessey is right to stress Augustine's function as a medium of professional accreditation; my argument places more emphasis on the importance of interpretive initiation. The *Confessions* provide a hermeneutic template which focuses on the exegete's inward spiritual disposition; although the *Essayes* ultimately use this *ethos* as a means of professional self-legitimation, Donne's text is primarily concerned with interpretation rather than *praedicatio*.

[53] Augustine, *Confessions*, ed. O'Donnell, 3.264.

knew'.[54] Peacham further notes that personification is often used as a last resort, when all other options have failed:

> the vse of it ought to be very rare, then chiefly, when the Orator hauing spent the principall strength of his arguments, is as it were constrained to call for helpe and aide else where, not vnlike to a Champion hauing broken his weapons in the force of his conflict calleth for new of his frendes, or of such as fauour his person and cause, or to an army hauing their number diminished, or their strength infeebled, do craue and call for a new supply.[55]

Donne summons Augustine's presence at a point of acute spiritual crisis, hoping that his voice will 'giue strength to the fainting cause': to resurrect the *Confessions* is to breathe new life into Donne's interpretive project.[56] He calls upon Augustine not just as a patristic authority but as a spiritual mediator here, a tutelary presence whose faith can revive his own.

At a vital point of transition and conversion, the *Essayes* stage a leap of faith and abandon themselves to the saving force of the Augustinian text. By entrusting his hermeneutic fate to the *Confessions*, Donne attempts to bridge the gap that separates him from Augustine, Moses, and God. Faith, humility, and empathy, encapsulated in the re-enunciation of Augustine's words, transport Donne out of his limited hermeneutic position and into Augustine's place. From this superior vantage point, Donne can '*say confidently to Moses, Thou say'st true*' (19). Being Augustine is a way of overcoming not only history but interpretation itself: it is to partake in the direct apprehension of divine truth which Augustine describes in the *Confessions*: '*for within me, within me there is a truth . . . which without organs, without noyse of Syllables, tels me true*' (19). Giving voice to his trust in Augustine allows Donne to share in the immediate languageless dialogue with God, gives him a glimpse of the inward conviction that defines exemplary believers (Donne cites, in this context, the case of 'that most devout Abbot *Antony* . . . of whom Saint *Augustine* says, that without knowledge of letters, he rehearsed, and expounded all the Scriptures').[57]

OUT-AUGUSTINING AUGUSTINE

When he ventriloquizes Augustine's encounter with Moses in *Confessions* 11.3, Donne is in fact engaged in an act of double emulation: he borrows Augustine's language, but he also copies a master trope of the *Confessions*. Speaking in another person's voice is a crucial spiritual coping strategy in Augustine's autobiographical meditations; the voice that he most persistently and successfully impersonates is

[54] Henry Peacham, *The Garden of Eloquence (1593)*, 2nd edn. (London, 1593), ed. Beate Maria Koll (Frankfurt am Main, 1996), 134. On *prosopopoeia* in early modern literature more generally, see Gavin Alexander, 'Prosopopoeia: The Speaking Figure', in *Renaissance Figures of Speech*, ed. Sylvia Adamson, Gavin Alexander, and Katrin Ettenhuber (Cambridge, 2007), 96–112.
[55] Peacham, *Garden of Eloquence (1593)*, 135.
[56] Ibid.
[57] *Essayes*, 74; the marginal reference in the *Essayes* is to paragraph 4 of the prologue to *De Doctrina Christiana*.

that of the apostle Paul. The most significant scenes in Augustine's *repraesentatio Pauli* are staged in Book 8, the part of the *Confessions* which recounts the story of his conversion. The climactic scene of the book takes place in the garden at Milan, where Augustine's climb towards conversion is initiated by reading (with his friend Alypius) Romans 13:13–14. This moment is explicitly designated as a leap of faith. Augustine's decision to open the Bible is inspired by two visions: 'Lady Continence' admonishes him to 'make the leap without anxiety; he will catch you and heal you' ('proice te securus! excipiet et sanabit te', 8.11.27), and he imagines hearing the voice of a child which instructs him to 'Pick up and read' ('tolle, lege!', 8.12.29) the first scriptural passage he can find.[58] (Once again, Augustine—like Donne—imagines interpretation both as an active intervention and as a moment of inward spiritual illumination.)

As James O'Donnell aptly observes in his introduction to Book 8 of the *Confessions*, 'true to the programme set out at 7.21.27, the whole of Book 8 is a record of reading Paul, particularly *Romans*'.[59] 'With avid intensity I seized the sacred writings of your Spirit and especially the apostle Paul', Augustine announces, with an emphatic rejection of 'the Platonic books'. He finds this humility and faith by submitting himself to '"the least" of your apostles' (7.21.27); once he has entrusted his fate to Paul, he feels ready to embark on the spiritual and exegetical journey that will lead him to God.[60] Augustine, then, uses Paul as a guiding light on the road to hermeneutic insight, just as Donne uses Augustine as a means of gaining access to 'Gods fairest Temple, his Word' (47).

However, the parallels between Augustine's Paul and Donne's Augustine go even further. Augustine, like Donne, frequently replaces argument and proof with citation and re-articulation at important points of his text. We find a crucial example of this practice in the fifth chapter of Book 8, where a sequence of quotations from Romans 7:22–5 finally enables Augustine to 'tell the story . . . of the way in which you delivered me from the chain of sexual desire, by which I was tightly bound, and from the slavery of worldly affairs'.[61] Here, Augustine turns the ending of Romans into an impassioned plea for his own salvation ('miserum ergo me'), but otherwise the Pauline text remains intact. By reiterating Paul's words, Augustine does not just avow his sense of self-identification with the apostle; he actively performs it. Augustine's Pauline impersonation acts as an important catalyst for conversion. For Augustine, speaking in another person's voice is the ultimate act of trust and belief, so much so that he even seeks to attribute this practice to Paul, his own source of spiritual solace. This emerges in a key moment at the end of the *Confessions* (13.13.14), which considers the possibilities of the ascent to God for the baptized soul. There, Augustine imagines a moment of direct, unmediated communion between Paul and his creator, a vision of future glory when God will be beheld face to face. For Augustine, however, the only way of envisioning this flash of insight is by imagining an investment of hermeneutic faith

---

[58] *PL* 32.762, 32.761.
[59] *Confessions*, ed. O'Donnell, 3.3.
[60] See *Confessions* 7.21 (*PL* 32.747–8).
[61] See *Confessions* 8.6 (*PL* 32.754), and see Romans 7:22–5.

on Paul's part: at the moment of ascent to God, Paul is not speaking in his own voice, but through a string of citations from the Scriptures. It is this act of faithful repetition, as Augustine's formulation makes clear, that puts him in touch with God—'vocat . . . non in voce sua; in tua enim':

> But now he is speaking not with his own voice but with yours. 'You sent your Spirit from on high' (Wisdom 9:17) through him who 'ascended on high' (Psalms 67:19), and opened the 'cataracts' of his gifts (Malachi 3:10). . . . . What a beautiful light that will be when 'we shall see him as he is' (1 John 3:2).[62]

It is worth retracing this complex series of ventriloquisms in some detail: in Book 13 of his *Confessions*, Augustine imagines Paul's vision of God; this is achieved by speaking through the voices of inspired scriptural texts. In Book 8 of the *Confessions*, Augustine uses Paul's voice to initiate his own exegetical journey of discovery, which ultimately leads to his conversion. And in the *Essayes in Divinity*, an exercise in 'Unvocall preaching' (47) for the future Dean of St Paul's, Donne seeks to be initiated into God's word by citing a passage from Book 11 of the *Confessions*, which in turn derives its inspiration from an avowal of faith in the truth and saving power of Moses' own wisdom. Given Donne's intimate knowledge of the *Confessions*, I think that it is not too fanciful to assume that Paul's speaking in God's voice—'in voce tua'—is the real target of Donne's leap of faith in the *Essayes*.

That leap is backwards in history and upwards in spirit; from Donne's new perspective, the scriptural map can be interpreted comfortably and authoritatively. This is one way of reading Donne's invocation of *Confessions* 11.3.5: his demonstration of faith in the Augustinian text transports him into a privileged position, which allows him to see the textual patterns of the *Confessions* more clearly. In other words, the interpretive route that I have just laboriously plotted here, collating *Confessions* 11.3.5 with 7.21.27, 8.5.12, and 13.13.14 (which in turn evokes the ascent of the soul in the vision of Ostia at 9.10.23–5—the intertextual parallels are almost infinite), is comprehended by Donne in a single flash of understanding that follows his avowal of trust in Augustine's text. This process recalls, but ultimately transcends, the model of scriptural collation advocated throughout the *Essayes*. Donne traverses landmark 'places' in the *Confessions*, collects, compares, and synthesizes key passages as he follows in Augustine's footsteps and retraces his journey towards illumination—once again, interpretation is embedded in a complex textual topography. But in moments of perfect understanding such as this one, the process of reading is accelerated to the point where it gives way to something else: a more immediate sense of communion with the spirit of the text. This intuitive, holistic, panoramic model of perception, as we will see, is delineated more precisely in Donne's definition of interpretive faith; it is also, as we saw in the Introduction, a mode of reading that Donne persistently attributes to Augustine—as when his 'misreading' of Ecclesiastes is saved by his knowledge of the Psalms (see Introduction, pp. 9–10).

---

[62] *Confessions* 13.13.14 (*PL* 32.851): 'Sed jam non in voce sua; in tua enim, qui misisti Spiritum tuum de excelsis per eum qui ascendit in altum.'

These insights can be consolidated when we read the *Essayes* against a passage from one of Donne's sermons on the Feast of the Conversion of St Paul. Preaching at St Paul's in January 1624/5, on Acts 9:4, Donne portrays the moment of conversion as a flash of spiritual illumination; importantly, however, the 'blindness' which results evokes the epistemological and hermeneutic reflections of the *Essayes*:

> *Saul* was struck blinde, but it was a blindnesse contracted from light. . . . This blind-nesse which we speak of, which is a sober and temperate abstinence from the immoderate study, and curious knowledges of this world, this holy simplicity of the soule, is not a darknesse, a dimnesse, a stupidity in the understanding, contracted by living in a corner, it is not an idle retiring into a Monastery, or into a Village, or a Country solitude, it is not a lazy affectation of ignorance[.][63]

Donne's account of Paul's transformation—from worldly knowledge to Christian wisdom—recalls his comments on 'ascending humility' in the *Essayes*: 'not such a groveling, frozen, and stupid Humility, as should quench the activity of our under-standing', but one which, when allied with 'Studiousnesse', breeds *'Temperance'*. The echoes from the *Essayes* grow stronger as Donne parses his text: in Acts 9:4, of course, Paul is reported to have 'heard a voyce, saying, Saul, Saul, why persecutest thou me'. Donne's sermon insists that Paul did not just hear a 'noyse', but a 'sound' (217); he was not distracted—as Donne put it in his translation of *Confessions* 11.3.5 in the *Essayes*—by the *'noyse of Syllables'*, but he 'understood' (6.218) God's message fully. At this point, Donne activates the submerged link between the *Essayes* and his sermon by delivering an explicitly Pauline reading of *Confessions* 11.3.5:[64]

> S. *Augustine* puts himselfe earnestly upon the contemplation of the Creation, as *Moses* hath delivered it; he findes it hard to conceive, and he sayes, *Si esset ante me Moses,* If *Moses* who writ this were here, *Tenerem eum, & per te obsecrarem,* I would hold him fast, and beg of him, for thy sake, O my God, that he would declare this worke of the Creation more plainly unto me. But then, sayes that blessed Father, *Si Hebræa voce loqueretur,* If *Moses* should speake Hebrew to mee, mine eares might heare the sound, but my minde would not heare the voyce; I might heare him, but I should not heare what he said. This was that that distinguished betweene S. *Paul,* and those who were in his company at this time[.][65]

In the *Essayes*, Donne the lay exegete strains to hear Paul's voice, and the inner truth of his message can be made available to him only at two removes, through his hermeneutics of Augustinian quotation. Donne's sermon, by contrast, uses the *Confessions* to validate the convert's faith explicitly: Paul 'heares' not with his ears, but with his heart and mind; he understands not because he is a superior linguist, but because he is now ready 'to feele' God's 'hand in every accident, and to discerne his presence in everything that befals us' (6.219).[66]

---

[63] *Sermons,* 6.215.
[64] *Confessions* 11.3.5 (*PL* 32.811).
[65] *Sermons,* 6.218.
[66] On the sermons Donne preached on the Feast of the Conversion of St Paul, see Gregory Kneidel, 'John Donne's *Via Pauli*', *Journal of English and Germanic Philology*, 100 (2001), 224–46.

Donne's emulation of Augustine's 'ascending humility' (8) and 'pious . . . credulity' (15) in the *Essayes* has a defining impact on his topographical model of reading. It moves him from the horizontal axis of rational, methodological exegesis (the slow and laborious progress from one scriptural place to another), into a higher, quasi-divine position, which offers a panoramic perspective on the biblical landscape. From this bird's-eye view, the hidden hermeneutic links and connections, the larger patterns of conceptual coherence, emerge with a sudden and total clarity. At the beginning of the second part of the *Essayes* ('Of God'), Donne elaborates on the interpretive possibilities opened up by faith:

> Men which seek God by reason, and naturall strength . . . are like Mariners which voyaged before the invention of the Compass, which were but Costers, and unwillingly left the sight of the land. . . . But by these meditations we get no further, then to know what he *doth*, not what he *is*. But as by the use of the Compass, men safely dispatch *Ulysses* dangerous ten years travell in so many dayes, and have found out a new world richer then the old; so doth Faith, as soon as our hearts are touched with it, direct and inform us in that great search of the discovery of Gods Essence, and the new *Hierusalem*, which Reason durst not attempt. . . . [A]ll acquired knowledg is by degrees, and successive; but God is impartible, and only faith which can receive it all at once, can comprehend him. (24–5)[67]

In the quest to return to God, faith offers the quickest mode of transport; while reason forces us to acquire and apply knowledge 'by degrees' (in another modulation of the compass image), faith operates through a more comprehensive process of perception and can 'receive . . . all at once'. It is therefore more suited to 'Gods Essence', which is indivisible or 'impartible'. (God's unity is matched, of course, as Donne frequently reminds us in the *Essayes*, by the 'integrity' of his Word, the Scriptures.) Where reason's hermeneutic steps are faltering and insecure, and consistently try to define, contract, and limit the textual horizon, faith commands the broad, expansive viewpoint that offers a comprehensive and reassuring prospect of the scriptural map. The sermons frequently reflect on the different types of spiritual insight available to Christian believers. A late sermon at St Paul's, for instance, distinguishes between knowledge 'delivered to the Apostles, as from a print, as from a stampe, all at once, and to us, but as by writing, letter after letter, syllable after syllable, by Catechismes, and Sermons'.[68] Donne's analogy with the material modes of textual production, contrasting a single impression with the sequential execution of handwritten characters, plays a variation on the epistemological model developed in the *Essayes*. The submerged reference to other meanings of the word 'print', notably 'perfection' and 'completion', may indicate that the sudden, panoramic nature of apostolic understanding is closer to God's own knowledge, but Donne reminds us in his sermon that degrees of wisdom must be apt and 'sufficient' for audience and occasion. In a similar fashion, the *Essayes* emphasize the importance of the preparatory hermeneutic processes that enable

---

[67] See also *Essayes*, 36: 'O Eternall and Almighty power, which being infinite, hast enabled a limited creature, Faith, to comprehend thee.'
[68] *Sermons*, 9.244–5.

the reader to attempt a leap of faith, and to see the world through apostolic eyes. If his affective and intuitive interpretations are to have any validity as an active and informed choice rather than just 'a stupid and lazy consideration' (13), and are to avoid the extremes of subjectivism, they need to be supported by a strong methodological framework. Donne's willingness to keep exercising the rules of prudent, contextual judgement lends credibility and hermeneutic weight to his visions of faith. As he observes in his 'Elegie upon the untimely death of the incomparable Prince Henry', 'reason, put to'her best extension,/Almost meetes faith'.[69] Donne's reading acts in the *Essayes* derive their moral justification from a dual strategy: the tools of rational enquiry must be used to take him to the brink of truth, but at the edge of reason, only faith can provide the final assurance the exegete craves.

In this chapter, I have argued that Donne's *Essayes* are best understood as an act of hermeneutic initiation conceived of in the broadest sense (as a devotional discipline as well as a reading exercise), and that the outlines of this interpretive philosophy emerge more clearly when we situate the *Essayes* in their Augustinian context. Recovering the Augustinianism of Donne's work has entailed looking in detail at the *Confessions*, the text which builds the public dimension of Augustine's ministry on the foundation of a rectified hermeneutic and spiritual disposition, but also at the reception of Augustinian precepts of interpretation in Renaissance guides to Scripture reading. As I suggested at the start of the chapter, however, the more universal ontological ramifications of Donne's hermeneutic can only be understood by attending to a second aspect of Augustine's early modern reception: the processes of spiritual rectification outlined in Renaissance manuals of meditation. Within this category, it is useful to consider guidebooks which draw on Augustine as the prime authority on meditation, often through his *Soliloquies*, as well as the enormously successful industry of pseudo-Augustinian works in translation such as Thomas Rogers's *A Pretious Booke of Heauenly Meditations* (1597), *S. Augustines Manuel* (1581), and *S. Augustines Praiers* (1581).[70] In the opening sentence of the *Essayes*, and then again in the first lines of the prayer which concludes the work, Donne describes himself as engaged in an act of textual meditation:

> I do not therefore sit at the door, and meditate upon the threshold, because I may not enter further. (7)
> O Eternal God . . . since by Thy grace, I have thus long meditated upon Thee and spoken of Thee, I may now speak to Thee. As Thou hast enlightened and enlarged me to contemplate Thy greatness, so, O GOD, descend Thou and stoop down to see my infirmities and the Egypt in which I live; and (if Thy good pleasure be such) hasten mine Exodus and deliverance, for I desire to be dissolved, and be with Thee. (104)

---

[69] 'Elegie upon the untimely death of the incomparable Prince Henry', ll. 15–16.
[70] See also John Day, *Godly Meditation Made in the Form of Prayers* (*c.*1570) and *Certain Select Prayers Gathered out of S. Augustines Meditations . . . Also his manuell* (1574). On the popularity of these pseudo-Augustinian meditation manuals, see Ian Green, *Print and Protestantism in Early Modern England* (Oxford, 2000), 258–9.

Early modern manuals on meditation such as Greenham's *Grave Counsels* identify three related stages of Scripture-based devotional exercises: the reader moves from reading to meditation to prayer, with the ultimate aim of reaching a contemplative state.[71] Greenham also advises that we 'reade, and conferre much with reuerence and diligence, else our meditation may be erronious'.[72] Joseph Hall's *The Arte of Diuine Meditation* (1606) further defines the spiritual benefits of achieving such depths of contemplation: 'by this we ... get more light to our knowledge, more heate to our affections, more life to our deuotion: by this we grow to be (as wee are) straungers vpon earth, and out of a right estimation of all earthly things, into a sweet fruition of inuisible comforts: by this, wee see our Sauiour with *Steuen*, we talke with God as *Moses* and by this we are rauished with blessed *Paul* into Paradise; and see that heauen which we are loath to leaue, which we cannot vtter.'[73]

This is precisely the hermeneutic trajectory charted by Donne's *Essayes*, which move from extended formal meditations 'Of God' to a final prayerful and affective colloquy, in which he addresses himself 'to Thee' directly. His re-enunciation of Augustine's imagined encounter with Moses prepares for this encounter with God; Augustine's realization that it is not Moses but God who '*sayst true*' is the crucial preparatory stage which has 'enlightened and enlarged' him 'to contemplate' God's greatness. Donne's private meditations seek precisely the transcendental dialogue that Hall describes: a liberation from the horizontal axis of history and a vertical ascent to God, communion with Moses and Paul. Guides to meditation also trace in detail the spiritual topography that Donne rehearses in the *Essayes*. Hall affirms that in meditation, '[h]umiliation truly goes before glory. For the more we are cast downe in our conceit, the higher shall GOD lift vs vp at the ende of this exercise, in spirituall reioicing.'[74] And he adds that 'the soule, which at the beginning of this exercise did but creepe and grouell vpon earth, ... now in the Conclusion soare[s] aloft in heauen; ... now find[s] it selfe neere to God, yea with him, and in him'.[75] In his own scriptural meditations, Donne starts by 'grovelling' upon the threshold and by the end, with Augustine's help, finds himself 'neere to God' through a hermeneutic discipline of 'ascending humility'. Augustine's paradoxical dynamic of exaltation and humiliation is at the heart of Hall's and Donne's rhetoric: God's 'humility', as the *Essayes* insist, 'was to be like us, was a Dejection; but ours, to be like him, is our chiefest exaltation'. Manuals of private meditation reveal the broader context of early modern devotional literature and culture to which the *Essayes* belong, and which supplements the focus on the pragmatic rules and exigencies of interpretation articulated in manuals of Scripture reading.

The final prayers of the *Essayes* dwell on the 'reverent devotions and pious affections' inspired by the spiritual exercise of reading God's Word, while they 'humbly acknowledge and confesse ... that glory which his [Christ's] humiliation purchased for us' (107). At this point, Donne most explicitly references the biographical circumstances which attended the composition of his text:

---

[71] Richard Greenham, *Grave Counsels*, in *Works* (1599), 37–41 (41).
[72] Ibid. 40.　　[73] Hall, *Arte*, 3–4.　　[74] Ibid. 154–5.　　[75] Ibid. 185.

And thou hast put me in my way towards thy land of promise, thy Heavenly Canaan,
by removing me from the Egypt of frequented and populous, glorious places, to a more
solitary and desart retiredness, where I may more safely feed . . . upon contemplation of
thee. (104)

The social isolation of the Mitcham years is here redefined and converted into an
opportunity for spiritual growth through devotional discipline. As Donne is
removed from the worldliness of 'frequented and populous, glorious places' he
achieves the 'solitary . . . retiredness' which, according to Hall, is the outward
foundation and internal precondition for successful meditation. Standing on the
shoulders of Augustine, Donne achieves the 'contemplation' of God which leads
him to set his sights on the English Church.

AUGUSTINE REVISITED

In a 1629 sermon at St Paul's on Genesis 1:2 ('And the Spirit of God moved upon
the face of the waters'; see also Chapter 6), Donne recapitulates some of his
fundamental ideas about faith-based interpretation. The occasion is Whitsunday,
the day which celebrates 'the third Person of the Holy, Blessed, and Glorious
Trinity, the Holy Ghost . . . the Spirit of Comfort'.[76] But Donne's preaching
performance, I would suggest, does not only commemorate the workings of the
Holy Spirit; it also pays homage to the tutelary spirit of the *Essayes* and thus relives
Donne's exegetical initiation at the hands of Augustine more than a decade
previously. Textually speaking, Donne's sermon takes up the thread where the
Essayes left off: while his solitary scriptural musings had invoked Augustine to reveal
the meaning of Genesis 1:1, the Whitsunday sermon aims to explicate Genesis 1:2.
There are further parallels between these two Donnean works: like the *Essayes*,
which established the need for interpretive humility and faith by way of an
Augustinian intervention, Donne's sermon uses some key texts from the *Confessions*
to illustrate the dangers of interpretive curiosity. Augustine makes a well-timed
appearance in a section on 'generall considerations' regarding 'the exposition of
darke places', for instance, lending his voice to confer authority on Donne's
discourse. He uses the *Confessions* to define the parameters of licit hermeneutic
engagement: 'within these limits [i.e. the ones set by Augustine] wee shall containe
our selves'.[77]

As in the earlier scriptural meditations, Augustine provides the hermeneutic
platform for Donne's conversation with the Scriptures: 'First then, undertaking the
consideration of the literall sense, and after, the spirituall, we joyne with
S. *Augustine, Sint castæ deliciæ meæ Scripturæ tuæ*; Lord I love to be conversant in
thy Scriptures.'[78] As in the *Essayes*, *Confessions* 11.3.5 sets the general framework for
Donne's exegesis:

---

[76] *Sermons*, 9.92–108 (92).   [77] Ibid. 9.95.
[78] Ibid. 9.94.

Thus that blessed Father meditates upon the word of God; he speakes of this beginning of the Book of *Genesis*; and he speaks lamenting, *Scripsit Moses & abiit*, a little *Moses* hath said, and alas he is gone; *Si hic esset, tenerem eum, & per te rogarem*, If *Moses* were here, I would hold him here, and begge of him, for thy sake to tell me thy meaning in his words, of this Creation. But sayes he, since I cannot speake with *Moses*, *Te, quo plenus vera dixit, Veritas, rogo*, I begge of thee who art Truth it selfe, as thou enabledst him to utter it, enable me to understand what he hath said.[79]

In the spirit of a Whitsunday sermon, Donne's focus is on the third person of the Trinity. The Holy Ghost's association with charity is here transposed—through *Confessions* 11.3.5—into a hermeneutic key: in his exegesis of Genesis 1:2, Donne develops an interpretive ethos of charitable liberty which enables him to recover Moses' intentions, but will ultimately lead to a more profound inward truth. Once again, Augustine unlocks Donne's love for the Scriptures.

The Seventh Expostulation of Donne's *Devotions upon Emergent Occasions* (1623) marks yet another attempt *'to hold on'* to Moses. Almost one third into the account of his illness, Donne anxiously reports his physician's failure to make sense of the symptoms; he cannot discern the underlying causes of Donne's condition and therefore *'desires to have others joyned with him'*.[80] Paradoxically, the idea of a *'multiplication of . . . helps'* offers no comfort to Donne, but only serves to heighten his sense of isolation from his friends, colleagues, the world of business, and the 'communion of thy *Catholique Church'*.[81] Donne's fear of becoming a *'schismatical singularit[y]'* is expressed in hermeneutic terms,[82] as the opening lines of the Seventh Expostulation hark back to Donne's earlier engagement with *Confessions* 11.3.5 in the *Essayes*:

My God, my God, thy blessed *Servant Augustine* begg'd of thee, that *Moses* might come, and tell him what hee meant by some places of *Genesis*: May I have leave to aske of that *Spirit*, that writ that Booke, why when *David* expected newes from *Joabs* armie, and that the Watchman tolde him, that *hee sawe a man running alone*, *David* concluded out of that circumstance, *That if hee came alone, hee brought good newes* [2 Samuel 18:25]?[83]

Donne uses 'grammar', 'logic', and 'rhetoric' to work out the meaning of God's word, but fails to resolve the interpretive dilemma. His sense of isolation coincides with a moment of acute hermeneutic crisis: Donne has yet to read the text of his illness properly and to discover the spiritual significance of his symptoms. In the Seventh Prayer, Donne wonders 'whether thy *Mercy*, or thy *Correction*, were thy primary, and original intention in this sicknes';[84] without faith in the 'gracious purpose' of his predicament, Donne is lost in the gap between *'signe'* and *'signified'*, *'Word'* and *'Sacrament'*—the very hermeneutic gulf that his trust in Augustine, Moses, and Paul had previously enabled him to overcome.[85] There is no inward illumination here, no guiding conviction that *'thou sayst true'*. Fallen language obscures, philological remedies fail, and the Scriptures remain a closed book

[79] *Sermons*, 9.94.
[80] John Donne, *Devotions Upon Emergent Occasions*, ed. Anthony Raspa (Montreal, 1975), 35.
[81] Ibid. 39.   [82] Ibid.   [83] Ibid. 37.   [84] Ibid. 40.   [85] Ibid. 37.

without faith. Separated from the 'communion' of the Church and the community of interpreters, Donne finds himself not simply in a precarious physical state, but also in a form of interpretive limbo.[86] In many ways, this passage stands in polar opposition to the project of the *Essayes*, which find comfort and inspiration in the notion of a timeless hermeneutic community, where no reader is an island.

The *Essayes in Divinity* enact a process of hermeneutic and epistemological initiation. When Donne speaks of the '*offices . . . which thou enjoynest amongst us in this life*' (43–4) he means, above all, the office of interpretation. This includes complex methods of textual judgement, but also sudden, intuitive leaps of faith. When Donne 'channels' the *Confessions*, textual communication gives way to 'unvocall' communion; local complication yields to a panoramic comprehension of Scripture, connects textual places that seemed to lie worlds apart. Augustine's 'ascending humility' is the model for this approach, which affords glimpses of eternity in the plodding narrative of history, and offers moments of revelation and inward illumination when the interpretive quest seems at its most laborious. For fallen readers these moments of total scriptural clarity are rare: even 'the faithfullest heart is not . . . constantly upon God' (20). It takes, characteristically, another act of intercession to stabilize this panoramic hermeneutic vision: '*the mediation of thy Son, our Saviour Christ Jesus*' (99), which will save mankind by 'assuming us into [the angels'] places' (100) and restore the writing 'in the *Tables* of our Heart' (9).

Donne's *Essayes* are deeply private meditations, but as the poet-preacher recognizes in one of his most explicit reflections on priestly vocation, the heights of inner contemplation are the very foundations upon which the public profession of God's Word is built. Donne's explicit adherence to Protestant forms of exegesis should encourage us to think afresh about the nature and degree of his conformity at this point in his career. In his verse letter 'To Mr Tilman after he had taken orders', Donne once again ponders the topographical implications of his metaphysics, remarking that preachers 'as angels out of clouds, from pulpits speak' (l. 43). In the *Essayes*, Donne aspires to just such an elevated station; since he cannot yet 'speake with *Moses*', Augustine must find the words for him. Reading and re-enunciating Augustine's texts is a conduit to self-knowledge in the *Essayes*; the transhistorical hermeneutic community established in Donne's text offers a path towards self-transformation, which is ultimately actuated in his career as a professional divine. To return to the Herbert analogy with which this chapter began: the *Essayes* situate Donne on 'The Church-Porch', but also resonate with that poem's alternative title, 'Perirrhanterium'—a Greek term for a sprinkling brush used in the ritual cleansing before a ceremony. In the *Essayes*, Donne prepares the ground for a spiritual and hermeneutic discipline that stayed with him throughout his career. He finds a new beginning in the very first words of Genesis, the biblical text that inaugurates Augustine's eschatological journey back to God in Book 11 of the

---

[86] For two different accounts of hermeneutic implications of Donne's illness, see Janel M. Mueller, 'The Exegesis of Experience: Dean Donne's Devotions upon Emergent Occasions', *Journal of English and Germanic Philology*, 67 (1968), 1–19; and Stephen Pender, 'Essaying the Body: Donne, Affliction, and Medicine', in David Colclough (ed.), *John Donne's Professional Lives* (Cambridge, 2003), 215–48.

Confessions. These two extreme points of the providential narrative will define Donne's engagement with Augustine in his writings, from the creation of the world to the eternal bliss of the beatific vision. Before we see this dynamic in action, however, we need to turn to the chronological beginnings of Donne's Augustinianism, which can be found in the rather less rarefied rhetorical atmosphere of *Biathanatos*.

4

The Bad Physician
Casuistry and Augustinian Charity in *Biathanatos*

> Some thought it mounted to the lunar sphere,
> Since all things lost on earth are treasur'd there.
> . . . .
> The courtier's promises, and sick man's prayers,
> The smiles of harlots, and the tears of heirs,
> Cages for gnats, and chains to yoke a flea,
> Dried butterflies, and tomes of casuistry.
>
> (Alexander Pope, *The Rape of the Lock*, Canto 5)

> [T]he intent and end conditions every action, and infuses the poyson or the
> nourishment.
>
> (Donne, *Biathanatos*, 127)

> And I am by no means sure that a person would feel much less sorry to see
> himself brutally killed by an infuriated villain than to find himself conscien-
> tiously stilettoed by a devotee.
>
> (Blaise Pascal, *Provincial Letters*, Letter 7)

Pope's final rhyme tells us much about casuistry's fate in the eighteenth century. In
a moment of resounding metrical anticlimax, his closed couplets spell out a
message of redundancy and superfluity: 'tomes of casuistry' have about as much
cultural value as 'chains to yoke a flea'. In *The Rape of the Lock*, the art of case-
based reasoning finds itself in the dubious company of cynical opportunists,
inhabiting a world of crocodile tears. The final epigraph to this chapter, from
Pascal's *Provincial Letters* (1656–7), is part of a more comprehensive attack on
casuistical thought, but equally emphasizes its time-serving, Machiavellian dimensions. Pascal's text exposes the fault-lines of a system of moral accountability which
relies entirely on the fragile categories of motive and intent. His Jesuit caricatures
are made to deliver a biting parody of casuistry's most cherished principles: its
near-obsessive attention to the specific circumstances of a case, and its intense
preoccupation with the question of moral intent. The religious figures satirized in
Pascal's *Letters* commit a whole series of crimes, all the while insisting on the piety
of their motives. Sheltered by 'our great method of *directing the intention*', the
Jesuit Fathers literally get away with murder; indeed, killing for the right reasons

can be a laudable expression of faith.[1] Under the Church's laws of conscience, true believers remain protected; as long as they abstain from 'sinning just for the sake of sinning', anything goes.[2] And even though secular jurisdictions may show a regrettable interest in the facts and the damage caused to the victim, Pascal's Jesuit stands firm in his defence of casuistical reasoning: '"Judges," said the Father, "who do not delve into the consciences, judge only of the externals of an action, whereas we mainly look at the intention. And that is why our principles are sometimes slightly different from theirs."'[3]

Donne, of course, was to launch his own attack on Jesuitical forms of argument and rhetoric in *Pseudo-martyr*. But the polemical concerns of that text are adumbrated even earlier: in *Biathanatos*, Donne's treatise on 'selfe-homicide', which mutually implicates suicide and martyrdom at every turn. The treatment of casuistry in *Pseudo-martyr*, as A. E. Malloch observes, depends on genre and occasion: there, Donne 'construes their [the Jesuits'] intentions' purely 'in terms of the political-religious brawl in which he was taking part'.[4] It is true that *Pseudo-martyr*'s position on Roman traditions of casuistry is firmly embedded in its controversial context; as a consequence, the text achieves a clarity of perspective which inevitably verges on distortion. This polemical decisiveness, however, stems from a far more complicated and morally problematic engagement with casuistical thinking in *Biathanatos*. In this chapter, I argue that the rhetorical 'structuration' of *Biathanatos*, its form and purpose, emerges more precisely when it is considered in relation to the ethics of intent—the mode of thought so vigorously caricatured by later seventeenth-century writers like Pascal. 'Intent' or motive is a key component in the resolution of casuistical problems, alongside the investigation of contextual and circumstantial evidence. The situational emphasis of casuistical analysis also, importantly, includes adjudicating the claims of competing jurisdictions and laws—secular, ecclesiastical, and scriptural: *Biathanatos* investigates all these legal codes in an attempt to determine (as Donne's title states) whether suicide can ever

---

[1] Blaise Pascal, *The Provincial Letters* (*Les Provinciales*), trans. A. J. Krailsheimer (Harmondsworth, 1967), 112. The best introduction remains Louis Cognet's in his 1965 Paris edition of the text, republished in Philippe Sellier's edition of Pascal, *Les Provinciales, Pensées et Opuscules divers*, Librairie Générale Française (Paris, 2004). On Pascal's views on Augustine, see Philippe Sellier, *Pascal et Saint Augustin*, 2nd edn. (Paris, 1995), and Vincent Carraud, 'L'Anti-Augustinisme de Pascal', in Laurence Devillairs (ed.), *Augustin au XVIIᵉ Siècle* (Florence, 2007), 151–201.

[2] Pascal, *Provincial Letters*, 103.

[3] Ibid. 112. On casuistry in the early modern period see, for instance, *Conscience and Casuistry in Early Modern Europe*, ed. Edmund Leites (Cambridge, 1988); Lowell Gallagher, *Medusa's Gaze: Casuistry and Conscience in the Renaissance* (Stanford, 1991); P. J. Holmes (ed.), *Elizabethan Casuistry* (London, 1981); Thomas Woods, *English Casuistry of the Seventeenth Century and its Relations with Medieval and Jesuit Casuistry* (Leeds, 1947). On the culture and politics of conscience, see Harald E. Braun and Edward Vallance (eds.), *Contexts of Conscience in Early Modern Europe, 1500–1700* (Basingstoke and New York, 2004); Stefania Tutino, *Law and Conscience: Catholicism in Early Modern England, 1570–1625* (Aldershot, 2007); Harald E. Braun and Edward Vallance (eds.), *The Renaissance Conscience*, special issue of *Renaissance Studies*, 23 (2009); and Ceri Sullivan, *The Rhetoric of the Conscience in Donne, Herbert, and Vaughan* (Oxford, 2008).

[4] A. E. Malloch, 'John Donne and the Casuists', *Studies in English Literature, 1500–1900*, 2 (1962), 57–76 (62).

be 'otherwise' than 'naturally sin'. The primacy of the law of charity, as we will see, is the most complex, and the most problematic, legacy of *Biathanatos*.

The category of intent is closely correlated, in Donne's text, with charity; and *Biathanatos* defines both concepts in explicitly Augustinian terms. Like the idea of interpretive faith in the *Essayes in Divinity*, the notion of Augustinian charity signifies a whole penumbra of principles and reading techniques; and, as in the *Essayes*, these hermeneutic processes have wide-ranging moral implications and applications. But this is where the parallels between the 'Augustinianisms' of these two texts end. Where the *Essayes* focus their attention on one major Augustinian text, the *Confessions*, and follow it closely to the point of citation, translation, and re-enunciation, *Biathanatos* displays a wholesale disregard for Augustine's meanings and contexts, in letter and in spirit. This is not a sign of ignorance: while a significant number of references in *Biathanatos* suggest second-hand recourse to texts such as *Against Gaudentius, a Donatist Bishop*,[5] *On Nature and Grace*, and the *Homilies on John's Epistle to the Parthi*,[6] it is clear that Donne took the time to engage with at least one text in detail: Augustine's *City of God*.[7]

Far from indicating scholarly negligence, then, Donne's misrepresentation of Augustine's text (the first systematic refutation of suicide in Christian philosophy) is part of a deliberate attempt to push the intentionalist ethics of casuistry to its absolute limits. Donne's hostile attitude towards the Augustinian position on suicide is framed by insistent affirmations of his own charitable motives: his (mis-)reading of the *City of God* and other Augustinian texts is tempered and justified by 'a charitable interpretacion of theyr Action, who dye so [i.e. by self-homicide]' (29).[8] The collision of intents provoked by this approach dogs Donne's treatise throughout, but is especially blatant in the final part of *Biathanatos*, where Donne discusses scriptural prohibitions against suicide. As Donne continues to extend the perimeters of charitable 'misinterpretation', his textual equivocations, omissions, and misprisions begin to question and subvert his casuistical, intent-based philosophy, threatening to convert moral 'nourishment' into 'poyson' (127). *Biathanatos*, in other words, interrogates the category of intent itself, but it also

---

[5] *Contra Gaudentium Donatistarum*, PL 43.
[6] *In Epistolam Johannis ad Parthos*, PL 35.
[7] John Donne, *Biathanatos*, ed. Ernest W. Sullivan II (Newark, Del., 1984). Subsequent references to *Biathanatos* in this chapter are to this edition and will appear parenthetically in the text. *Biathanatos* provides ample evidence of Donne's use of secondary or mediating sources, but also of the related habit of tracing such mediated references back to the original texts. See, for instance, *Biathanatos*, 38, where a reference from Augustine's *Contra Faustum Manichaeum* is credited to Lombard, but the precise formulation of Donne's quotation shows that he returned to the original (the word 'Aeternum' is found in Augustine, but not in Lombard; see A. E. Malloch, 'The Definition of Sin in Donne's *Biathanatos*', *Modern Language Notes*, 72 (1957), 332–5). At p. 60 of *Biathanatos*, Alphonsus a Castro's *Adversus Omnes Haereses* (1560) is used to mediate Augustine's controversial exchanges with Petilianus the Donatist, but the next reference in Donne's text—Augustine's letter to Boniface about the Donatists, 'De Correctione Donatistarum'—again suggests that the mediating source inspired direct recourse, since the letter is not included in Alphonsus's work.
[8] The full title of Donne's text is *Biathanatos. A Declaration of that Paradoxe, or Thesis, that Selfe-homicide is not so naturally Sinne, that it mau neuer be otherwise. Wherein The Nature, and the extent of all those Lawes, which seeme to be violated by this Act, are diligently Surueyd* (1644).

scrutinizes the boundary between licit and illicit action which is contested in every act of casuistical interpretation; it asks, with Pascal, how far 'the purity of the end' can be stretched in order to legitimize 'the viciousness of the means' by which it is achieved.[9] At the same time, Donne's use of Augustine in *Biathanatos* demonstrates that he was more than capable of appropriating Augustinian modes of argument and thinking without sharing the assumptions and moral purposes of his source texts.

Re-examining *Biathanatos* from an Augustinian perspective is a necessary project, not simply because it allows for a fresh evaluation of the role of casuistry in Donne's work, but also because it provokes an investigation of the concepts which underlie the exercise of casuistry as a moral and interpretive practice. 'Discretion' and 'judgement' have already made an appearance in Donne's scriptural hermeneutics in the *Essayes*; as I noted in my analysis of that text, both terms have played a crucial role in revisionist readings of Donne's sermons, most notably in the work of Jeanne Shami. From her first major piece on 'Donne and Discretion' to her monograph on Donne's late-Jacobean preaching, Shami has emphasized the importance of discretion and good judgement as principles of religious conduct and political accommodation; casuistry, whether implicitly or explicitly, often furnishes the interpretive mechanisms for the implementation of discreet judgement.[10] Shami's readings of Donne's casuistry shore up faith in the efficacy of its hermeneutic proceedings; while the political and ethical challenges posed by key scriptural texts such as Esther 4:16 are considerable, the operations of casuistical procedure are relatively transparent and unproblematic. This is, as Shami's more recent work implies, a function of the sermons' pastoral emphasis: while they are committed to confronting complex religio-political issues, Donne's sermons are also mindful of the broader task of providing comfort and edification to their audiences—where ruptures in the moral fabric are exposed and debated, the preacher also faces the duty of healing them.

Biathanatos, by contrast, has no such pastoral responsibilities; its methods of casuistical 'physick' are, therefore, of a rather more experimental kind. First of all, it is worth re-stating that, unlike the sermons, *Biathanatos* is not formally an example of a specifically Protestant brand of casuistry. This observation was made by Camille Slights in her 1981 monograph on *The Casuistical Tradition in Shakespeare, Donne, Herbert, and Milton*, but does not receive sufficient attention in the only book-length work on Donne's casuistry, Meg Lota Brown's *Donne and the Politics of Conscience in Early Modern England* (1995).[11] Brown's otherwise excellent account of Donne's casuistical practice is too quick to dismiss the conspicuously Catholic or Jesuitical (and, relatedly, scholastic) elements of *Biathanatos*: for instance, while Protestant manuals of conscience such as Perkins's, Ames's, and Hall's (discussed below) proceed with minimal proof-texting and focus on a limited

[9] Pascal, *Provincial Letters*, 104.
[10] Jeanne Shami, 'Donne on Discretion', *English Literary History*, 47 (1980), 48–66; *John Donne and Conformity in Crisis in the Late Jacobean Pulpit* (Cambridge, 2003).
[11] Camille Wells Slights, *The Casuistical Tradition in Shakespeare, Donne, Herbert, and Milton* (Princeton, 1981); Meg Lota Brown, *Donne and the Politics of Conscience in Early Modern England* (Leiden, 1995).

number of model cases that can be applied to a broad range of moral challenges, Donne's text follows the Catholic model of accumulating clouds of authorities and witnesses, and envelops his case studies in a shroud of scholastic distinctions and qualifications.

A dualist model of casuistical approaches—'[f]or [Rome's] penance, legalism, and authority, Reformers substituted reason, individual conscience, and Scripture'—thus cannot do full justice to the complex interaction of the two discourses in *Biathanatos*.[12] While Donne acknowledges the procedural differences that separate Roman and Reformed models of casuistry, and their different views on the relationship between authority and individual conscience, *Biathanatos* is more profoundly concerned with the fundamental principles of casuistical thought: the idea of a hierarchy of laws and, as we have seen, the primacy of hermeneutic intent. The epistemological critique mounted by *Biathanatos* is fuelled by just such a return to first principles: when viewed as a set of arguments and rhetorical manoeuvres, Jesuitical and Reformed approaches to casuistry prove surprisingly difficult to disentangle; this is a deeply troubling notion, which the polemical momentum of *Pseudo-martyr* works hard to suppress. *Biathanatos*, then, is not a straightforward endorsement of casuistical principles and procedures. Donne's text confronts contingency and uncertainty at every turn, arguing—at times to its own detriment—that moral boundaries can be redrawn and shifted in the act of interpretation. In so doing, Donne's casuistical edifice ultimately runs the risk of self-sabotage and subverts its function as an instrument of pastoral support and edification. By destabilizing the concept of intent, as we will see, *Biathanatos* undermines the very structures upon which discreet judgement and deliberation are built.

In Donne's works, we find a consistent preoccupation with the category of intent; he is particularly interested in the applications of intent-based reasoning in legal and theological forms of argument. Walton's biography notes, for instance, that in considering Bishop Morton's proposal that he should take orders, Donne fell back on the judgement of 'the best of *Casuists*'

> that *Gods Glory should be the first end, and a maintenance the second motive to embrace that calling;* and though each man may propose to himself both together; yet the first may not be put last without a violation of Conscience, which he that searches the heart will judge. And truly my present condition is such, that if I ask my own Conscience, whether it be reconcileable to that rule, it is at this time so perplexed about it, that I can neither give my self nor you an answer.[13]

Walton's report isolates two key criteria for casuistical judgement which will occupy Donne throughout *Biathanatos*: the examination of an agent's intent, and the 'end' or purpose of advancing God's glory. In the biographical narrative, Donne's priorities are presented as ultimately clear-cut: in a pious display of moral probity, Walton's subject refuses to permit a usurpation of religious by secular concerns; he will not join the ranks of the clergy for financial gain. A few years later, however, in a sermon preached to the members of the Virginia Company (1622), the relationship between primary

---

[12] Brown, 46.   [13] Walton, *Lives*, 34.

and secondary intent appears less comfortingly transparent. The merchants, notorious for their focus on worldly '*maintenance*' rather than missionary zeal, are invited to
scrutinize the underlying motives of their colonial project:

> whether . . . a probable imagination of future profit, or a willingnes to concurre to the
> vexation of the Enemie, what collaterall respect soever drew thee in, if now thou art in,
> thy principall respect be the glory of God, that occasion, whatsoever it was, was
> *vehiculum Spiritus Sancti*, that was the Petard, that broke open thy Iron gate . . . and
> now hee is fallen upon thee, if thou do not *Depose*, (lay aside all consideration of profit
> for ever, never to looke for returne) . . . but if thou doe but *Post-pose* the consideration
> of temporall gaine, and study first the advancement of the *Gospell* of *Christ Iesus*, the
> *Holy Ghost* is fallen upon you[.][14]

In his Virginia sermon, Donne presents a notion of intention which is multi-
layered and composite, and which acknowledges that various motives can coexist
and shape our responses to an event in different, and potentially conflicting, ways.
His rhetoric works hard initially to adjust the balance of motives so as to make it
conform to Walton's binary model: greed and aggression are rendered 'collateral' to
the 'principall' end of serving 'the glory of God'. But this idea of qualitative
differentiation is immediately re-complicated, as Donne's language moves from a
qualitative to a merely chronological model of moral priorities. By the end of the
passage, Donne is content to have the explorers '*Post-pose*' their desire for material
profit, rather than '*Depose*' and supplant it entirely with the more salutary Christian
motives of enlightenment and conversion. This may be no more than an instance of
pastoral realism, but it nevertheless alerts us to a continuing, and morally troubling,
preoccupation with the ethics and politics of intent in Donne's texts.

AUGUSTINE AND CHARITY IN *BIATHANATOS*

Charity is at the centre of Donne's moral argument in *Biathanatos*. Donne's text
begins and ends by exhorting its readers to charitable interpretation, and the
analysis of legal principles and specific cases is punctuated, at crucial points, by
reminders of the speaker's own charitable credentials. Donne's opening meditation
sets out the parameters for this rhetorical strategy:

> I haue often such a sickly inclination [i.e. to suicide] . . . Often Meditation of this, hath
> wonne me to a charitable interpretacion of theyr Action, who dye so: and prouok'd me
> alitle [*sic*] to watch, and exagitate theyr reasons, which pronounce so peremptory
> iudgements vppon them. A deuout, and godly man hath guided vs well, and rectified
> our vncharitablenesse in such cases, by this remembrance *Scis lapsum etc. Thou knowest
> this mans fall, but thou knowest not his Wrastling, which perchance was such, that allmost
> his very fall is iustefied, and accepted of God.* . . . An vncharitable Misinterpreter vnthrif-
> tely demolishes his owne house, and repayres not another. He looseth without any
> gaine or profit to any. (29)

---

[14] *Sermons*, 4.273–4.

This inaugural moment associates charity with the qualities of empathy and mercy, but proceeds to outline a more specific set of interpretive techniques. The phrase *'thou knowest not his Wrastling'* prepares for the scrutiny of circumstance and motive which is typical of casuistical enquiry. Donne also clarifies at once that this procedure involves some degree of ethical latitude and flexibility, a further characteristic of charitable exegesis; this is no pedants' paradise: 'so do I wish, (and as much as I can effect) that to those many learned and subtile men, which haue trauayld in this poynt, some charitable and compassionate men might be added' (32). Further validation is found in charity's moral lineage; Christ's example of unselfish love adds unimpeachable authority to Donne's argument: *'Ne iudices proximum, donec ad eius locum pertingas*; Feele and wrastle with such tentations, as he hath done, and thy zeale will be tamer. For *Therefore* (saith the Apostle) *it became Christ to be like vs, that he might be mercifull'* (30). In the final moments of *Biathanatos*, Donne resumes his focus on charitable judgement and takes pre-emptive action against 'vncharitable Misinterpreters': 'Against the reasons whereof, and against Charity, if preiudice . . . haue so precluded any, that they haue not bene pleasd to tast, and digest them, I must leaue them to theyr drowsinesse still' (146). Hostile readers, Donne slyly concludes, resist his ministrations to their own detriment.

Even to the most charitable readers of Donne's text, it is clear that his frequent recourse to the term charity encompasses a plurality of motives. Ernest W. Sullivan II argues that the text presents 'a general plea for charity towards suicides', but also readily appreciates the tactical usefulness of such rhetoric: Donne 'proclaims his own Christian charity and intimates that his opponents are uncharitable, evil, zealous, easily susceptible to sin, choleric, malicious, lazy, ignorant, and foolish'.[15] In recognizing the strategic efficacy of charity, Donne was drawing on august patristic precedent. During the prolonged conflict with the Donatist Church, Augustine appropriated the language of charity as a polemical tool in his exchange with the Donatist bishop Gaudentius. Augustine's *Against Gaudentius* confronts rhetorical challenges not dissimilar to those faced by Donne in *Pseudo-martyr*: both texts revolve around the attempt to wrest discursive control over key terms from their opponents, and both pivot on the re-definition of martyrdom as suicide. In Augustine's treatise *Against Gaudentius* (which Donne cites), the Donatists are portrayed as a splinter group who, rather than expressing dissatisfaction with Augustine's policies, has chosen to sever all ties with the spirit of Christianity itself—a decision Augustine purports to view with profound sadness and regret: 'because we feel such deep Christian charity in our hearts', he argues, 'we feel all the more pain at seeing you rebel against the peace of Christ'.[16] Having claimed Christian charity for his side, Augustine goes on to re-describe the Donatist

[15] *Biathanatos*, pp. xxx, xxvii.
[16] 'Proinde, quanto major est in nobis charitas Christi, tanto majore cum dolore animi vos videmus . . . rebellare contra pacem Christi' (*Contra Gaudentium Donatistarum* 1.22; *PL* 43.720). See also James J. O'Donnell, *Augustine, Sinner and Saint* (London, 2005), 221–4; Donne's reference to *Contra Gaudentium Donatistarum* Book 1, chapter 31 comes at p. 104 of *Biathanatos* (Sullivan II, 226) and he mistakenly identifies his reference as Book 2, chapter 23.

position as a factional rebellion against the true Catholic Church, and re-frames a potential act of political repression and usurpation as a gesture of loving reconciliation: the Donatists, though 'covered in crimes', are offered the support of their Augustinian brethren, whose charity covers a multitude of sins—'*caritas cooperit multitudinem peccatorum.*'

The idea that 'charity covers a multitude of sins' will come to haunt Donne's own moral discourse in *Biathanatos*. Before moving on to this problematic territory, however, we need to establish further the Augustinian pedigree of Donne's charity, and examine its connections with the intent-based strategies of casuistical reasoning. The third part of *Biathanatos* discusses scriptural strictures against suicide, including the seemingly unambiguous prescription, from Exodus 20:13, 'Thou shalt not kill'. Moving on from civil and ecclesiastical jurisdictions to divine law, this section provides Donne with the toughest casuistical nuts to crack yet. It is no surprise, then, that the discussion of scriptural prohibitions begins with an invocation of charity, which now emerges as the very incarnation of equitable and discreet judgement:

> To prepare vs therefore to a right vnderstanding, and application of these places of Scripture, we must arest a while vpon the Nature, and degrees and effects of Charity; the Mother and the forme of all Vertue; which shall not onely lead vs to heauen (for faith opens vs the Dore) but shall continue with vs when we are there, when both faith, and hope are spent and vselesse. We shall no where find a better portrait of Charity, then that *which S' Aug:* hath drawne, *She loues not that, which should not be loued; She neglects not that which should be Loued; She bestowes not more Loue vpon that which deserues lesse; Nor doth she æqually Loue more and lesse Worthynesse; Nor vpon æquall Worthinesse, bestowe more and lesse Loue....* Vppon assurednesse therefore, and a testimony of a rectified Conscyence, that we haue a charitable purpose, let vs consider how farre we may aduenture vpon authority of Scripture, in this Matter which we haue in hand. (125–6)[17]

Donne's discussion is based on *De Doctrina Christiana* 1.27, a key passage for Augustine's definition of charity.[18] Charitable judgement assigns to each element its true value and weight, not in a rigorously literalistic sense, but in a way that recognizes its spirit and essence. By the end of the passage, these virtues have been moved out of the abstract realm of definition and absorbed into the *ethos* or persona of Donne's speaker, who is thus able to confront the scriptural challenges to his case with the best possible accreditation: 'a testimony of a rectified Conscyence, that we haue a charitable purpose'. Throughout the final section of *Biathanatos*, charitable deliberation is closely allied with the concept of hermeneutic intent. Shortly after announcing, with programmatic pith, that 'the intent and end conditions every

[17] On charity as the mother of all virtues, see *Confessions* 13.6.7 and 13.14.15; on charity as eternal and transcending faith and hope, see *De Doctrina* 1.37–8 and *Confessions* 7.10.16.

[18] *De Doctrina Christiana* 1.27, on the order of love ('ordo dilectionis'): the godly person 'does not love what is wrong to love, or fail to love what should be loved, or love too much what should be loved less (or love too little what should be loved more), or love two things equally if one of them should be loved either less or more than the other, or love things either more or less if they should be loved equally' (see *PL* 34.29).

action, and infuses the poyson or the nourishment' (127), Donne turns his attention to the Pauline position on suicide. Donne observes that Paul himself had an inclination to suicide—he 'desir'd to be loose, and to be with *Christ*'—but renounced his desire for the sake of 'his Brethren', because of a 'generall resolution of doing euer that which should premoue theyr happinesse'.[19] This is the right choice in Augustine's system of moral action, where the love of one's neighbour trumps self-love: '*Charity* must be the Rule of our wish, and actions' (131); motive determines the quality of every act.

Donne's idiosyncratic brand of voluntarism also derives inspiration from Augustinian theories of motive, will, and intent. Augustine's theory of Christian ethics builds on the close connection between love and the will. As Albrecht Dihle notes, 'the notion of will, as it is used as a tool of analysis and description in many philosophical doctrines from the early Scholastics to Schopenhauer and Nietzsche, was invented by St Augustine'; 'everything in the view of Augustine, depends on *voluntas* in religious and moral life'—the will is as foundational to Augustine's anthropology as it is to his ethics and hermeneutics.[20] The concept of will also plays a crucial part in Augustine's doctrine of grace and salvation. There, original sin is seen to cause a perversion of man's will and converts charity into self-love.[21] Humanity's liberation from this state of entrapment, Dihle argues, can only be effected by a voluntary sacrifice of love on the part of its creator:

> The grace of God can renew the human will and restore its original freedom of choice.... The intervention of divine grace is, however, unpredictable, inexplicable, and not to be provoked or influenced by human activity. It is merely due to God's sheer love, out of which he has elected a number of human beings to be saved.... God's love has been revealed in the life and death of Christ, which becomes the model of the renewed will of the elect. St Augustine's famous precept for the Christian conduct of life becomes clear from this doctrine: *Dilige et quod vis fac!* 'Love, and do what you will.'[22]

For Dihle, Augustine's idea of redemption is founded on the twin bases of 'voluntas' and 'caritas': God's love enables Christ to give himself freely to mankind. This ultimate act of charity represents the guiding example for all Christians. The terminological link between love and will is first cemented in *On the Trinity* 15.29—'For what else is charity, if not the will' ('Nam quid est aliud caritas, quam voluntas')—but the idea appears, in a variety of contexts, throughout Augustine's writings. In his commentary on Galatians 6:1, the maxim is adapted to a homiletic

---

[19] Paul's desire for death and reunion with Christ is frequently discussed in Donne's sermons; the phrase 'cupio dissolvi' (as a shorthand for Paul's desire 'to be loose, and to be with *Christ*') occurs nearly a dozen times, and with particular frequency in St Paul's sermons preached in 1626 and 1627.

[20] Albrecht Dihle, *The Theory of Will in Classical Antiquity* (Berkeley, 1982), ch. 4, 'St Augustine and his Concept of the Will', 122–44 (122, 129).

[21] See Oliver O'Donovan, *The Problem of Self-Love in St. Augustine* (New Haven, 1980), 45–8; and John Burnaby, *Amor Dei: A Study of the Religion of St. Augustine*, 2nd edn. (Norwich, 1991), 123–5.

[22] Dihle, *Theory of Will*, 131. The concluding quotation is from Augustine's *Homilies on John's Epistle to the Parthi* 7.8 (*PL* 35.2033).

context: '*Dilige & dic quod voles*'—'Love, and say what you will.' It is this homiletic application which Donne invokes in a sermon delivered during the diplomatic mission to The Hague on 19 December 1619, to an audience mindful of the complex interrelations of legal, political, and religious counsel:

> Let the Congregation see that thou studiest the good of their soules, and they will digest any wholesome increpation, any medicinall reprehension at thy hands, *Dilige & dic quod voles.* . . . So also the Congregation sayes to the Minister, *Dilige & dic quod voles,* shew thy love to me, in studying my case, and applying thy knowledge to my conscience . . . deal thus with me, love me thus, and say what thou wilt; nothing shall offend me.[23]

In evidence here is, once again, Donne's tendency to reduce complex moral challenges and pastoral interactions to first principles; the difficult task of 'studying' an individual 'case' can be facilitated through recourse to a limited set of fundamental rules, in this case, the law of charity. Donne's idea that love is best manifested through diligent attention to particular lives and actions is a recurrent motif in early modern casuistical discourse. Joseph Hall's influential treatise *Resolutions and Decisions of Divers Practicall Cases of Conscience* (1649), for instance, builds his discussion of 'humane and civill' commerce on the principle of charitable interpretation:

> Shortly, for the guidance of our either caution, or liberty in matter of borrowing, and lending, the onely Cynosure is our *Charity;* for in all humane and civill acts of Commerce, it is a sure rule, That whatsoever is not a violation of Charity cannot be unlawfull, and whatsoever is not agreeable to Charity can be no other then sinfull: And as Charity must be your rule, so your selfe must be the rule of your Charity; Look what you could wish to be done to you by others, doe but the same to others, you cannot be guilty of the breach of Charity: The maximes of Trafique are almost infinite; onely Charity (but ever inseparable from Justice) must make the application of them[.][24]

Charity is portrayed as the 'sure' and 'onely' rule, the 'Cynosure' or guiding star which guarantees the equity of financial transactions; it emanates from a properly rectified moral disposition—'as Charity must be your rule, so your selfe must be the rule of your Charity'. At the close of his analysis, Hall forges a familiar connection with questions of motive and intent:

> it is not the mere act of buying, or of not selling, that in it selfe is accused for unjust, but to buy, or not to sell, with an intention, and issue of oppressing others, and undue enriching themselves by a dearth. For what can be more unjust then for a man to indevor to raise himself by the affamishing of others?[25]

Hall, like Donne before him, attempts to fence in the messy circumstantial details of individual cases by appealing to the timeless precept of charitable intent. In the

---

[23] *Sermons*, 2.277.
[24] Hall, *Resolutions*, 12–13. Hall did not publish the *Resolutions* until 1649, but Brown (*Politics of Conscience*, 10) convincingly argues for Donne's familiarity with Hall's casuistical thought.
[25] Hall, *Resolutions*, 48.

second of two Lincoln's Inn sermons preached on Matthew 18:7, Donne traces the roots of this idea, whilst also recognizing some of its inherent fault-lines and risks. Drawing a contrast with the laws of 'ancient Rome', Donne observes that

> howsoever I say, various occasions may vary their Laws, adhere we to that Rule of the Law, which the Apostle prescribes, that we always make *Finem præcepti charitatem, The end of the commandment charity:* for, no Commandement, (no, not those of the first Table) is kept, if, upon pretence of keeping that Commandement, or of the service of God, I come to an uncharitable opinion of other men.[26]

Where Roman law is compromised by an excessive responsiveness to political and social 'occasions', the law of charity answers to God's eternal 'Commandement' alone. Donne's observation also reveals one of the main paradoxes of casuistical rhetoric: it attempts to counter the contingency of case-based reasoning with a language of permanence and metaphysical transparency. The sustaining ideal for this narrative is Christ, whose voluntary sacrifice represents the ultimate act of charity.[27] While articulating this ideal, however, Donne's sermon is disrupted by the possibility of moral dissimulation, equivocation—the mere 'pretence of keeping' God's commandments. This fear of duplicity and hidden motives is explored in much greater detail in *Biathanatos*.

While charity is universal and stable, serving 'the fix'd and permanent law of promoting God's glory', its vital function in casuistry arises from the notion that the contexts and circumstances of human actions are varied and potentially infinite.[28] William Perkins's *Hepieíkeia: or, a Treatise of Christian Equitie and Moderation* argues, for instance, that both equity and casuistry stem from our inability to 'foresee, or set downe all cases that may fall out'.[29] Therefore, 'when the case altereth, then must the discretion of the law-maker show itself'.[30] The appeal here is to 'the intent of the law' rather than its strict letter, and therefore also to the interpreter's discretion;[31] as William Ames further explains, 'Legall Iustice taken strictly, considereth the words just as they are written, but Equity considereth the End, scope and intent of the Law, and so hath more Law in it, then Legall Iustice, when taken strictly.'[32] The 'stiffe wickednesse' of literalism must be tempered by charitable latitude to avoid injustice. In practice, casuistical procedure is the mirror image of these precepts, prescribing due attention to the agent's intent and to the circumstances of the case. *Biathanatos* displays just such an attention to

---

[26] *Sermons*, 3.185–6 (the Scripture reference is to 1 Timothy 1:5).

[27] See Harald E. Braun and Edward Vallance, 'Introduction', *Renaissance Studies*, 23 (2009), 413–33 (414): 'Renaissance divines worked hard to embed and sustain the individual conscience as the locus of authoritative and objectively binding precepts.' In casuistical terminology, timeless precepts such as charity fall under the remit of 'synderesis'. As Gallagher (*Medusa's Gaze*, 8) notes, while 'synderesis' and its circumstantial adjudication are envisaged by casuistical thinkers as complementary, interpretive practice rarely sustains this fiction of timeless truth and authority.

[28] *Sermons*, 5.225.

[29] William Perkins, *HEPIEÍKEIA: or, a Treatise of Christian Equitie and Moderation* (1604), 10.

[30] Ibid.

[31] Ibid. 31.

[32] William Ames, *The Workes of the Faithfull and Reverend Minister of Christ, William Ames* (1643), 111 (Book 5, 'Of Iustice').

circumstantial detail: '[T]here is no externall act naturally Euill', Donne insists: 'Circumstances condition them [moral acts], and giue them theyr Nature' (120).

The discourse of casuistry, as we have seen, is frequently implicated in moral boundary disputes, and defenders of situational reasoning are fiercely protective of its status as a guarantor of just and godly Christian action. *Biathanatos* displays similar territorial instincts in its constant recourse to the rhetoric of charity, which at once invigorates and attenuates the complex dynamic of its casuistical negotiations. However, the vulnerability of Donne's hermeneutic system is adumbrated precisely at the points where its ethical norms are celebrated most enthusiastically, as in his claim '[t]hat Charity will recompence, and justify many excesses, which seeme vnnaturall, and irregular and enormous transportations' (132). Donne explicitly acknowledges cases where interpretive latitude may transport him beyond the boundaries of justifiable conduct. This is a crucial assertion, not least because it opens up a rupture in the fabric of casuistical thought, and thus potentially subverts the clean separation between charity and self-interest, good and evil intent, which he elsewhere affirms. Charity is initially seen to provide critical 'recompence' for such transgressions, reining in disruptive impulses and re-establishing familiar lines of demarcation. But a closer look at the language of casuistical deliberation proves destabilizing to this binary model at a more fundamental level. Rather than identifying two distinct zones of ethical conduct, one within the bounds of legitimacy, the other outside it, Donne sets up a third, and much more flexible perimeter, where 'Exception' becomes a rule of Christian life. In mounting his attack on Exodus 20:13, Donne explains that while an action can be 'within the Circuit of the Command, it may allso be within the Exception thereof. For though the Words be generall *Thou shalt not Kill*, we may kill beastes, Magistrates may kill Men' (116). This alternative moral territory falls under the jurisdiction of charity, but comes under increasing pressure as the argument of *Biathanatos* proceeds: just how far, Donne asks, can the perimeters of charitable exception-making be extended before the doctrinal foundations of his moral system are themselves called into question?

Donne's self-reflexive interrogation of the hermeneutics of charity is at its most acute in his treatment of Augustine, which comes to epitomize the weaknesses of casuistical procedure. Donne knows, of course, that any defence of suicide, however limited, will find a formidable opponent in Augustine. As he concedes in preparation for his first engagement with Augustine, 'from him are deriued allmost all the reasons of the others [i.e subsequent opponents of suicide], he writing purposely thereof, from the 17 to the 27 Chap: of his first Booke *De Ciuitate Dei*' (76–7). The majority of Donne's references to Augustine in *Biathanatos* are to the *City of God*; the detail of these quotations, and the contextual knowledge demonstrated by Donne's discussion, suggest that he encountered Book 1 of *City of God* directly and studied it in depth, while tracking down passages from other parts of the text through more cursory reading or through a patristic mediator. Interestingly, however, Donne's analysis begins not with an explication of Augustine's intellectual position on suicide, but with an assessment of his moral character and overall theological achievement:

[T]hough St *Aug:* for sharp insight, and conclusiue Iudgement, in exposition of places of Scripture, which he allways makes so liquid, and peruious, . . . hath scarse bene æquald therein, by any of all the writers of the Church of God . . . yet in practique Learning, and morall diuinity he was of so nice, and refind, and rigorous a conscyence (perchance to redeeme his former Licenciousnes, as it falls out often in such Convertites, to be extreamly zealous) that for our direction in actions of this Life, St *Hierome,* and some others may be thought sometymes fitter to adhere vnto, then St *Aug:* (77)

Donne's verdict on Augustine is breathtaking in its lack of charity, empathy, and sympathy, and shows complete disregard for the standards of judgement he has set himself in the preface to *Biathanatos.* A complement to his claim that Augustine was possessed of a 'most zealous and startling tendernes of Conscyence' (107), this portrait of the convert as priggish zealot could not be further from the hermeneutic philosophy that Donne so persistently advertises and defends in the rest of his text. The tonal dissonances created by Donne's approach are heightened by the fact that his argument consistently and provocatively draws attention to its own disingenuousness, both in the 'peremptory' judgement passed by one prominent 'Convertite' upon another, and in the strategic separation of exegesis and ethics—upon whose conjunction, as we have seen, the entire rhetorical strategy of *Biathanatos* is built. In Donne's characterization, Augustine manages to be erratic and dogmatic at the same time: a wide and generically diverse range of pronouncements on suicide is reduced to a biographical pathology—a desperate attempt 'to redeeme his former Licenciousnes'. Far from showing any interest in the occasion, circumstances, and motives that underlie Augustine's statements on 'selfe-homicide', as the rules of casuistical judgement would demand, Donne concentrates solely on discrediting his moral authority.

At a superficial level, the casuistical logic of Donne's discourse offers a solution by permitting him to revert to a hierarchical system of moral imperatives: once the primary objective—to demonstrate charity towards suicides—has been formulated, and the value of that objective reified, all other rhetorical strategies can be marshalled in its service.[33] Augustine can be attacked because he has proved himself to be an 'vncharitable Misinterpreter' of suicide. Yet this recourse offers cosmetic help at best: a sticking plaster is an insufficient remedy to the potential damage of Donne's poisonous casuistical infusion. The conspicuous viciousness of the 'means' deployed in Donne's attack on Augustine is bound to reflect on the quality of the 'end'; after all, what is the status of a charity-based argument whose first major casualty is charity itself? As Donne reminds us in his second sermon on Matthew 18:7, '*The end of the commandment is charity:* for, no Commandement, (no, not those of the first Table) is kept, if, upon pretence of keeping that Commandement, or of the service of God, I come to an uncharitable opinion of other men.'[34]

Donne's problematic engagement with the category of charitable intent manifests most starkly in his treatment of Augustine's texts. His approach is best

---

[33] See *Biathanatos,* 29, on the text's professed desire to promote 'a charitable interpretacion of theyr Action, who dye so'.

[34] *Sermons,* 3.185–6.

described as an escalating series of citational misrepresentations, ranging from mild cases of selective quotation to the active and deliberate distortion of Augustine's meaning. It is at this point also that the significance of Donne's formal and generic choices resurfaces: the complexities of motive and intent reveal themselves most acutely in casuistical works which allege, in Donne's words, 'clouds of witnesses'— those that are, at least in their structural features, more closely aligned with Roman traditions of casuistical thought. This enables contemporary theorists of casuistry to re-imagine the language of ethics in textual terms: Richard Eedes's critique of casuistical latitude, for instance, warns of evil 'glosses . . . [which] corrupt the text of truth'.[35] However, for Donne the principal use of these text-centred forms of casuistry is that they allow for a close and difficult calibration of moral and readerly intent. *Biathanatos* applies the same standards of judgement to the interpretation of laws as it does to the textual authorities that articulate and frame them. Charity is not simply about reading, it is about virtuous conduct, and thus Donne's interpretation of his authorities—charitable or otherwise—serves as a litmus test for the value of his discursive system more broadly. When he stretches and distorts his sources, in other words, this rhetorical stress test also puts pressure on the entire moral fabric of *Biathanatos*. The central dilemma of Donne's argument obtains at the level of ethics and interpretation alike, and thus restates the challenge of Pascal's *Provincial Letters* in a different key: how far can virtuous ends justify vicious means, and how far can the perimeter of meaning be extended before the normative substructure of Donne's charitable philosophy is permanently compromised?

In order properly to understand and contextualize Donne's treatment of Augustinian texts in *Biathanatos*, we need to make a brief excursus to the outer reaches of casuistical thought. The place where the moral limits of charitable intent and interpretation are tested most rigorously is in discussions of lying, deception, dissimulation, and equivocation. It should be noted from the outset that theorists and practitioners of casuistry in the period often conceive of these categories in textual terms, if for polemical reasons alone: thus, in the printed controversial exchanges between Bishop Morton and the Jesuit Robert Parsons, for instance, debates about political conformity and spiritual probity are fought out through contests over scholarly and hermeneutic practices. Deception and equivocation are identified with citational selectivity and manipulation, for instance, since these moral and textual vices equally involve the withholding of critical evidence—an analogy that Donne will come to exploit in *Biathanatos*.

Renaissance casuists' views on the moral status of lying and equivocation draw on the language of motive, interest, and intent we have already seen at work in *Biathanatos*. William Perkins's 1604 commentary on Galatians (the Pauline text from which Augustine derives his maxim 'Love, and do what you will') presents a usefully compact summary of issues which are analysed at much greater length in his *Discourse of Conscience* (1596), and which also inform the practical applications

---

[35] Richard Eedes, *A sermon of the difference of Good and Euill. Preached before Queene Elizabeth, at Whitehall in Lent. 1596*, in *Six learned and godly sermons preached some of them before the Kings Maiestie, some before Queene Elizabeth* (1604), sig. N4r.

presented in *The Whole Treatise of Cases of Conscience* (1606). Drawing on the Augustinian distinction between mendacious and fallacious statements, Perkins defines a lie, and its conceptual neighbours—'concealment', 'fayning' and 'deceit'—in the following terms:

> *A lie is when we speake contrarie to that we thinke with an intention to deceiue*. . . . [D]ifference must be put betwene a lie and *the concealement of a thing*, for it is one thing to speake against our knowledge, and another to speake that which we knowe. And concealments, if there be reasonable cause, and if it be not necessary for vs to reueale the thing concealed, are not vnlawfull. . . . [A] difference must be made between lying and *fayning*: which some call *simulation*: not *dissembling*, but rather *sembling*. And that is, when something is spoken not contrary, but beside, or diuers to that which we thinke. And this kind of fayning, if it be not to the preiudice of truth, against the glory of God, and the good of our neighbour, & some conuenient and reasonable cause, is not vnlawfull. . . . There is a kind of deceit called *dolus bonus*, that is, *a good deceit*. . . . Thus Physitians for their good, vse to deceiue the senses of their impotent patients.[36]

It is important to note that Perkins defines a lie *not* as the mere statement of an untruth, but as the malicious intent to mislead and deceive. This conviction is echoed, at the opposite end of the doctrinal spectrum, by the Jesuit Robert Parsons, who posits a related theory of moral culpability in response to Bishop Morton's attacks on Roman doctrine and practice: Parsons argues that without the 'intention or cupidity of deceauing, as *S. Augustines* wordes are', a lie can be re-classified as a mere 'dissimulation or fiction'.[37] As long as there is 'reasonable cause' and a charitable concern for 'the glory of God, and the good of our neighbour', in other words, the territorial distinctions between truth and lie, good and evil choices remain intact. In his commentary on Galatians, Perkins adds a further layer to this precarious rhetorical structure by elaborating on his final example, the *'good deceit'* of his 'Physitians'. There, moral integrity is predicated on 'a conformitie, and consent, betweene the tongue, and the minde'; while good motives obtain, this sustaining unity of thought and speech can be preserved, even in the case of the doctor whose 'tongue' belies what the 'minde' knows to be true.[38]

Throughout his text, Perkins works hard to suppress the idea that truth may reside not simply within the mind and intent of an individual moral agent, but may be constituted through a rather more complex trajectory of motive, act, and effect, in which multiple parties intervene. Parsons is a little more candid in acknowledging the complications of such a multilateral perspective, but equally quick to de-escalate its moral implications: 'it is no lye or fallacy at all, when a man speaketh that which in his owne sense is true, though it be false in the sense which the hearer conceiueth, so that the speaker doe not vtter those ambiguous words with intention

[36] William Perkins, *A commentarie or exposition, vpon the fiue first chapters of the Epistle to the Galatians* (1604), 62–4. The connections between equivocation and casuistry are analysed in Gallagher, *Medusa's Gaze*, 65–7, with reference to Perkins and Parsons.
[37] Robert Parsons, *A Treatise Tending to Mitigation towards Catholicke Subiectes in England* (1607), 397. On Parsons, see Michael L. Carrafiello, *Robert Parsons and English Catholicism* (London, 1998).
[38] Perkins, *Galatians*, 64.

to deceaue another, but only to conceale profitably some truth'.[39] One may note in passing the epistemological problems raised by Parsons's approach here: the idea of truth, rather than leading to a stable centre of ethical certainty, is revealed as a mere approximation, a constant process of re-negotiation which is itself subject to the shifting tides of circumstance. The truth in my 'owne sense' is responsive to context, determined by what is judged to be 'reasonable' or 'profitable' at any given time; often, this places it, in Perkins's ambiguous formulation, 'beside, or diuers to' known facts: moral negotiations do not yield a firm metaphysical footprint, but involve either a nervously evasive shuffle or the breathless pursuit of a moving target.

But the language of 'reasonable' causes and 'profitable' ends also raises questions of substantial ethical import. This is nowhere more apparent than in the vast doctrinal differences which separate Perkins's and Parsons's perspectives, and which illustrate the vulnerability of their intentionalist philosophies. It is clear, even on the most cursory inspection, that the Calvinist and the Jesuit subscribe to radically diverse notions of 'reason' or 'profit'; and at times it seems as though the rhetoric of good intent simply puts them in an endless aporetic loop of mutual recriminations. Parsons's text, speaking from the margins of the dominant cultural and religious discourse, betrays a greater sense of tonal dissonance in his treatment of intent. His views of 'reasonable cause' oscillate between charitable motive ('to stirre vp . . . love') and the drive to self-preservation, the tutiorist reflex 'to deliuer himselfe by concealing a truth only', rather than telling an outright lie.[40] Once again, this illuminates the unsettling flexibility of the terminological perimeter, and the wider problematic of a casuistical ethics in which the ability to create a rhetoric of definitional certainty is at once crucial to the validation of an ideology and always open to subversive re-interpretation. In this sense, casuistry also mirrors the deep structure of early modern religious discourse as delineated in recent scholarship. Anthony Milton has drawn our attention to the ways in which controversies of the period depend not so much on a stable core of doctrinal convictions as on the skilful and occasion-centred manipulations of polemical labels and stereotypes.[41] The intent-based language of casuistry operates within a similar atmosphere of terminological fluctuation, where the assessment of a moral act is predicated on the ascription—or, more complexly, the (retrospective) re-description—of motive. One person's 'reasonable cause' is an unforgivable transgression to another; the language of charity can cover a multitude of sins.

In the quest for definitional supremacy, Renaissance controversialists were able to draw on a vast and powerful arsenal of Augustinian examples. The Donatist Petilianus, as we have seen, was painfully aware of Augustine's polemical expertise—his ability to hide under a 'veil of goodness', 'wage war with kisses', and

[39] Parsons, *Mitigation*, 397; see Gallagher, *Medusa's Gaze*, 66.

[40] Equivocation emerges as a major social and ideological concern in the sixteenth century around the issue of missionary priests from the Continent; this is the background against which Morton constructs his anti-Roman argument.

[41] Milton, *Catholic and Reformed, passim.*

appropriate key labels such as 'peace and unity' for his own cause.[42] Carol Quillen remarks that Augustine's writings 'reveal him carefully redefining words and drawing the relationships among concepts to create a language for talking about religion the very terms of which render heretical discourse difficult'.[43] In the *City of God*, the entire first chapter of Book 10 is devoted to the re-definition of key words such as 'cultus', 'religio', and 'pietas', as Augustine attempts to wrest conceptual control from his 'pagan' opponents.

Donne's representation of Augustine in *Biathanatos* participates in the casuistical dispute over the relative status of lying, feigning, re-definition, and dissimulation. The textual practices at work in Donne's treatise echo discussions of interpretive equivocation and concealment in the controversial exchanges between Morton and Parsons. Donne's citational manipulations pit the truth 'in his owne sense'— directed by an increasingly brittle plea for charity—against the truth as conceived by Augustine. The resulting impasse calls into question not simply the ethos of Donne's persona, but the very criteria on which moral judgement is founded.

The maxim '*Dilige & dic quod voles*' underlies Donne's negotiations with Augustine in *Biathanatos*, and the treatise as a whole charts an increasingly flagrant series of textual 'excesses . . . and transportations', which strategically problematize the philosophy of charity that frames Donne's argument. As a starting-point, and as an example of a relatively mild infraction, we might turn to a quotation from *City of God*, Book 1, chapter 26, which Donne knew in detail and likely consulted in the original. There, he consolidates the terminology of charitable 'disinterest' by confronting a core question: are there any conditions in which suicide may be regarded as 'Lawfull'? Donne argues that

> neyther to auoyd occasion of Sinne, nor for any other cause wherein my selfe am meerly or principally interested, I may do this act. . . . And so, as S* Aug:, we with as much earnestnesse say *Hoc asserimus, hoc dicimus, hoc omnibus modis approbamus, That neither to auoyd temporall troubles, nor to remoue from others occasion of Sinne, nor to punish our owne past Sinnes, nor to preuent future, nor in a desire of the next Life* (where these considerations are only or principally) *it cannot be Lawfull for any man to kill himselfe*. But neyther S* Aug. nor we denye but that if there be cases, wherein the party is disinterested, and onely, or primarily the glory of God is respected and aduanced, it may be Lawfull[.] (77)

Donne's main point is that suicide can be permitted if it does not serve selfish ends, but is motivated by a religious cause: when 'the glory of God is respected and aduanced'. He will go on to build towards the issue of martyrdom via a series of case studies which implement the principles set out here; the first of these alone, a rather suspect excursus on simony—'*euer do it, with an Intention to do it so, as God knowes it may be done*'—would be enough to raise doubts about the tonal stability of Donne's discourse. The treatment of Augustine's quotation raises additional concerns. First of all, Donne misrepresents what one might classify as Augustine's

[42] *Contra Litteras Petiliani* 2.17 (*PL* 43.270); see above, p. 12.
[43] Quillen, *Rereading the Renaissance*, 56.

illocutionary intent. *City of God* 1.26 focuses on a prescriptive warning against self-inflicted death; its discussion of martyrdom concedes that there might be some exceptions to the general law against suicide, but it places much stricter limitations on these exceptions than Donne's argument admits. Augustine, in a manoeuvre which was itself to prove highly controversial, condones suicide only when the agent is manifestly moved by divine inspiration. This is why he concludes his chapter with such a firm caution against suicide: martyrs may be exemplary in their devotion, but the manner of their death cannot be separated from the divine intervention which inspired it; this intervention cannot be provoked nor should the act itself therefore be emulated. The purpose of Augustine's passage, in other words, is not to highlight cases where 'selfe-homicide . . . may be Lawfull', but to address the majority of cases when it is definitely otherwise. Donne is fully aware of this fact—he goes on to describe the idea of divine inspiration as a cowardly 'retrait' ('*S: Aug:* was euer prouided for this retrait, that it was a speciall inspiration', 104)—but chooses to suppress it because acknowledging Augustine's tougher strictures simply does not serve the interest of his argument. As Donne prepares for a more generous definition of 'disinterested' suicide, Augustine's categorical pronouncements are radically adapted to Donne's rhetorical agenda.

This is a strategy which Donne brings to bear on many Augustinian passages in *Biathanatos*, especially those that derive from intermediary sources. An Augustinian quotation gleaned from Lombard's *Sentences*, which Lombard traces back to Augustine's *Homilies on John's Epistle to the Parthi* (6.1), illuminates yet another facet of charity: 'For *P: Lombard*', Donne notes, 'allowing Charity this growth *Beginning, Proficient, Perfect, More, and most Perfect* he cites *St Aug:* who calls *That perfect Charity to be redy to dy for another*' (125). In *Biathanatos*, this extract prepares for a praise of martyrs both past and present; in Augustine, by contrast, it serves as an illustration of divine love, manifested in Christ's supreme—and *unique*—sacrifice: it is another demonstration of Augustine's conviction that Christ's death cannot, and should not, be imitated. The fact of textual mediation may serve as an excuse in this case, since Lombard supplies only the snippet that Donne quotes; however, in the broader context of Donne's citational tactics, his failure to follow up the reference is, if not deliberate and functional, then certainly convenient, and provides a further clue that the scholarly means and techniques deployed in the text are firmly subordinated to a larger polemical end.

Donne's most egregious misuse of the vocabulary of charity comes in the conclusion of his treatise, where he interprets Augustine's 'double love' command ('cherish God and neighbour') as inviting a consideration of suicide:

> But it is well noted by *Alcuinus,* (and I think from *St Aug:*) *That though there be foure things which we must Loue, Yet there is no precept giuen vpon any more then two, God, and our Neighbor.* So that the other, which conscerns our selues, may be pretermitted in some occasions. (144)

Donne's use of the term 'pretermit' casts a sideways glance at the citational manipulations at work in this passage. Neither Alcuin's twenty-third epistle, to which Donne refers, nor Augustine himself, read the absence of a specific injunction to self-love as a potential justification for suicide; both authors articulate the imperative of charity and devotion, and are in no way concerned with the circumstances which might validate the neglect ('pretermission') of self-preservation. Augustine simply posits at *De Doctrina Christiana* 3.10.16 that love is 'the impulse of one's mind to enjoy God on his own account and to enjoy oneself and one's neighbour on account of God'.[44] In both cases, therefore, context reveals Donne's interpretation to be a deliberate misrepresentation of the writer's intent. But Donne's argument from omission (the second meaning of the verb 'pretermit') also has a secondary function in that it draws attention to a discursive strategy which is characteristic of his treatise as a whole: the tendency to put rhetorical pressure on terms that are hidden, implied, unstated, or—quite simply—absent from the texts he alleges in favour of his position. Like the category of intent itself, the language of omission can initiate a process of infinite hermeneutic regress, as Donne's exegesis withdraws from argument and proof to dissimulation, concealment, and even deceit.

Donne's tendency to blur Augustine's distinctions, and to elide crucial differences with his own argument, continues with a passage from Book 4, chapter 13 of Augustine's *On the Trinity*. There, Augustine explains the manner of Christ's death, noting that

> it was not through punishment of sin that he came to the death of the flesh, because he did not leave life against his will, *but because he willed, when he willed, as he willed.* For because he is so commingled [with the flesh] by the Word of God as to be one, he says: I have power to lay down my life, and I have power to take it again. No man takes it from me, but I lay down my life that I might take it again.[45]

Donne's perspective on this extract initially looks innocent enough. 'To expresse the abundant, and overflowing charity of our *Sauyour,*' Donne argues 'all words are defectiue . . . *His soule* sayth *St Aug: did not leaue his body constraynd, but because he would, and when he would, and how he would*' (129). This is a fairly straightforward translation of Augustine's Latin original: 'non . . . invitus sed quia voluit, quando voluit, quomodo voluit'. The inference Donne draws from the text, however, could not be further from Augustine's intent. Donne relies on the assumption that 'the act of our *B: Sauyor* . . . was the same as *Sauls* and these Martyrs actuall furtherance' (130)—and could thus conceivably be used as a justification for suicide. By contrast, Augustine's entire argument pivots on the uniqueness of Christ's case: because he is one with God and—unlike humanity—free from sin, the otherwise illegitimate act of offering 'violence' to oneself is converted into a charitable sacrifice. Once again, Augustine's reasoning depends on critical distinctions that Donne's text wilfully ignores.

---

[44] *De Doctrina Christiana* 3.10.16: 'Charitatem voco motum animi ad fruendum Deo propter ipsum et se atque proximo propter deum' (*PL* 34.72); see also *De Doctrina Christiana* 1.27.38, and Dany Dideberg, 'Caritas', in *Augustinus-Lexikon*, ed. Cornelius Mayer et al., 5 vols. (Basel, 1986–), 1.730–43 (738, 740, and 734–5 for further examples).
[45] *De Trinitate* 4.13 (*PL* 42.898).

However, the most blatant example of citational equivocation is presented by the final case study of *Biathanatos*, as Donne invokes Augustine's testimony in support of the notion that some cases of suicide manifest 'greatnesse of Mind'. Donne's Augustinian case study centres on one Cleombrotus, whose suicide was inspired by Plato's remarks on the immortality of the soul in *Phaedo*:

> For *S^t. August:* who argues as earnestly as *Aristotle,* that this is not greatnesse of Mind, Confesseth yet, that in *Cleombrotus* it was: who onely vpon reading *Plato* his *Phedo,* killd himselfe; for sayth *St Aug: where no calamity vrged him, No Crime, either true, or imputed, nothing but greatnes of mind moued him to apprehend Death, and to breake the sweet bands of this Life.* And though he ad *that it was done rather Magne, then bene* yet by this, that which we seeke now is in Confession, that sometymes there is in this act Greatnesse and Corage. (142)

The detail of Donne's account suggests that he consulted Cleombrotus's case in the original, rather than culling the quotation from an intermediary source (the episode does not feature prominently in the Augustinian anthologies I have examined). This extract from *City of God* 1.22 is one of half a dozen passages taken from the section of Augustine's work that Donne has identified as critical to the issue of suicide, and which he most likely consulted directly: chapters 17–27 of Book 1. Donne's phrase 'that which we seeke now is in Confession' is perhaps a first indication that his interpretation of Augustine is overdetermined by a particular agenda and hermeneutic perspective; even a superficial reading of the case shows that, while Augustine attempts to muster some Christian sympathy, he is far from condoning Cleombrotus's actions. First of all, Donne's version of *City of God* 1.22 completely sidesteps the scope of the original argument, which clearly privileges prescription over description: Augustine states unequivocally of Cleombrotus's case that 'we are not now asking whether this was done but whether it should have been done'. (The answer, unsurprisingly, is 'no'.) But perhaps more crucially, having conceded in the first instance that Cleombrotus's act may have been regarded by some as an expression of magnanimity, Augustine immediately proceeds to complicate this position and subverts the entire moral foundation upon which the idea of 'greatness' is based:

> But perhaps those who have perpetrated this crime upon themselves, though not to be praised for the soundness of their wisdom, are nonetheless admired for their greatness of soul? . . . Plato himself, whom he had read, could have told him that he [Cleombrotus] had acted greatly rather than well. For Plato, of all people, would have been the first to act in the same way had he not, with that mind with which he had seen the soul's immortality, also perceived that this should not be done: and should, indeed, be forbidden.[46]

Augustine's argument reinforces the contrast between greatness—associated throughout the text with 'pagan' culture—on the one hand, and true Christian wisdom on the other. R. W. Dyson, the Cambridge editor of the *City of God*, goes

---

[46] Augustine, *The City of God against the Pagans,* ed. and trans. R. W. Dyson (Cambridge, 1998), 34–5.

so far as to place the phrase 'greatness of soul' in inverted commas in order to indicate the dismissive force of Augustine's rhetoric.[47] Magnanimity may be a foundational virtue of classical civilizations, but it has little moral traction in a Christian universe. The most crucial aspect of Cleombrotus's example, however, is the sense of bitter irony it confers on Donne's own interpretive practices in *Biathanatos*: Augustine insists that Cleombrotus's fate is decided through a misreading of Plato; had he listened more carefully to Plato's text, he might not have been so quick to put his soul in mortal peril. Donne, in extolling 'magnanimity', misses the point of Augustine's text in equally dramatic fashion.

This last example of Augustinian misrepresentation is arresting not least because it sets up strong resonances with the rhetoric of casuistical equivocation at work in the Parsons–Morton controversy. Parsons's *Treatise Tending Towards Mitigation*— a polemical reply to Bishop Morton published in 1607—concludes its defence of James's Catholic subjects with a series of chapters detailing examples of Protestant equivocation.[48] As a representative parallel to Donne's treatment of *City of God* 1.22, we might look at Parsons's discussion of John Jewel's citational practices in the 1560s, and more particularly at his use of Augustine's treatise *On the Good of Widowhood*. Parsons builds on the Augustinian doctrine, articulated earlier in his treatise, that lies and equivocations are constituted through the considered and deliberate intent to deceive and mislead, against one's better knowledge and judgement. To consolidate the case against Jewel, Parsons starts by eliminating other possible causes of textual misrepresentation, such as ignorance: Jewel, he explains, was present at a controversial disputation with the Catholic theologians Ridley and Latimer in 1554 and has been presented with the patristic evidence that speaks on the Roman side. In Parsons's eyes, Jewel has no factual excuse for claiming that the Catholics will not be able to allege 'one Father, one Doctor' in support of their cause—as he had famously done in his 'Challenge Sermon'; his rhetoric must, therefore, stem from a malicious desire to bring the opposition into disrepute. In the case of Augustine's *On the Good of Widowhood*, Parsons first asserts that 'the whole drifte of this holy Father in that place, is directly against *M. Iewell*', but then adduces more specific evidence. Jewel had claimed that 'it was no synne to marrie after vowes made of Chastity', drawing support from Augustine's treatise;[49] Parsons exposes the tendentiousness of Jewel's quotations through close analysis, showing how Jewel consistently suppresses inconvenient passages from Augustine's text:

[47] *City of God*, 35. Augustine owes this anecdote to Cicero's *Tusculan Disputations* 1.34.84.

[48] On Walton's claim that Morton sought Donne's scholarly services shortly after being presented to the Deanery of Gloucester in June 1607, see Bald, *Life*, 205; for Donne's likely collaboration on Morton's *A Catholicke Appeale* (1609), see ibid. 210–12. It is intriguing to note that this research work for Morton coincides chronologically with the composition of *Biathanatos*. On the composition date of Donne's treatise, see Ernest W. Sullivan, 'The Genesis and Transmission of Donne's *Biathanatos*', *The Library*, 5 (1976), 52–72: 'Donne finished the holograph of *Biathanatos* between 1607 and the summer of 1609' (52). On the Canterbury manuscript of *Biathanatos*, see Peter Beal, *In Praise of Scribes: Manuscripts and their Makers in Seventeenth-Century England* (Oxford, 1998), ch. 2.

[49] Parsons, *Mitigation*, 504–5 ('Six Examples of *Maister Iewels* particuler Equiuocation').

So then heere is great wilfull falsity, to alleadge *S. Augustine* as though he fauoured the marriages of Votaries, whereas throughout this whole booke he doth purposely impugne the same, yea that which is more, in the very next immediate wordes that follow in the same sentence before alleadged by *M. Iewell S. Augustines* expresse wordes do ouerthrow all that is alleadged for Votaries.... [L]et the Reader consider what Equiuocation this might be in *M. Iewell,* and whether it be possible to imagine that he was so occupyed, and distracted, as he did read the one halfe of the sentence, and not the other, or that he was so simple as he did not vnderstand, what was the whole drifte, and argument of *S. Augustine* in that booke: and if he did, and yet alledged him to the contrary, yow see what ensueth.[50]

Jewel's citational selectivity is redefined by Parsons as unlawful equivocation; by ignoring the drift of Augustine's argument and suppressing evidence that blatantly contradicts his thesis, Jewel has made himself vulnerable to a more general attack on his scholarly and moral integrity: '*S. Augustines* expresse wordes do ouerthrow all that is alleadged for Votaries'. Donne's own descent into sharp textual practice is a mirror image of the flaws Parsons exposes here: Donne, too, distorts the scope and intent of Augustine's reasoning by omitting information which qualifies some of his assertions and flatly undermines others. Parsons's verdict on Jewel also applies to Donne's treatment of *City of God* 1.22: 'in the very next immediate wordes that follow in the same sentence before alleadged' by Donne, '*S. Augustines* expresse wordes do ouerthrow all that is alleadged'—through a crushing dismissal, as we have seen, of the very idea of 'magnanimity' at a later point in the same chapter. Donne rightly attributes to Augustine the notion that Cleombrotus acted '*through greatnes of mind*',[51] but it is hard to see how he could have missed Augustine's clear prescription, only a few lines on, that 'this should not be done: and should, indeed, be forbidden'.[52]

There is, however, a crucial difference between Jewel's and Donne's citational practices. Unlike Jewel, Donne persistently draws attention to his textual procedures. His manipulations and intertextual misprisions are made conspicuous, and thus encourage reflection on the central premise of *Biathanatos*, '[t]hat Charity will recompence, and iustify many excesses, which seeme vnnaturall, and irregular and enormous transportations' (132). The escalation of Donne's interpretive transgressions provokes suspicions of special pleading, and their distorting effect ultimately undermines the reader's faith in the integrity of the author's motives. Donne's infractions originate in the system of hermeneutic latitude on which casuistical negotiations are predicated. While recognizing the usefulness of extending or restricting the scope of the law, and departing from the letter to fulfil its spirit, casuistical commentators also expressed some nervousness about the possibility of controlling the interpretive freedoms offered by this approach. Richard Eedes's *Sermon of the difference of Good and Euill*, preached to the queen in Lent 1596, for instance, notes 'how many sleights this witlesse wittie, and learnedly vnlearned age hath deuised to make the rules of good and euill like that *leaden rule of Lesbia,*

---

[50] Parsons, 505.   [51] *Biathanatos*, 142.   [52] *City of God* 1.22.

pliable to purposes, and to serue turnes . . . how many shadowes vngodlinesse hath found to shroud it selfe vnder the law of God'.[53] Donne's *Biathanatos* bends the leaden rule of exegesis to the point where such textual infractions begin to cast a shadow over his charitable protestations. His discourse thus becomes a textbook example of Hall's casuistical caution: 'take good heed that your heart beguile you not in mis-applications; for we are naturally too apt out of our self-love to flatter our selves with faire glozes of bad intentions; and rather to draw the rule to us, then our selves to the rule'.[54] Donne himself remarks on the slippery and uncertain relations between charity and self-interest in a sermon preached for the commemoration of Lady Danvers on 1 July 1627. Once again, the theme is suicide, but two decades after the composition of *Biathanatos* Donne takes a very different view both on Christ's death and man's 'desire' to leave the world behind:

> If we could wish our owne *death*, as innocently, as harmlesly, as they did the day of *Iudgement*, if no ill *circumstances* in us, did *vitiate* our desire of *death*, if there were no *dead flies in this oyntment* (as *Salomon* speakes) if we had not, at least, a *collaterall* respect, (if not a *direct*, and *principall*) to our owne *ease*, from the incumbrances, and grievances, and annoyances of this world, certainly wee might safely desire, piously wish, religiously pray for our owne *death*. But it is hard, verie hard to devest those circumstances that infect it. For if I pretend to desire *death*, meerly for the fruition of the *glorie*, of the sight of *God*; I must remember, that my *Saviour* desir'd that *glorie*, and yet staid his time for it. If I pretend to desire *death*, that I might see no more *sinne*, heare no more blasphemies from *others*, it may be I may do more good to *others*, than I shall take harme by *others*, if I live. If I would die, that I might be at an end of *temptations*, in my selfe, yet, I might lose some of that glory, which I shall have in Heaven, by resisting another yeeres tentation, if I died now.[55]

Yet again, Donne's anxieties about the medicinal value of martyrdom—the '*dead flies*' in the ointment of charity—converge around questions of self-interest. In his sermon for Lady Danvers, he is deeply sceptical about the possibility of truly selfless moral action; purity of motive appears inevitably and fundamentally compromised by 'a *collaterall* respect, (if not a *direct*, and *principall*) to our owne ease'. This is the core dilemma which *Biathanatos* articulates through its suspect citational practices. There, the rhetoric of charity, as we have seen, may aspire to metaphysical transparency and inviolability, but in the murky regions of Donne's intertextual manipulations, the language of charitable latitude acquires a doubtful kind of opacity. Donne's character assassination of Augustine and the subsequent attack on his textual legacy do not inspire confidence in the accuracy of his moral compass; at times, the course of his argument on suicide seems openly directed by the circumstantial modulations of expediency rather than by a staunch commitment to 'a charitable interpretacion of theyr Action, who dye so'. This is not the firm voice of spiritual resolve, but a language of mixed motives which can come dangerously close to Jesuit caricatures of the lax conscience. In Richard Eedes's

---

[53] Eedes, sigs. N3v–N4r. See Gallagher, *Medusa's Gaze*, 148.
[54] Hall, *Resolutions*, 14.   [55] *Sermons*, 8.79.

formulation, the wavering soul is 'glad to be deceiued with an *euill opinion of good*' so that it may 'deceiue' itself '*with a good opinion of euill*'.[56]

In *Biathanatos*, Donne explores the worryingly porous boundary between '*good*' and '*euill*'; he does so chiefly by impersonating textual and moral practices which his next prose treatise, *Pseudo-martyr*, will condemn unequivocally: hermeneutic concealment, dissimulation, and, above all, the 'peremptory' direction of charitable intent in the face of scandalous scholarly infractions. 'Motive', in *Biathanatos*, cannot ultimately separate itself from the vagaries of context and occasion ('those circumstances that infect it'), and the recourse to a stable set of core precepts—here crystallized by the idea of charity—rarely provides a reliable cure. It is instructive, in this regard, to conclude with a brief look at the remedy suggested by Donne in a sermon preached at St Paul's more than a decade after the completion of *Biathanatos*, on 13 October 1622. Those who suffer from a doubting or scrupulous conscience should 'labour to recover the conscience, and devest it of those scruples, by *their* advise, whom God hath indued with knowledge, and power, for that purpose'.[57] Donne argues for the possibility of rectifying the conscience, but instead of asking the congregation to search their souls for guiding moral principles, he redirects them to an external source of counsel. Although he is careful to distinguish the guidance provided by Protestant ministers from the tyrannical influence of a Catholic confessor, Donne's reluctance to draw on the resources of the individual conscience is nevertheless suggestive.

In this chapter, I have argued that *Biathanatos* self-consciously questions the ethics of charitable intent; in the process, it also examines the epistemological basis on which the categories of conscience and discreet judgement are founded. The result of Donne's deliberations is neither scepticism nor relativism, but the definitional isolation of a fraught moral category—charity—which would be re-deployed and re-complicated in a variety of polemical and political contexts throughout his career.

To state this is not to sidestep a weightier judgement on the work's purpose and scope, but to take a clear-eyed view of the kinds of conclusions that *Biathanatos* admits and those it actively forestalls. Donne's treatise on suicide is at once the most probing discussion of the fundamental terms of his thought—discretion, decorum, and intent—and a highly occasional text, whose insistence on case, circumstance, and context limits opportunities for extrapolation and generalization. At the risk of frivolity, we might describe *Biathanatos* as a serious exercise in moral and hermeneutic calisthenics. This is a text concerned at every level with the activity of stretching and expanding: in a crucial and under-appreciated sense, *Biathanatos* flexes its rhetorical muscles in preparation for the polemical battle over martyrdom and suicide which informs *Pseudo-martyr*. In his discussion of 'selfe-homicide', Donne experiments with, and at times inhabits, positions he will summarily refute in his role as a professional controversialist in 1610. The systematic attack on Augustine's character and textual legacy is crucial to this process of discursive over-

---

[56] Eedes, sig. O4v.   [57] *Sermons*, 4.222.

extension, which moves far beyond the conventional boundaries of polemical training as its author limbers up for the challenges of *Pseudo-martyr*.

Biathanatos is not simply an example of an argument 'in utramque partem'; it is a thought experiment which sees Donne venture to the outer reaches of his deepest convictions, where Augustine, his most revered authority and tutelary spirit, emerges as the ultimate enemy and where the rhetoric of Jesuitical equivocation can be his best friend. It maps out a series of preparatory steps to anticipate controversial attack by the Roman opposition in *Pseudo-martyr*, at precisely the time when Donne was also working as a professional polemicist for Bishop Morton; in this sense, *Biathanatos* is a thoroughly occasional work, whose pronouncements on theology and ethics are not easily mapped onto the rest of Donne's *oeuvre*. Yet at the same time, it is precisely in this insistence on the situational, circumstantial, and perspectival aspects of reading and writing that the broader philosophical implications of the text reveal themselves most acutely. It is a critical commonplace to observe that Donne's works are firmly rooted in their time and place, that they are endlessly attentive to the rules of rhetorical decorum. The sermons present the clearest examples of such contextual embeddedness, tailored as they are to specific audiences, preaching venues, and liturgical contexts. In the *Songs and Sonets*, the same preoccupations are readily felt; rather than chasing a timeless Platonic ideal, Donne's love poems are vigorously situational: snapshots of relationships which are either on the cusp of change, or anticipate, analyse, and seek to come to terms with its effects.[58]

Less well articulated in scholarly discussion is the sense that Donne's concern with context and circumstance extends into the deep structures of his thought; it is no accident that the two early modern discourses which shape Donne's approach to emotional, moral, legal, and theological problems—casuistry and equity—are devoted, above all, to the complex mechanisms by which individual circumstances affect and modify universal laws. Donne is preoccupied with ideas of interpretive latitude and discretionary judgement, with the ways in which a specific case impacts on the application of global principles and precepts. In *Biathanatos*—to return to the idea of intellectual calisthenics—this process of accommodation and adjudication is imagined as a stretching and extension of legal boundaries in the interests of particular justice: Donne deliberately pushes too far and provokes a collision of legitimate liberties with licentious infractions. At the simplest level, Donne's text acknowledges the fact of change—personal, situational, and historical. As an earlier Continental theorist of equity, Jean Gerson, observed with some trepidation, 'the diversity of human temperament is incomprehensible—not just in several men, but in one and the same man—and not, I say, in different years or months or weeks, but in days, hours, and moments'.[59] But the practice of extending moral perimeters becomes most fraught not in the midst of fluctuating circumstances but when it

---

[58] This concern with situation and emotional occasion also finds expression in Donne's generic choices, such as his predilection for valediction poems and aubade forms.

[59] Cited in Thomas N. Tentler, *Sin and Confession on the Eve of the Reformation* (Princeton, 1977), 159.

impinges on the timeless categories which legitimize and contain such situational negotiations—most notably, as we have seen, in the case of Augustinian charity. As Donne explores the double-edged assertion that charity can 'cover a multitude of sins', and exploits its authority to justify an escalating series of interpretive 'excesses' and 'transportations', he ultimately questions his own ability to draw clear lines of distinction between acts that are truly 'disinterested' and those that are merely expedient and convenient. The problem is, of course, that we rarely have palpable proof to distinguish between these two states of mind: Donne insists, both in the sermon to the Virginia Company and in the commemoration of Lady Danvers, on the difficulty of separating 'collaterall' or 'principall' elements of self-interest. More than anything else, perhaps, *Biathanatos* draws out the subversive consequences arising from this opacity of motive and thus accentuates preoccupations that arise in less explicit form in Donne's other works. The *Songs and Sonets*, for instance, despite unfolding a poetics of love that is based on circumstance and change, seek a similar kind of stability in constancy of motive and commitment. 'The Good-Morrow' gives expression to this desire in its most idealistic form when it imagines the physical manifestation of true devotion: 'My face in thine eye, thine in mine appeares,/And true plaine hearts doe in the faces rest'.[60] 'Twicknam Garden', by contrast, is just as energetic in denying this possibility: 'Alas, hearts do not in eyes in shine,/Nor can you more judge womans thoughts by teares,/Then by her shadow, what she weares.'[61]

Biathanatos, the most supremely occasional of Donne's texts, thus spells out a fundamental difficulty in his occasion-centred method of writing and thought. Casuistical reasoning is built on the discretionary judgements of its practitioners; as recent scholarship has demonstrated, the discretion that characterizes Donne's negotiation of case theology is a vital building block of his politics, ethics, and theology. The lasting value of *Biathanatos* lies in its careful interrogation of the epistemological and moral frame which holds up these principled and contextually sensitive modes of decorous judgement. Donne's treatment of Augustinian charity leads us back to a conscience whose workings are opaque and unaccountable, which struggles to banish self-interest, and which sometimes barely seems to know itself at all. These are the problematic parameters Donne sets for himself in his treatise of 'selfe-homicide'. When he mounts the pulpit at Lincoln's Inn for the first time, almost ten years later, his sermons still struggle to digest the implications of this casuistical deconstruction. Preaching to an audience of lawyers, Donne revisits the difficult process of adjudicating between occasion and principle, case and law, and confronts the challenge of evolving a set of interpretive responses which are at once transparent and contextually self-aware, and sensitive to the specific contexts and needs of his congregation. It is to this new Augustinian setting that I now turn.

[60] 'The Good-Morrow', ll. 15–16.   [61] 'Twicknam Garden', ll. 23–5.

5

'Medicinall Concoctions'
Equity and Charity in the Lincoln's Inn Sermons

Chapter 4 examined the interrelations of charity and casuistry in *Biathanatos*. In Donne's treatise on 'selfe-homicide', charitable interpretation emerged as a complex religio-ethical concept which both facilitated and problematized the mechanisms of casuistical enquiry. Donne's sermons continue this preoccupation with charity in a variety of contexts; one of the most significant applications can be found in a set of Lincoln's Inn sermons, preached around 1620, which focus on the idea of judgement. *Biathanatos*, as we have seen, meditates extensively on the motives of casuistical judgement; it complicates the concept of charitable discretion by exploring the outer perimeters of mixed motives and collateral self-interest. Donne's Lincoln's Inn sermons transpose these concerns into a different key, exploring the political and legal dimensions of judicial (or judicious) reasoning. Intention still looms large in these discussions, and charity even larger. But charity proves an especially useful thinking tool in the Lincoln's Inn period because its processes overlap with a legal term that every member of his audience would have known: the controversial and much contested notion of equity, or legal discretion. The language of equity in turn recalls the discourses of conscience anatomized in *Biathanatos*. Some courts of law, especially Chancery and Requests, came to be known as courts of conscience; and in trying to justify the revisiting of a judgement at common law in Chancery, for instance, Lord Chancellor Ellesmere argued that his concern was not with the judgement itself, but 'with the hard conscience of the party'.[1] Conscientious interpretation, then, remains a persistent concern for Donne, but the Lincoln's Inn sermons examine such issues of motive and intent in the more public forum of equity.

Some brief remarks on methodology are needed before we proceed to an analysis of Donne's texts. The interpretive challenges and conflicts articulated in the Lincoln's Inn sermons emerge primarily from the fraught analogical relations between equity and charity. This is by no means an unfamiliar phenomenon: the tendency to think through an issue by analogizing it with something else— explaining the intricacies of love's constancy by recourse to a pair of compasses, for instance—is a recurrent one in Donne's poems.[2] One of the central contentions

---

[1] Cited in J. H. Baker, 'The Common Lawyers and Chancery', in *The Legal Profession and the Common Law: Historical Essays* (London, 1986), 205–29 (214).
[2] 'A Valediction forbidding mourning', ll. 25–36.

of this chapter is that this habit of thought persists in Donne's preaching: that his sermons mobilize contextual knowledge in particular ways, and therefore demand a particular kind of analogical, or inter-disciplinary, approach from us. One way of putting this would be to say that what they ask for is not so much a cross-disciplinary as a criss-cross disciplinary methodology: that when we try to analyse and evaluate Donne's theological, political, and philosophical positions in the sermons, we need to take account of the fact that his thoughts often emerge by thinking across and between a variety of discourses, rather than about any given issue in isolation.

The case study that I have chosen here is intended to clarify this approach. Equity places Donne's performance in the sphere of technical legal debate, but also puts it in touch with the politics of the law—the relative claims of common law and the king's prerogative justice were subject to intense public debate during James's reign.[3] Charity is a principle of Christian conduct, but was also deployed, as we will see, as a powerful polemical tool in early seventeenth-century controversy: an insistence on impartiality, tolerance, and moderation frequently served to discredit opposing views as partisan and narrowly factional. What equity and charity have in common, however, is a shared set of interpretive processes. Both terms inscribe hermeneutic strategies that revolve around the relationship between particulars and universals, letter and spirit, expression and intent; all of these concepts are crucial to the processes of secular and divine judgement discussed in Donne's Lincoln's Inn sermons. The flexible relations between charity and equity help to illuminate the complexities of moral and political decision-making; even more importantly, however, they impact on the ways in which Donne's own performance can be judged by showing how polemical arguments are constructed, articulated, resisted, or deflected. It is in the *analogy* between these two modes of judgement—in the parallels, similarities, and contrasts between equity and charity—that Donne's own rhetorical position begins to take shape. My main case study, Donne's sermon on Genesis 18:25, illuminates habits of thought that operate throughout his Lincoln's Inn preaching: a persistent interest in exegetical processes of judgement and interpretation and the ways in which they can acquire or resist polemical significance; a concern with the legal concept of equity and its significance for contemporary debates about the nature of prerogative justice and its

---

[3] Recent work on Donne's Lincoln's Inn sermons includes Shami, *Controversy*; Emma Rhatigan, 'Knees and Elephants: John Donne Preaches Ceremonial Conformity', *John Donne Journal*, 23 (2004), 185–213; Rhatigan, 'John Donne's Lincoln's Inn Sermons' (unpublished D.Phil. dissertation, Oxford, 2006); Hugh Adlington, 'The Preacher's Plea: Juridical Influence in John Donne's Sermons, 1618–1623', *Prose Studies*, 26 (2003), 344–56. The relations between law and literature in the early modern period are now the subject of much scholarly interest. For an overview of recent developments in this field, see Erica Sheen and Lorna Hutson (eds.), *Literature, Politics and Law in Renaissance England* (Basingstoke, 2005), and Victoria Kahn and Lorna Hutson (eds.), *Rhetoric and Law in Early Modern Europe* (New Haven, 2001). See further the seminal work of Luke Wilson (*Theaters of Intention: Drama and the Law in Early Modern England* (Stanford, 2000)), Peter Goodrich, Bradin Cormack, and Andrew Zurcher. On equity more particularly see Fortier (below, n. 14); also Daniela Carpi (ed.), *The Concept of Equity: An Interdisciplinary Assessment* (Heidelberg, 2007) and Carpi (ed.), *Practising Equity, Addressing Law* (Heidelberg, 2008).

claims upon the conscience; and an emergent notion of civic engagement, addressed to Donne's legal audience and built on a joint foundation of equitable and charitable interpretation.[4]

The Lincoln's Inn sermons represent yet another permutation of Donne's Augustinianism. Here, as we will see, the idea of charitable interpretation—derived from the first book of *De Doctrina Christiana* (a text invoked in *Biathanatos*) and the final books of the *Confessions*—provides the foundation for Donne's discussion of the moral, epistemological, and political complications of equity. In order to place Donne's engagement with Augustinian charity in its proper context, however, it is necessary first of all to illuminate the connections between equity and charity in early modern discussions of law and religion; I will then set the scene for the political implications of Donne's sermons by glancing at contemporary debates about the virtues and risks of equity—notably the contest between Chief Justice Coke and Lord Chancellor Ellesmere in 1616, and a crucial intervention by James VI and I in a Star Chamber speech delivered in the same year. My route to the Augustinian debt of Donne's Lincoln's Inn preaching is therefore a more circuitous one than that taken in previous chapters. This indirect approach is informed by the distinctive nature of Donne's Augustinian recourse in the Lincoln's Inn sermons. The dominant rhetorical mode of these homiletic performances is analogical; they deal in global hermeneutic precepts and processes; and their mode of citational reference is allusive and selective rather than specific and cumulative. Donne relies on familiar and well-rehearsed Augustinian formulations on charity which were known to his audience through their overlap with the legal discourse of equity; some of these concepts are referenced only implicitly, while others derive from a (suppressed) mediating source. Donne builds on fundamental Augustinian princi-ples which operate at a submerged analogical level as well as in the context of overt, acknowledged, and specific quotation.

CHARITY AND EQUITY

Charity and equity were frequently linked in the religious and legal discourses of the period. An early example is provided by the anonymous Tudor interlude *Kynge Daryus* (1565), whose principal character Equytie joins forces with Charytie, 'a brother of myne', to drive out Iniquytie and Importunytie. Both virtues are associated, characteristically, with the quality of 'good intent'. Unlike their enemies, Equytie and Charytie experience no disjunction between motive and act: their

---

[4] Donne was well placed to deal with the terminology of the law: although he was never called to the bar, Donne went through the usual course of common law education, first at Thavies Inn (one of the Inns of Chancery, essentially a prep school for the Inns of Court), and then, from 1592 to 1594, at Lincoln's Inn itself. He returned to preach at the Inn between 1616 and 1621. On the biographical background see Bald, *Life*, 53–79; Potter and Simpson, 'Introduction' to vol. 2 of the *Sermons*, 1–20; and Geoffrey Bullough, 'Donne the Man of Law', in *Just So Much Honor: Essays Commemorating the Four Hundredth Anniversary of the Birth of John Donne*, ed. Peter Amadeus Fiore (University Park, Pa., 1972), 57–94 (*passim*).

'thoughtes' and 'mouth' are perfectly at one with each other and thus embody the scriptural precept 'one to loue another'.[5] William Ames's *Marrow of Sacred Divinity* similarly uses charity and equity interchangeably to describe the mitigation of strict justice. He argues that while 'some offices are said to belong to Iustice strictly taken', others come within the purview of 'charity; of which difference and formall distribution we have Christ the author. Luke 11. 42. Ye passe by judgement and the love of God.'[6]

Finally, Thomas Scott's sermon *Salomons Puritan* (printed 1616), on Ecclesiastes 7:18, 'Bee not too iust', exploits the parallels between charity and equity, and between divine and secular jurisdictions, in ways which prepare for Donne's more complex engagement with the same issues. Scott's comparative account of 'politicall Iustice' and 'Christian Iustice' serves a particular political agenda: his sermon emphasizes the connection between equity and charity in order to voice support for the king's position on ceremonial conformity. The links between charity and equity also affirm Scott's conviction that things indifferent such as children's baptism 'and many other points concerning the doctrin, discipline and ceremonies vsed in our Church' should be governed by the wise and discreet judgement 'of Princes and Prelates'.[7] Scott sets up his *divisio* by outlining a core principle of divine justice, which he derives from an Augustinian sermon on almsgiving (*De Generalitate Eleemosynarum*, not now attributed to him): 'If the Lord God himselfe doth allow that his owne law should be dispensed withall in cases of charity, it is lawfull for the Magistrate to vse the like liberty in the like matters and cases of the lawes of man for charities sake.'[8] God dispenses with his laws in the interests of charity; in human society, the same latitude expresses itself in the process of equity: 'the Interpreter of the Law, making a fauourable exposition of the intention of the Law, to auoyd the inconueniences and extremities, which may sometime bee drawn from the precise words of the Law'.[9] The need for equitable flexibility is strongest in cases where the law does not provide for every detail or circumstantial modulation, and this argument prepares the ground for Scott's central point. Scripture does not legislate on all aspects of worship; this is why the king must be granted interpretive authority on certain matters: 'giue to *Caesar* the things that are *Caesars* . . . according to the equity of obedience'.[10] Scott warns against 'leaning too much to the letter of the Scripture, as though nothing were to bee allowed, which is not found in the very letters and sillables of the Scripture'; what matters is the deeper 'meaning of the Scripture, though it be not in the expresse words of the Scripture'.[11] He concludes with an axiomatic summation of princely equity: 'Bee iust in your religion, but bee not too iust.'[12]

---

[5] *Kynge Daryus*, ed. James O. Halliwell (London, 1860), 27, 22, 19.

[6] William Ames, *The Marrow of Sacred Divinity* (London, 1642), 351.

[7] Thomas Scott, *Christs politician, and Salomons puritan. Deliuered in two sermons preached before the Kings Maiestie* (1616). On this sermon see Peter E. McCullough, *Sermons at Court: Politics and Religion in Elizabethan and Jacobean Preaching* (Cambridge, 1998), 147, 175–8.

[8] Scott, *Christs politician*, 6.

[9] Ibid. 5.   [10] Ibid. 22.   [11] Ibid. 21.   [12] Ibid.

If Scott uses the secular language of equity to press a polemical point about religious practice, Donne's sermon rehearses the mirror image of that analogy: in his sermon on Genesis 18:25, preached at Lincoln's Inn on Trinity Sunday 1620, the rhetoric of Christian charity serves as a means of articulating concerns about political and legal issues of judgement and interpretation. These are raised explicitly by the biblical text in question, 'Shall not the Iudge of all the earth do right?', but are given more specific contextual contours as Donne develops the comparison between divine and human modes of judicial enquiry:

> The Pope may erre, but then a Councell may rectifie him: The King may erre; but then, God, in whose hands the Kings heart is, can rectifie him. But if God, that judges all the earth, judge thee, there is no error to be assigned in his judgement, no appeale from God not throughly informed, to God better informed, for hee alwaies knowes all evidence, before it be given. And therefore the larger the jurisdiction, and the higher the Court is, the more carefull ought the Judge to be of wrong judgement; for *Abrahams* expostulation reaches in a measure to them, *Shall not the Iudge of all* (or of a great part of the earth) *do right?* (3.147–8)

CONTEXTS

In 1620, a sermon preached to the members of Lincoln's Inn on the topic of appeal and final judgement, equity and law, would have recalled a debate over precisely these issues four years previously—the spectacular altercation between Chief Justice Coke and Lord Chancellor Ellesmere in 1616. This landmark conflict soon developed into a wider debate regarding the respective authorities of the King's Bench and Chancery, common law and equitable jurisdiction, and, ultimately, parliament and the royal prerogative. The gist of the matter was this: should the king command a special form of jurisdiction (embodied mainly in the Court of Chancery) that was distinct from the common law (represented by the common lawyers and judges who sat on the King's Bench)? Among defenders of the common law, the constitutional implications of such prerogative justice were a subject of fraught debate. An extreme (if in some ways prescient) view was expressed by Timothy Tourneur, a barrister at Gray's Inn, who regarded the growing powers of Chancery as a threat to ancient liberties and parliamentary privileges. Tourneur deplored

> the high power of the Chancellors who persuade the King that they are solely instruments of his prerogative, and insinuate with the King that his prerogative is transcendant to the common law. And thus in a short time they will enthrall the common law ... and by consequence the liberties of the subjects of England will be taken away[.] ... And if these breeding mischiefs are not redressed by Parliament the body will in a short time die in all the parts.[13]

[13] Tourneur's notes are recorded in BL MS Add. 35957, cited in Baker, 'Common Lawyers and Chancery', 222: 'Nul particuler disgrace fuit fait a ceo temps al ascun des judges come le common people a cep temps expect, nec come spero unquam serra, car lour disgrace est ter al ley mesme.' See also, on the constitutional implications of Coke's position, Alan Cromartie, *The Constitutionalist Revolution: An Essay on the History of England, 1450–1642* (Cambridge, 2006), 179–233.

The legal argument about the reach of equity centred on widely divergent interpretations of two statutes, 7 Edward III, chapter 1, and 4 Henry IV, chapter 23.
While Chief Justice Coke claimed that the statutes prohibited recourse to Chancery
after a cause had been determined at common law, Ellesmere maintained in *The
Earl of Oxford's Case* that 'the Statute of 4 *H* 4, *Chap*. 23, was never made nor
intended to restrain the power of the *Chancery* in Matters of Equity'.[14]

The quarrel between King's Bench and Chancery had flared up, intermittently, for
more than a century. One of the most pressing issues in this controversy centred on
the place and function of equitable justice: who was to administer it, and what kinds
of procedures and rules were to govern its execution. One of the most important
contributors to the debate about the role of equitable justice during Henry VIII's
reign had been Christopher Saint German, a lawyer at the Middle Temple, whose
definition of equity in the dialogue *Doctor and Student* in many ways set the
parameters for the dispute between common law and Chancery. Saint German's
account of equitable interpretation invoked some of the crucial topoi of equitable
judgement first articulated by Aristotle in the *Rhetoric* and the *Nicomachean Ethics*.
Aristotle presents equity as an instrument of hermeneutic mitigation designed to
compensate for the unavoidable disparities between general laws and individual cases;
as Saint German explains, 'syth the dedes and actes of men/for whiche lawes ben
ordayned happen in dyuers maners infynytlye. It is not possyble to make any generall
rewle of the lawe/but that it shall fayle in some case.'[15] As an interpretive mechanism,
equity allows for a law to be constructed according to its reason and spirit, rather than
the letter, so as to make it applicable to cases for which it does not expressly provide:
'in some cases it is *good* and *even* necessary to leue the wordis of the lawe/& to folowe
that reason and Justyce requyreth/& to that intent equytie is ordeyned/that is to say
to tempre and myttygate the rygoure of the lawe'. In practice, as we saw in
Biathanatos, equitable enquiry involves attention to 'all the pertyculer cyrcum-
staunces of the dede' and puts especial emphasis on the agent's intent.[16]

At the time Donne composed his sermon on Genesis 18:25, anxieties about the
political impact of equity were localized in the figure of the Lord Chancellor.
Reviewing the role of Chancery during Francis Bacon's administration, the legal
writer George Norbury noted that '[i]t cannot be denied, but that the boundless

[14] *The Earl of Oxford's Case. The Third Part of Reports of Cases Taken and Adjudged in the Court of
Chancery* (London, 1716), 1–16 (15). See Mark Fortier, 'Equity and Ideas: Coke, Ellesmere, and James
I', *Renaissance Quarterly*, 51 (1998), 1255–81 (1263). On Ellesmere, see Louis A. Knafla,
'Mr Secretary Donne: The Years with Sir Thomas Egerton', in David Colclough (ed.), *John Donne's
Professional Lives* (Cambridge, 2003), 37–71. Ellesmere was, of course, Thomas Egerton, Donne's
former employer, so Donne may have had a particular interest in his dispute with Coke.
[15] Christopher Saint German, *Doctor and Student*, ed. T. F. T. Plucknett and J. L. Barton (London,
1974), 95. The treatise was originally published as *Dialogus de Fundamentis Legum Angliae et de
Conscientia* in Latin in 1523 and 1528. The English version followed in 1530. STC records that it was
reprinted frequently throughout the sixteenth and seventeenth centuries, and this in turn suggests that
Saint German's arguments were considered to be relevant to the juristic issues of the 1610s and 1620s.
On the political and constitutional issues raised by Saint German's work, see John Guy, *Politics, Law
and Counsel in Tudor and Early Stuart England* (Aldershot, 2000) and *Christopher St German on
Chancery and Statute* (London, 1985).
[16] Saint German, *Doctor and Student*, 95, 97.

power of chancery . . . is the cause of much discontent and distraction to the king's subjects, and clamours against the lord chancellor'.[17] Bacon was able to draw support from the king's official pronouncements on equitable justice. In a Star Chamber speech of June 1616, for instance, James had effectively reified the authority of Chancery when he warned the common law judges to 'keepe within your limits and Iurisdictions':

> It is Atheisme and blasphemie to dispute what God can doe: good Christians content themselues with his will reuealed in his word. So, it is presumption and high contempt in a Subiect, to dispute what a King can doe, or say that a King cannot doe this, or that; but rest in that which is the Kings reuealed will in his Law. . . . [T]here [is] a Chancerie Court; this is a Court of Equitie, and hath power to deale likewise in Ciuill causes: It is called the dispenser of the Kings Conscience, following alwayes the intention of the Law and Iustice . . . And where the rigour of the Law in many cases will vndoe a Subiect, there the Chancerie tempers the Law with equitie, and so mixeth Mercy with Iustice, as it preserues men from destruction. . . . The Chancerie is vndependant of any other Court, and is onely vnder the King: There it is written *Teste meipso; from that Court there is no Appeale.*[18]

In Chancery, the king acts as the ultimate judge of consciences and intentions, and answers only to God: 'the seat of Iudgement is properly Gods, and Kings are Gods Viceregents'.[19] James concluded that 'That which concernes the mysterie of the Kings power, is not lawfull to be disputed; for that is to wade into the weaknesse of Princes, and to take away the mysticall reuerence, that belongs vnto them that sit in the Throne of God.'[20] Soon after this speech, Bacon spelled out the institutional consequences of this philosophy, putting the common lawyers firmly in their place: 'the twelve judges of the realm are as the twelve lions under Solomon's throne. They must be lions, but yet lions under the throne. They must show their stoutness in elevating and building up the throne.'[21] Armed with this contextual information, we can now turn to Donne's sermon on Genesis 18:25, which subtly but determinedly engages the conditions of prerogative justice, and debates precisely the terms upon which it can be 'disputed'.

DONNE'S TEXTS

Donne's sermon on Genesis 18:25 takes on a text with explicitly legal resonances, 'Shall not the Iudge of all the Earth do right?' and considers the proposition that the

---

[17] 'The Abuses and Remedies of Chancery', in *A Collection of Tracts Relative to the Law of England*, ed. Francis Hargrave (Dublin, 1787), 430.

[18] James VI and I, 'Speech in Star Chamber of 20 June 1616', in James VI and I, *Political Writings*, ed. Johann P. Sommerville (Cambridge, 1994), 204–28 (214; my emphasis).

[19] Ibid. 205.

[20] Ibid. 213. For a fascinating (but very different) account of the connections between equity, absolutism, and Christian justice see Debora Kuller Shuger, *Political Theologies in Shakespeare's England: The Sacred and the State in Measure for Measure* (Basingstoke, 2001), esp. chs. 3 and 4.

[21] Francis Bacon, *The Works of Francis Bacon*, ed. James Spedding, Robert Leslie Ellis, and Douglas Denon Heath, 14 vols. (London, 1857–74), 13.201–2.

'King may erre...but then, God...may rectifie him'. In doing so, it confronts some of the urgent moral and political issues connected with the problem of equitable jurisdiction in the years immediately following the 1616 conflict between Chancery and King's Bench. The opening section of his sermon sums up the main concerns of Donne's enquiry, casting Genesis 18 in the language of equitable appeal:

> That God appeared to *Abraham* in the plaine of Mamre, in the persons of three men; three men so glorious, as that *Abraham* gave them a great respect: That *Abraham* spoke to those three, as to one person: That he exhibited all offices of humanity and hospitality unto them[;] ... that they imparted to *Abraham*, upon their departure, the indignation that God had conceived against the sins of Sodome, and consequently the imminent destruction of that City; That this awakened *Abrahams* compassion, and put him into a zeale, and vehemence; for, all the while, he is said, *to have been with him that spoke to him*, and yet, now it is said, *Abraham drew near*, he came up close to God, and he sayes, Peradventure, (I am not sure of it) but peradventure, there may be some righteous in the City, and if there should be so, it should be absolutely unjust to destroy them; but, since it may be so, it is too soone to come to a present execution; *Absit à te*, sayes *Abraham*, *Be that far from thee*; And he repeats it twice; And upon the reason in our text, *Shall not the Iudge of all the Earth do right?* ... [H]e thinks it unjust, that God should wrap up just and unjust, righteous and unrighteous, all in one condemnation. (3.134–5)

Donne rewrites the account of Abraham's encounter in a way that invites his audience to draw parallels with the processes of judgement at law and equitable correction. It is worth stating, however, that neither here nor anywhere in the sermon does he employ the term 'equity'. This is by no means unusual: Donne's sermon on Esther 4:16, which is a textbook example of casuistical deliberation, nowhere mentions the word 'casuistry'. Instead, he saturates his text with the language of the law, expecting his audience to hear the continual resonances between his exegesis and the practices of equitable reasoning in which they had been trained: the psalmist is a 'petitioner'; God is a judge who will undertake a 'visitation' and go on a 'Circuit', and as such is compared with a mere 'Arbitrator' or even 'Chancellor' (3.146, 147). In the passage just cited, the parallels with equitable interpretation are made clear. Donne begins by recounting the initial verdict, 'the imminent destruction of that City', and then retraces Abraham's movement from one judicial instance to the next: 'he came up close to God' to plead, in Saint German's words, for a judgement that 'is temperyd with the swetnes of mercye'. Abraham's argument in Donne's representation closely follows two *loci classici* of equitable interpretation: he notes, first, the deficiencies arising from the generality of the law (as Saint German had observed, '[i]t is not possyble to make any generall rewle of the lawe/but that it shall fayle in some case'), and then refers to the classic legal maxim *summum ius, summa iniuria*—'it should be absolutely unjust ... that God should wrap up just and unjust, righteous and unrighteous, all in one condemnation'. When Abraham demands that God consider the claims of the righteous minority in a corrupt city, he is effectively pleading a case of restrictive equity: the rules of fairness imply the possibility of an exception from the general 'condemnation'. There are 'some cases', as Saint German had affirmed, where it is *'good* and *even* necessary . . . to tempre and myttygate the rygoure of the lawe'. Donne suspends the resolution of the problem—'it may be so, it is too soone to come to a present execution'—and thus opens up a hermeneutic space in which his own assessment of the case can unfold.[22]

Against the background of Abraham's eloquent pleading, the *divisio* of Donne's sermon reads like a typical example of equitable enquiry into the circumstances of the case. Invoking the spirit of the lawgiver, as Aristotle had specified, he also considers the motives of the two main parties, Abraham and God:

> The person who is *the Iudge of all the Earth*, submits us to a necessity of seeking, who it is that *Abraham* speaks to; and so, who they were that appeared to him: whether they were three men, or three Angels, or two Angels, and the third . . . were Christ: Or whether in these three persons, whatsoever they were, there were any intimation, any insinuation given, or any apprehension taken by *Abraham*, of the three blessed Persons of the glorious Trinity? (3.135)

As well as demonstrating his command of legal terminology, however, Donne's text is concerned with probing and (in the words of *Biathanatos*) 'vexing' the ethical problems surrounding equitable reasoning. The figure of Abraham plays a crucial part in this project. He is presented as, at once, the ideal interpreter and as an exemplary text that embodies the best meaning of God's law: 'he is our copie' (3.137), Donne insists in a characteristic conflation of textual and moral spheres. Throughout his account of Genesis 18, Donne focuses on Abraham's charity: '*Abraham* entreated them [the three men] faire, and entertained them well: he spoke kindly, and kindly performed all offices of ease, and refocillation to these way-faring strangers. . . . Give really, and give gently; Doe kindly, and speake kindly too, for that is Bread, and Hony' (3.137). Equitable judgement is pre-figured in charitable acts of doing and speaking 'kindly'.

In the next part of his *divisio*, Donne's sermon builds towards a test of the preacher's own judgement, which crystallizes in one key question: 'whether he [Abraham] apprehended not an intimation of the three Persons of the Trinity' (3.142). It is in this exercise of hermeneutic adjudication that the ethical and political implications of equity become most pressing:

> But yet, betweene them, who make this place, a distinct, and a literall, and a concluding argument, to prove the Trinity, and them who cry out against it, that it hath no relation to the Trinity, our Church hath gone a middle, and a moderate way, when by appointing this Scripture for this day, when we celebrate the Trinity, it declares that to us, who have been baptized, and catechised in the name and faith of the Trinity, it is a refreshing, it is a cherishing, it is an awakening of that former knowledge which we had of the Trinity, to heare that our onely God thus manifested himselfe to *Abraham* in three Persons. (3.143)

---

[22] For another sermon that confronts Abraham with a legally and theologically significant conflict of conscience, see *Sermons*, 6.186–204 (preached at St Dunstan's on 1 January 1624/5, on Genesis 17:24). This sermon is analysed by Jeanne Shami in 'Donne's Sermons and the Absolutist Politics of Quotation', in *John Donne's Religious Imagination*, ed. Frontain and Malpezzi, 380–412 (esp. 400–3).

Donne initially expresses doubt about the possibility of discovering definitive proof of the Trinity at the 'literall' level of the text. Trinitarian meditations, Donne argues, could not have been part of Moses' historical intention: in the most obvious sense, encountering Christ at this point in the narrative creates problems with the scriptural timeline. Working out the literal sense of the text is certainly a crucial element of Donne's task, but there are other obligations in play. Donne notes immediately that by discarding the Trinitarian reading on Trinity Sunday, he may not 'doe this congregation the best service'.[23] A conflict of interpretive interests emerges between the literal sense on the one hand, and the sense that will be most edifying to Donne's audience on the other. In the context of Donne's legal argument, the conflict can be re-framed as one of textual letter against spirit, and thus evokes a classic issue in equitable enquiry: can Donne afford to deviate from the strict *letter* of Old Testament law to refresh and advance the lawyers' faith in the *spirit* of the New Dispensation? The answer is a qualified 'yes', but Donne's solution remains enmeshed in the moral complexities of both equity and charity.

Donne justifies his audience-orientated deviation from the literal sense by appealing to the ultimate 'voluntas' (will, intent) of the lawgiver. In this, he follows a common precept of equitable reasoning. As Aristotle notes in the *Nicomachean Ethics*, any departure from the law must be undertaken in the spirit of the legislator's intent: 'as the lawgiver would himself decide if he were present on the occasion'.[24] Donne also deploys a more specific technique of equitable investigation: the legal fiction. To explain this idea, we need to look to Book 5 of Quintilian's *Institutio Oratoria*. There, Quintilian remarks that legal 'arguments are drawn not merely from admitted facts, but from fictitious suppositions. . . . When I speak of fictitious arguments I mean the proposition of something which, if true, would either solve a problem or contribute to its solution.'[25] Donne's sermon closely follows this distinction between 'admitted facts' on the one hand (the external circumstances of a case, or the literal sense of a statute at law), and the practical moral applications derived from 'fictitious arguments' on the other. He interprets Genesis 18:25 as the religious equivalent of a legal fiction—a 'figure', as he puts it, an instance of 'similitudinary, and comparative reasons' (3.144). And, as in Quintilian's example, admitting this useful hermeneutic 'proposition' helps to 'solve' a textual 'problem'. But the main function of Donne's exegetical fiction is a devotional one: 'renewing the Trinity to our Contemplation, by the reading of the Scripture, this day'. As he observes in the same passage, 'there are places of Scripture for direct proofes, and there are places to exercise our meditation, and devotion' (3.144). Donne's legal fiction-making is justified by appeal to a higher authority, the lawgiver's intent: Moses' historical meaning is overruled by God's overriding desire 'to exercise our . . . devotion' (3.144); this superior interpretation emerges through equitable deviation from the letter of the text.

---

[23] *Sermons*, 3.143.
[24] Aristotle, *The Nicomachean Ethics*, trans. H. Rackham, 2nd edn. (Cambridge, Mass., 1934), 5.10.5.
[25] Quintilian, *Institutio Oratoria*, trans. H. E. Butler, 4 vols. (Cambridge, Mass., 1920–2; repr. 1993–6), 5.10.95–6. Russell's more recent translation obscures the legal reference.

Donne's sermon articulates these processes of exegetical latitude through recourse to the Augustinian hermeneutics of charity. As he argues, with an explicit invocation of Augustine, '*Figura nihil probat,* A figure, an Allegory proves nothing; yet, sayes he, *addit lucem, & ornat,* It makes that which is true in it selfe, more evident and more acceptable' (3.144). The truth identified by Donne in Genesis 18:25 is the truth of charity and peace: as Augustine insists in *De Doctrina Christiana* and the *Confessions,* figurative readings of Scripture texts can be rendered legitimate if they serve to instruct and edify. I will turn to the relevant passages from *De Doctrina* and the *Confessions* in a moment; for now, it is important to reflect on the specific provenance of Donne's maxim that 'A figure . . . proves nothing'. Although explicitly referenced as Augustinian, Donne's quotation is in fact taken from Luther's commentary on Genesis (on which see more below). As Hans-Ulrich Delius has observed, the phrase '*Figura nihil probat*' has no exact verbal equivalent in Augustine's works, despite the fact that Luther, on ten different occasions, treats it as a literal quotation from Augustine.[26] Donne seems to have accepted Luther's attribution; this is chiefly, of course, because 'Augustine's' remark about the probative value of figurative readings is so acutely responsive to the overlap of legal and religious discourses at issue in Donne's sermon: it places the argument at the intersection of charitable and equitable interpretation, where both Luther and Augustine felt at home. In this sense, the pilfered 'Augustine' reference from Luther could not have been a more valuable discovery.

But the maxim '*Figura nihil probat*' is useful to Donne also because its sentiments resonate with the hermeneutic philosophy carved out by more familiar Augustinian texts: *De Doctrina Christiana* and the *Confessions.* In his exegesis of Genesis, Donne stresses the importance of interpretive conditioning: his reading is built on a '*Communicatio pacis*, a peaceable disposition, a charitable interpretation' (3.139). At a later point in the sermon, Donne re-emphasizes the moral implications of his approach when he remarks that '*Sed non sic agendum cum auditoribus, ac cum adversariis*, We must not proceed alike with friends and with enemies' (3.144). Throughout this key section of the sermon, Donne relies completely on Luther's exposition of Genesis 18 in his *Lectures on Genesis*, which serves as the chief mediator of Augustinian principles in his Lincoln's Inn performance. Donne quotes and explicates five Lutheran passages at length (introduced by the phrase '*Luther* sayes well' at 3.143); in doing so, he follows his characteristic method of concentrating on the beginning and end of a scholarly text. He starts with an extract from Luther's commentary on Genesis 18, which focuses on the very first verse, and then draws the majority of his quotations from the concluding paragraphs in Luther's reading of Genesis 18:2–5, including all of the passages quoted above.[27] But Donne's debt to Luther goes further still: the Augustinian precepts of edifying interpretation, and the distinction between probative and useful arguments, can be

---

[26] Hans-Ulrich Delius, *Augustin als Quelle Luthers* (Berlin, 1984), 53. According to Delius, the most likely source is *On the Unity of the Church* 5.9 (a text now recognized as spurious).

[27] Luther is quoted from the Weimar edition of his Complete Works ('Kritische Gesamtausgabe'): *Vorlesungen über I. Mose von 1535–1545*, ed. Karl Drescher, vol. 43 (Breslau, 1912), 2.

traced back to the *Lectures on Genesis*. Luther commends the Trinitarian reading as 'apposite' and 'useful' ('aptum', 'utile'), and notes further that arguments drawn from rhetoric, while not serving as irrefutable proof, can nevertheless support and adorn an argument.[28] Throughout his engagement with Luther's lectures, Donne carefully adapts the source text to his thematic concerns, omitting (for instance) the satire against the Anabaptists which is a major preoccupation of Luther's discourse.

Donne's aim in the Lincoln's Inn sermon is to forge a sense of interpretive community with his legal audience, to offer a moral contract with mutual obligations and benefits: unless the lawyers open themselves, charitably, to Donne's textual negotiations, they cannot reap the spiritual rewards offered by Abraham's example. Donne's formulation 'a charitable interpretation' consolidates the Augustinian subtext of his hermeneutic meditations: the system of charitable exegesis as formulated in Book 1 of *De Doctrina Christiana*—a text cited, albeit in mediated form, as early as *Biathanatos* (see p. 144). Unlike *Biathanatos*, however, which opts for a strategic misrepresentation of Augustine's position, the Lincoln's Inn sermon offers a reading which—though far from straightforward—is more attentive to the meaning and context of its source, *De Doctrina Christiana* 1.36. It is at this point that the crossover between the discourses of charity and equity begins to emerge more clearly in Donne's sermon. As Kathy Eden has shown, Augustine's approach to the hermeneutics of charity offers close parallels with equitable interpretation. Like equity, Augustine's description of charity radically privileges interpretive objective and intent over literal and historical meaning, for instance:[29]

> [A]nyone who thinks that he has understood the divine scriptures or any part of them, but cannot by his understanding build up this double love of God and neighbour, has not yet succeeded in understanding them. Anyone who derives from them an idea which is useful for supporting this love but fails to say what the writer demonstrably meant in the passage has not made a fatal error, and is certainly not a liar. In a liar there is a desire to say what is false, and that is why we find many who want to lie but nobody who wants to be misled.[30]

Reading, on Augustine's terms, is about educating oneself to find love in a text. The main criterion of success is the usefulness of an interpretation in the task of 'build[ing] up this twofold love of God and our neighbour'; or, as Donne puts it, to 'exercise . . . devotion'. This intention, the will towards love, is the decisive factor in any reading act, even if it entails a misconstruction of the text's historical sense. Augustine's argument, then, like Donne's, is founded on a hierarchy of intentions: God's ultimate will to 'build up . . . love' may outweigh 'what the writer demonstrably meant' in a specific passage; and in the quest for this underlying sense, readers frequently depart from the literal meaning of the text. As Augustine

---

[28] Luther, *Vorlesungen*, 14.

[29] For a more extensive account of the parallels between charitable and equitable interpretation see Kathy Eden, 'The Rhetorical Tradition and Augustinian Hermeneutics in *De Doctrina Christiana*', *Rhetorica*, 8 (1990), 45–63.

[30] Augustine, *De Doctrina Christiana* 1.36.40 (*PL* 34.34).

observes in Book 3 of *De Doctrina Christiana*, '[g]enerally speaking, it is this: anything in the divine discourse that cannot be related either to good morals or to the true faith should be taken as figurative. Good morals have to do with our love of God and our neighbour, the true faith with our understanding of God and our neighbour.'[31] If the surface meaning of a scriptural passage does not advance the love of God and neighbour, Augustine argues, it is legitimate to deviate from the literal sense in order to discover more edifying readings. Both charity and equity insist on the necessity of departing from the literal (historical or semantic) dimension of the written word in order to recover the spirit or *dianoia* of its author. Where Aristotle's equitable exegetes contribute to 'the rectification of law', Augustine's loving latitude seeks to advance the 'reign of charity'. Both transactions rely on the moral commitment of a human reader, without whom God's charitable intent cannot be realized. Interpretive fictions may be admitted in the interest of a 'fide non ficta' and of true justice, but the only safe access to God's loving plan is through the reader's good intentions.

While this exegetical mechanism ensures devotional efficacy by allowing the possibility of non-literal interpretation, it also points to a central element of hermeneutic indeterminacy that is common to equity and charity. Because the legislator is absent, his intentions cannot be verified directly, and this in turn opens up an exegetical space that could be claimed, potentially, by benign and malicious interpreters alike. Saint German's account of equity hints at the problem when he states that the principle of 'excepcion is secretly vnderstande in euery generall rewle of euery posytyue lawe'.[32] Equity depends on the assumption that the law contains hidden pockets of signification, but this hermeneutic opacity also makes it vulnerable to abuse. As Ian Maclean has pointed out, equitable and malicious interpretations are distinguished 'not in their formal or material elements (i.e. their argument or premises) but solely in their purpose', and Renaissance lawyers thus confronted 'the problem of providing adequate notation' to distinguish between contrary motives of interpretation.[33] In view of these issues, it is hardly surprising that Donne should reflect at such length on the audience's hermeneutic disposition.

In his sermon on Genesis 18:25, Donne tries to negotiate the competing needs of law and case, text and audience, through complex processes of interpretive accommodation. In a 1629 Whitsunday sermon, Donne resumes discussion of these issues. There, he considers the problem of multiple Scripture senses, wondering whether competing interpretations endanger the integrity of God's common law. Once again, Augustine's law of charity offers a ready solution. Scripture can encompass a range of readings, provided that they all 'conduce . . . to edification':

---

[31] *De Doctrina Christiana* 3.10.14 (*PL* 34.71). On the role of charity more generally, and the link between charity and non-literal interpretation in particular, see Karla Pollmann, *Doctrina Christiana: Untersuchungen zu den Anfängen der christlichen Hermeneutik unter besonderer Berücksichtigung von Augustinus, De Doctrina Christiana* (Fribourg, 1996).

[32] Saint German, *Doctor and Student*, 97.

[33] Ian Maclean, *Interpretation and Meaning in the Renaissance: The Case of Law* (Cambridge, 1992), 139.

Where divers senses arise, and all true, (that is, that none of them oppose the truth) let truth agree them. But what is Truth? God; And what is God? Charity; Therefore let Charity reconcile such differences. *Legitimè lege utamur,* sayes he [Augustine], let us use the Law lawfully; Let us use our liberty of reading Scriptures according to the Law of liberty; that is, charitably to leave others to their liberty, if they but differ from us, and not differ from Fundamentall Truths. . . . So far I will goe, saies he, so far will we, in his modesty and humility accompany him, as still to propose, *Quod luce veritatis, quod fruge utilitatis excellit,* such a sense as agrees with other Truths, that are evident in other places of Scripture, and such a sense as may conduce most to edification.[34]

Donne's phrase 'the Law of liberty' crystallizes many of the concerns that trouble him in the Lincoln's Inn sermon on Genesis 18:25.[35] What he argues in his 1629 sermon is that Scripture caters for the exceptions to its own rules. God's timeless Word anticipates equitable or charitable deviations from its literal meaning: it allows for 'divers senses', which may 'all' be 'true'. This is a kind of perfect textual justice, in which every eventuality is already implicit in God's laws: although these exceptions are only actuated as history unfolds, certain deviations from the letter of Scripture are latent within it from the inception of time. Donne invokes *Confessions* 12.30 in support of his argument, a text which already informed the exegetical negotiations of the *Essayes* and which also connects with the hermeneutic philosophy of *De Doctrina Christiana*: both Augustinian texts prescribe and rehearse the controlled liberty of charitable reading. On the terms of this model, an interpreter can realize figurative readings that benefit his audience whilst still respecting the integrity of the Scriptures: the Bible thus means many different things to different readers, and yet remains perfectly at one with itself.

As Donne is quick to emphasize, however, such liberty is not to be confused with hermeneutic licence. The law of liberty is synonymous with the law of charity, which is governed by the ultimate intent of the legislator: God 'is . . . Charity', and the true end of his law is 'edification'; human readers participate in this process by putting Augustine's model into practice.[36] Non-literal readings are only admissible, in other words, if they conduce to devotion and edification. Donne's system of hermeneutic circulation, then, depends on an exegetical ethos, predisposition, or mentality rather than the technical specificities of interpretation. Charity is the concept that enables textual diversity, whilst at the same time 'reconcil[ing] . . . differences'. Donne stresses the difficulty of implementing the law of exegetical liberty: any deviation from the literal sense must be examined in

---

[34] *Sermons*, 9.92–108 (94–5).

[35] Donne's Augustinian notion of the law of charity has complex scriptural and legal resonances. It relies on the shifts of interpretive emphasis implicit in the transition from the Old Testament covenant to the New Dispensation: 1 John 4:8 ('God is love') encapsulates the spirit of interpretive liberty that licenses deviation from the literal meaning of a text. At the same time, however, Donne's definition of the law of liberty carries clear contractual overtones; Donne, as we will see, draws his audience into a hermeneutic bond designed to safeguard charity against potential abuses. On Donne's interest in the law of contract see Jeremy Maule, 'Donne and the Words of the Law', in Colclough (ed.), *John Donne's Professional Lives*, 19–36.

[36] Books 1–3 of *De Doctrina Christiana* outline specific rules of interpretation for implementing Augustine's 'rule of charity'.

the light of its devotional value and must link back to the unified plurality of God's intention(s).

APPLICATIONS

In his Lincoln's Inn sermon on Genesis 18:25, Donne seeks to demonstrate that the equitable liberties he takes are not outside the Scripture law, but fall firmly within its scope. The discourse of scriptural charity helps to justify this claim: Augustine's rule of charity can accommodate a plurality of occasions and audiences; at the same time, it preserves the integrity of the Bible's message by uniting divergent readings under the aegis of the double love command. But Donne's complex calibration of metaphysical and hermeneutic languages also has more immediate implications for the topical relevance of his performance. Donne's dual insistence that exceptions to a law are implied in its spirit or reason, and that equity and charity are forms of hermeneutic 'liberty' which can be contained by the law, would certainly have appealed to the common lawyers of Lincoln's Inn. His suggestion that the spirit of the law is capable of catering for 'all in one' (3.135) resonates richly with Saint German's conviction that exceptions are 'secretly vnderstande in euery generall rewle of euery posytyue lawe', and that equity, therefore, should be administered in the common law courts rather than through an independent system of prerogative justice. This position is confirmed by a closer inspection of Donne's legal rhetoric in the Lincoln's Inn sermon, which expresses doubts over the capacity of human judgement:

> The Pope may erre, but then a Councell may rectifie him: The King may erre; but then, God, in whose hands the Kings heart is, can rectifie him. But if God, that judges all the earth, judge thee, there is no error to be assigned in his judgement, no appeale from God not throughly informed, to God better informed, for hee alwaies knowes all evidence, before it be given. And therefore the larger the jurisdiction, and the higher the Court is, the more carefull ought the Judge to be of wrong judgement; for *Abrahams* expostulation reaches in a measure to them, *Shall not the Iudge of all* (or of a great part of the earth) *do right?* (3.147–8)

Donne, unlike James and Ellesmere during the legal quarrel of 1616, chooses to stress the differences between divine and human justice. Although the king has powers vested in him by God, he is by no means infallible. Donne's warning to those who would defend the prerogatives of 'higher' courts over the law, and to those who judge 'a great part of the earth', 'reaches in a measure' to James VI and I, who had stated in the Star Chamber speech of 1616, that 'there is no Appeale' from Chancery.[37] Donne insists on the complexity of equitable interpretation and warns the king to be 'carefull . . . of the wrong judgement'.

---

[37] James VI and I, '1616', 214. For two influential accounts that emphasize Donne's critical stance towards the prerogative rights of absolute monarchs, see David Norbrook, 'The Monarchy of Wit and the Republic of Letters: Donne's Politics', in *Soliciting Interpretation: Literary Theory and Seventeenth-Century English Poetry*, ed. Elizabeth D. Harvey and Katharine Eisaman Maus (Chicago, 1990), 3–36;

The sermons of the Lincoln's Inn period are persistent in their attempts to
delimit the scope and reach of equitable jurisdiction. An undated sermon on
2 Corinthians 1:3, for instance, describes the proliferation of jurisdictions as a
form of idolatry, and condemns those who 'pray the Virgin *Mary* to assist her Son,
nay to command her Son, and make her a Chancellor to mitigate his common Law'
(3.263). In this trenchant critique of 'false intercession', Donne's satirical swipe
combines anti-Catholic polemic with anti-prerogative argument. He objects to two
kind of 'exception-making', as the Virgin Mary's role is firmly subordinated to
Christ's, and the chancellor's authority curtailed in favour of the common law.
Equitable exceptions also come under critical scrutiny in a sermon on Psalms 2:12,
which features a damning indictment of 'fat Equity['s]' tendency to transgress 'the
limits of precedent' (3.330) and claim for itself the prestige which belongs to God's
'common law'. The 'fat' equity of the prerogative courts is associated with 'Subtilty'
and 'Craft'—a tendency 'To go towards good ends, by ill ways' (3.329). Restrictions on interpretive latitude are also advocated by the sermon on Genesis 18:25,
where Donne relies on the 'argumentation of S. *Augustines*' that when a text 'may
be interpreted . . . by an ordinary way, it is never necessary, seldome safe to induce
an extraordinary' (3.141). The clearest parallels with Donne's political position in
the Genesis 18:25 sermon, however, emerge in a sermon speculatively dated by
Potter and Simpson to 30 January 1620, on John 5:22: 'The Father judgeth no
man, but hath committed all judgement to the son.' There, Donne's argument is
once again founded on the key distinction between divine and human knowledge:
human jurisdictions are plural and fragmented, hampered by a limited grasp of
circumstance, context, and motive. God, however, who 'will judge the world, and
the Judges of the world' (2.313), is truly equitable in his proceedings. He is a judge
'*Sine Appellatione*', who 'knows my heart', possesses 'the power of discerning all
actions, in all places', and assigns all elements of the case their proper place and
weight:

> Earthly Judges have their distinctions, and so their restrictions; some things they
> cannot know, what mortall man can know all? Some things they cannot take knowl-
> edge of, for they are bound to evidence: But God hath *Iudicium Discretionis,* no mist,
> no cloud, no darknesse, no disguise keeps him from discerning, and judging all our
> actions, and so he is a Judge too. . . . [F]or the office of a Judge who judges according to
> a law, being not to contract, or extend that law, but to declare what was the true
> meaning of that Law-maker when hee made that law, God hath this judgement in
> perfection, because hee himself made that law by which he judges[.] . . . Who shall
> think to delude the Judge, and say, Surely this was not the meaning of the Law-giver,
> when he who is the Judge was the Law-maker too. (2.316–17)

Donne's language speaks directly to the technical procedures of equity. The office
of a human judge is only to implement the law ('declare'), not to alter it through
interpretation ('contract, or extend'). Men have a duty to explicate the law; God has

the power to make it. Equity is perfect justice, but perfect justice is predicated on perfect knowledge, and 'the true meaning of the Law-maker' can only be known by God. In Donne's sermon, the conventional distinction between human and divine knowledge is transformed into a highly polemical position on the relationship between conscience and equity. Only God has *'Iudicium Discretionis'*, the ability to scrutinize the soul and penetrate to the depth of motive. Donne seems to object particularly to courts of conscience (Chancery, Requests), where judges presumed to enquire not only into what had been done, but into the states of mind and consciences of the people who might have committed, or might have considered committing, an unlawful act. He keeps intact a distinction between equity and conscience that came under increasing pressure as the king and his chancellors sought to extend the reach of prerogative justice. The 'power of discerning all actions, in all places' is God's, not the king's or the chancellor's, and this has profound implications for the scope of equitable jurisdiction. In defending the authority of the prerogative courts, James's chancellors frequently referred to their superior powers in examining the conscience. Suits in equity were presented, according to J. H. Baker, not as 'an appeal to correct a legal decision, but a means of correcting the corrupt conscience' of parties who sought 'to avail themselves of a judgement contrary to equity'.[38] Donne's sermon may not deny the need for a system of equity that can be embedded within the operations of the common law, but it certainly restricts its scope: by questioning the premise of quasi-divine knowledge upon which Chancery's claims were founded, and by insisting that the *'Iudicium Discretionis'* belongs to God alone.[39] In God's court, all the circumstances of the case are at the judge's fingertips: this is why 'there is no error to be assigned in his judgement' and 'no appeale from God not throughly informed, to God better informed' (3.147–8).

As a preacher and a lawyer, Donne must also stand trial in God's court. Is his spiritual reading, designed to edify the audience on Trinity Sunday, really consonant with 'the true meaning of that Law-maker'? Through explicit reflection on the methods and motives of interpretation, Donne's argument seeks to establish and defend the preacher's own judicial discretion. He is confident that he will receive a fair verdict at God's hand, and not simply because 'hee alwaies knowes all evidence, before it be given'. God invites active engagement with his Word and decree, and tolerates even the most speculative enquiries into his actions:

> God admits, even expostulation, from his servants; almost rebukes and chidings from his servants. . . . Now, *Offer this to one of your Princes*, says the Prophet, *and see whether he*

---

[38] Baker, 'Common Lawyers and Chancery', 208.

[39] Donne's concern with equity may have been inspired, in part, by Calvin's treatment of Genesis 18:25. Calvin remarks that 'God by nature loueth equitie' and that his 'will is a lawe of equitie'. Such purity of motive cannot be relied upon in the case of 'earthly Judges, who are nowe and then through errour deceived, either moued with fauour, either kindled with hatred, and displeasure . . . or else are brought by some other meanes to iniustice'. Donne's treatment of the issue is rather more discreet, but also more concerned with the legal implications of human judgement. *A Commentarie of John Caluine, vpon the first booke of Moses called Genesis*, trans. Thomas Tymme (London, 1578), 398. See, on Donne's discretion more generally: Shami, *Conformity*, and Shami, 'Donne on Discretion', *English Literary History*, 47 (1980), 48–66 (56, 50).

will take it. . . . [W]hat Prince would not (and justly) conceive an indignation? . . . And yet our long-suffering, and our patient God, (must we say, our humble and obedient God?) endures all this . . . [and] as long as Abraham kept himselfe upon this foundation, *It is impossible that the Iudge of all the earth should not do right,* God mis-interpreted nothing at *Abrahams* hand, but received even his Expostulations[.] (3.145–6)

Donne once again finds validation for his procedures in the contrast between human and divine judgement. He evidently did not need reminding that James thought it 'contempt and high Presumption in a Subiect, to dispute what a King can doe', and he is far from advocating a stance of open resistance to royal authority (see especially 3.146). Nevertheless, the political reverberations of Donne's comparison are readily felt: if God can muster the humility to admit 'expostulation' and disputation, perhaps James would be well advised to do the same. Donne argues his case eloquently, mustering the collective support of scriptural precedent. Jacob, David, Amos, Paul, and Abraham are all shown to debate with God, and thus help to articulate an alternative model of political engagement: one that is grounded in active deliberation, dialogue, and good faith.

Donne's sermon emphasizes the difficulties of equitable judgement, especially in relation to questions of conscience, motive, and intent. At the same time, he knows that such introspection is necessary to his audience, not least because it contributes to the upkeep of a healthy soul:

Tell thy selfe that thou art the Judge, as *Abraham* told God that he was, and that if thou wilt judge thy selfe, thou shalt scape a severer judgement. He told God that he was Judge of all the earth; Judge all that earth that thou art; . . . Mingle not the just and the unjust together; God did not so; Doe not thinke good and bad all one; Doe not think alike of thy sins, and of thy good deeds, as though when Gods grace had quickned them, still thy good works were nothing, thy prayers nothing, thine almes nothing in the sight and acceptation of God[.] (3.155)

Donne recommends an attitude of intense self-analysis here, insisting that the lawyers keep a close eye on the motives and consequences of their actions. But he also reminds them of the rules of charitable enquiry: the idea of a fair hearing implies discretion—'Doe not thinke good and bad all one'. Judgement also falls to other paternal figures: 'a Magistrate', 'a father', and, above all, 'a Preacher' (3.154). Throughout the Lincoln's Inn sermons, Donne stresses his role as a mediator of God's justice, in a gesture that seeks to shore up his own interpretive authority. This is especially apparent in his concluding exhortations to the lawyers, a conscious and deliberate attempt to write after Abraham's hermeneutic 'copie':

though Gods appearing thus in three persons, be no irrefragable argument to prove the Trinity against the Jews, yet it is a convenient illustration of the Trinity to thee that art a Christian: And therefore . . . accustome thy selfe to meditations upon the Trinity . . . and seeke a reparation of that thy Trinity, by a new Trinity, by faith in Christ Jesus, by hope of him, and by a charitable delivering him to others, in a holy and exemplar life. (3.154)[40]

[40] On this 'Trinity' of faith, hope, and charity see 1 Corinthians 13.

By charitably admitting a Trinitarian reading that will edify the audience, and by advising the lawyers to practise the rule of charity, Donne aims to establish himself as a worthy heir to Abraham's hermeneutic and ethical legacy. Once again, he is keen to stress that Genesis 18:25 offers 'a convenient illustration of the Trinity' for Christians believers; his reading has no probative or suasive value outside this circle of the faithful. To the initiated, however, Abraham's legacy always already entails an element of legal responsibility, as the text of Genesis 18 implies: God reveals his judgement of Sodom to Abraham in recognition of his future role as the founding father and principal law-keeper of the Israelite community: 'For I know him, that he will command his children and his household after him, and they shall keep the way of the LORD, to do justice and judgment' (Genesis 18:19). Donne's discourse aims to found a different kind of community: one that ties the lawyers to the preacher through the bonds of charity, creating good faith through displays of pastoral equity and discreet but politically committed acts of judgement. This represents a solution of sorts to the crisis of intent and motive played out in *Biathanatos*: in the Lincoln's Inn sermons, mutual obligation replaces the unilateral interpretive action of Donne's casuistical negotiations, and stabilizes the shifting tides of self-interest and circumstance precisely (and paradoxically) by insisting on the occasional and contextual situatedness of Donne's discourse.

IMPLICATIONS

The Lincoln's Inn sermons demonstrate Donne's active and principled participation in the political affairs of early Stuart England. His analysis of the possibilities and limitations of prerogative justice makes full use of his own and the audience's legal expertise, and analogizes the languages of the law, politics, hermeneutics, and ethics to formulate a powerful critique of the king's claim to occupy the ultimate 'seate of Iudgement'.[41] Against James's attempt to silence the 'curious wits' who would enquire into 'my Prerogatiue or mystery of State', Donne asserts the right—and indeed the duty—of the lawyers and judges 'to dispute what a King can doe'.[42] Donne insists on the importance of discussing, debating, and 'vexing' the defining political issues of his day. As he observes in the preface to *Biathanatos*, 'as in the Poole of *Bethsaida*, there was no health till the Water was troubled, so the best way to find the truith . . . was to debate and vex it, (for *we must as well dispute De veritate, as pro veritate*)'.[43]

The Donne of the Lincoln's Inn sermon subtly but resolutely argues the case for a model of homiletic engagement which encourages active deliberation about essential political 'truths' and the institutions that embody them. Is this a radical stance? If we read the sermon in the context of James's 1616 Star Chamber speech, which establishes the Chancery as the supreme 'dispenser of the Kings conscience'

---

[41] James VI and I, '1616', 205.
[42] Ibid. 204, 213, 214.
[43] John Donne, *Biathanatos*, 30.

and prohibits discussions about 'the mysterie of the Kings power', then the answer
is probably yes. But there are other criteria to be applied here: that Donne did not
suffer any consequences for his intervention in matters of controversy, for instance,
or that he did not advocate (or implicitly suggest) any concrete measures for
curtailing the king's prerogative rights.[44] On these terms, the answer is probably
no. What we can say with some certainty, however, is that the evidence of the
Lincoln's Inn sermons shows us a preacher who is intensely engaged in matters of
politics and governance. That Donne was preoccupied with the politics of religion
and doctrine is well known. But the Lincoln's Inn sermons also show him grappling
with the politics of the law, with hard-nosed debates about the scope of jurisdictions and the relations between parliament and crown. The complex analogies
constructed in these sermons between legal and religious discourses, equity and
charity, deny a tidy separation of pulpit and lawcourt, Church and State.

But these contextual implications also re-focus attention on the concept of
charity itself. In the Lincoln's Inn sermons, Augustinian charity is no longer a
caricature of casuistical thought, but it remains imbricated in a complex discourse
of conscience and moral intent. Charity is politicized through its parallels with
equitable interpretation, but it also serves a pastoral function in that it helps Donne
discover edifying readings of his scriptural text. The modes of Augustinian recourse
have also been re-configured: the importance of figurative reading is attributed to
Augustine but actually mediated through Luther, and the double-love command
which sustains the interpretive framework of the entire sermon only emerges
through allusion and analogy. Yet despite this circuitous approach to Augustine's
thought, the moral, political, and spiritual ramifications of charity could not be
more crucial.

Donne's treatment of charity has occasioned considerable critical debate. For
Jeanne Shami, Donne's approach to charity encompasses ethics and exegesis: where
other 'players in the religious debates vied for interpretive control of their common
authority—scriptures—Donne continues his unusual practice of emphasising that
his "interpretations" of controversial religious matters are merely interpretations'.[45]
Donne, Shami goes on to observe, is a remarkably 'impartial' reader, whose
exegetical tolerance aims to encourage doctrinal inclusiveness, 'a capacious vision
of the English church' which would 'integrate and convert all but the most
determined recusants'.[46] Donne's charitable exegesis, then, is political but not
polemical. Achsah Guibbory, on the other hand, arguing for Donne's affiliation
with the anti-Calvinist party of Montagu and Laud in the mid and late 1620s, sees
Donne's use of the term charity as merely strategic, a useful means of denigrating
his Calvinist opponents as extremist: 'Donne's emphasis on "charity" is not simply
a generic Augustinian formulation: rather, it aligns him with the Arminians who

---

[44] For a summary of some influential attempts to delimit the monarch's equitable discretion, see
Mark Fortier, *The Culture of Equity in Early Modern England* (Aldershot, 2005), 99–101.

[45] Shami, *Conformity*, 140.

[46] Ibid. 20.

repeatedly invoked the ideal of "charity" in attacking predestination and who attacked Puritans and Calvinists as rigid and uncharitable.'[47]

Donne's use of charity in the Lincoln's Inn pulpit at once confirms and destabilizes these positions. Charitable exegesis in these sermons is both interested and disinterested, and can be put to political as well as pastoral purposes. Donne, as we have seen, employs the hermeneutics of charity to 'advance' the lawyers' 'devotion', and there is no reason to doubt the sincerity of this endeavour. At the same time, however, Donne deploys these interpretive processes to shore up his own authority, to ensure that his sermon is received in good faith; and he discovers a highly polemicized application in the problem of equity. The complexity and richness of this stance arises from Donne's ability to find connections between discourses that seem worlds apart; to bring them home to specific audiences and create a 'nearnesse' with them that allows for a uniquely effective communication of the homiletic message.[48]

Jeremy Maule has shown us how the Holy Sonnets deploy the language of early modern property law to negotiate the terms of Christian salvation.[49] The Lincoln's Inn sermons demonstrate that, years later, Donne was still alive to the rich intellectual, ethical, and political resonances of the legal vocabularies he commanded. But the sermons also remind us that if the parallels between law and religion provide opportunities for topical commentary, the relationship between these discourses is neither stable nor mono-dimensional. Augustinian charity, as it weaves in and out of specific legal and political applications, provides the hermeneutic foundation for Donne's approach to the lawyer's souls and the soul of the law: it is, at once, a timeless law of love and a highly occasion-specific instrument of ideological engagement. It is in this dual dynamic, finally, that Donne reveals himself to be a faithful heir to Augustine's own habits of thought.

---

[47] Achsah Guibbory, 'Donne's Religion: Montagu, Arminianism and Donne's Sermons', *English Literary Renaissance*, 31 (2001), 412–39 (422).
[48] On 'nearenesse', see Shami, *Controversy*, 21–2, 38; 76, 91, 111, 145, 278.
[49] Maule, 'Donne and the Words of the Law', 36.

6

'Keeping the Peace'

Donne, Augustine, and the Crisis of 1629

In his Lincoln's Inn sermons of the early 1620s, as we have seen, Donne engages closely with the politics of charity, re-configuring and re-invigorating that Augustinian term to probe the legal and moral ramifications of equitable justice. Through his terminological manoeuvres, Donne scrutinizes the operations of political discourse, and explores the ways in which key terms such as charity and equity accrue or deflect polemical significance. This chapter charts Donne's return to the Augustinian rhetoric of charity towards the end of his preaching career, in a Whitsunday sermon of 1629, delivered at St Paul's on Genesis 1:2, 'And the spirit of God moved upon the face of the waters' (*Sermons*, 9.92–108).

Donne mounted the pulpit during a time of acute crisis which extended from the domestic to the international sphere, and which embraced religious and political concerns. The most immediate contexts for Donne's sermon of 24 May 1629 were the dissolution of parliament two months earlier, on 10 March, and the controversial peace with France in April of the same year. The dissolution of parliament had been precipitated by debates about the reach and scope of the royal prerogative and, more particularly, Charles I's right to exact tonnage and poundage from parliament. However, as the Commons Resolution of 2 March makes clear, the conflicted relationship between parliament and crown was put under equal strain by questions of religious doctrine and practice. A week before parliament was disbanded, for instance, MPs declared as a capital enemy of the kingdom anyone who 'shall bring in innovation in religion, or by favour seek to extend or introduce Popery or Arminianism'.[1] Discussions held in the Commons between January and March 1629 document repeated attempts to push religious concerns to the top of the political agenda, not least because—in the mind of many—matters of doctrine and state were inextricably linked. Sir Walter Erle argued in a Commons speech of 27 January, for example, that 'never was there (in a point of subsistence) a more neare conjunction between matter of Religion and matter of State in any Kingdom in the world then there is in this Kingdom at this day'.[2] Parliamentary deliberations on the issue of doctrinal 'innovation' focused on the dual (and related) threats of Arminianism and 'Popery', which were seen to be embodied at the institutional level in the 1628

---

[1] 'The Protestations of the Commons in Parliament on Monday 2 March', in *Commons Debates of 1629*, ed. Wallace Notestein and Frances Helen Relf (Minnesota, 1921), 101–2.

[2] *Commons Debates of 1629*, 14.

Declaration on Religion accompanying the re-issue of the Thirty-Nine Articles, and—in a more tangible sense—in the persons of the Bishops of London and Winchester, William Laud and Richard Neile.[3] In these debates, the language of doctrinal peace, charity, and moderation played a crucial part. Donne's Whitsunday sermon of 1629 anatomizes this new register of charity and seeks to infuse it with fresh currency. He takes on another project of terminological re-definition, which tests the polemical rhetoric of moderation associated with Laud's policies in the late 1620s, and ultimately attempts to rehabilitate the language of charity for the twin purposes of comfort and pastoral edification. In doing so, Donne draws on Augustinian precepts of interpretation articulated in the final books of the *Confessions*; he tries to catch glimpses of God's eternal love through localized ruptures in the fabric of political discourse, and re-casts the crisis of 1629 as a temporary digression from the broader providential narrative of creation and salvation.

Before we move on to a discussion of the politics of charity, however, a brief analysis of the language of the 1628 Declaration illustrates the extent to which the political crisis of 1629 was implicated in a crisis of interpretation. '*His maiesties declaration*' stipulated 'that all curious search' into contentious doctrines 'be layd aside', in an attempt to silence disputation of controversial topics from the pulpit and in lecture-halls.[4] The wholesome antidote to such corrosive wrangling was located in 'the true usuall literall meaning' of the Thirty-Nine Articles, the 'plain and full' scope of doctrinal fundamentals. Despite its rhetoric of natural semantic plenitude and lucidity, however, the 1628 Declaration clearly enjoined that the 'true' meaning of the articles could only be established by the proper authorities: 'the settled continuance of the doctrine and discipline of the Church of England' was to be overseen by 'the clergie in their convocation'.[5] Yet this question of

---

[3] On the 1628 Declaration in the context of parliament and censorship, see Cyndia Susan Clegg, *Press Censorship in Caroline England* (Cambridge, 2008), 84–5, and S. Mutchow Towers, *Control of Religious Printing in Early Stuart England* (Woodbridge, 2003), 210–12. For two radically opposed views of the religio-political effect of the 1628 Declaration, see Nicholas Tyacke, *Anti-Calvinists: The Rise of English Arminianism c.1590–1640* (Oxford, 1989) and Peter White, *Predestination, Policy and Polemic: Conflict and Consensus in the English Church from the Reformation to the Civil War* (Cambridge, 1992). While Tyacke argues that the 1628 Declaration was effectively the final step by which Calvinism was outlawed (50–1), White contends that, 'far from inaugurating an Arminian regime, [the Declaration] was substantially successful in preventing further controversy' (204). See further, Julian Davies, *The Caroline Captivity of the Church: Charles I and the Remoulding of Anglicanism, 1625–1641* (Oxford, 1992); L. J. Reeve, *Charles I and the Road to Personal Rule* (Cambridge, 1989); and Kenneth Fincham and Peter Lake, 'The Ecclesiastical Policies of James I and Charles I', in Fincham (ed.), *The Early Stuart Church 1603–1642* (Basingstoke, 1993), 23–50. My aim is not to gauge the political motives or effects of the 1628 Declaration, but to create a contextual framework for Donne's sermon by highlighting some responses to its publication. It is clear from the parliamentary debates that many key figures in the Commons read the Declaration as an anti-Calvinist document—or, importantly, thought it would be conducive to their own political purposes to be seen to do so. My focus in this chapter is on the implications of these assumptions for the shaping of polemical discourses in 1629.

[4] 'Royal Declaration for the Peace of the Church, 1628–9', prefixing articles of religion of 1562, in Kenneth Fincham, *Visitation Articles and Injunctions of the Early Stuart Church*, 2 vols. (1603–42) (Woodbridge, 1998), 2.33–4. The Declaration was composed in late December 1628 and printed at the turn of the year; it was available to newsletter writers by 7 January 1629 (ibid. 33).

[5] Ibid. 34.

interpretive authority proved a crucial point of dissension between monarch and parliament. While the 1628 Declaration construed Convocation as a natural institutional extension of the articles—and the clergy collectively as inhabiting the spirit of its doctrinal laws—many in the Commons regarded Convocation as an external and decidedly partial body, whose interests and motives required constant supervision. On the terms of this argument, interpretation was not simply a reactive process of elucidation, but could actively shape a more global religio-political agenda. Sir Walter Eliot's speech of 29 January represents this position in its most fully articulated form:

> If there be any difference in the opinion concerning the sense and interpretation, the Bishops and the Clergy in the Convocation have power admitted to them to do anything that shall concern the continuance and maintenance of the Truth professed; which Truth being contained in these Articles, and these Articles being different in the sense, so as if there be any dispute about it, it is in them to order which way they please; and for aught I know, Popery and Arminianism may be a sense introduced by them, and then it must be received.[6]

Eliot's speech pulls together a number of points which summarize the position taken by the parliamentary committee on religion in the early weeks of 1629. While the 1628 Declaration had sought to emphasize the impartial nature of its injunctions in a language of unity, peace, and moderation, Eliot presented it as a highly sectarian initiative designed to introduce 'Popery and Arminianism'. Where the Declaration insisted on the king's desire 'to conserve and maintain the Church . . . in the unity of true religion, and in the bond of peace', Eliot argued that its stipulations put 'our Faith and Religion . . . in danger'. Both the Declaration and Eliot's response, then, were engaged not only in driving a political agenda, but in devising discursive strategies that would be most conducive to its realization. The rhetoric of the Declaration leans heavily on its context, the re-publication of a classic document in the Church of England's history: the 1562 Articles, carrying timeless authority and transcending local controversy. Eliot, on the other hand, insisted on the highly acute and contemporary significance of the royal re-issue, and pursued its potential religio-political ramifications in a hyperbolical idiom designed to appeal to his audience's worst fears (including the somewhat cryptic claim that the Thirty-Nine Articles might serve as a conduit for the introduction of Catholicism). The reference to 'the bonds of peace' invokes a biblical proof-text which was fundamental to debates over religious unity in 1628 and 1629. Ephesians 4:3, 'Endeavouring to keep the unity of the Spirit in the bond of peace', was the passage that Laud had selected for his sermon at the opening of the previous parliament on 17 March 1628;

[6] *Commons Debates*, 26. This is particularly interesting in light of Donne's election as prolocutor of Convocation in 1626. Donne's address to Convocation is printed in Bald, *Life*, 573–5; his participation there is discussed in Jeanne Shami, 'Speaking Openly and Speaking First: John Donne, the Synod of Dort, and the Early Stuart Church', in Mary A. Papazian (ed.), *John Donne and the Protestant Reformation* (Detroit, 2003), 35–65; see also Nigel Bawcutt and Hilton Kelliher, 'Donne through Contemporary Eyes: New Light on his Participation in the Convocation of 1626', *Notes & Queries*, NS 42 (1995), 441–4.

the same scriptural text was frequently cited as the central terms of the conflict over interpretive jurisdiction were evolved and contested.[7] To many members of the parliamentary committee on religion, the act of ceding exegetical authority to Convocation potentially put Protestantism itself at risk, and the king's and Laud's exhortations to peace were merely part of a broader strategic plan to suppress dissent. Laud, by contrast, drawing on Augustine's authority and mobilizing the rhetoric of charitable inclusiveness, insisted on a commitment to moderation, in an effort to create 'one mind in the Church and one mind in the State':

> The 'unity,' then, 'of the Spirit' . . . includes both; both concord in mind and affec-
> tions, and love of charitable unity, which comes from the Spirit of God, and returns to
> it. And, indeed, the grace of God's Spirit is that alone which makes men truly at peace
> and unity with one another. *Ei tribuendum non nobis;* to Him it is to be attributed, not
> to us, saith Saint Augustine.[8]

Donne's Whitsunday sermon of 1629, I would suggest, is best considered as a contribution to this discourse of religio-political charity, peace, and moderation. His most extensive homiletic meditation on the conditions and aims of scriptural interpretation, Donne's exposition of the second verse of Genesis richly resonates with the terminology that defined the hermeneutic controversies of 1628–9. In a more immediate sense, however, Donne's sermon squarely positions itself at the centre of the disputed rhetorical territory of peace and unity: '*Contendunt & dimicant, & nemo sine pace videt istam visionem*', Donne argues with a reference to *Confessions* 13.11, '[t]hey dispute, and they wrangle, and they scratch, and wound one anothers reputations, and they assist the common enemy of Christiani-ty by their uncharitable differences, *Et sine pace* [13.11], And without peace, and mildnesse, and love, and charity, no man comes to know the holy Ghost, who is the God of peace, and the God of love' (9.101).

Donne's emphasis on the 'God of peace', 'the holy Ghost' was, of course, inspired by the liturgical occasion, Whitsunday, the feast commemorating the descent of the Holy Spirit on the Apostles, fifty days after the resurrection of Christ. But his focus on the Holy Ghost as an instrument of hermeneutic comfort and charity owes as much to the more localized political context I have outlined above. Donne's engagement with the discourse of unity and moderation is thor-ough and complex; and, once again, his deployment of Augustinian material directs the purpose and function of his preaching. While evidently conforming to the ecclesiastical injunctions promulgated since December 1628, Donne also uses his

---

[7] e.g. by the king in his opening address to that parliament, and by Attorney General Heath in his admonition to Montagu after his appointment to the See of Chichester, on 7 October 1628: 'You are now a father of our Church; and, as a father, you will, I know, tender the peace and quiet of the Church. . . . [C]onsult first with Almighty God, the God of peace, the bond of peace, the spirit of peace' (cited in Samuel Gardiner, *History of England from the Accession of James I to the Outbreak of the Civil War 1603–1642*, 10 vols. (London, 1884), 7.19).

[8] William Laud, *Works*, ed. William Scott and James Bliss, 7 vols. (Oxford, 1847–60), vol. 1, ed. William Scott, 162. The reference is to Augustine's *Homilies on the Gospel of John* (Homily 110, on John 17:21–3; *PL* 35.1921). See n. 29 for an account of scholarly work on the rhetoric of charity and peace in Donne, and in early modern preaching and politics more generally.

pulpit performance to redefine the meaning of religious peace; crucially, he does so by re-configuring Laud's use of Augustine and, with it, the vocabulary of charity and moderation more generally. While Laud's sermon at Westminster presents Augustine as a custodian of institutional Church order—chiefly with reference to *De Ordine*—Donne uses the final books of the *Confessions* and the first book of *On the Literal Interpretation of Genesis* to open up a more comprehensive metaphysical perspective. The prospect of heavenly peace with God adumbrated at the end of the *Confessions* offers glimpses of a higher providential order, which transcends the sense of political chaos and unrest attendant upon the dissolution of parliament in 1629. Donne's Whitsunday sermon thus ultimately marks a withdrawal from the polemical fray and, in many ways, inaugurates the final phase of his ministry: by adopting a homiletic approach that is characterized not so much by active participation in political debate as by meditation, devotional introspection, and anticipation of eternal rest in heaven.

Donne's 1629 Whitsunday sermon differs from his other preaching performances on that festival in a number of significant ways. First of all, it is unique in selecting an Old Testament passage as its scriptural text. The other nine surviving Whitsunday sermons concentrate on the New Testament; of these, more than half were preached on the Gospel of John.[9] The reasons for this choice will become clearer when we attend in more detail to the sermon's emphasis on scriptural plenitude and plurality, which arises from Donne's engagement with Augustine's hermeneutics. For now, it is sufficient to note that Genesis 1:2 testifies to Donne's interest in the creation narrative, which he reads above all as an epitome of God's providential plan: creation history is cosmic history and eschatology. Donne clocks up a total of thirty-four acknowledged references to Augustine's expositions of Genesis 1 in his sermon, citing six different Augustinian approaches to the first book of the Pentateuch and alluding through more remote echoes to a further four. Genesis was the scriptural text to which Augustine returned most consistently at crucial points of his career, from the early *On Genesis against the Manichees* (388–90),[10] via the *Incomplete Commentary on Genesis* (393–4)[11] and Books 11–13 of the *Confessions* (398), to his final two attempts to explicate the creation account in *On the Literal Interpretation of Genesis* (401/2–416) and the *City of God* (413–26). Another substantial departure from Donne's Whitsunday conventions is the thematic focus of the 1629 sermon. As recent scholarship has demonstrated, Donne's pentecostal rhetoric tends to foreground one or both of two prominent ideas: the office of preaching and the art of memory.[12] Donne's 1629

[9] The Gospel of John occupies the top spot among Donne's favourite scriptural source texts jointly with Matthew's Gospel.

[10] *De Genesi adversus Manichaeos*, PL 34.

[11] *De Genesi adversus Manichaeos*, PL 34.

[12] On preaching, see Hugh Adlington, 'Preaching the Holy Ghost: John Donne's Whitsunday Sermons', *John Donne Journal*, 22 (2003), 203–28; on memory, see the text of the 1627 Whitsunday sermon, John 14:26, 'the Holy Ghost ... shall teach you all things, and bring all things to your remembrance'. See also, for a discussion of Donne's theory of memory from an Augustinian perspective, Guibbory, Guite, Hickes, and Mueller; and for the Thomistic case, Masselink (all cited on p. 16 n. 54).

190   *'Keeping the Peace'*

discourse marks a complete departure from these patterns: it has nothing to say about memory and counsels against overenthusiastic sermon attendance. Instead, it devotes itself wholly to exegesis and interpretation as activities of existential and political import, and as sources of metaphysical comfort. In doing so, it transforms the 1628 Declaration's emphasis on 'the true usuall literall meaning' into an alternative hermeneutic approach: one which redefines the contested category of the 'literal' as superficial and aspires to a 'transcendental' form of reading, which develops a new spiritual sense under the tutelage of the Holy Ghost, 'the spirit of Comfort'.

'Comfort' is the attribute of the Holy Spirit which attracts the greatest attention in Donne's 1629 Whitsunday sermon.[13] He opens with an emphatic reminder that the 'Holy Ghost is the God, the Spirit of Comfort... the intire, the onely Comforter; and more than all that, The Comfort it selfe' (9.92). Donne also— and in an equally timely fashion—stresses 'the office of the Holy Ghost... to gather, to establish, to illumine, to governe the Church which the Son of God... hath purchased with his blood' (9.92). In his *divisio*, Donne proposes to consider both the literal and the spiritual sense of Genesis 1:2, 'And the Spirit of God moved upon the face of the waters'. His 'literal' exposition refers to the first creation, God's 'making the world for us' (9.93); the text's 'spiritual' significance is revealed through reflections on the second creation, man's regeneration, or God's 'making us for the other world' (9.93). Within this bipartite structure, Donne concentrates on three key questions: (1) '*Quid Spiritus Dei?* What this Power, or this person, which is here called *the Spirit of God*, is'; (2) '*Quid ferebatur?* What this Action, which is here called a *Moving*, was'; and (3) '*Quid super faciem aquarum?* What the subject of this Action, *the face of the waters*, was'.

Donne's sermon makes explicit reference to six Augustinian texts: the *Confessions* (Books 11–13); *On the Literal Interpretation of Genesis*; the *Enarrations on the Psalms*; the *Incomplete Commentary on Genesis*; an Easter sermon on Genesis 1; and *On the Incarnation of the Word*.[14] Lingering in the background of Donne's sermon are four other works by Augustine which offer suggestive comments on Genesis and which are referenced elsewhere in his sermons: the *City of God*, *On Genesis against the Manichees*, *Eighty-Three Various Questions*, and *Of the Immortality of the Soul*.[15] In his Whitsunday performance of 1629, Donne showcases a whole range of responses to Augustine's texts, from cases of simple 'fact-checking', as he collates and reports Augustine's various explications of Genesis 1:2, to the complex structural elaboration of ideas that are latent in Augustine's works but prove foundational to Donne's own account of the two creations. To the first

[13] 'Paraclete', the alternative designation of the Holy Spirit, derives from the Greek word for 'comfort', *parakletos*.
[14] *De Incarnatione Verbi ad Januarium Libri Duo*, PL 42. This text, and the Easter sermon, are not now attributed to Augustine.
[15] *On Genesis against the Manichees* 1.8 (PL 34.179), for instance, provides the recurring motif of God as 'artifex'. See Stanislaus J. Grabowski, 'Spiritus Dei in Gen. 1:2 According to St. Augustine', *Catholic Biblical Quarterly*, 10 (1948), 13–28, for a comprehensive summary of Augustine's shifting pronouncements on Gen. 1:2. For Augustine's exposition of the creation narrative more generally, see Christopher O'Toole, *The Philosophy of Creation in the Writings of St. Augustine* (Washington, DC, 1944); J. J. O'Meara, 'Saint Augustine's Understanding of the Creation and Fall', in *Studies in Augustine and Eriugena*, ed. Thomas Halton (Washington, DC, 1992), 233–43.

category of synopsis and fact-checking we can consign a cluster of references found in the opening section of Donne's *divisio* under the question '*Quid Spiritus Dei*': the question of whether the word 'Spirit' merely denotes a power 'proceeding from God' or represents 'God himselfe' (9.96). Here, Donne presents a brief conspectus of Augustinian positions to illustrate the complexity of this issue. He begins by citing two passages which show Augustine advocating the first position (Spirit as 'power'), then reviews the competing viewpoint (that the 'Spirit' of Genesis 1:2 is an example of direct divine intervention), and finally has Augustine affirm that the Holy Spirit was indeed 'a Creator' (9.97):

> some great men in the Christian Church have imagined it to be ... *Operatio Dei, The power of God working upon the waters,* (so some) or, *Efficientia Dei, A power by God infused into the waters;* so others. And to that S. *Augustine* comes so neare, as to say once in the negative, *Spiritus Dei hic, res dei est, sed non ipse Deus est,* The Spirit of God in this place is something proceeding from God, but it is not God himselfe; And once in the affirmative, *Posse esse vitalem creaturam, quâ universus mundus movetur;* That this Spirit of God may be that universall power, which sustaines, and inanimates the whole world.... This Spirit of God gave life, therefore this Spirit was a Creator; therefore God. S. *Augustine* prints his seale deepe; *Secundùm quod eo intelligere possum, ita est,* as far as my understanding can reach, it is so; and his understanding reached far. But he addes, *Nec ullo modo, &c.* Neither can it possibly be otherwise. (9.96–7)

The three brief quotations from Augustine in this passage are taken, in order, from the first sermon on the Easter Vigil; from the fourth chapter of the *Incomplete Commentary on Genesis*; and from Book 1, chapter 17 of *On the Incarnation of the Word*.[16] It is clear that none of these Augustinian references serves a significant structural or thematic purpose in Donne's sermon; they are adduced purely to build up a useful summary of Augustinian positions on Genesis 1:2, a strategy which itself prepares for the disquisition on hermeneutic plenitude and variety that follows. All of this suggests that Donne probably distilled these citations from a mediating source.[17]

Hugh Adlington has reminded us of the close connection, in sermon theory and practice, between the office of the Holy Ghost and that of the preacher.[18] Andreas Hyperius's *The Practis of Preaching* (1577), for instance, comments on the

---

[16] (1) Augustine, *Sermo* 157 (De Tempore), *In Vigilia Paschae (I), On Genesis 1.1–61*, ch. 3: 'Spiritus super aquas, non Deus, sed res Dei' (*PL* 39.2056); (2) Augustine, *De Genesi ad Litteram Liber Imperfectus*, chapter 4: 'Potest autem et aliter intelligi, ut spiritum Dei, vitalem creaturam, qua universus iste visibilis mundus atque omnia corporea continentur et moventur, intelligamus[.]' (*PL* 34.226); (3) *De Incarnatione Verbi*, Book 1.17 (also not by Augustine): 'puto quod non sit alius quam Spiritus sanctus, secundum quod ego intelligere possum' (*PL* 42.1184).

[17] It is interesting to note, however, that entries under 'creatio' or 'spiritus sanctus' in mainstream Augustinian anthologies by Corvinus, Andreas Musculus, and Crespin do not provide a single reference to the Augustinian expositions cited by Donne in his sermon. Erasmus's Index, by contrast, under the heading 'spiritus Dei ferebatur super aquas', sends the reader straight to chapter 4 of Augustine's *Incomplete Commentary on Genesis* (in vol. 3 of Erasmus's edition), which offers the precise wording of the passage cited by Donne, and also references *On the Incarnation of the Word*.

[18] Adlington, 'Preaching the Holy Ghost', 207.

rhetorical effectiveness of the Apostle Peter who, 'filled with the holy ghost, is had in admiration for his libertie in speaking'.[19] Donne himself notes in an undated Whitsunday sermon on Acts 10:44 that 'the Holy Ghost leads and places the words, and sentences of the Preacher';[20] and, preaching on the same occasion in 1628, on John 14:26, he explains that the Holy Ghost 'came in the form of Tongues, and they that received him, were thereby presently enabled to speak to others'.[21] Donne's Whitsunday sermon of 1629 contains no such praise of the Holy Spirit as 'Teacher' and model preacher, nor does it make any attempt to foreground the importance of sermon delivery and sermon attendance to its audience. If anything, Donne's sermon works hard to devalue the importance of preaching in relation to prayer and other forms of religious observance. He speaks disparagingly of those who 'will not be satisfied with Manna, but will needs have Quailes, that is, cannot make one meale of Prayers, except he have a sermon' (9.102), and criticizes those members of his congregation who 'may offend God in running after many working dayes Sermons' and, in so doing, neglect 'the sustentation' of their families. Though conventional and unobjectionable in themselves, these pronouncements on preaching represent subtle yet significant alterations to viewpoints expressed at other crucial moments in Donne's preaching career, which emphasize the symbiotic relationship of prayer and preaching—often in explicitly Augustinian terms—and the compatibility of sermon attendance and professional vocation.[22]

Donne's sermon downplays the significance of preaching and highlights instead the importance of exegesis. He turns inward and seeks devotional comfort in the act of reading: the exposition of Genesis serves to unlock the wider providential meaning of God's creation. In the Whitsunday sermon of 1629, these concerns are foregrounded through a series of reflections on 'the exposition of darke places' in the opening section of Donne's discourse. There, Donne shores up his interpretive principles with sixteen references from the final three books of the *Confessions*—that portion of the work which, as Augustine remarked in the *Retractations*, marked the turn from biography ('de me') to scriptural interpretation ('de scripturis sanctis').[23] Of these, seven are taken from the second and third chapters of Book 11 alone. Robert P. Kennedy has argued that 'Book 11 may be regarded as the interpretive key to the *Confessions* because it sets out the groundwork for

---

[19] Andreas Hyperius, *The Practis of Preaching* (1577), sig. 6r.
[20] *Sermons*, 5.40.
[21] Ibid. 8.260.
[22] Donne's fourth Prebend sermon, for instance, preached at St Paul's on 28 January 1626, cites 'S. Augustines holy circle, in which he walks from Prayers to Sermon, and from the Sermon, next day to Prayers againe' (7.312). See also *Sermons*, 3.128: 'We cannot inherit the kingdom of God if we possess not the preaching of the Word'; 6.93, where preaching is described not as a 'courtesy . . . but a duty'; 7.157, where 'slackening of preaching' is said to lead to 'a danger of losing Christ'; 4.195: '[preaching is] God's ordinance to beget faith, to take away preaching were to disarm God'; 5.45: 'howsoever God may afford salvation to some in all nations, yet he hath manifested to us no way of conveying salvation to them, but by the manifestation of Christ Jesus in his ordinance of preaching'. (All cited in P. M. Oliver, *Donne's Religious Writing: A Discourse of Feigned Devotion* (Harlow, 1997), 240–1.)
[23] *Retractations* 2.6.1 (*PL* 32.632).

discovering the eternal within the temporal, and for transforming the desire for God into the activity of attaining communion with him. The path that will guide him to God is Scripture; by uniting his mind with its words, he can shape his life for an identity that can sustain the vision of God.'[24] Donne's hermeneutic project in the Whitsunday sermon also builds towards the ultimate goal of discovering the eternal within the temporal. Scripture interpretation is the path that will lead Donne to God, and reading the creation narrative through the *Confessions* will become the chief source of comfort in Donne's sermon, a spiritual coping strategy which at once enables continued participation in a crisis-ridden world and sustains belief in a broader salvific perspective. Donne begins the main part of the sermon with a lyrical meditation on scriptural exegesis; once again, he interweaves Augustine's voice and his own, invoking key passages from Book 11 of the *Confessions*:

> First then, undertaking the consideration of the literall sense, and after, of the spirituall, we joyne with S. *Augustine, Sint castæ deliciæ meæ Scripturæ tuæ* [*Confessions* 11.2]; Lord I love to be conversant in thy Scriptures, let my conversation with thy Scriptures be a chast conversation; that I discover no nakednesse therein; offer not to touch any thing in thy Scriptures, but that, that thou hast vouchsafed to unmask, and manifest unto me: *Nec fallar in eis, nec fallam ex eis* [11.2]; Lord, let not me mistake the meaning of thy Scriptures, nor mis-lead others, by imputing a false sense to them. *Non frustra scribuntur* [11.2], sayes he; Lord, thou hast writ nothing to no purpose; thou wouldst be understood in all: But not in all, by all men, at all times; *Confiteor tibi quicquid invenero in libris tuis* [11.2]; Lord I acknowledge that I receive from thee, whatsoever I understand in thy word; for else I doe not understand it. (9.94)

Donne's choice of the word 'conversation' sums up Augustine's attempt to forge a relationship between God-as-author and his human readers in *Confessions* 11. This connection, as Donne's modulations on Augustinian charity will make is established and preserved by the Holy Spirit, whose operations are imagined in textual and hermeneutic terms. Donne's riff on *Confessions* 11.2 envisages a more direct encounter with God's Word; he fuses several early modern meanings of the term 'conversation' to construct an interpretive trajectory which leads from textual communication to metaphysical communion: from the idea of exegetical order (avoiding the imputation of 'a false sense') to the loving receptivity and tentative intimacy of incipient dialogue.[25] At the same time, Donne is keen to emphasize the difficulty of reading, as well as the partiality and inadequacy of human cognition: 'thou wouldst be understood in all: But not in all, by all men, at all times.' From the recognition that time-bound human interpretations are necessarily fragmented, Donne moves to a consideration of semantic plurality:

[24] Robert P. Kennedy, 'Book 11: *The Confessions* as Eschatological Narrative', in *A Reader's Companion to the Confessions*, ed. Kim Paffenroth and Robert P. Kennedy (Louisville, Ky., 2003), 167–83 (168).
[25] *OED* 2: 'commerce, intercourse, society, intimacy'; 6: 'manner of conducting oneself in the world, behaviour, mode/course of life'; 7: 'interchange of thoughts and words, familiar discourse or talk'. For Donne on holy conversation and the Holy Ghost, see his sermon on Matthew 9:13, preached to the household at Whitehall, on 30 April 1626 (7.141–63).

So difficult a thing seemed it to that intelligent Father, to understand this history, this mystery of the Creation. But yet though he found, that divers senses offered themselves, he did not doubt of finding the Truth: For, *Deus meus lumen oculorum meorum in occulto* [*Confessions* 12.18], sayes he, O my God, the light of mine eyes, in this dark inquisition, since divers senses, arise out of these words, and all true, *Qui mihi obest, si aliud ego sensero, quam sensit alius, eum sensisse, qui scripsit* [12.18]? What hurt followes, though I follow another sense, then some other man takes to be *Moses* sense? . . . Where divers senses arise, and all true . . . let truth agree them. But what is Truth? God; And what is God? Charity; Therefore let Charity reconcile such differences. . . . [The solution is] charitably to leave others to their liberty, if they but differ from us, and not differ from Fundamentall Truths. (9.94–5)

Donne's observation that even Augustine struggled with the exposition of Genesis, and his insistent reminders that our exegetical efforts are (at best) a 'dark inquisition', recall both the *Essayes in Divinity* (which rely heavily on the *Confessions*) and the interpretive contortions of the Lincoln's Inn sermons. But this passage also casts a shadow of wry pessimism over the 1628 Declaration's faith in the value of clerical interpretation. In Donne's model, the only comfort and effective antidote to cognitive fragmentation is the work of the Holy Spirit.

Any impression that Donne's sermon may be dissenting from prevailing opinions on interpretive authority, however, is defused and contained by the conclusion of this passage. Here, Donne confines the scope of permissible difference to matters *in*different; in the case of 'Fundamentall Truths', 'diverse' voices must be harmonized into an expression of orthodoxy. This movement represents one of many significant attempts on Donne's part to demonstrate conformity with the ecclesiastical policies articulated in the first half of 1629. In May, bishops without court or household offices were ordered back to their dioceses to police pulpits and enforce the 1628 Declaration against controversial preaching, encourage prayers and catechizing, and impose conformity on lecturers. Donne, as we have seen, certainly does not encourage excessive sermon-going (in April 1627, by contrast, he had claimed that 'if a man could have six Sermons a day, all the days of his life, he might die without having heard all the Scriptures explicated in Sermons'[26]). In its place, he extols the virtues of doctrinal fundamentals, recommends a 'love of peace, and holy assurance, and acquiescence in Gods ordinance' (9.105), and dwells in detail on the sacrament of baptism.[27]

---

[26] *Sermons*, 7.401.

[27] As Peter McCullough has noted, by the late 1620s, 'Andrewes and his acolytes had . . . ranked the administration of the two sacraments, baptism and the eucharist, as superior conduits of divine grace to preaching', thus reversing the Elizabethan Calvinist insistence on the primacy of the Word preached ('Donne as Preacher at Court: Precarious "Inthronization"', in Colclough (ed.), *John Donne's Professional Lives*, 179–204 (198)). See Lancelot Andrewes on preaching: 'the corps, the whole body of some mens profession, all godliness with some, what is it but hearing a sermon? The ear is all, the ear is all that is done, and but by our ear-mark no man should know us to be Christians', quoted in Peter Lake, 'Lancelot Andrewes, John Buckeridge, and Avant-Garde Conformity at the Court of James I', in Linda Levy Peck (ed.), *The Mental World of the Jacobean Court* (Cambridge, 1991), 113–33 (116). But see also McCullough, *Sermons at Court*, 159–66, on the court-dependence of this critique (Andrewes was criticizing James I's sermon-gadding in particular, not sermons in general).

Donne's eagerness to display his conformist credentials, I would suggest, can also be gauged by the sermon's conspicuous avoidance of controversial topics, whether doctrinal or political. His performance is devoid of polemical comment; nor does it implicate any faction—Puritan, Calvinist, Laudian—through favourable or unfavourable comparisons with the Church of Rome. Instead it vigorously pursues the rhetoric of peace, charity, and moderation that was the hallmark of official proclamations in 1628–9, through constant recourse to the final books of the *Confessions*: *'Contendunt & dimicant, & nemo sine pace videt istam visionem* [*Confessions* 13.11], They dispute, and they wrangle, and they scratch, and wound one anothers reputations, and they assist the common enemy of Christianity by their uncharitable differences, *Et sine pace* [13.11], And without peace, and mildnesse, and love, and charity, no man comes to know the holy Ghost, who is the God of peace, and the God of love' (9.101).[28]

A word of caution is needed before we pursue this line of enquiry further. The language of irenicism, conciliation, and pacifism, as recent scholarship has recognized, was a staple of polemical discourse in the 1620s and 1630s. Peter Lake in particular has revealed to us the ubiquity and versatility of these tropes of moderation, which could be used, on the anti-Calvinist side, to counsel against English involvement in a Continental religious war, while enabling moderate Calvinists to appeal in the same terms for active participation in that conflict.[29] Laud's own deployment of the rhetoric of peace and charity at the end of the 1620s was far from disinterested. A letter to Gerhard Vossius of 14 July 1629 presents Laud as an advocate of 'moderation':

> I have turned over every stone so that these treacherous and perplexed questions should not be discussed before the people, lest we should do violence to piety and charity under the appearance of truth ('ne pietatem et charitatem sub specie veri violaremus'). . . . This has not, perhaps, always given pleasure; but I remember how seriously our Saviour recommended charity to his followers. . . . I will try with all my strength so that peace and truth might kiss each other ('dabo operam, ut veritas et pax se invicem exosculentur').[30]

Laud places 'truth' in a complex relationship with 'piety and charity'. While the final sentence of the extract expresses some hope that 'peace and truth' might be united, Laud's reflections on the practical implementations of doctrinal peace suggest a more problematic picture. In his 1628 sermon at the opening of

[28] Donne draws on the Augustinian association between charity and the spirit; see e.g. *Confessions* 13.7.8 (*PL* 32.847): 'Against this background the reader can grasp your apostle's meaning when he is saying that "love is diffused in our hearts by the Holy Spirit who is given to us" (Rom. 5.5). Teaching us concerning the things of the Spirit he demonstrates that the way of charity is "supereminent" (1 Cor. 12.1).' See also *Confessions* 13.9.10 and 13.31.46.
[29] Lake, 'Lancelot Andrewes', 113–33; Lake, 'The Moderate and Irenic Case for Religious War: Joseph Hall's *Via Media* in Context', in *Political Culture and Cultural Politics in Early Modern England*, ed. Susan Amussen and Mark Kishlansky (Manchester, 1995), 55–83; Lake, 'Joseph Hall, Robert Skinner and the Rhetoric of Moderation at the Early Stuart Court', in Ferrell and McCullough (eds.), *The English Sermon Revised*, 167–85. Achsah Guibbory, as we have seen, has shown how the term charity was used as a polemical tool by anti-Calvinist divines in the mid-1620s to redefine elements of Calvinist theology as Puritan zealotry.
[30] Laud, *Works*, vol. 6, ed. James Bliss, 265–6.

parliament on Ephesians 4:3, Laud expresses a definitive preference for 'peace'—a virtue which is equated throughout with order, compliance, and submission. Augustine and the Holy Spirit, the twin sources of solace and spiritual comfort in Donne's 1629 Whitsunday sermon, are Laud's custodians of discipline in Church and State. Peace, in Laud's sermon, 'stands for a calm and quiet dispose of the hearts of men, and of their carriage': 'The "peace" then here spoken of, differs not much from the virtue of meekness.... It is an ancient rule for kingdoms and a good, *iisdem artibus quibus parta sunt facile retinentur,*—they are kept in subjection, order, and obedience, by the same virtues by which they were first gotten.'[31] The country, Laud warns, will only be preserved in peace and unity if its citizens display the virtues associated with the Holy Ghost, ' "humility" [lowliness] at the heart; "meekness" in the carriage; "patience" [long-suffering] in point of forbearance; and "charity" [forbearing one another in love]'.[32] The enemies of the peace, Laud continues in more ominous tones, are those who 'would have a little more liberty that have too much already'.[33] The Fathers of the Church are presented by Laud as holy enforcers, whose mission is to warn against breaches of the peace, lest we incur 'the wrath of the Lord': 'For the Church; nothing, saith Saint Chrysostom, doth so provoke God to anger, as to see *divisam Ecclesiam* ... And for the commonwealth; a people is as one city, yet such a one, saith Saint Augustine, *cui est periculosa dissensio,* as to whom all breach of "unity" is full of danger.'[34] Laud's Fathers are guarantors of 'calm', 'quiet', and 'meekness'; 'charity, which is the glue of the Spirit' manifests chiefly as a form of mutual neighbourly surveillance, a means of policing the enemies of national and ecclesiastical unity—'pride and disobedience'.[35] Laud's Augustine in particular is a relentless and dedicated enforcer of Church order.

The significance of Donne's own rhetoric of peace in May 1629—including the potentially contentious equation of 'truth' and 'charity'—can be delineated more accurately through comparison with his last sermon before the dissolution of parliament, preached at Whitehall on 20 February, on James 2:12: 'So speak ye, and so do, as they that shall be judged by the Law of Liberty.' On the first Friday in Lent, Donne highlighted the importance of political counsel and active dialogue: 'we are bound to speak: speech is the Glue, the Cyment, the soul of Conversation, and of Religion too.... *Loquimini Deo,* speak to God; And ... those that have the Honorable office to do so, are bound to speak to Kings by way of Counsel' (8.338–9). As David Colclough has shown, Donne stresses the importance of regulated, discreet speech, and strikes a balance between *'multi-loquio'* and *'nulli-loquio'* (8.337)—perhaps as a more diplomatic alternative to the more strident tones of Commons protests.[36] Nevertheless, the contrast between Donne's vocal defence of

---

[31] Laud, *Works*, vol. 1, ed. William Scott, 173.
[32] Ibid. 172.   [33] Ibid. 180.
[34] Ibid. 160, an exact citation from Augustine's *De Ordine* (Book 2, chapter 18).
[35] Ibid. 167, 178.
[36] David Colclough, *Freedom of Speech in Early Stuart England* (Cambridge, 2005), 97–101; see also Paul W. Harland, 'Donne's Political Intervention in the Parliament of 1629', *John Donne Journal*, 11 (1992), 21–37.

political speech and counsel in February and, following the dissolution of parliament, the deafening silence of May, is a striking one.

Donne's approach to the controversial language of peace and charity emerges most clearly through detailed examination of his exegetical philosophy in the Whitsunday sermon. His opening disquisition on scriptural interpretation models itself on the rules prescribed by '[t]hat heavenly Father', Augustine, but also responds to the local debates about hermeneutic and political authority I explored at the beginning of the chapter. Donne notes that 'a right exposition of Scripture' must establish 'such a sense as may violate no confessed Article of Religion'; but while this notion firmly embeds Scripture readers in the institutional, human, 'earth-bound' context of exegesis, Donne's next stipulation reaches out into a different hermeneutic dimension. In the second part of his sermon, Donne homes in on the second creation, man's regeneration, and attempts to excavate 'such a sense, as may carry us most powerfully to the apprehension of the next life' (9.95). The sermon's transition from physical to metaphysical creation corresponds to a movement from literal to spiritual interpretation, and from textual surface to depth. This hermeneutic and perspectival gear change is announced at the half-way mark of the sermon, where Donne launches the second part of his *divisio*—as he did the first—with a meditation on scriptural difficulty and the cognitive limitations of human readers:

> *Mira profunditas eloquiorum tuorum* [*Confessions* 12.14]; The waters in the creation, were not so deep as the word of God, that delivers that creation. *Ecce, ante nos superficies blandiens pueris* [12.14], sayes that Father; We, we that are but babes in understanding, as long as we are but naturall men, see the superficies, the top, the face, the outside of these waters, *Sed mira profunditas, Deus meus, mira profunditas* [12.14], But it is an infinite depth, Lord my God, an infinite depth to come to the bottome. (9.100)

The source behind Donne's reflections on textual profundity is Book 12 of the *Confessions*. Throughout that book, and in Chapter 14 more particularly, Augustine charts the enhancement of human knowledge through a progression from hermeneutic surface to depth. Donne's Whitsunday sermon models itself on this process of interpretive regeneration, as it draws out the spiritual meanings of the key terms it has established in the first, literal exposition of Genesis 1:2.

More particularly, Donne seeks to re-claim and rehabilitate ideas of charity and peace, which had been identified with recognizably conformist Laudian terminology in the first section of his discourse. He divests these terms of their immediate polemical significance and re-invests them with more universal devotional implications. This re-evaluation entails a firm re-positioning of Augustine and the Fathers more generally vis-à-vis the Laudian attempt to present the patristic tradition as a magisterium—a means of enforcing Church discipline. Donne, by contrast, presents Augustine as a kind of eschatological enabler, a textual facilitator who helps him connect 'to the next life', and opens up a long view of history in which local, historical conflict ultimately resolves into eternal peace and comfort through the work of the Holy Spirit. To this end, the second part of Donne's sermon focuses on Augustinian texts which describe, invoke, and enact moments of (self-)

transcendence: the *Enarrations on the Psalms, On the Literal Interpretation of Genesis*, and the final books of the *Confessions*. By pressing these self-consuming texts into service, Donne seeks to transform strategic and polemical uses of charity into a notion of 'super-eminent' divine love, which lifts us out of the waters of sin, and converts the peace of political 'meekness', compliance, and silence into a vision of eternal rest in heaven. In all these respects, Donne builds his performance on the exegetical principles of Augustine's own approach to Genesis. For uniting the various occasions and settings of Augustine's readings of the creation narrative— polemical, methodological, pastoral, to name but a few—is a commitment to its deeper soteriological and eschatological implications. The opening words of *On the Literal Interpretation of Genesis*, for instance, announce Augustine's intent to discover 'intimations of eternity' in the first book of the Pentateuch ('quae ibi aeterna intimentur', 1.1.1); Book 11 of the *Confessions* similarly declares the importance of Genesis to our understanding of human and providential history, '[f]rom the beginning in which you made heaven and earth until the perpetual reign with you in your heavenly city'.[37] Augustine's hermeneutic, as Aimé Solignac observes, always already includes a metaphysical dimension.[38]

Donne's sermon examines the ways in which the Holy Spirit makes 'us for the other world' (9.93), and his discussion emulates the metaphysical outlook of *Confessions* 11–13. The spiritual sense of the creation narrative that Donne discovers in Augustine's text liberates from the pressures of contemporary history (indeed, as Augustine argues at *Confessions* 13.13.14, from time itself) and opens up the prospect of a return to God, and a conversion of human mutability and restlessness into the hope of eternal bliss. As Augustine maintains in all his writings on Genesis, the explication of creation history must ultimately be put in the service of a return to our homeland and to God, the source of heavenly peace.[39] This model of providential action involves a dual dynamic of motion and rest, and of rest through motion: God continually works in the world through the Spirit while being perfectly at peace with himself; conversely, the work of the Spirit lifts man out of the chaos and restlessness of sin and enables a peaceful union with the creator. This paradoxical interplay of rest and motion is frequently identified in Augustine as an attribute of God (for example, at *Confessions* 13.37: 'always working and always resting'; *Homilies on the Gospel of John* 17.14: God 'works in peace and rests while he works').[40] In Donne's sermon, the motion–rest dynamic becomes foundational to the structure of the argument, the key which unlocks the meaning of cosmic history. 'Motion and rest' animate the actions of the Holy Spirit in the world:

---

[37] *Confessions* 11.2.3 (*PL* 32.810).

[38] Aimé Solignac, 'Exégèse et Métaphysique, Genèse I, 1–3 chez Augustin', in *In principio, Interprétations des premiers versets de la Genèse* (Paris, 1973), 153–71 ('une herméneutique qui enveloppe toujours une métaphysique'), 154.

[39] 'Redire in patriam' (*De Doctrina Christiana* 1.4.4), 'redire ad creatorem' (*Literal Interpretation of Genesis* 4.18). See also *Retractations* 1.10.1: God is the highest good ('summum bonum'), the 'immutable creator of all of mutable nature' ('immutabilem creatorem . . . omnium mutabilium naturarum').

[40] See also *Confessions* 1.4.4, *Literal Interpretation of Genesis* 4.8 and 9.17.

[t]he Action of the Spirit of God, the Holy Ghost, in this place, is expressed in a word, of a double, and very diverse signification; for it signifies *motion*, and it signifies *rest*. And therefore, as S. *Augustine* argues upon those words of *David, Thou knowest my downe sitting, and my uprising,* That God knew all that he did betweene his downe sitting and his uprising; So in this word which signifies the Holy Ghosts first motion, and his last rest, we comprehend all that was done in the production, and creation of the Creatures. (9.98)

In drawing the grand narrative arc from the 'first motion' of creation to the 'last rest' on the eternal Sabbath, Donne invokes Augustine's *Enarration* on Psalm 139. He takes some liberties with his source text: Augustine produces a Christological reading of the psalm, likening the 'downe sitting' to the voluntary humiliation of the Passion and the 'uprising' to the 'resurrection'. In Donne, the motion–rest dynamic is transferred from the second to the third person of the Trinity, from Christ to the Holy Spirit. But Donne echoes Augustine's conviction that without Christ's 'motion', humanity cannot be saved. His sacrifice enables our rest: man 'rises up when his sins are forgiven, and he is lifted up to the hope of everlasting life'.[41] As Donne continues to explicate the actions of the Holy Ghost, this process is uppermost in his mind:

Now the word in our Text is not truly *Ferebatur,* The Spirit *moved,* which denotes a thing past; but the word is *Movens, Moving,* a Participle of the present; So that we ascribe first Gods manifestation of himself in the creation, and then the continuall manifestation of himself in his providence, to the holy Ghost; for God had two purposes in the creation, *Vt sint, ut maneant,* That the creature should be, and be still ... The holy Ghost moves, he is the first author; the holy Ghost perpetuates, settles, establishes, he is our rest, and acquiescence, and center; Beginning, Way, End, all is in this word, *Recaph; The Spirit of God moved, and rested.* (9.99)

The Spirit moves in the process of creation and provides 'rest, and acquiescence, and center'; this movement takes place in time but also—crucially for Donne— transcends it: the operations of God through the Spirit occur in an eternal 'present', as a 'continuall manifestation of himself in his providence'. Donne's final Augustinian reference in this passage, '*Vt sint, ut maneant*', is from *On the Literal Interpretation of Genesis*;[42] that text supplies the 'divine rationale' for the act of creation and for the continuous unfolding of eternal providence in time: God creates because God loves.

Non amor ita egenus & indigus, ut rebus quas diligit subjiciatur, sayes S. *Augustine* excellently: The love of God to us is not so poore a love, as our love to one another; that his love to us should make him subject to us, as ours does to them whom we love; but

---

[41] *Enarrations on the Psalms* 138.3 (*PL* 37.786–7). See, on this transcendental dynamic, Robert Alter, *Art of Biblical Poetry* (New York, 1985), 117: because of their paratactic, repetitive structure, the psalms are a literary form capable of 'neutralizing the temporal movement inherent in all verbal artworks'. This, Alter argues, can be used to subvert linear ideas of movement and cause and effect, and evoke non-linear relationships such as that between time and eternity.

[42] *On the Literal Interpretation of Genesis* 1.8 (*PL* 34.251): 'Duo quippe sunt propter quae amat Deus creaturam suam; ut sit, et ut maneat. Ut esset ergo quod maneret, *Spiritus Dei superferebatur super aquam*; ut autem maneret, *Vidit Deus quia bonum est.*'

Superfertur, sayes that Father, and our Text, he moves above us; He loves us, but with a Powerfull, a Majesticall, an Imperiall, a Commanding love. (9.104)[43]

Donne's re-definition of charity works through a change of perspective, discovers an alternative reading of the creation narrative. The 'Imperiall' project established by God's providence is 'Powerfull' yet unencumbered by self-interest; true king-ship, Donne argues with more than a cursory glance at local concerns, is animated by 'Majesticall' love. But yet again, any note of overt political dissonance is quickly reined in as Donne applies this concept of charity to the sacrament of baptism, administered through the institution of 'the Christian Church':

> The water of Baptisme, is the water that runs through all the Fathers. . . . And for our selves, *Mergimur & emergimus*, In Baptisme we are sunk under water, and then raised above the water againe; . . . *Affectus, & amores*, sayes he, our corrupt affections, and our inordinate love of this world is that, that is to be drowned in us; *Amor securitatis*, A love of peace, and holy assurance, and acquiescence in Gods Ordinance, is that that lifts us above water. (9.104–5)

Donne's Augustinian quotations ('*Mergimur & emergimus*'; '*Affectus, & amores*'; '*Amor securitatis*') derive from Book 13, chapter 7 of the *Confessions*, which con-nects the idea of charity with the work of the Spirit.[44] The redemptive effect of the Holy Ghost is predicated, once again, on the idea of converting one type of love into another: in baptism, 'inordinate love of this world' turns into 'A love of peace', as man is lifted above the waters of sin.[45] The parallels with Augustine's own language at *Confessions* 13.7 are instructive:

> with what words can I express, the weight of cupidity pulling us downwards into the precipitous abyss and the lifting up of love given by the Spirit who was 'borne above the waters'. To whom can I communicate this? How can I speak about it? For it is not about literal places when we sink down and rise up ('mergimur et emergimus'). . . . [It is about] our feelings and our loves ('affectus sunt, amores sunt'). The impurity of our spirit flows downwards because of our love of anxieties, and the holiness which is yours draws us upwards in a love of freedom from anxiety ('amore securitatis').[46]

Once again, processes of conceptual re-definition are the sustaining force behind Augustine's argument; a similar process will undergird Donne's attempt to recu-perate the language of charity. In *Confessions* 13.7, the 'weight of cupidity' ('pon-dere cupiditatis') is counterbalanced by 'the lifting up of love' ('sublevatione caritatis'). And it is this supreme love that will ensure eternal peace, as Augustine argues through another forceful parallelism in *Confessions* 13.7: the 'supereminent way of charity' ('supereminentem viam charitatem') will direct us, ultimately, 'to the supereminent resting place' ('supereminentem requiem'). Just as in the

---

[43] *On the Literal Interpretation of Genesis* 1.7 (*PL* 34.251).
[44] *Confessions* 13.6–7 (*PL* 32.847): 'Why, therefore, was it inappropriate to introduce the Spirit except with the words that he was "borne above"?' . . . 'Teaching us concerning the things of the Spirit he [St Paul] demonstrates that the way of charity is "supereminent"' ('supereminentem viam charitatis', 1 Cor. 12:1).
[45] *Sermons*, 9.105, and Augustine, *Enarrationes in Psalmos* 123, both identify water with sin.
[46] *Confessions* 13.7 (*PL* 32.847–8).

Confessions the spirit 'was borne above the waters' to effect liberation from sin and reunion with God, so Augustine in Donne's sermon points the way to a better place, where the soul can be at one with itself and its creator in eternal peace and charity. The Whitsunday sermon of 1629 was by no means the first time that Donne had invoked the help of Augustine's spirit in the quest for comfort and rest. In his second sermon preached at the churching of the Countess of Bridgewater, on Micah 2:10 ('Arise and depart, for this is not your rest'), Donne draws on *Confessions* 13.9 to describe the Holy Ghost as 'the *Pondus animæ*, the weight, the ballast of our soule, *rest*, and peace of Conscience'.[47] And the closing moments of the same sermon introduce Augustine's *Enarration* on Psalm 85 to launch their prayerful vision of peace and love in the heavenly city: 'To end all, though there be no Rest in all this world, no not in our *sanctification* here, yet this being a Consolation, there must be rest some where; And it is, *In superna Civitate, unde amicus non exit, qua inimicus non intrat,* In that City, in that Hierusalem, where there shall never enter any man, whom we doe not love, nor any goe from us, whom we doe love.'[48]

But in May 1629, as I have argued, reflections on the metaphysical dimension of peace and on Augustine's Christian doctrine of love must have seemed especially timely. The peace with France of April 1629 struck many Protestants as an apocalyptic defeat; Laud's language of peace and moderation was construed, in Calvinist circles, as a victory of order and discipline over truth. The dissolution of parliament marked the termination of 'conversations' with the king and, I would suggest, also contributed to the silencing of Donne's political voice. The comfort offered by Donne's Whitsunday sermon stems from an appeal to 'Truth it selfe' (9.94), from an imagined transportation to a realm where factionalism and self-interest give way to a holy conversation with those 'whom we love'. Nevertheless, it is indicative of Donne's political situation in May 1629 that these inward truths could only be articulated from a position of outward conformity.

Peter McCullough has argued that April 1627 marked a watershed moment in Donne's court preaching. After a confrontation with Laud which forced Donne to submit a copy of his sermon of 1 April to the king's scrutiny, Donne's preaching style saw a dramatic change. The remaining nine court sermons Donne preached before Charles 'are striking as a group for their complete avoidance of . . . politically charged opinions', displaying instead 'an introspective eloquence on themes of universal import'.[49] Donne's performance at Whitehall in February 1629, as we have seen, with its vigorous emphasis on the importance of political counsel, is a rare deviation from this pattern, perhaps inspired by the increasing escalation of the conflict between parliament and crown. By May 1629, however, Donne had given

---

[47] *Sermons*, 5.199. See, on the rest of the soul in Augustine, Alberto Di Giovanni, *L'inquietudine dell'anima* (Rome, 1964); Alberto Pincherle, 'Et inquietum est cor nostrum. Appunti per una lezione agostiniana', *Augustinus*, 13 (1968), 353–68; George Lawless, 'Interior Peace in the "Confessiones" of St. Augustine', *Revue des Études Augustiniennes*, 26 (1980), 45–61.

[48] *Enarrationes in Psalmos* 84: 'Quis non desideret illam civitatem, unde amicus non exit, quo inimicus non intrat' (*PL* 37.1076); *Sermons*, 5.215.

[49] McCullough, 'Donne as Preacher at Court', 202.

up the political fight altogether. The concluding words of the 1629 Whitsunday sermon focus on Christ, 'who as he doth presently lay our soules in that safe Cabinet, in the Bosome of *Abraham* . . . keepes an eye upon every graine, and atome of our dust . . . and keepes a roome at his owne right hand for that body, when that shall be re-united in a blessed Resurrection' (9.108). All that remains for Donne, after 'civill Conversation' has ceased, is a steadfast faith in his saviour and in Augustine, the Father who represents the bonds of peace, the 'glue' and 'cyment' between this world and the next.

Donne's Augustinian exegesis of Genesis 1:2 takes two key ideas in the controversies of 1628–9 and converts them to his own uses. The first of these is the centrality of the literal sense, vigorously articulated in the 1628 Declaration. Donne rejects the fiction of the 'true usuall literall meaning', which came to be appropriated by all parties and was patently vulnerable to abuse; instead, he creates a deeper, spiritual, metaphysical sense which can provide comfort to his audience. At the same time, however, the Whitsunday sermon objects to the uncoupling of charity from truth that looms large in Laud's correspondence. As Debora Shuger has recently observed, 'what mattered to Laudians . . . were the bonds of charity, not the search for truth'.[50] The problem with this argument, as Donne saw it in *Biathanatos*, was that charity could cover a multitude of sins: in the minds of his detractors, Laud's rhetoric of loving forbearance masked a rather more oppressive register of political compliance. Donne's re-definition of charity in the Whitsunday performance, then, harks back to a familiar dilemma: once charity is separated out from truth, all that remains are the pious and highly unstable assurances of good intent. The events of 1629, it seems, had eroded whatever remnants of faith Donne may have had in the value of *human* charity. His sermon, however, finds solace in a re-orientation of perspective and a re-calibration of terminology: Donne's Augustinian reading of the creation narrative reveals an unimpeachable motive in God's providential plan, 'a Powerfull . . . Love'. And unlike the Laudian philosophy of charity, Donne's need not choose between the love of truth and the truth of love because they are one and the same: 'But what is Truth? God; And what is God? Charity' (9.94).

This is a deceptively simple solution to a complex problem; in some ways, perhaps, it is even an unsatisfing one. And it cannot ultimately escape the charge of self-interest: Donne is too obviously concerned to keep the peace with Laud, and consciously avoids any appearance of dissent.[51] But if we listen to the sermon in good faith, we may nevertheless discover an inward truth within the shell of

---

[50] Debora Shuger, 'Literature and the Church', in David Loewenstein and Janel M. Mueller (eds.), *The Cambridge History of Early Modern Literature* (Cambridge, 2002), 512–43 (540).

[51] I agree with McCullough's assessment that Donne's silence on controversial topics after 1627 was tactical, and further evidence of Laud's growing control over ecclesiastical patronage in the late 1620s. Donne's treatment of charity in the Whitsunday 1629 sermon does not suggest any degree of sympathy with *political* Laudianism. See 'Donne as Preacher at Court', 202, and Kenneth Fincham, 'William Laud and the Exercise of Caroline Ecclesiastical Patronage', *Journal of Ecclesiastical History*, 51 (2000), 69–93. For the competing viewpoint, that Donne subscribed to the political programme of Arminianism in the later part of his career, see Guibbory, 'Donne's Religion', 412–39.

outward conformity. Donne's Pauline dialectic of surface and depth ultimately allows us—perhaps with more charity than his discourse warrants—to read the external compliance with Laudian policies as surface phenomenon, as a preliminary stage in the journey towards the depths and heights of God's providential love. Whether we take this opportunity may well turn out to be a test of our own charity.

7

'The evidence of things not seen'
Donne, Augustine, and the Beatific Vision

Donne's meditation on cosmic and providential history on Whitsunday 1629 ends with the anticipation of an everlasting present; his idealized vision of a loving communion with God attempts to relegate contemporary political conflict to the status of a digression, a local rupture in the fabric of eternity. Donne's metaphysical perspective on the events of 1629 provides comfort to his audience by expanding spiritual and hermeneutic horizons; religious controversy is revealed as a mere pre-text, the surface meaning of human existence which ultimately yields to the more profound implications of eschatology. During the final years of his ministry, Donne was frequently preoccupied with the theology of last things; in these closing stages of the journey towards the heavenly city, Augustine was once again his mentor and guide. Donne's sermon on Genesis 1:2, as we have seen, figures ideas of eternal rest and peace in recognizably Augustinian terms.

This chapter will concentrate on a different aspect of Donne's eschatological thought: the identification of eternal happiness with the beatific vision—the unmediated, direct apprehension of God in the resurrection. This is the strand of Augustine's theology that Donne comes to rely on most explicitly and most intensively between 1627 and 1631. Donne's definition of heavenly felicity depends on Augustinian notions of patefaction and revelation; the prospect of an immediate encounter with God, and the supreme fruition of seeing him face to face, are inevitably perceived—with more than a hint of Donnean paradox—through the eyes of Augustine. For Donne, as for Augustine, divine self-revelation represents the completion of a lifelong hermeneutic quest: the vision of God heralds the advent of a completely new mode of knowledge, cognition, and comprehension. The beatific vision inaugurates a reformation of knowledge, offering an unmediated, 'experimentall' form of perception. The 'actuall seeing' of God rectifies man's faculties and enables, in the words of a Paul's Cross sermon of 22 November 1629, the possession of a '*continuitatem Intuendi*' (*Sermons*, 9.128)—'an un-interrupted, un-intermitted, an un-discontinued', intuitive apprehension of divine glory.[1] The pre-texts that are being shed in Donne's homiletic meditations on the sight of God, in other words, are textuality and mediation, and, finally,

---

[1] This is an improvement on our cognitive abilities before the Fall; even Adam, as theologians of all persuasions insisted, never saw God in paradise. See, for instance, Richard Montagu, *A gagg for the new Gospell? No: a new gagg for an old goose* (London, 1624), sig. 2Q4v.

interpretation itself. This process continues, but ultimately transcends, the leaps of faith into God's presence evoked by the *Essayes in Divinity*; but it builds on, and extends, the reach and significance of charity as an eschatological category: the perfection of vision, as Donne's Easter sermon of 1628 makes clear, depends on the perfection of love. Lest we be too quick to elevate Donne to the status of a neo-Augustinian (or indeed Neoplatonic) saint, however, it should be noted from the outset that his textual practices are concerned with worldly display as well as otherworldly bliss: the sermons discussed in this chapter enact moments of perfect understanding and interpretive clarity which are intended to dazzle the professional members of Donne's audience while skilfully obscuring the citational mechanics that prop up his spectacle. The congregation comprehends but dimly and 'in part', yet Donne is in complete command of his Augustinian performances.

Donne's reflections on 'visio dei' (the sight of God), and on the recuperation of intuitive, 'experimentall knowledge' it implies, are characterized by an unusual degree of rhetorical self-consciousness. In many ways, this is hardly surprising: the project of imagining unmediated communion with God in a fallen language takes Donne to the very limits of representation, and in their attempts to provide a glimpse of the highest glories, his sermons anxiously contemplate the inadequacy of their own expressive possibilities. Donne's preaching on divine patefaction manifests the aesthetic and communicative frustrations of ineffable beauty and peace in their most acute form: 'I would say something of the beauty and glory of [God's] eyes', he laments while preaching on Matthew 5:8 on Candlemas 1627, but 'can find no words but such, as I my selfe have mis-used in lower things' (7.348). The Augustinian references deployed in Donne's sermons on the sight of God attempt to counteract this gravitational pull of fallen rhetoric; they enable, yet again, a re-direction of perspective, thus facilitating spiritual ascent.

In crafting a discourse of divine illumination, Donne mirrors key theological ideas through his citational practice. His Easter sermon of 1628 on 1 Corinthians 13:12 is a case in point. In this sermon, Donne addresses the scriptural *locus classicus* for Augustinian treatments of the beatific vision: 'For now we see through a glass darkly, but then face to face; now I know in part, but then I shall know, even as also I am known.' His citations, as we will see, reflect the themes of his Scripture text, and trace the journey from spiritual darkness to insight through a series of intertextual adumbrations and revelations. Donne's performance on Candlemas 1627, on Matthew 5:8—'Blessed are the pure in heart, for they shall see God'— narrows the focus of discussion and, in the process, also contracts the horizon of Augustinian reference. While the Easter sermon surveys Augustine's textual universe from a lofty, panoramic perspective, taking in a broad range of pronouncements on the universal spiritual ramifications of the beatific vision, the 1627 sermon on Matthew 5:8 concentrates on one specific question—whether God can be seen with bodily eyes—and brings to bear on it the intense gaze and focus of a single Augustinian text, the epistle to Fortunatianus. Both sermons provide unique insights into the occasion-centred nature of Donne's intertextual transactions with Augustine; but they also illuminate the final stages of the hermeneutic process initiated by the *Essayes in Divinity*: the return to God, envisaged as the immediate experience of his 'essence', which at once transforms and transcends the activity of interpretation.[2] The Whitsunday 1629 sermon chronicles Donne's estrangement from the world of politics and articulates a desire for eschatological rest and peace. It works hard to discover a deeper meaning in the obscure narrative of history. Donne's late sermons on the beatific vision trace the next stage of this journey; their textual negotiations simulate a superior form of communion with God.

Augustine's identification of happiness ('beatitudo') with the vision of God is articulated most cogently in Book 1, chapter 2 of his *Retractations*. There, he reviews his early philosophical work *The Happy Life*, which associated happiness with the Ciceronian ideal of wisdom ('no one can be happy unless he has wisdom')[3] and re-casts 'beatitudo' in eschatological terms: 'there is no greater bliss for man', Augustine argues, than 'the perfect vision of God . . . in a future life'.[4] This definition of happiness is first adumbrated by Paul at 1 Corinthians 13:12 and elaborated, through constant reference to that core scriptural text, by Augustine in a series of influential writings.[5] Chief among these are the final books of *On the Trinity* and the *City of God*, a number of key passages from the *Confessions*, *On the Lord's Sermon on the Mount*,[6] and two letters on the origin and destination of the soul to St Jerome (Letters 166 and 167).[7] It is important to note immediately that Donne does not cite any of these classic texts in his 1627 and 1628 sermons on 'visio dei'.[8]

On a cursory inspection, these omissions may seem curious. Donne, as the use of Augustinian quotations in *Biathanatos* and the *Essayes in Divinity* demonstrates, was familiar with parts of the *City of God* and with the *Confessions* by the time of his ordination in 1615, for instance. More careful investigation of Donne's textual strategies in these sermons, however, suggests that his exclusion of the

---

[2] 1 Corinthians 13:12 and Matthew 5:8 are key texts for Donne's treatment of the beatific vision and are frequently combined in his preaching (see *Sermons*, 1.189, for instance).

[3] *De Beata Vita*, chapter 2 (*PL* 32.966).

[4] *Retractationes* 1.2 (*PL* 32.588).

[5] 'Perfecta cognitio dei . . . in futura vita.' See Henrique de Noronha Galvão, 'Beatitudo', in *Augustinus-Lexikon*, 1.624–38; see also Goulven Madec, 'Ascensio, ascensus', *Augustinus-Lexikon*, 1.465–75. On Augustine's notion of 'beatitudo' see further, Werner Beierwaltes, *Regio Beatudinis. Zu Augustins Begriff des glücklichen Lebens* (Heidelberg, 1981); Ragnar Holte, *Béatitude et sagesse. Saint Augustine et le problème de la fin de l'homme dans la philosophie ancienne* (Paris, 1962); Rudolf Lorenz, 'Fruitio dei bei Augustin', *Zeitschrift für Kirchengeschichte*, 63 (1950/51), 75–132; Noronha Galvão, *Die existentielle Gotteserkenntnis bei Augustin. Eine hermeneutische Lektüre der Confessiones* (Einsiedeln, 1981).

[6] *De Sermone Domini in Monte*, *PL* 34.

[7] These two letters are referenced in a different context in Donne's 18th Meditation; see *Devotions*, 91–2.

[8] Other key passages cited in patristic anthologies (such as Jean Crespin, *Bibliotheca Studii Theologici ex Plerisque Doctorum Prisci Seculi Monumentis Collecta*, 3 vols. (1565) and Johann Piscator, *Diui Aurelii Augustini Episcopi . . . Epitome*, 3 vols. (Augsburg, 1537)) include: *De Spiritu et Littera*, ch. 33; *De vera innocentia*, ch. 27; *De Moribus Ecclesiae Catholicae* 1.25; *De Fide et Symbolo*, ch. 6; *De Videndo Deo* (= Epistle 147, to Paulina); *Enarrationes in Psalmos* 85 and 86. Of all these, Donne only makes explicit reference to *De Videndo Deo*; expert listeners might also have spotted a submerged reference to *De Civitate Dei* 22.39 (see below). The most significant omissions from Donne's point of view are the passages from *De Moribus Ecclesiae Catholicae* and *Enarrationes in Psalmos*, both texts he knew well and used elsewhere in his sermons.

better-known Augustinian proof-texts may have been pointed and deliberate: Donne's mimetic patterning of theological concept and rhetorical strategy extends to his citational manoeuvres. The spiritual narrative charted by both sermons is predicated on the deferral of fruition, and on the promise of a mode of vision that is less carnal and more rarefied than the cognitive processes in this life. Preaching on two feast days and in the presence of the Bishop of London and the chapter of clerics Donne worked with throughout the liturgical year, he makes serious textual play of the principal themes of his discourse.[9] The Easter 1628 sermon is structured around the grammatical dichotomy dictated by Paul's text: 'now we see ... darkly, then ... face to face'. As Donne anticipates these eschatological events, 'the *Then,* the time of *seeing face to face,* and *knowing as we are knowne*' (8.219), his own discussion of the patefaction is constantly deferred, to be brought to fruition at a much later point in the sermon than the binary *divisio* indicates, well after the half-way mark, and with an air of sudden revelation. On Candlemas Day 1627, as we have seen, Donne debates a more technical aspect of the beatific vision—'with what eyes I shall see him'—a development of 1 Corinthians 13:12, 'S. *Pauls Cognoscam, I shall know him as I am knowne*' (7.342). This leads, by way of an elaborate set of Augustinian quotations, to the conclusion 'That our bodily eyes should never see God': only the eyes of the soul, our 'spirituall' faculties, will behold God in his essence. Donne's sermon is built on this distinction between the carnal and the spiritual, the material and the ineffable/invisible: it is completely in tune with these structural principles that his intertextual system should eschew the patent, obvious, and visible, that it relies, in the words of the 1628 Easter sermon, on *'the evidence of things not seen'* (8.230). To cite Augustine's most commonplace pronouncements on 'visio dei', in other words, would be to work against the spirit of the text and drag Donne down from the heights of intuitive apprehension to the much maligned region of 'lower things' (7.348).[10]

That Donne's citational manipulations would only have been apparent to a select minority of the audience is crucial to his rhetorical strategy in both sermons; in fact, the Candlemas sermon of 1627 explicitly addresses this very issue. Before expounding the complexities of the beatific vision, Donne dwells in detail on the cognitive and moral parameters that frame sermon reception and delivery. One of the main planks of his argument is that listening to the preacher's discourse involves a crucial element of selective perception on the congregation's part. This is because the ministry of the word deals with the specifics of sin as well as devotional universals: 'for the rectifying of ... one soul, God poures out the Meditations of the Preacher, into such a subject, as perchance doth little concern the rest of the Congregation' (7.328). But the impact and accuracy of the preacher's discourse is also determined by the audience's intellectual capacities, emotional receptivity, and

[9] For information on the cathedral's personnel, which would have made up a significant part of Donne's professional audience, see W. Sparrow Simpson, *Registrum Statutorum et Consuetudinum Ecclesiae Cathedralis Sancti Pauli Londoniensis* (London, 1873), and John LeNeve, *Fasti Ecclesiae Anglicanae, 1541–1857,* vol. 1, St Paul's London, compiled by Joyce M. Horn (London, 1969).
[10] Terry Sherwood discusses Donne's views on beatitude in *Fulfilling the Circle* (60–2); see also Jeffrey Johnson, *The Theology of John Donne* (Cambridge, 1999), 85–8.

the early modern equivalent of a horizon of expectation. In a congregation as mixed as that of St Paul's on a major feast day, it is thus no surprise 'if they do not understand all, or not remember all the Sermon. Scarce any Sermon is so preached, or so intended, as that all works upon all, or all belongs unto all' (7.327). The main theme of these sermons—the idea of partial vision, and of obscure intimations of full perception—is thus replicated at the level of intertextual representation and display: the theologically informed members in Donne's congregation would have noticed the absence of acknowledged references to the obvious Augustinian proof-texts (the *City of God* and the *Confessions* make appearances through more remote and obscure allusions), but they are not exempt from the limitations of earth-bound cognition. Donne's professional colleagues, too, are left hunting for clues as he assembles his complex Augustinian jigsaw. Not seeing things, or only seeing them obscurely, is precisely the point at issue here.

A closer examination of Donne's Augustinian quotations in the Easter 1628 sermon illustrates the profound connections between hermeneutics, epistemology, and intertextuality. But in order to achieve a fuller understanding of Donne's citational techniques, it is necessary first to explicate in more detail the new mode of knowledge afforded to the resurrected souls in heaven. The Easter sermon of 1628, as I have already observed, works with a bipartite *divisio* which follows the chronological and topographical distinctions constructed in 1 Corinthians 13:12: 'now' and 'then'. Donne further subdivides the category of 'now' into the 'place', 'medium', and 'light' which define our cognitive abilities. In the 'now', our place is 'the whole world'; our media are 'Naturall Reason' (to interpret 'the Book of Creatures') and 'the Ordinance of God in his Church, Preaching and Sacraments' (to interpret the Scriptures); our light is 'the light of faith'. At this stage, we know God 'by obscure representations, and therefore it is called a *Knowledge but in part*' (8.220). By contrast, 'for our sight of God in heaven, our place, our Spheare is heaven it selfe, our *medium* is the Patefaction, the Manifestation, the Revelation of God himselfe, and our light is the light of Glory' (8.220). Donne tracks a movement of absolute cognitive and spiritual re-orientation: 'in the life to come', we command 'another manner of knowledge' altogether (8.220); there, we experience '*Patefactio sui*, Gods laying himself open, his manifestation, his revelation, his evisceration, and embowelling of himselfe to us' (8.231).

The contours of this perfected knowledge are more clearly delineated in another Easter sermon, preached at St Paul's in the evening of Easter day 1624, on Revelation 20:6. Once again, Donne makes a radical distinction between 'the knowledge of the soule' in the 'here' on the one hand, and in the 'hereafter' on the other. While on earth, Donne argues, the soul is not strong enough to behold the truth, and habitually retreats into the shadows of opinion and speculation: 'Here saies S. *Augustine*, when the soule considers the things of this world, *Non veritate certior, sed consuetudine securior;* She rests upon such things as she is not sure are true, but such as she sees, are ordinarily received and accepted for truths: so that the end of her knowledge is not Truth, but opinion, and the way, not Inquisition, but ease' (6.76). Life in heaven, by contrast, fills the soul with the dazzling light of truth:

But then in her Resurrection, her measure is enlarged, and filled at once; There she reads without spelling, and knowes without thinking, and concludes without arguing; she is at the end of her race, without running; . . . She knowes truly, and easily, and immediately, and entirely, and everlastingly; . . . In Heaven we shall have Communion of Joy and Glory with all, alwaies; *Vbi non intrat inimicus, nec amicus exit,* Where never any man shall come in that loves us not, nor go from us that does. (6.76)

Donne relies, for his vision of understanding and cognition, on Book 1, chapter 7 of *On the Values of the Catholic Church* (there are three other quotations from this text in the passage just cited), and for his account of heavenly 'Joy and Glory' on *Enarrations on the Psalms* 84.10.[11] In the Candlemas sermon of 1627, Donne similarly describes the 'Beatificall vision' as a quality of perception far removed from somatic experience, an immediate form of apprehension that transcends 'those lazy degrees of the senses, and the phantasie, and discourse, and reading, and medita-tion, and conversation' (7.334).[12]

Donne's 1622 Easter sermon enacts such a moment of vision by staging a metaphysical encounter between Donne's spiritual mentor, Augustine, and Augus-tine's own tutelary spirit, Jerome. An apocryphal letter from Augustine to Cyril of Jerusalem recounts how, one evening, Augustine sat down to compose a letter to Jerome in order to debate the 'last and everlasting joy and glory of heaven'.[13] Jerome had died that same morning but 'as soon as he dyed at Bethlem, he came instantly to Hippo, then S. *Augustines* Bishoprick' (4.86) to instruct him on the matter. After confirming his identity—'*Hieronymi anima sum*'[14]—Jerome advises Augustine to abstain from further enquiries: the fate of the soul is 'incomprehensi-ble to us in this life' and Augustine will find out about heavenly joys soon enough, when he comes to experience them: 'As all knowledge in this world is causall, (we know a thing, if we know the cause thereof) so the knowledge in heaven, is effectuall, experimentall, we know it, we have found it to be so' (4.87).[15]

---

[11] Another crucial Augustinian *locus* is *Confessions* 12.13, where Augustine's exposition of Genesis 1 leads him to the consideration of 'the intellectual, non-physical heaven where the intelligence's knowing is a matter of simultaneity—not in part, not in an enigma, not through a mirror, but complete, total openness, "face to face" (1 Cor. 13:12). This knowing is not of one thing at one moment and of another thing at another moment, but is concurrent without any temporal successiveness' (*PL* 32.832–3). Other crucial passages on 1 Cor. 13:12 in the *Confessions* not cited by Donne include 8.1.1, 10.5.7, 13.5.6, 13.15.18, 12.15.21. On the transition from earthly to heavenly knowledge, see also Book 1 of Hooker, *Lawes of Ecclesiasticall Politie* (1604), which describes faith as 'beginning here with a weake apprehension of things not seene' and ending 'with the intuitiue vision of God in the world to come' (80). See also the address to the reader by Richard Sibbes, in Paul Baynes, *A commentarie vpon the first chapter of the epistle of Saint Paul, written to the Ephesians* (1618), sig. A2v–3r: 'how God conceiues things, which differs in the whole kind from ours, he conceiuing of things, altogether and at once without discourse, we one thing after another, and by another. Our comfort is, that we cannot see in the light of nature, and grace, we shall see in the light of glory, in the Vniuersitie of heauen.'
[12] In this passage, Donne rebuts Roman claims that a state of perfect cognition can be achieved in this life.
[13] *Sermons*, 4.86.
[14] 'I am the soul of Jerome.'
[15] An undated Candlemas sermon on Matthew 5:16 recounts the same episode; there, Donne also acknowledges doubts about Augustine's authorship of the letter: 'Blessed S. *Augustine* reports, (if that

There is something mildly comical in the notion of Jerome's rushing to Hippo just to tell Augustine to stop bothering him (Augustine and Jerome had been exchanging letters on the origin, nature, and destiny of the soul for some time), but Donne's portrait of the encounter also makes two serious points. First, the meeting of minds that occurs in the pseudo-Augustinian account—Jerome's spirit appears to Augustine at the very moment Augustine most ardently craves his counsel— speaks to a Donnean desire for transcendental interpersonal communion that unites his sacred and secular writings. One way of describing these ideal experiences is to call them ecstatic: Donne's visions of perfect understanding are always relational and directive; even the patefaction is an expression of mutual love between creator and creature, an effortless act of the will precipitated by charity. Donne, as we will see, concludes both his Easter sermon of 1628 and the Candlemas performance of 1627 with an Augustinian paean to God's love. In the sermons, a key paradigm for this kind of relationship is *Confessions* 9.10, the vision at Ostia, which describes a mystical experience shared by Augustine and his mother, Monica, shortly before her death:

> S. *Augustine* speaking of discourses that passed between his mother, and him, not long
> before her death, sayes, *Perambulavimus cuncta mortalia, & ipsum cœlum,* We talked
> our selves above this earth, and above all the heavens; *Venimus in mentes nostras, &*
> *transcendimus eas,* We came to the consideration of our owne mindes, and our owne
> soules, and we got above our own soules; that is, to the consideration of that place
> where our soules should be for ever. (8.232)

As Brian Stock has pointed out in his analysis of *Confessions* 9.10, it is crucial that Augustine shares this moment with Monica, a symbol of absolute, unconditional love, and of untutored (and therefore textually unmediated) religious wisdom; she does not read the Scriptures but believes intuitively. Stock's gloss continues: 'as the pair of speakers interpenetrate each other's minds, they cease to be mother and son and become spiritual kin'.[16] The episode at Ostia charts a progress towards emotional union and intellectual ascent; it is a dialogue of two minds that have become one. Donne's own reporting of this ecstatic experience is direct and unfiltered; his voice fuses with Augustine's as he attempts to describe how 'we got above our own soules'. At times, Donne's determined pursuit of visionary states in the sermons can seem like a rarefied version of obsessive stalking, in his impatient attempts to summon Augustine's spirit or provoke a sudden revelation in the style of Jerome. But even if Augustine's soul seems disinclined to make the journey to London, the traces of his mind are everywhere apparent in Donne's work. *Confessions* 9.10, for instance, re-works elements of the Plotinian ecstasy, a Neoplatonic tradition which is often cited as the source for Donne's most famous *poetic* attempt

---

Epistle be S. *Augustines*) that when himselfe was writing to S. *Hierome*, to know his opinion of the measure and quality of the Joy, and Glory of Heaven, suddenly in his Chamber there appeared *ineffabile lumen* . . . and out of that light issued this voyce, *Hieronymi anima sum,* I am the soul of that *Hierome*' (10.93).

[16] Brian Stock, *Augustine the Reader* (Cambridge, Mass., 1996), 118.

to capture the meeting of two minds, 'The Extasie'. That poem depicts the fusion of the two lovers' souls into a common, 'abler soule', a silent 'dialogue of one', which initiates a scene of transcendental communion:

> This Extasie doth unperplex
>   (We said) and tell us what we love,
> Wee see by this, it was not sexe
>   Wee see, we saw not what did move:[17]

'Unperplex' is an important word in Donne's hermeneutic vocabulary. It evokes the *Essayes in Divinity*, and their emphasis on the limits of rational enquiry: 'perplexing' matters can only be unravelled by an act of faith, which brings the soul to a more intuitive understanding of God. In such moments, Donne stages a dual movement of cognitive clarification, through hearing and sight. In 'The Extasie', Donne's speaker first alludes to the soul's silent language (it 'tell[s] us what we love') and then transforms this inward voice of truth into the light of vision: 'Wee see by this, it was not sexe/Wee see, we saw not what did move'. Donne's lovers have overcome mediation; their souls meet face to face, in an anticipation of the soul's direct apprehension of the beatific vision. Augustine and his mother also progress through a combination of visual and auditory experience, through 'internal reflection and dialogue and vision'.[18] It is important to register the fact that neither Donne's nor Augustine's accounts are Neoplatonic in the strict sense of that term. Stock notes that instead of the Neoplatonic hierarchy of the senses, which proceeds from images of hearing to those of outer and inner sight, the Ostia narrative presents 'a visual framework . . . [which] acts as a background for an ascent described largely in auditory terms'.[19] In Donne's 'Extasie', the force that enables this fusion of souls and integrates fragments of knowledge into a greater unity is 'good love'; that love—refined in the furnace of divine sacrifice and revelation—also animates the immediate encounter between God and man in heaven in Donne's preaching.

The ecstasy topos occurs in a hermeneutic modulation in one of Donne's letters to his friend Henry Goodyer. There, Donne describes letter-writing between friends as 'a kind of extasie, and a departure and secession and suspension of the soul, which doth then communicate it self to two bodies'.[20] On the terms of the ecstasy argument, the shared space or meeting-place of the souls is the page, where the correspondents—like the two lovers—exist for each other. To compose and to receive letters is to encounter an other that is also oneself, or one's other self. In establishing the possibility of ecstatic communion between human beings, 'The Extasie' presents a crucial link between the secular and sacred elements of Donne's poetics. It deploys the idea of religious ecstasy to express the speaker's conviction that his love possesses mysterious, transcendental qualities, and creates a moment of

---

[17] 'The Extasie', ll. 29–32.
[18] *Confessions* 9.10.24: 'interius cogitando et loquendo et mirando' (*PL* 32.774).
[19] Stock, *Augustine the Reader*, 119.
[20] *Letters*, sig. C2r.

complete understanding, free from the perplexing complications of human communication. In doing so, it also reveals some of the fundamental mechanisms of the hermeneutics of charity, and tells us something about the kinds of sympathetic responses Donne may have expected from his own readers. Among the many examples of the ecstasy genre, Donne is unique in foregrounding the role of the witness or observer in the ecstatic moment he describes:

> If any, so by love refin'd,
>   That he soules language understood,
> And by good love were growen all minde,
>   Within convenient distance stood,
> He (though he knowes not which soul spake,
>   Because both meant, both spake the same)
> Might thence a new concoction take,
>   And part farre purer then he came.[21]

In return for this spiritual purification, Donne's observer testifies to the strength of the lovers' bond, thus ensuring the faithful communication of their message to posterity:

> To'our bodies turne wee then, that so
>   Weake men on love reveal'd may looke;
> Loves mysteries in soules doe grow,
>   But yet the body is his booke.
> And if some lover, such as wee,
>   Have heard this dialogue of one,
> Let him still marke us, he shall see
>   Small change, when we'are to bodies gone.[22]

Donne's witness 'marke[s]', guards, and maintains the two aspects of love celebrated in the poem: the letters that spell out the book of the body, and the spirit of the soul. An observer who approaches the lovers' mystery in the right spirit will be able to ensure the preservation, dissemination, and continued survival of the 'abler soule'. Donne's love cannot exist without such a sympathetic observer; the same is true of his texts, which often depend on a faithful reader's willingness to project himself (or herself) into Donne's silences and activate his 'dialogue of one'. It is illuminating to note at this point that Donne is not, in fact, the only writer who portrays the ecstasy as a witnessed event. Augustine concludes his account of the vision at Ostia with a similar invocation to Donne's: 'if anyone has silenced the tumult of the flesh, if . . . all language and every sign and everything transitory is silent', they would be able to join in their ecstatic communion with the divine.[23] This is a close approximation, in terms of syntax and idea, to Donne's formulation: 'If any, so by love refin'd,/That he soules language understood,/And by good love

---

[21] 'The Extasie', ll. 21–8. (I have amended Patrides' misprint from 'concotion' to 'concoction'.)
[22] Ibid., ll. 69–76.
[23] *Confessions* 9.10.25: 'Si cui sileat tumultus carnis . . . omnis lingua et omne signum, et quidquid transeundo fit, si cui sileat omnino' (*PL* 32.774).

were growen all minde,/Within convenient distance stood'. In the context of such parallels, Augustine's vision at Ostia appears a likely candidate in the ongoing search for the sources of 'The Extasie'.

Donne's hermeneutics of charity is built on his 'second religion, friendship', and his reading instructions to friends often have quasi-religious overtones.[24] Donne deploys the conventions of scriptural exegesis to solicit sympathetic responses from his recipients, transplanting some of its key terms into a variety of secular discourses. This is demonstrated by a letter from Donne to Henry Goodyer, probably composed in 1612:

> Therefore give me leave to end this, in which if you did not finde the remembrance of my humblest services to my Lady *Bedford*, your love and faith ought to try all the experiments of pouders, and dryings, and waterings to discover some lines which appeared not; because it is impossible that a Letter should come from me, with such an ungratefull silence.[25]

In Donne's conceit, Goodyer will reveal his good wishes to the Countess through an act of physical intercession, by bringing to light a passage written in invisible ink, which 'appeared not' on an initial, casual reading. Donne's hermeneutic instructions to his friend hark back to contemporary definitions of Christian love and faith as articulated in homiletic and devotional manuals. His tongue-in-cheek suggestion that Goodyer put his faith in something he cannot see and give form to a hidden message in invisible ink, for instance, is reminiscent of texts like the 1547 homily *Of the True and Lively Faith*, which praises Moses for 'settyng hys hart upon the invisible God, as if he had seen hym ever present before hys eyes'.[26] Goodyer can put his faith in the letter's missing lines not simply because he has privileged access to Donne's intentions but because—on the terms of the ecstasy argument—he has and is a piece of his mind. Love, as Donne puts it in an earlier letter to Goodyer, has 'made us so much towards one',[27] that we 'both meant, both spake the same'.[28] This hermeneutic faith, however, can only gain validity through works of charity: these are Goodyer's 'experiments of pouders, and dryings, and waterings', which give voice to a silent message and complete an incomplete utterance. They literally incarnate and revive the spirit of love, thereby creating an 'abler' text. While on earth, the manifestations of love are perforce material; in heaven, by contrast, souls express affection, sympathy, and kinship more directly, through the eyes of the mind and the heart.

Donne's 'pouders' are merely the most physical manifestations of the mediated, sign-bound rhetoric which defines communication. His prose writings articulate a constant anxiety about the expressive capacities of human language; such fears are magnified, unsurprisingly, at moments when Donne attempts to give visible shape

---

[24] *Letters*, sig. M3r.
[25] Ibid., sig. L2v–L3r.
[26] *Certain Sermons or Homilies (1547) and A Homily against Disobedience and Wilful Rebellion (1570)*, ed. Ronald B. Bond (Toronto, 1987), 95.
[27] *Letters*, sig. I1v.
[28] 'The Extasie', l. 26.

and form to the invisible and ineffable. An Easter sermon of 1622, having summoned up the image of Jerome's soul, proceeds to a consideration of heavenly beatitude which laments the poverty of human discourse: 'How infirme, how impotent are all assistances, if they be put to expresse this Eternity?', Donne asks, in the face of everlasting communion with God's essence, 'How empty a thing is Rhetorique' (4.87).[29] The mediated nature of human communication is brought into sharper focus when we examine the material contexts in which the sermon is situated. The ecstatic dialogue between Jerome and Augustine—an unmediated experience in itself—is presented in a verbal redaction by Donne, which itself derives from a written account: the spurious letter to Cyril of Jerusalem. A further layer of representation is introduced when the sermon passes into writing—a process characterized by Donne, despite the residual presence of the writer's 'hand', as a fatal depletion of life-force: 'I know what dead carkasses things written are, in respect of things spoken', he writes in the dedicatory epistle to a sermon preached to the Countess of Montgomery.[30] Donne moves on, however, to a recuperation of the written word under the guidance of the Holy Spirit: 'But in things of this kinde, that soul that inanimates them, receives debts from them: The Spirit of God that dictates them in the speaker or writer, and is present in his tongue or hand, meets himself again (as we meete our selves in a glass) in the eies and eares and hearts of the hearers and readers: and that Spirit, which is ever the same to an equall devotion, makes a writing and a speaking equall means to edification.'[31] Under the auspices of the Spirit, the human medium becomes a conduit for God's message; the obscure shadows of 1 Corinthians 13:12 give way to perfect illumination in 'the eies and eares and hearts of the hearers and readers'.

Donne's texts aspire to such intuitive communication, but ultimately remain tethered, of course, to the fragile resources of language. Ideal interpretive transactions depend on 'an equall devotion', but achieving this state—as his prose works frequently testify—is a supremely difficult challenge for earth-bound readers. The *Essayes in Divinity* remind us that even 'the faithfullest heart is not ... constantly upon God',[32] and the Candlemas sermon of 1627 vividly portrays the complex

---

[29] Donne's critique of rhetoric is conditional and relative rather than absolute and universal. Rhetoric's resources cannot but fail to express eternal bliss, simply because it operates under the cognitive and expressive limitations outlined by 1 Corinthians 13:12. Donne does not dispute its general usefulness; as he observes in the same sermon, rhetoric aids in the preacher's task of edification by making 'absent and remote things present to our understanding' (4.87).

[30] See D. F. McKenzie's account of how the material modes of textual production and dissemination affect sermon reception, in 'Speech-Manuscript-Print', *The Library Chronicle of the University of Texas at Austin*, 20 (1990), 87–109. The writer's presence is 'greatest in speech, still implied by script, least of all in print' (96), despite attempts, on the part of writers and printers, 'to limit the difference of print by devising ways to suggest its affinities with speaking and writing' (101). Neither the Easter sermon of 1628 nor the Candlemas sermon of 1627 were printed during Donne's lifetime; in manuscript, they were one step above print, on a ladder of medial obfuscation that proceeds from manuscript to voice to vision. On the need to hear the Word preached to reap its full spiritual benefits, see e.g. Edward Vaughan, *A plaine and perfect Method, for the easie vnderstanding of the whole Bible* (2nd edn., 1617), 25–6 (cited by McKenzie, 91).

[31] *Sermons*, 2.179. The passage recurs verbatim in *Letters*, sig. E1r, but omits the reference to the 'eares' of its recipients.

[32] *Essayes*, 20.

landscapes of temptation and sin which daily confront Donne's audience. In the face of such difficulties, Donne's texts frequently resort to the idea of an enabling middle ground, a linguistic zone located somewhere between the elusive goal of intuitive apprehension and the dead weight of fallen speech. This region is populated by rhetorical tropes and devices which can function as a link between the world of human discourse and the joys of heavenly vision. Chief among these facilitating rhetorical 'platforms' is hyperbole: a self-transcending figure whose functional excesses were seen by Christian theorists of eloquence as a rare means of evoking the glories of divinity. John Prideaux's *Sacred Eloquence* praises the spiritual expressivity of 'sublime Hyperboles', while Thomas Traherne explains that 'All Hyperbolies are but little Pigmies, and Diminutiv Expressions, in Comparison of the Truth'.[33] Donne expands both of these definitions when he extols the '*third Heavens of Hyperbole*' in his panegyric to scriptural beauty in the *Devotions upon Emergent Occasions*.[34]

As Anthony Raspa explains, the 'third heaven' refers to the paradisal visionary state described by St Paul in 2 Corinthians 12:2.[35] Augustine's gloss on that phrase in *On the Literal Interpretation of Genesis* provides further useful insights: although we 'do not . . . rashly determine whether Paradise is in the third heaven',[36] it is clear that the third heaven brings us closer to God and symbolizes spiritual regeneration. Hyperbole for Donne is a means of connecting with such processes of self-transcendence, a material sign invested with metaphysical significance. Because, as its etymology indicates,[37] hyperbole always overshoots the mark, breaking the bounds of conventional discourse, it can afford poetic intimations of eternity.

Another such metaphysical conduit, as we have seen in the *Essayes in Divinity*, is the invocation and re-enunciation of Augustinian texts, which function as channels between Donne and his maker through which the spirit of charity can operate. This strategy is also vital to Donne's sermons on the vision of God, which address a specific representational challenge: how to evoke the sight of God with flawed rhetorical tools, 'words . . . as I my selfe have mis-used in lower things'. Both the Candlemas and the Easter sermon attempt to solve this dilemma by borrowing Augustine's voice. Donne's explication of Matthew 5:8 'end[s] all with S. *Augustines* devout exclamation, *Deus bone, qui erunt illi oculi!* Glorious God, what kinde of eyes shall they be! *Quam decori, quam sereni!* How bright eyes, and how well set! *Quam valentes! quam constantes!* How strong eyes, and how durable!' (7.348). And the Easter sermon on 1 Corinthians 13:12 concludes

---

[33] John Prideaux, *Sacred Eloquence* (1659), sig. A2r; Thomas Traherne, *Centuries, Poems and Thanksgivings*, ed. H. M. Margoliouth, 2 vols. (Oxford, 1972), Century II, §52. See Katrin Ettenhuber, 'Hyperbole', in *Renaissance Figures of Speech*, ed. Sylvia Adamson, Gavin Alexander, and Katrin Ettenhuber (Cambridge, 2007), 196–213 (206).

[34] *Devotions*, 99.

[35] Ibid. 128.

[36] *On the Literal Interpretation of Genesis* 12.34 (*PL* 34.482).

[37] Hyperbole: from Greek 'huper', 'over', and 'ballein', 'to throw': a 'throwing beyond' or 'overshooting'. See Henry George Lidell, Robert Scott et al. (eds.), *Greek–English Lexicon* (Oxford, 1996), 'hyperbole', 1.1, 1.2.

with an easie request of S. *Augustine; Fieri non potest ut seipsum non diligat, qui Deum diligit;* That man does not love God, that loves not himself; doe but love your selves: *Imo solus se diligere novit, qui Deum diligit,* Only that man that loves God, hath the art to love himself . . . for if he love God, he would live eternally with him, and, if he desire that, and indeavour it earnestly, he does truly love himself, and not otherwise. (8.236)[38]

'The Extasie', as we have seen, transposes a defining element of the beatific vision into the realm of human love: intuitive cognition animated by the forces of charity. Another discussion of the soul's knowledge is found in *The Second Anniversarie.* In his poetic eulogy for Elizabeth Drury, Donne contrasts the superior quality of Elizabeth's existence in heaven with 'us slow-pac'd snailes, who crawle upon/Our prisons prison, earth' (ll. 248–9). Yet again, Donne is in hot pursuit of an ecstatic experience when he chides his soul for its sluggishness; he aspires to Elizabeth's spiritual alacrity instead:

> When wilt thou shake off this Pedantery,
> Of being taught by sense, and Fantasy?
> Thou look'st through spectacles; small things seeme great,
> Below; But up unto the watch-towre get,
> And see all things despoyld of fallacies:
> Thou shalt not peepe through lattices of eies,
> Nor heare through Laberinths of eares, nor learne
> By circuit, or collections to discerne.
> In Heaven thou straight know'st all, concerning it,
> And what concernes it not, shalt straight forget.[39]

Donne's language evokes the rhetoric of obscurity and revelation, as well as the tension between partial and comprehensive knowledge, which inform Paul's language in 1 Corinthians 13:12. The phrase 'lattices of eies' alludes to Song of Solomon 2:9, a text which was frequently combined with the Pauline passage to comment on the differences between human and divine cognition. While inhabiting 'our prisons prison, earth', knowledge is somatic and, above all, laboriously processual.[40] A 'collection' is an enquiry which proceeds from gathering evidence to logical inference,[41] while a 'circuit' describes a roundabout mode of reasoning or simply a detour.[42] In any case, it is the *modus operandi* of 'slow-pac'd' minds, prone to succumbing to 'fallacies'. Heavenly knowledge, by contrast, provides a superior

---

[38] The references are taken, in the 1627 sermon, from Augustine's *On Order* 2.19 (*PL* 32.1019), and in the Easter 1628 sermon, from the *On the Values of the Catholic Church* 1.26 (*PL* 32.1331).

[39] *The Second Anniversarie,* ll. 291–300. Heavenly knowledge is also characterized as an open book: see e.g. *Devotions,* which construes death as God's translation of man 'into a better *language*'; in the resurrection, 'his hand shall binde up all our scattered leaves againe, for that *Librarie* where every *booke* shall lie open to one another' (*Devotions,* 86). See, on this passage, and the epistemological implications of Donne's book metaphors more generally, Thomas A. Festa, 'Donne's *Anniversaries* and his Anatomy of the Book', *John Donne Journal,* 17 (1998), 29–60.

[40] On the difference between somatic and spiritual knowledge in this text, and for an excellent account of the relationship between body and soul in Donne's writings more generally, see Ramie Targoff's excellent discussion: *John Donne, Body and Soul* (Chicago, 2008), esp. 102.

[41] *OED,* 'collection': 1, 5.

[42] *OED,* 'circuit': 3b, 8b.

vantage-point in the literal and metaphysical sense: secure in its panoramic perspective, our gaze is 'straight', and safe from the misdirections of crooked 'fallacies'.

It is this accuracy and breadth of vision that Donne's Augustinian citations in the Easter sermon of 1628 seek to simulate. Donne presents twelve quotations from eleven Augustinian texts, combining range of quotation with an almost implausible level of precision. His selection of texts is at once comprehensive and suited exactly to the themes and ideas he treats in his sermon: it mimics, in other words, the processes of perfect knowledge described in *The Second Anniversarie*.

Donne's Augustinian quotations steer clear of the obvious and commonplace; instead, from his imagined vantage-point, he peers into every nook and cranny of Augustine's vast textual topography. In order to assemble these remote textual places and better illustrate Donne's citational techniques, I will start by listing some of the key references deployed in the sermon. In each case, Donne has selected a portion of the work which speaks 'straight' to the aspects of 1 Corinthians 13:12 he wishes to emphasize. For ease of reference, I include the chapter titles added by Donne's late seventeenth-century editors, the Benedictines of St Maur, which are reproduced in Migne's *Patrologia Latina*. Donne's range of references comprises (1) chapter 27 of the (spurious) *Meditations*, which speaks of the 'incomprehensible glory of the blessed' and of the soul's transition from earthly 'stupor' to perfect insight;[43] (2) Augustine's sermon on Psalm 72, subtitled 'De Visione Dei';[44] (3) chapter 36 of the *Soliloquies of the Soul*, entitled 'Of the light of glory. Seeing God face to face and the complete bliss of the beatific vision';[45] (4) Epistle 147, 'That it is impossible to see God with the eyes of the body';[46] and (5) *On the Literal Interpretation of Genesis*, Book 12, chapter 27, 'What was the nature of Moses' vision of God?'[47]

---

[43] *Meditationum Liber Unus*, chapter 27 (*PL* 40.921). See *Sermons*, 8.235–6: 'And so it shall be a knowledge so like his knowledge, as it shall produce a love, like his love, and we shall love him, as he loves us. . . . *Qualis sine fine festivitas!* what a Holy-day shall this be, which no working day shall ever follow! By knowing, and loving the unchangeable, the immutable God, *Mutabimur in immutabilitatem*, we shall be changed into an unchangeablenesse, sayes that Father, that never said any thing but extraordinarily.'

[44] See *Sermons*, 8.236: 'He [Augustine] sayes more, *Dei præsentia si in inferno appareret*, If God could be seene, and known in hell, hell in an instant would be heaven' (*PL* 36.926).

[45] *Soliloquiorum Animae*, chapter 36 (*PL* 40.896; a spurious text). See *Sermons*, 8.235: 'But in heaven there is no materiall thing to be assumed, and if God be seen face to face there, he is seen in his Essence. S. *Augustine* summes it up fully, upon those words, *In lumine tuo, In thy light we shall see light, Te scilicet in te*, we shall see thee in thee; that is, sayes he, *face to face.*'

[46] See *Sermons*, 8.234 (*PL* 33.597; Classis Tertia): 'S. *Augustine* calls it a debt, a double debt, a debt because she asked it, a debt because he promised it, to give, even a woman, *Paulina*, satisfaction in that high point, and mystery, *how we should see God face to face in heaven*.' (Paulina is the addressee of Epistle 147.)

[47] *Sermons*, 8.226 (*PL* 34.477): 'Therefore saies S. *Augustine*, that *Moses* saw God, in that conversation which he had with him in the Mount, *Sevocatus ab omni corporis sensu*, Removed from all benefit and assistance of bodily senses, (He needed not that Glasse, the helpe of the Creature) And more then so, *Ab omni significativo ænigmate Spiritus*, Removed from all allusions, or similitudes, or representations of God, which might bring God to the understanding, and so to the beliefe; *Moses* knew God by a more immediate working, then either sense, or understanding, or faith.' Other Augustinian texts cited in the sermon besides the ones already discussed (*De Moribus Ecclesiae Catholicae* 1.26, *Confessions* 9.10, *De Trinitate* 10.1) are: a sermon on Luke 14:16–24 (also cited in the Candlemas sermon), and a sermon on Paul's letter to the Philippians 3:3–16.

Collectively, this set of citations simulates a moment of perfect comprehension, as Donne steps out of Paul's 'dark glass' to behold the glory of God more directly. It is another example of a self-transcending rhetorical device, a connection which, although bound 'in body' to the tools of mediated, representational language, endeavours to open up a spiritual connection through which eternal verities can be apprehended more immediately. The pointed omission of Augustine's more 'visible' reflections on 'visio dei' would have attracted the attention of the theological experts among Donne's audience, but the exact operations of his referential play remain hidden from view. Although all quotations are openly declared as Augustinian (the single exception being Donne's favourite maxim—the canonical pronouncement from *On the Trinity* 10.2 that we cannot love a thing unless we know it ('amari nisi nota non posse')), further details of provenance are characteristically withheld. Donne thus speaks from a position of complete citational clarity while the congregation deals, in the language of his Pauline text, with 'partial' and 'obscure' intimations of his textual strategy. Donne is the only one who beholds Augustine face to face. This, however, is not the end of Donne's intertextual manipulations. It is crucial to note at this point the most obvious fact about Donne's use of Augustine in the Easter sermon of 1628: that the breadth and the precision of his references points to the exact opposite of a direct encounter with Augustine, and overwhelmingly indicates the use of a mediator—a printed patristic anthology, Donne's own commonplace book, or Erasmus's Index. Indeed, the evidence suggests that he used a combination of the three: the patristic sentence collections include Epistle 147 to Paulina and the letters to Jerome, while Erasmus points, under 'beatitudo', 'videre Deum', and 'visio intellectualis', to the *Soliloquies of the Soul* and *On the Literal Interpretation of Genesis*, among others. In addition to these auxiliary tools, Donne also draws on Aquinas's and Calvin's commentaries on 1 Corinthians 13:12 to supplement his discussion.[48] Donne's reliance on patristic mediators reveals a knowledge of Augustine's *oeuvre* that deals 'but in parts'; paradoxically, this mediated form of recourse is also absolutely foundational to the fiction of total clarity and comprehension which his sermon constructs. He uses a crib precisely to demonstrate complete command of his subject, and lifts the veil of ignorance with the help of 'despised' and inadequate scholarly 'assistances'.

Donne's sermon on Matthew 5:8, 'Blessed are the pure in heart, for they shall see God', also concerns itself with the rectification and perfection of human vision. God, Donne argues, is 'invisible in this world only, and visible in the

[48] See Aquinas, *Commentary on 1 Corinthians*, Lectio 4, expounding Augustine's reading of 1 Corinthians 13:12. Aquinas notes that our knowledge of God in the resurrection is similar, but not equal, to the quality of God's cognition ('non importat hic aequalitatem cognitionis, sed similitudinem tantum'); Aquinas, *Super Epistolas S. Pauli Lectura*, ed. Raphael Cai, 2 vols. (Turin, 1953). Compare *Sermons*, 8.235, 'But it is *Nota similitudinis, non aequalitatis.*' Calvin is the likely source for Donne's analogy between Church ordinances (and the work of preachers especially) and Paul's 'glass'; see Calvin, *Commentary vpon the first Epistle of S. Paule to the Corinthians*, trans. Thomas Tymme (London, 1577), fol. 156r: 'there is no doubt but that the ministerie of the woord, and those Instruments which are required to exercise the same, are compared here by the Apostle to a glasse. For God which is otherwise inuisible, hath ordayned these meanes, to make hym selfe knowen vnto vs.'

next' (7.344); the promise of the scriptural text, that the blessed 'shall see', is 'principally intended' of the 'Visio Beatifica': 'videre Essentiam ... we shall see God in his Essence' (7.341). Within this broad thematic framework, Donne focuses on a more specific issue, 'with what eyes I shall see him' (7.342)—the eyes of the body or the eyes of the mind. To this end, Donne proposes (with a glancing pun) to 'look a little into the Fathers, and into the School, and conclude so, as may best advance our edification' (7.342). Once again, it is vital to note the close correlation between theme, doctrine, and intertextual strategy. As the focus of his enquiry into the beatific vision contracts to a question of detail, so does Donne's citational horizon: 'For the Fathers, it may be sufficient to insist upon S. *Augustine;* not because he is alwayes to be preferred before all, but because in this point, he hath best collected all that were before him, and is best followed of all that come after' (7.342). The promise to incorporate a range of patristic and scholastic viewpoints is retracted almost immediately: the School does not really get a look in at all and the Fathers are reduced to Augustine. But Donne goes further still in refining his intellectual target. The Candlemas sermon of 1627 includes a total of thirteen Augustinian references from four different texts;[49] in the 'technical' analysis of bodily and spiritual eyes, however, a single text dominates: here, Donne relies exclusively on Augustine's epistle to Fortunatianus, introducing eight specific citations and gutting (without explicit acknowledgement) the second chapter of Augustine's letter to supply a conspectus of further patristic authorities.

Donne's sermon betrays other signs of scholarly focus and efficiency. One of his key points is that 'only the heart of man can see God' (7.344). Donne supports this argument with the first quotation from the epistle to Fortunatianus, which explains that 'our bodily eyes, howsoever glorified, should never see God' (7.342). But Donne requires further proof: 'S. Augustine ... S. Ambrose, and S. Hierome, and S. Chrysostome ... [all] agree in this resolution, *Solus Deus videt cor, & solum cor videt Deum*' (7.344). This is an exact overlap with the range of authorities cited for Matthew 5:8 in Aquinas's *Catena Aurea.* Aquinas's patristic conspectus also includes an extract from *On the Lord's Sermon on the Mount*, in which Augustine excoriates the 'stupidity of those who seek God with bodily eyes, when he can only be seen with the eyes of the heart'.[50] The *Catena* further supplies the next unacknowledged source in Donne's sermon: Augustine's *City of God.* In the penultimate chapter of that text, Augustine considers the quality of vision in the next life, with particular reference to Matthew 5:8: 'Blessed are the pure in heart, because they shall see God. But now is in question, whether hee [God] may be

[49] They are, in chronological order of citation, (1) Augustine's Epistle 148, to Fortunatianus (eight references); this letter comes immediately after Epistle 147 to Paulina, which has just been discussed in relation to the Easter 1628 sermon—another indication, perhaps, of scholarly economy; (2) a sermon on Luke 14:16–24 (two references), also cited in the Easter sermon of 1628; (3) a sermon on Matthew 5:3–8 (one reference); (4) *De Ordine* 2.19 (two references).

[50] 'Quam ergo stulti sunt, qui Deum istis exterioribus oculis quaerunt, cum corde videatur' (*De Sermone Domini in Monte* 1.2). Thomas Aquinas, *Catena Aurea in Quatuor Evangelia*, ed. Angelico Guarienti, 2 vols. (Turin, 1953).

seene there [in heaven] also with corporall eyes.'[51] Crucially, Augustine also
connects that text with Luke 2:29–32, Simeon's prophecy that the child Jesus
would save the world: 'mine eyes have seene thy salvation'. This biblical scene takes
place at Christ's Presentation at the Temple—the alternative title for the Feast of
Candlemas. *City of God* 22.29, the penultimate chapter of this massive work, thus
provides the main ideas and the liturgical anchor for Donne's Candlemas reflections on 'visio dei', but the reference is nowhere acknowledged and was probably
mediated through Aquinas, even though Donne knew Augustine's text at first
hand.

Donne's sermon opens with a reminder that Candlemas is 'a day of purification
to us, and a day of lights'. But if his discourse is designed to purify the hearts of his
hearers, Donne also brings a purer and more direct focus to his citational procedures, especially by comparison with the Easter 1628 sermon. Instead of a panoramic overview, we find the detailed investigation of a single Augustinian text.
Donne proceeds chronologically through Augustine's letter to Fortunatianus in the
first half of his analysis (7.342–3); he starts by distilling two quotations from
chapter 1 and then paraphrases Augustine's synopsis of patristic opinion from
chapter 2 (Jerome, Athanasius, Gregory Nazianzen). Donne's discussion uses five
further quotations from the same epistle, derived from chapters 3 and 5.[52] In some
ways, it is difficult not to feel that this is the intertextual version of a neat recycling
job and that Donne was, at least to some extent, responding to the pressures of time
and occasion. Indeed, while he suppresses the more obvious source—*City of God*
22.29—he makes no attempt to conceal his dependence on Augustine's letter to
Fortunatianus. As we have seen, he openly acknowledges that Augustine, in this
point, 'hath best collected all that were before him' and, perhaps a little more glibly,
that he 'is best followed of all that come after'. He also readily points his audience to
the source of his material: 'S. *Augustine* had written against a Bishop who was of the
Sect of the Anthromorphists[.] . . . In that Treatise S. *Augustine* had been very bitter
against that Bishop, and being warned of it, in another Epistle to another Bishop,
Fortunatianus, he repents, and retracts his bitternesse, but his opinion, his doctrine,
That our bodily eyes should never see God, S. *Augustine* never retracted' (7.342).
However, Donne is equally keen to justify these citational choices, and ends up with
an extremely creative explanation for those strategy. His sermon offers an in-depth
analysis of another act of homiletic recycling, one derived from a precedent more
venerable even than the Bishop of Hippo's. Matthew 5:8 is part of Christ's sermon
on the mount and, as Donne notes, 'there is doubt . . . whether this Sermon which S.
Matthew records here, be the same which S. *Luke* mentions in his sixth Chapter, or
whether they were preached at severall times' (7.327). If it is the same sermon,
Donne further argues, this proves that 'Christ did not, and therefore we need not

[51] 'J.[ohn] H.[ealey], *St. Avgvstine Of the Citie Of God: with the Learned Comments of Io. Lod. Vives*
(1610), 916. On Healey and this translation more generally, see Mark Vessey, 'The *Citie of God* (1610)
and the London Virginia Company', *Augustinian Studies*, 30 (1999), 257–81.
[52] Augustine, Epistle 148, To Fortunatianus (*PL* 33.622; Classis Tertia).

forbeare to preach the same particular Doctrines, or to handle the same particular points, which we, or others, in that place, have handled before' (7.329).

'[P]oints, which we, *or others*... have handled before': Christ's example of homiletic self-repetition justifies or 'purifies' Donne's reliance on Augustine in the 1627 Candlemas sermon; the intense spiritual gaze described in the exegesis of Matthew 5:8 finds its citational counterpart in the direct, focused encounter with a single Augustinian text—just as the panoramic quality of 'visio dei' in the Easter 1628 sermon is expressed by a unique breadth and accuracy of intertextual comprehension. Donne's referencing systems, then, are rigorously occasion-centred—tailored, in their selection of texts and in their modes of recourse, to precise thematic purposes and rhetorical contexts. But this intense preoccupation with context serves, paradoxically, to articulate a desire for self-transcendence: in constructing his occasional spectacle, Donne reaches out to timeless, eternal truths. In both sermons, Augustine is the principal source for Donne's treatment of the beatific vision, through direct and mediated consultation. The majority of Donne's citations on this topic, especially in the later years of his ministry, are heavily indebted to Augustinian texts. But Augustine cannot claim complete exclusivity. When questions of eternal bliss and heavenly vision appear in a controversial context, for instance, Donne tends to invoke Aquinas, especially on the connections between 'beatitudo' and 'visio dei'.[53] Donne also relies on redactions of medieval controversies on the subject of heavenly vision (usually between the camps of Aquinas and Duns Scotus); for details of such scholastic disputes, Donne often depends on an early modern tertiary mediator such as the Italian Capuchin scholar Zacharias Boverius (1568–1638; see, for example, *Sermons*, 4.168).

Donne's Easter sermon of 1628 concludes with an exhortation to those who 'endeavour to see God in heaven... as he is loved' (8.236). Throughout his Augustinian reflections on the beatific vision, charity is presented as the conduit to perfect cognition and comprehension; it is also the theological virtue that endures even after faith has been superseded by the light of glory. As Donne observes on the perfection of love in the beatific vision: 'as S. *Augustine* saith, *Sunt quasi cunabula charitatis Dei, quibus diligimus proximum,* The love which we beare to our neighbour is but as the Infancy, but as the Cradle of that love which we beare to God; so that sight of God which we have *In speculo, in the Glasse,* that is, in nature, is but *Cunabula fidei*... and yet that knowledge which we have in faith, is but *Cunabula visionis,* the infancy and cradle of that knowledge which we shall have when we come to see God *face to face*' (8.230).[54] Donne's invocations of Augustine, and his habit of eavesdropping on the most intimate and devotionally exalted moments of Augustine's biography (the encounter with Jerome, the vision at Ostia), mark points of continuity with the *Essayes in Divinity*, especially the

---

[53] See e.g. *Sermons*, 9.127–8. See e.g. Aquinas, *Commentary on the Epistle to the Hebrews*, ed. Chrysostom Baer (South Bend, Ind., 2006), 1.11, 'the essence of beatitude is nothing other than the vision of God ('essentia enim beatudinis nihil aliud est, quam visio Dei'). Aquinas is indebted to Augustine, of course, but Donne chooses to ignore the connection.
[54] *On the Values of the Catholic Church* 1.26 (*PL* 32.1331).

anguished re-creation of Augustine's imaginary interview with Moses. But if the *Essayes'* leaps of faith provide momentary glimpses of a higher order, Donne's sermons on the beatific vision imagine a still more glorious ascent: eternal heavenly communion with a loving God. It is a peculiarly Donnean paradox that he is most dependent on his favourite Church Father when he envisages a direct, unmediated vision of his father in heaven. This sense of paradox intensifies when we realize that his continued reliance on another human being in fact constitutes Donne's most significant departure from Augustine's example. Brian Stock has argued that the vision at Ostia is Augustine's 'final attempt to see his image of himself taking shape with another living person'.[55] From this moment onwards, Augustine only enters into dialogue with himself and with God. Donne's vision of glory, by contrast, remains interpersonal to the last; he is in dialogue with Augustine's living spirit even as he prepares to meet his maker, and relies on hermeneutic mediation even as interpretation gives way to revelation. In this sense, Donne also remains true to what Elaine Scarry has described as his ongoing preoccupation with 'tracing and retracing the passage between the material and immaterial worlds'.[56]

Scarry's account of Donne brilliantly anatomizes the material dimensions of his poetics, epistemology, and spirituality, stressing his insistence on 'the obligation to touch the human body, whether acutely alive or newly dead, with generosity and fierce decency'.[57] It is interesting to note that Scarry's analysis rests mainly on four of Donne's Easter sermons, which dwell in detail 'on the Easter miracle of the resurrected body' and 'the willful materialism of the Judeo-Christian God'.[58] In the context of this discussion, it hardly comes as a surprise to learn that 'for Donne, touch is the model for all the senses'.[59] But the evidence of the Easter sermons I have examined here offers an important counterbalance to this material dimension; time and again Donne argues, with Augustine, that vision matters, especially the kind that enables glimpses of a higher reality: 'The sight is so much the Noblest of all the senses, as that it is all the senses.... [S]o, sayes, S. Augustine... *Visus per omnes sensus recurrit*, All the senses are called Seeing.'[60] It is true that Donne stays in touch with the world while he preaches in it—through Augustine, and through the decidedly worldly textual play that characterizes his interaction with the audience in the Candlemas and Easter sermons. At one level, these citational performances are doubtless designed to astonish and impress. Donne is no Neo-platonist: he thoroughly enjoys the pleasures provided by argument and rhetoric— the 'cyment' and 'glue' which hold together a community of the fallible and the

[55] Stock, *Augustine the Reader*, 118.
[56] Elaine Scarry, 'Donne: "But Yet the Body is his Booke"', in Scarry (ed.), *Literature and the Body: Essays on Populations and Persons* (London, 1986), 70–106 (88).
[57] Ibid. 70.
[58] Ibid.
[59] Ibid. 88.
[60] *Sermons*, 8.221 (from Augustine's Sermon on Luke 14:16–24, ch. 6; *PL* 38.646). There are three other occurrences of this quotation, one in Donne's Easter sermons, one in the Candlemas sermon of 1627, and one in a Whitehall sermon of 4 March 1625. In this last sermon, Donne also works closely with Book 1 of *On the Values of the Catholic Church* (1.20 and 1.26) and reflects on the beatific vision: he was clearly re-using familiar material when he returned to the topic of heavenly bliss in 1628.

fallen. His textual displays, then, are supremely occasional demonstrations of skill and intellectual poise, but they are also expressive of a desire for grace, revelation, and self-transcendence. Augustine's perspective on 'visio dei' enables Donne to imagine an escape from the sinful self and the language that entraps it. And this vision is no less genuine for Donne's constant acknowledgement of the gravitational forces which preclude its realization, at least for now.

Conclusion

> Thy sacred Academe above
> Of Doctors, whose paines have unclasp'd, and taught
> Both bookes of life to us (for love
> To know thy Scriptures tells us, we are wrought
> In thy other booke) pray for us there
> That what they have misdone
> Or mis-said, wee to that may not adhere,
> Their zeale may be our sinne. Lord let us runne
> Meane waies, and call them stars, but not the Sunne.[1]

Donne's 'Litanie' postdates the composition of *Biathanatos*, with its unflattering portrait of Augustinian 'zeale', and precedes the patristic anatomy of Genesis and Exodus in the *Essayes in Divinity*.[2] But the 'love/To know thy Scriptures' connects all these texts. The *Essayes* also supply a gloss for Donne's metaphor of the 'bookes of life'; in his opening disquisition 'Of the Bible', Donne explains that

> God hath two Books of life; that in the *Revelation,* and else where, which is an eternall Register of his Elect; and this Bible. For of this, it is therefore said, *Search the Scriptures, because in them ye hope to have eternall life.* . . . [O]ur orderly love to the understanding this Book of life, testifies to us that our names are in the other.[3]

As so often in Donne's works, the process of Christian history is folded back into the process of reading: when suffering gives way to '*Revelation*', the meaning of God's Word is made clear, and his 'bookes' are laid open. But the intertextual resonances do not stop there. Donne's *Devotions* conceive of humanity's salvation in similarly bookish terms: in the resurrection, God's 'hand shall binde up all our scattered leaves againe, for that *Librarie* where every *booke* shall lie open to one another'.[4] Christ re-edits our story in the ultimate act of loving sacrifice, but it is the 'sacred Academe'—the Fathers and Doctors of the Church—who have 'unclasp'd' the 'bookes of life', whose 'love to know thy Scriptures' teaches us to become better

---

[1] Donne, 'The Litanie', 109–17. Patrides prints 'Academie', following the 1633 edition of Donne's *Poems*, but this is clearly a mistake. Donne's poem is in twenty-eight stanzas of nine lines each and sticks to a strict tetrameter pattern in the first line of each stanza; Robbins is thus right to amend to 'Academe' (507).

[2] Robbins's edition (496) tentatively dates the poem to autumn 1608 and summarizes the contextual evidence from Donne's letters.

[3] *Essayes in Divinity*, 8–9.

[4] *Devotions*, 86.

readers of God's providential narrative. While lauding the Fathers' contribution, however, Donne also keeps the patristic tradition firmly in its place, as he did throughout his preaching career. John Jewel supplied the classic formulation which Donne invokes in his 'Litanie': '[the Fathers] are stars, fair and beautiful and bright; yet they are not the sun: they bear witness of the light, they are not the light.'[5] The Fathers are part of a hierarchy of 'orderly love', in another Augustinian trope which connects Donne's early religious thought with his mature preaching. 'The person who lives a just and holy life', Augustine observes in Book 1 of *De Doctrina Christiana*, is a 'person who has ordered his love, so that he does not love what it is wrong to love . . . or love too much what should be loved less[.] . . . Every human being, *qua* human being, should be loved on God's account; and God should be loved for himself.'[6] *Biathanatos*, as we have seen, turns this passage to highly ingenious casuistical uses, while the *Essayes* and the sermons attempt to find more orthodox applications. A Trinity Sunday sermon preached on 1 Corinthians 16:22, for instance, notes that 'God forbids us not a love of the Creature, proportionable to the good that that creature can do us. . . . But because God does all this, in all these severall instruments, God alone is centrically, radically, directly to be loved, and the creature with a love reflected and derived from him.'[7] Donne's 'Litanie', however, treads 'Meane waies' of the slightly uncomfortable variety. While piously affirming Jewel's patristic formula, the poem also deviates from Protestant convention through the simple gesture of including the Fathers in the first place: as P. M. Oliver observes, invocations of the great theologians 'had been part of the Roman litany, but not of the English versions of 1544 or 1549'.[8]

Although it may not quite be a case of loving 'too much what should be loved less', Donne's desire to find a place for Augustine, to carve out a niche for him even in the contested territory of liturgical politics, attests to a profound and lasting sense of attachment: to return to the quotation with which this study began, 'I am loath to part from this father, and he is loath to be parted from.'[9] The sermons are the most remarkable textual monument to Donne's Augustinian reading; through Donne's preaching, we can chart his changing relationship with Augustine's thought as well as his continuous and acknowledged spiritual debt. The earliest sermons of the period 1615–18, for instance, offer some relatively rare glimpses of Augustine's theology of grace: even there, however, Donne is concerned with the moral ramifications of sin, rather than with the minutiae of soteriology.[10] God

---

[5] Jewel, *Works*, 4.1173–4.
[6] *De Doctrina Christiana* 1.27 ('Ordo dilectionis'): 'Ille autem juste et sancte vivit, qui rerum integer aestimator est: ipse est autem qui ordinatam dilectionem habet, ne aut diligat quod non est diligendum . . . aut amplius diligat quod minus est diligendum[.] . . . omnis homo in quantum homo est, diligendus est propter Deum, Deus vero propter seipsum' (*PL* 34.29).
[7] *Sermons*, 3.303. Donne's sermon continues with an extended meditation on Augustine's epistle to a young man, Licentius, which applies the doctrine of ordered love to particular examples (Epistle 26, *PL* 33.104–7; Prima Classis).
[8] P. M. Oliver, *Donne's Religious Writing: A Discourse of Feigned Devotion* (London, 1997), 86.
[9] *Sermons*, 9.102.
[10] See e.g. Donne's sermon preached at Greenwich on 30 April 1615, on Isaiah 52:3 (*Sermons*, 1.151–67), and the two sermons preached at Whitehall on 19 April 1618, on 1 Timothy 1:15

appears as omnipotent judge in these sermons, with the occasional glance at controversial tracts such as *On Genesis against the Manichees*, but one also senses that Donne is actively concerned to keep Augustine out of his theology of sin; the uncomfortable truths of Christianity are rarely communicated by his favourite Father.[11] Reflections on the preacher's office constitute another major preoccupation in Donne's early preaching, especially in the Lincoln's Inn years. Perhaps unsurprisingly, Augustine's sermons are Donne's main ports of call for this theme, and he often homes in on passages which discuss homiletic techniques, or show Augustine meditating on his own early experiences as a preacher.[12] At this time, Donne also seems to have discovered Augustine's *Enarrations on the Psalms*, taking his cue from 'Saint *Augustines* protestation, that he loved the *Book of Psalms*'.[13] The initial impetus for his reading may well have emerged from the daunting task of preparing a whole series of sermons on Psalm 38 at Lincoln's Inn (see *Sermons*, vol. 2, nos. 1–6), which draw in detail on Augustine's exposition of that Scripture text; the *Enarrations*, at any rate, with their characteristically Christological readings of the Psalms, make regular appearances in Donne's sermons of 1618–19. After his appointment to St Paul's, Donne's focus shifts to other Augustinian concerns. To his regular audience at the cathedral, Donne's Augustine provides edifying disquisitions on the sacraments—especially baptism—and on the office of the Holy Ghost.[14] In some respects, Donne's patristic recourse depends heavily on audience and place, of course. As David Colclough shows in a comparative analysis of two court sermons of April 1626, Donne was as alert to the intellectual capacities of his congregation as to their spiritual and pastoral needs. Donne's sermon of 18 April 1626 was preached to the king and his courtiers; in it, he deploys a range of patristic references, and is especially subtle in his use of Augustine. By contrast, when he preaches to the king's household 'below stairs' almost a fortnight later, Donne's references to the Fathers are pared down to a minimum and work towards audience edification rather than controversial or technical theology.[15]

While place of preaching matters, however, the most crucial changes in Donne's use of Augustine occur along biographical or chronological lines. The most seismic shift, without doubt, takes place in 1624/5, in the wake of the near-fatal illness chronicled in Donne's *Devotions*. Janel Mueller puts the case succinctly: when Donne 'returned to the pulpit of St. Paul's Cathedral in London at Easter

(*Sermons*, 1.285–318). References tend to be drawn from Augustine's preaching (e.g. the spurious *Sermo* 393, 'De Poenitentibus', *PL* 39.1714 (Sermones Dubii): 'If any such sinner seem to thee to repent at his end, *Fateor vobis non negamus, quod petit*, saith St. *Augustin*: I confess, we ought not to deny him, any help that he desires in that late extremity' (Donne, *Sermons*, 1.156)).

[11] See e.g. *Sermons*, 1.162, invoking *On Genesis against the Manichees* 1.2: 'Of which will of God, whosoever seeks a reason, *Aliquid majus Deo quærit*, says S. *Augustin*, he that seeks what perswaded or inclind the will of God, seeks for something wiser, and greater than God himself.' (*PL* 34.175: 'majus aliquid quaerit quam est voluntas Dei: nihil autem majus inveniri potest'.)

[12] See e.g. *Sermons*, 1.202, 1.250–1, 1.260, 2.172–3, 2.229, 2.274, 2.276.

[13] Ibid. 2.49.

[14] See e.g. ibid. 5.62–4, 5.73–4, 5.86, 5.101, 5.128, 5.164–7, 5.366.

[15] David Colclough, 'Upstairs, Downstairs: Doctrine and Decorum in Two Sermons by John Donne', *Huntington Library Quarterly*, 73 (2010), 163–91 (180).

1624 ... [he] spoke like a man brought back from the dead. . . . Donne's illness midway in his ministry led to a new clearsightedness of the soul.'[16] Donne's Augustinian references after 1624 overwhelmingly stress God's love, mercy, and goodness: God the creator, God the redeemer. In doing so, they draw on the *Enarrations*, as in a sermon preached in March 1624 on Matthew 19:17: 'But, *ineffabili dulcedine teneor cum audio, Bonus dominus;* I am, not transported with astonishment . . . but replenished with all sweetnesse, established with all soundnesse, when I hear of my God in that name, my good God.'[17] But other textual emphases begin to emerge alongside these Augustinian staples: Donne draws frequently on St Matthew's Gospel in this period and relies for exegetical guidance on Book 2 of Augustine's *Consensus of the Evangelists*.[18] And, above all, Donne celebrates divine providence through reference to the anti-Manichean tracts, which defend Augustine's loving God against His detractors through ever more enthusiastic songs of praise: '*Brevissima differentia Testamentorum, Timor & Amor;* This distinguishes the two Testaments, The Old is a Testament of *fear,* the New of *love*', Donne explains with a glance at Augustine's *Against Adimantus*, for instance.[19]

The sermons of 1626/7, meanwhile, present the densest structures of prooftexting and also offer Donne's most explicit reflections on the doctrinal status and scope of patristic theology. There, he stages extended disputations with Roman authors on the issues of purgatory and prayers for the dead, engaging in detail with Bellarmine's controversial writings.[20] Donne's patristic methodology follows Protestant guidelines on the use of the Fathers: they are firmly subordinated to the Scriptures and must be read in the context of their historical situation, rhetorical conventions, and polemical concerns.[21] Towards the end of 1627, Donne begins to turn his attention towards eschatology and epistemology: the sermons of this period often cite Augustine on the nature of angelic knowledge, on heaven, and on the vision of God.[22] Augustine's texts plot paths of faith through these complex ideas, and provide comfort in the midst of anxious contemplation. Preaching on 19 November 1627, on Matthew 22:30, Donne meditates on the question of 'what those *Angels* of God in heaven . . . are'.[23] After protracted discussion, Donne defers the solution until our arrival in heaven—when 'we shall be like them . . . then we shall know what they are'—but characteristically he shores up belief in the solidity of last things through Augustine: 'we know not; But we are content to say with S. *Augustine, Esse firmissimè credo, quænam sint nescio;* that there are . . . *Angels,* assuredly I beleeve; but what they are, I cannot tell.'[24]

---

[16]   Mueller, *Donne's Prebend Sermons,* 2.
[17]   *Sermons,* 6.232; *Enarrationes in Psalmos* 134.4 (*PL* 37.1740).
[18]   See e.g. *Sermons,* 6.148, 6.230.
[19]   *Sermons,* 6.112. See Augustine, *Contra Adimantum,* chapter 17 (*PL* 42.159).
[20]   See e.g. *Sermons,* vol. 7, nos. 4, 6, 7, and 13.
[21]   See *Sermons,* 7.203; discussed above, p. 18.
[22]   See e.g. 8.85, 8.105–8, 8.233–6, 8.360–3.
[23]   *Sermons,* 8.105.
[24]   Ibid. 105–6. The reference is to Augustine's *Enchiridion,* chapter 58 (*PL* 40.259–60).

In the final phase of his ministry, as we have seen, Donne continues this emphasis on the next life, with reference to Augustinian notions of beatitude and 'visio dei'. In anticipating these heavenly joys, Donne utilizes the sermons and *Enarrations*, and, increasingly, the final books of the *City of God.*[25] But these years also mark the high point of Donne's engagement with the hermeneutics of charity, through frequent references to Augustine's *Homilies on the Gospel of John*, *De Doctrina Christiana*, and the final books of the *Confessions.*[26] In many ways, Donne simply continues his long-lasting preoccupation with charity as the virtue that abides; as he asserts in an early Lincoln's Inn sermon,

> [t]his vertue then, *Charity,* is it, that conducts us in this life, and accompanies us in the next. In heaven, where we shall *know God,* there may be no use of *faith;* In heaven, where we shall *see God,* there may be no use of *hope;* but in heaven, where *God* the Father, and the Son, love one another in the Holy Ghost, the bond of charity shall everlastingly unite us together.[27]

The late sermons, as they eagerly anticipate this perfection of charity in the resurrection, perfect mimetic modes of recourse to Augustine's textual universe, as we saw in Chapters 6 and 7. At the same time, however, they also remain caught up in the complex dynamic of idealism and polemic, altruism and self-interest, which has characterized Donne's use of charity throughout. '*Charitas in via*', he argues, differs from '*Charitas in patria*': the Church Militant at times requires a militant kind of charity.[28] Thus, a late court sermon preached on Genesis 1:26 delivers a paean to Augustine's charity only to convert it swiftly into a polemical jibe against Rome. Augustine had defended Tertullian against imputations of heresy, the argument that God possessed a physical body:

> Because it was possible to give a good interpretation of *Tertullian,* that charitable Father Saint *Augustine,* would excuse him of heresie. I would Saint *Augustines* charity would prevaile with them, that pretend to be *Augustinianissimi,* and to adore him so much in the *Roman Church,* not to cast the name of Heresie upon every probleme[.] . . . Saint *Augustine* would deliver *Tertullian* from heresie in a point concerning God, and they will condemne us of heresie, in every point that may be drawne to concerne not the Church, but the Court of *Rome;* not their doctrine, but their profit.[29]

It would doubtless have been possible to give a charitable interpretation of the Catholic position here, but Donne chooses not to. At the same time, he manages to marginalize his opponents through the imputation of uncharitable pride: Rome's doctrinal and spiritual corruption is adumbrated in the refusal to grant any kind of

---

[25] See e.g. *Sermons*, 10.223–3 (*Enarrationes in Psalmos* 32, 67, 88); Donne's final sermon, 'Death's Duell', draws on Augustine's exegesis of Psalm 68 in *City of God* 17.18; for *De Doctrina Christiana*, see e.g. *Sermons*, 10.196, invoking Book 2, chapter 37 of Augustine's text (*PL* 34.61).

[26] On Augustine and charity, see e.g. *Sermons*, 8.360, 9.76–7, 9.141, 9.200.

[27] Ibid. 2.213–14.

[28] Ibid. 214.

[29] Ibid. 9.76–7. See Tertullian, *Adversus Praxeam*, 7 (*PL* 2.126C), where he suggests that God has a body. For Augustine's defence, see *De haeresibus* 86: 'Tertullianistae' (*PL* 42.47). (Augustine defends Tertullian again in *De Genesi ad Litteram* 10.25 (*PL* 34.427).)

forgiveness, even in non-fundamental matters: '*Augustine* would deliver *Tertullian* from heresie in a point concerning God', yet the Pope will not give an inch even in the pettiest disputes. Donne claims his place among the '*Augustinianissimi*'—the superlative Augustinians—through rhetorical manoeuvres such as this one, which combines polemical pragmatism with a wistful desire to read the world differently. *Biathanatos* and the Whitsunday sermon of 1629 anatomize the corruption of charity in different ways, but the sermons also imagine a resolution of these terminological difficulties in the heavenly vision of God. Charity is a controversial weapon; when it is mobilized '*in* via', along the route of human history, some of its applications will inevitably bear the marks of combat and conflict. But it is also an instrument of redemption. To observe the vocabulary of charity in action, to read it as dynamic argument and interpretive process, is to discover less saintly versions of Augustine; this in turn also saves us from canonizing Donne. Nevertheless, the bond of charity that connects him with Augustine is genuine, and so is Donne's commitment to reading as a form of philosophy, a spiritual discipline that detects signs of God's eternal love in the texture of fallen discourse.

Augustine's *Confessions*, as we have seen, are central to Donne's reading exercises: he draws on them more frequently than on any other Augustinian text. From the *Confessions*, Donne learns the symbolic importance of hermeneutic and providential time, and in the art of meditating on them he becomes attuned to the special resonances of beginnings and endings: throughout his career, he will gravitate towards opening and closing moments in the Scripture narrative, and in Augustine's own texts. From the vast *oeuvre* of Saint Augustine, Donne also learns, paradoxically, the value of scholarly economy and textual (self-)recycling. Donne cannot compete with the towering figures of Renaissance scholarship that have recently been revealed to us; nor, I suspect, would he have wanted to: he is no Casaubon, no Scaliger.[30] But he is a diligent student of Augustine, and deploys his knowledge with creative power and efficiency (in this, it is worth noting again, he resembles iconic religious thinkers such as Calvin). Unlike contemporary English divines such as Montagu and, to a lesser extent, Andrewes, Donne rarely delves into the technical details of patristic theology: when he summons Augustine to defend Tertullian against accusations of heresy, the most striking feature of Donne's discussion is the absence of doctrinal particulars—although disputes regarding the property of God's 'body' could easily have filled several libraries. Donne consults Augustine for global principles and interpretive fundamentals: his fascination with the logic of a priori assumptions, for instance, is matched by an ongoing preoccupation with the creation story, the ultimate manifestation of God's timeless love and eternal wisdom.

Across the range of Donne's works, these principles can be synthesized into a philosophy of quotation and interpretation; and although, as we have seen, textual practice tends to work across clear lines of systematization, Augustine brings out in Donne a unique sense of hermeneutic debt and obligation. His writings are subject

---

[30] See e.g. Anthony Grafton, *Joseph Scaliger: A Study in the History of Classical Scholarship*, 2 vols. (Oxford, 1983–93); Grafton, *Defenders of the Text: The Traditions of Scholarship in an Age of Science, 1450–1800* (Cambridge, Mass., 1981).

to closer scrutiny and care than those of any other authority: Donne quotes more frequently at first hand, and with a greater degree of accuracy; he is less dependent on memory, often checks references against a reliable source, and makes visible attempts to bypass obvious short cuts. While other Fathers often supply various types of patristic 'padding', in-depth examination of Donne's Augustinian references uncovers substantial modes of intellectual engagement. This complexity, as we have seen, extends to Donne's Augustinian sources, intricate tectonic structures which require a unique form of intertextual archaeology from their readers. Donne relied on Augustine's reading rules throughout his career: the language of faith and charity anchors his moral, political, and religious thought. But, above all, Donne recognized in Augustine the sustaining force of (inter)textual fictions, the power of interpretation to re-imagine the flow of time. The poetics of charity redefines the relationship between human and providential history; by making different temporal axes diverge or intersect, Donne can find glimpses of comfort and perspective in the fractured prism of fallen cognition. He accelerates time, breaks order and sequence in sudden leaps of faith, and sometimes allows himself to dream that history might stop altogether. In those moments, Donne can almost believe that '*Plato* and his Disciples should rise from the dead' to debate the Scriptures, that Moses 'were here' to explain the meaning of Genesis to him, and, more than anything, that he and Augustine should never be 'parted'.[31]

---

[31] For Plato, see *Sermons*, 9.145, translating a passage from chapter 4 of Augustine's *De Vera Religione*; on Moses, see *Essayes in Divinity*, 19, invoking *Confessions* 11.3: '*Moses writ this, but is gon from me to thee; if he were here, I would hold him, and beseech him for thy sake, to tell me what he meant*' (see discussion of this passage in Chapter 3).

List of Augustine's works cited by Donne

Ad Inquisitiones Januarii (*Answers to the Questions of Januarius*)
Confessionum (*Confessions*)
Contra Adimantum (*Against Adimantus*)
Contra Adversarium Legis et Prophetarum (*Against Adversaries of the Law and the Prophets*)
Contra Epistulam Parmeniani (*Against the Letter of Parmenianus*)
Contra Faustum Manichaeum (*Against Faustus the Manichee*)
Contra Gaudentium Donatistorum Episcopum (*Against Gaudentius, a Donatist Bishop*)
Contra Julianum (*Against Julian*)
Contra Litteras Petiliani (*Reply to the Letters of Petilianus*)
Contra Priscillianistas (*Against the Priscillianists*)
Contra Julianum Opus Imperfectum (*The Incomplete Work against Julian*)
De Bono Conjugali (*On the Good of Marriage*)
De Bono Viduitatis (*On the Good of Widowhood*)
De Catechizandis Rudibus (*On Instructing the Unlearned*)
De Civitate Dei (*City of God*)
De Consensu Evangelistarum (*Consensus of the Evangelists*)
De Correptione et Gratia (*On Admonition and Grace*)
De Diversis Quaestionibus ad Simplicianum (*Various Questions for Simplicianus*)
De Diversis Quaestionibus Octoginta Tribus (*Eighty-Three Various Questions*)
De Doctrina Christiana (*On Christian Teaching*)
De Genesi ad Litteram (*On the Literal Interpretation of Genesis*)
De Genesi ad Litteram Liber Imperfectus (*Incomplete Commentary on Genesis*)
De Genesi adversus Manichaeos (*On Genesis against the Manichees*)
De Gratia Christi et de Peccato Originali (*On the Grace of Christ and Original Sin*)
De Gratia et Libero Arbitrio (*On Grace and Free Will*)
De Haeresibus (*Heresies*)
De Immortalitate Animae (*Of the Immortality of the Soul*)
De Magistro (*On the Teacher*)
De Mendacio (*On Lying*)
De Moribus Ecclesiae Catholicae (*On the Values of the Catholic Church*)
De Natura et Gratia (*On Nature and Grace*)
De Nuptiis et Concupiscentia (*On Marriage and Concupiscence*)
De Octo Dulcitii Quaestionibus (*Eight Questions by Dulcitius*)
De Ordine (*On Order*)
De Origine Animae (*On the Origin of the Soul*)
De Patientia (*On Patience*)
De Peccatorum Meritis et Remissione (*On Punishment and Forgiveness of Sins*)
De Perfectione Justitiae Hominis (*The Perfection of Human Justice*)
De Praedestinatione Sanctorum (*On the Predestination of the Saints*)
De Sermone Domini in Monte (*On the Lord's Sermon on the Mount*)
De Trinitate (*On the Trinity*)

De Utilitate Credendi (*On the Advantage of Believing*)
De Vera Religione (*On True Religion*)
Enarrationes in Psalmos (*Enarrations on the Psalms*)
Enchiridion de Fide, Spe et Caritate ad Laurentium (*Enchiridion on Faith, Hope, and Charity to Laurentius*)
Epistulae (*Letters*)
Expositio Epistulae ad Galatas (*Explanation of the Epistle to the Galatians*)
In Johannis Evangelium Tractatus (*Homilies on the Gospel of John*)
Quaestiones Evangeliorum (*Questions on the Gospels*)
Quaestiones in Heptateuchum (*Questions on the Heptateuch*)
Retractationes (*Retractations*)
Sermones (*Sermons*)
Soliloquia (*Soliloquies*)
Tractatus in Epistolam Johannis ad Parthos (*Homilies on John's Epistle to the Parthi*)
Texts which Donne would have regarded as Augustinian but which are now recognized as *dubious* or *spurious*:
Ad Cyrillum Jerosolymitanum (*To Cyril of Jerusalem*)
De Incarnatione Verbi ad Januarium (*On the Incarnation of the Word to Januarius*)
De Scriptura Sacra Speculum (*Mirror of Holy Scripture*)
De Unitate Ecclesiae (*On the Unity of the Church*)
De Vera et Falsa Poenitentia (*On True and False Penitence*)
Meditationum Liber Unus (*Meditations*)
Soliloquiorum Animae (*Soliloquies of the Soul*)

Bibliography

PRIMARY SOURCES

(Unless otherwise specified, the place of publication is London.)

Ambrose, *Expositio in Psalmum CXVIII*, PL 15 (Paris, 1845).

—— *Seven Exegetical Works*, trans. Michael P. Hugh (Washington, 1972).

Ames, William, *The Marrow of Sacred Divinity* (1642).

—— *The Workes of the Faithfull and Reverend Minister of Christ, William Ames* (1643).

Ammianus, Sebastian, *Conclusiones catholicae ex divi Augustini dictis, quibus ostenduntur Lutheranorum mendacia* (Venice, 1553).

Andrewes, Lancelot, *Selected Sermons and Lectures*, ed. Peter McCullough (Oxford, 2005).

—— *Works*, ed. J. P. Wilson and James Bliss, 11 vols. (Oxford, 1841–54).

Aquinas, Thomas, *Catena Aurea in Quatuor Evangelia*, ed. Angelico Guarienti, 2 vols. (Turin, 1953).

—— *Commentary on the Epistle to the Hebrews*, trans. Chrysostom Baer (South Bend, Ind., 2006).

—— *In Quatuor Libros Sententiarum Commentaria*, 2 vols. (Paris, 1638).

—— *Summa Theologiae*, Blackfriars edition, 60 vols. (1964).

—— *Super Epistolas S. Pauli Lectura*, ed. Raphael Cai, 2 vols. (Turin, 1953).

Aristotle, *The Nicomachean Ethics*, trans. H. Rackham, 2nd edn. (Cambridge, Mass., 1934).

Ascham, Roger, *The Scholemaster* (1570).

Ashe, Thomas, *Epieikeia et table generall a les annales del ley* (1609).

Askew, Egeon, *Brotherly reconcilement preached in Oxford for the vnion of some, and now published with larger meditations for the vnitie of all in this Church and common-wealth: with an apologie of the vse of fathers, and secular learning in sermons* (1605).

—— *Saint Augustines Confessions Translated and with Some Marginal Notes Illustrated*, trans. William Watts (1631).

—— *St. Avgvstine, Of the Citie of God: with the Learned Comments of Io. Lod. Vives, Englished by J.H.* (1610).

Augustine, *De Beata Vita*, ed. W. M. Green, CC 29 (Turnhout, 1970).

—— *De Bono Coniugali*, ed. Joseph Zycha, CSEL 44 (Vienna, 1900).

—— *De Bono Viduitatis*, ed. Joseph Zycha, CSEL 41 (Vienna, 1901).

—— *The City of God against the Pagans*, ed. and trans. R. W. Dyson (Cambridge, 1998).

—— *De Civitate Dei*, ed. Bernhard Dombart and Alfons Kalb, CC 47–8 (Turnhout, 1955).

—— *The Confessions of the Incomparable Doctour S. Augustine*, trans. Toby Matthew (St Omer's, 1620).

—— *Confessions*, ed. James J. O'Donnell, 3 vols. (Oxford, 1992).

—— *Confessions*, trans. Henry Chadwick (Oxford, 1991).

—— *De Correptione et Gratia*, PL 44 (Paris, 1845).

—— *De Diversis Quaestionibus Octoginta Tribus*, ed. Almut Mutzenbecher, CC 44 (Turnhout, 1975).

—— *De Doctrina Christiana*, ed. Josef Martin, rev. Isabelle Bochet and Goulven Madec, CC 32 (Paris, 1997).

—— *De Doctrina Christiana*, trans. R. P. H. Green (Oxford, 1993).

—— *Enarrationes in Psalmos*, ed. Eligius Dekkers and Johannes Fraipont, 3 vols., CC 38–40 (Turnhout, 1956).

Augustine, *Enarrationes in Psalmos* [101–50], ed. Franco Gori, CSEL 95 (Vienna, 2002).
—— *Enchiridion*, ed. Michael P. J. van den Hout, CC 46 (Turnhout, 1969).
—— *Epistulae*, ed. Alois Goldbacher, 5 vols., CSEL 34/44/57–8 (Vienna, 1895–1923).
—— *Explanatio Libri Psalmorum*, 3 vols. (Basel, 1489).
—— *Expositions on the Book of Psalms*, ed. Charles Marriott et al., 6 vols. (Oxford, 1847–57).
—— *Contra Faustum Manichaeum*, ed. Joseph Zycha, CSEL 25 (Vienna, 1891).
—— *Contra Gaudentium Donatistarum*, ed. Michael Petschenig, CSEL 53 (Vienna, 1953).
—— *De Genesi ad Litteram Liber Imperfectus*, ed. Joseph Zycha, CSEL 28 (Vienna, 1895).
—— *De Genesi ad Litteram*, ed. Joseph Zycha, CSEL 28 (Vienna, 1894).
—— *De Genesi adversus Manichaeos*, ed. Dorothea Weber, CSEL 91 (Vienna, 1998).
—— *De Gratia Christi et de Peccato Originali*, ed. Karl Franz Urba and Joseph Zycha, CSEL 42 (Vienna, 1902).
—— *In Johannis Epistolam ad Parthos Tractatus*, ed. John William Mountain, CC 37 (Paris, 2008).
—— *In Epistulam Iohannis ad Parthos Tractatus*, ed. Paul Agaësse (Paris, 1961).
—— *In Iohannis Evangelium Tractatus*, ed. Radbod Willems, CC 36 (Turnhout, 1954).
—— *Tractates on the Gospel of John*, trans. John Gibb and James Innes (New York, 1888).
—— *Contra Julianum*, *PL* 44 (Paris, 1845).
—— *Contra Julianum Opus Imperfectum*, ed. Ernst Kalinka and Michaela Zelzer, CSEL 85 (Vienna, 1974).
——*Prima (-Undecima) Pars Librorum diui Aurelii Augustini*, 11 vols. (Basel, 1506) [Amerbach edition].
—— *Contra Litteras Petiliani*, ed. Michael Petschenig, CSEL 52 (Vienna, 1903).
—— *De Magistro*, trans. Robert P. Russell (Washington, 1968).
—— *De Moribus Ecclesiae Catholicae*, ed. Johannes B. Bauer, CSEL 90 (Vienna, 1992).
—— *De Natura et Gratia*, ed. Karl Franz Urba and Joseph Zycha, CSEL 60 (Vienna, 1913).
——*Opera D. Aurelii Augustini Hipponensis . . . tomis decem comprehensa* (Antwerp, 1576–7) [Louvain edition].
—— *Operum Omnium primus [-Decimus] tomus*, 10 vols. (Basel, 1528–9) [Erasmus edition].
—— *De Ordine*, ed. William M. Green, CC 29 (Turnhout, 1970).
—— *De Praedestinatione Sanctorum*, *PL* 44 (Paris, 1845).
—— *Retractationes*, ed. Almut Mutzenbecher, CC 57 (Turnhout, 1984).
—— *De Sermone Domini in Monte*, ed. Almut Mutzenbecher, CC 35 (Turnhout, 1967).
—— *Sermones*, *PL* 38–9 (Paris, 1841).
—— *Sermones*, ed. Cyril Lambot, CC 41 (Turnhout, 1961).
—— *Plura ac diuersa diui Aurelii Augustini Sermonum opera*, 2 vols. (Basel, 1494–5).
—— *De Trinitate*, ed. W. J. Mountain, CC 50 (Turnhout, 1970).
—— *De Utilitate Credendi—Über den Nutzen des Glaubens*, trans. Andreas Hoffmann (Freiburg, 1992).
—— *The Works of Saint Augustine: A Translation for the 21st Century*, gen. ed. John E. Rotelle [electronic resource] (Charlottesville, 2006–).
Bacon, Francis, *The Works of Francis Bacon*, ed. James Spedding, Robert Leslie Ellis, and Douglas Denon Heath, 14 vols. (1857–74).
Baronius, Caesar, *Annales Ecclesiastici*, 12 vols. (Rome, 1588–1607).
Bastwick, John, *The Vanity and Mischeife of the Old Letany* (1637).
Bayly, Lewis, *The Practise of Pietie Directing a Christian How to Walke That He May Please God* (1613).

Bayne[s], Paul, *A commentarie vpon the first chapter of the epistle of Saint Paul, written to the Ephesians* (1618).

Bellarmine, Robert, *Disputationes Roberto Bellarmini Politiani, Societatis Iesu, De Controversiis Christianae Fidei, adversus huius temporis haereticos*, 3 vols. (Ingolstadt, 1586–93).

—— *Explanatio in Psalmos* (Lyon, 1611).

—— *De Scriptoribus Ecclesiasticis* (Cologne, 1613).

Biblia Latina cum Glossa Ordinaria, 4 vols. (Turnhout, 1992; facsimile reprint of the editio princeps, 1480–1).

The Holie. Bible. (1568) [The Bishops' Bible].

The Holie Bible . . . out of the Authentical Latin (Douai, 1609–10) [Douai–Rheims].

The Bible . . . according to the Ebrew and Greeke (1587) [Geneva].

Biblia Sacra sive libri canonici . . . facti ab I[mmanuel] Tremellio & F[rancisco] Junio [Tremellius–Junius].

Biblia Sacra Iuxta Vulgatem Versionem, ed. Bonifatius Fischer et al. (Stuttgart, 1969).

The Holy Bible (1611) [Authorized, or 'King James' version].

The Bible: Authorized King James Version, ed. Robert Carroll and Stephen Prickett (Oxford, 1997).

St Blasius, Werner of, *Libri Deflorationum . . . Patrum, PL* 157 (Paris, 1854).

Bodius, Hermann, *Unio dissidentium . . . ex praecipuis ecclesiae christianae doctoribus* (Cologne, 1531).

—— *Unio locorum theologicorum conflata ex Scriptura et Patribus, Hieronymo, Augustino, Gregorio, Chrysostomo et aliis* (Constance, 1602).

Bolton, Robert, *Some Generall Directions for a Comfortable Walking with God* (1626).

Bond, Ronald B. (ed.), *Certain Sermons or Homilies (1547)* and *A Homily against Disobedience and Wilful Rebellion (1570)* (Toronto, 1987).

Bovosius, Alphonsus, *Dispvtationes Catholicae* (Bologna, 1607).

Boys, John, *An Exposition of Al the Principal Scriptures Vsed in our English Liturgie* (1610).

Brinsley, John, *The Preachers Charge. And Peoples Dvty. About Preaching and Hearing of the Word* (1631).

Byfield, Nicholas, *Directions for the Priuate Reading of the Scriptures* (1618).

Cajetan, Giacomo, *In Quinque Libros Mosi iuxta sensum literalem commentarii. & primum in Genesim* (Paris, 1539).

Cajetan, Tommaso de Vio, *Secunda Secundae Partis Summae Sacrosanctae Theologiae Sancti Thomae Aquinatis* (Lyon, 1562).

Calvin, John, *Commentary vpon the first Epistle of S. Paule to the Corinthians*, trans. Thomas Tymme (1577).

—— *A Commentarie of John Caluine, vpon the first booke of Moses called Genesis*, trans. Thomas Tymme (1578).

—— *Commentaries on the First Book of Moses Called Genesis*, trans. John King (Edinburgh, 1847).

—— *Institutes of the Christian Religion*, ed. John T. McNeill, trans. Ford Lewis Battles et al., 2 vols. (1961).

—— *The Commentaries of M. Iohn Caluin vpon the Actes of the Apostles*, trans. Christopher Fetherstone (1585).

Cano, Melchior, *De locis theologicis libri duodecim* (Cologne, 1585).

Cartwright, Thomas, *A Confutation of the Rhemists Translation, Glosses and Annotations on the New Testament So Farre As They Containe Manifest Impieties, Heresies, Idolatries, Superstitions, Prophanesse, Treasons, Slanders, Absurdities, Falsehoods and Other Evills. By*

Occasion whereof the True Sence, Scope, and Doctrine of the Scriptures, and Humane authors, By Them Abused, Is Now Given (Leiden, 1618).

Chamberlain, John, *The Letters of John Chamberlain*, ed. Norman Egbert McClure, 2 vols. (Philadelphia, 1939).

Chandos, John (ed.), *In God's Name: Examples of Preaching from the Act of Supremacy to the Act of Uniformity* (1971).

Chrysostom, John, *Homilies on the Gospel of Matthew*, trans. George Prevost, 3 vols. (Oxford, 1843–51).

Church of England, *Certaine Sermons or Homilies Appointed to be Read in Churches in the Time of Queen Elizabeth I. A Facsimile Reproduction of the Edition of 1623*, intr. Mary Ellen Rickey and Thomas B. Stroup (Gainesville, Fla., 1968).

—— *The Book of Common Prayer 1559. The Elizabethan Prayer Book*, ed. John T. Booty (Charlottesville, Va., 1976).

Colet, John, *John Colet's Commentary on First Corinthians*, ed. Bernard O'Kelly and Catherine A. L. Jarrott (Binghamton, NY, 1985).

Condognat, Martin, *Ioannis Maldonati Summula* (Lyon, 1604).

Coppenstein, Johann, *Dispositiones . . . ex D. Thomae de Aquino Commentariis in Matthaeum et Ioann.* (Mainz, 1616).

Corvinus, Antonius, *Augustini et Chrysostomi theologia . . . in communes locos digesta* (Schwäbisch Hall, 1539).

Crespin, Jean, *Bibliotheca Studii Theologici ex Plerisque Doctorum Prisci Seculi Monumentis Collecta*, 3 vols. (Geneva, 1565).

Cyprian, *De Unitate Ecclesiae*, ed. E. H. Blakeney (1928).

D'Averoultius, Antonius, *Catechismus Historicus, sive Flores Exemplorum Collectis ex Sacra Scriptura, Sanctis Patribus, aliisque Ecclesiae Doctoribus, ac Historicis* (Cologne, 1614).

Dawson, John, *A Right Intention the Rule of All Mens Actions, Converted out of Drexelius to our Proper Use* (1642).

Denison, John, *The Sinners Acqvittance. A Checke to Cvriositie. The Safest Seruice* (1624).

Donne, John, *A Sermon vpon the VIII. Verse of the I. Chapter of the Acts of the Apostles Preach'd to the Honourable Company of the Virginian Plantation, 13 Nouemb. 1622* (1622).

—— *Biathanatos*, ed. Ernest W. Sullivan II (Newark, Del., 1984).

—— Βιαθανατος. *A Declaration of that Paradoxe, or Thesis, that Selfe-homicide Is Not So Naturally Sinne, that It May Neuer Be Otherwise: Wherein the Nature, and the Extent of All Those Lawes, Which Seeme to be Violated by This Act, Are Diligently Surueyd* (1644).

—— *Devotions Upon Emergent Occasions*, ed. Anthony Raspa (Montreal, 1975).

—— *Donne's Prebend Sermons*, ed. Janel M. Mueller (Cambridge, Mass., 1971).

—— *Essayes in Divinity*, ed. Anthony Raspa (Montreal, 2001).

—— *Essayes in Divinity*, ed. Evelyn M. Simpson (Oxford, 1952).

—— *Essayes in Divinity; by the Late Dr Donne, Dean of St Paul's. Being Several Disquisitions, Interwoven with Meditations and Prayers: Before he Entred into Holy Orders. Now Made Publick by his Son J. D. Dr of the Civil Law* (1651).

—— *Fifty Sermons* (1649).

—— *Fiue Sermons vpon Speciall Occasions* (1626).

—— *Foure Sermons vpon Speciall Occasions* (1625).

—— *Ignatius his Conclave*, ed. T. S. Healy, SJ (Oxford, 1969).

—— *Letters to Severall Persons of Honour* (1651).

—— *LXXX Sermons* (1640).

—— *Poems, by J.D. With Elegies on the Authors Death* (1633).

Donne, John, *Pseudo-martyr. Wherein out of Certaine Propositions and Gradations, this Conclusion is Euicted. That Those Which Are of the Romane Religion in This Kingdome, May and Ought to Take the Oath of Allegiance* (1610).

—— *Pseudo-Martyr*, ed. Anthony Raspa (Montreal, 1993).

—— *Selected Prose*, chosen by Evelyn Simpson, ed. Helen Gardner and Timothy Healy (Oxford, 1967).

—— *Selected Prose*, ed. Neil Rhodes (Harmondsworth, 1987).

—— *Six Sermons upon Severall Occasions Preached before the King, and Elsewhere* (Cambridge, 1634).

—— *The Anniversaries and the Epicedes and Obsequies*, ed. Paul A. Parrish et al., The Variorum Edition of the Poetry of John Donne, vol. 6 (Bloomington, Ind., 1995).

—— *The Complete English Poems*, ed. C. A. Patrides, intr. Robin Hamilton, 2nd edn. (1994).

—— *The Complete Poems of John Donne*, ed. Robin Robbins (Harlow, 2010).

—— *The Divine Poems*, ed. Helen Gardner (Oxford, 1952).

—— *The Elegies, and The Songs and Sonnets*, ed. Helen Gardner (Oxford, 1965).

—— *The Elegies*, ed. Ted-Larry Pebworth et al., The Variorum Edition of the Poetry of John Donne, vol. 2 (Bloomington, Ind., 2000).

—— *The Epigrams, Epithalamions, Epitaphs, Inscriptions, and Miscellaneous Poems*, ed. Jeffrey Johnson et al., The Variorum Edition of the Poetry of John Donne, vol. 8 (Bloomington, Ind., 1995).

—— *The Poems of John Donne*, ed. Herbert Grierson, 2 vols. (Oxford, 1912).

—— *The Satires, Epigrams and Verse Letters*, ed. Wesley Milgate (Oxford, 1967).

—— *The Sermons of John Donne*, ed. George R. Potter and Evelyn M. Simpson, 10 vols. (Berkeley, 1953–62).

—— *The Songs and Sonets of John Donne*, ed. Theodore Redpath (Oxford, 1967).

—— *XXVI Sermons* (1661).

Drexel, Jeremias, *Aurifodina artium et scientiarum omnium: Excerpendi sollertia, omnibus litterarum amantibus monstrata* (Antwerp, 1638).

Drusius, Joannes, *Miscellanea Locutionum Sacrarum* (Franeker, 1586).

The Earl of Oxford's Case. The Third Part of Reports of Cases Taken and Adjudged in the Court of Chancery (1716).

Eedes, Richard, *Six learned and godly sermons preached some of them before the Kings Maiestie, some before Queene Elizabeth* (1604).

Erasmus, Desiderius, *Opus Epistolarum Des. Erasmi Roterodami*, ed. P. S. Allen, 12 vols. (Oxford, 1906–58).

Felicianus, Johannes, *Catena Explanationum Veterum Sanctorum Patrum, ab Oecumenio ex Diversis Commentariis Collecta* (Venice, 1545, 1556; Basel, 1552).

Ferrius, Paulus, *Scholastici Orthodoxi Specimen Hoc est Salutis nostrae Methodus Analytica* (Gotstad, 1616).

Filesacus, Johannes, *De Sacra Episcoporum Auctoritate Comment* (Paris, 1606).

Fincham, Kenneth (ed.), *Visitation Articles and Injunctions of the Early Stuart Church*, 2 vols. (1603–42) (Woodbridge, 1998).

Flacius Illyricus, Matthias, *Catalogus Testium Veritatis* (Strasbourg, 1562).

Gastius, Ioannes, *D. Aurelii Augustini . . . tam in vetus quam in novum testamentum commentarii* (Basel, 1542).

Gataker, Thomas, *Noah his Obedience, with the Ground of it . . . A Meditation on Hebrewes 11.7. Deliuered in a Sermon at Lincolnes Inne* (1637).

Gesta Collationis Chartageni Habitae Honorii Caesaris Iussu inter Catholicos et Donatistas (Paris, 1588).

Granger, Thomas, *The Application of Scriptvre. Or The Maner How to Vse the Words to Most Edifying* (1616).

Gratian, *Decretal, PL* 187 (Paris, 1855).

—— *Decretal* (Basel, 1500).

—— *Decretorum Collectanea* (Paris, 1552).

—— *Decretum* (Basel, 1500).

Greenham, Richard, *Grave Counsels and Godly Observations*, in *The Works of the Reuerend and Faithfull Seruant of Iesus Christ M. Richard Greenham* (Cambridge, 1599).

Hacket, John, *Scrinia Reserata* (1693).

Hake, Edward, *Epiekeia: A Dialogue on Equity in Three Parts*, ed. D. E. C. Yale, Yale Law Library Publications, 13 (New Haven, 1953).

Hales, John, *A Sermon Preached at St Maries in Oxford vpon Tuesday in Easter Weeke, 1617 Concerning the Abuses of Obscure and Difficult Places of Holy Scripture, and Remedies Against Them* (Oxford, 1617).

Hall, Joseph, *The Arte of Divine Meditation* (1606).

—— *Resolutions and Decisions of Divers Practicall Cases of Conscience* (1649).

Hargrave, Frances (ed.), 'The Abuses and Remedies of Chancery', in *A Collection of Tracts Relative to the Law of England* (Dublin, 1787).

Hofmeister, Johann, *Loci communes rerum theologicarum* (Ingolstadt, 1550).

Hooker, Richard, *Of the Lawes of Ecclesiasticall Politie Eight Bookes* (1604).

Hyde, Edward, *The life of Edward, earl of Clarendon . . . written by himself*, 3 vols. (1827).

Hyperius, Andreas, *The Practise of Preaching, Otherwise Called the Pathway to the Pulpet Conteyning an Excellent Method how to Frame Diuine Sermons, & to Interpret the Holy Scriptures According to the Capacitie of the Vulgar People*, trans. John Ludham (1577).

James VI and I, 'Speech in Star Chamber of 20 June 1616', in James VI and I, *Political Writings*, ed. Johann P. Sommerville (Cambridge, 1994).

James, Thomas, *A Treatise of the Corrvption of Scripture, Councels, and Fathers, by the Prelats, Pastors, and Pillars of the Church of Rome, for Maintenance of Popery and Irreligion* (1611).

Jewel, John, *Certaine sermons preached before the Queenes Maiestie, and at Paules crosse* (1583).

—— *A Replie vnto M. Hardinges Answeare* (1565).

—— *The Works of John Jewel*, ed. John Ayre, 4 vols. (Cambridge, 1845–50).

—— *The Works of the Very Learned and Reuerend Father in God Iohn Iewell* (1609).

Keynes, Geoffrey, *A Bibliography of Dr. John Donne, Dean of Saint Paul's*, 4th edn. (Oxford, 1973).

Kristeller, P. O., et al. (eds.), *Catalogus translationum et commentariorum: Medieval and Renaissance Latin Translations and Commentaries, Annotated Lists and Guides*, vols. 1–7 (Washington, DC, 1960–).

Kynge Daryus, ed. James O. Halliwell (1860).

Laud, William, *Works*, ed. William Scott and James Bliss, 7 vols. (Oxford, 1847–60).

LeNeve, John, *Fasti Ecclesiae Anglicanae, 1541–1857*, vol. 1: St Paul's, London, compiled by Joyce M. Horn (1969).

Lérins, Vincent de, *Pro Catholicae Fidei Antiquitate et Universitate* (Paris, 1544) [= the *Commonitorium*].

de Lille, Alain, *Liber in Distinctionibus Dictionum Theologicalium, PL* 210 (Paris, 1855).

Lombard, Peter, *Sententiarum Libri IV* (Paris, 1163).

—— *Sententiarum Libri Quattuor, PL* 192 (Paris, 1855).

Luther, Martin, *A Commentarie of M. Doctor Martin Luther vpon the Epistle of S. Paul to the Galathians* (1575).

—— *Vorlesungen über I. Mose von 1535–1545*, ed. Karl Drescher and Weimarer Ausgabe, vol. 43 (Breslau, 1912).

Lyra, Nicolaus de, *Postilla Super Bibliam* (Cologne, 1485).

Marlorat, Augustin, *Novi Testamenti Catholica Expositio Ecclesiastica* (Geneva, 1561).

Montagu, Richard, *Appello Caesarem. A iust appeale from two vniust informers* (London, 1625).

—— *A gagg for the new Gospell? No: a new gagg for an old goose* (1624).

Musculus, Andreas, *Enchiridion Sententiarum* (1528).

Musculus, Wolfgang, *Common places of Christian religion, gathered by Wolfgangus Musculus, for the vse of such as desire the knovvledge of godly truth. Translated out of Latine into English, by Iohn Man of Merton Colledge in Oxforde* (1578).

—— *In Divi Ioannis Evangelium . . . Commentarii* (Basel, 1580).

—— *Loci communes sacrae theologiae* (Basel, 1564).

Nashe, Thomas, *The Anatomie of Absurditie*, in *Works*, ed. R. B. McKerrow, rev. F. P. Wilson, 5 vols. (Oxford, 1958).

Notestein, Wallace, and Relf, Frances Helen (eds.), *Commons Debates of 1629* (Minneapolis, 1921).

Paez, Balthasar, *Commentarii in Epistolam B. Iacobi Apostoli* (Lyon, 1617).

Parker, Matthew, *De Antiquitate Britanniae Ecclesiae* (Hanover, 1605).

Parsons, Robert, *A Treatise Tending to Mitigation towards Catholicke Subiectes in England* (St Omer, 1607).

Pascal, Blaise, *The Provincial Letters*, trans. A. J. Krailsheimer (Harmondsworth, 1967).

—— *The Provincial Letters*, trans. Thomas McCrie (New York, 1850).

Patrologiae cursus completus . . . series latina, ed. J.-P. Migne et al., 221 vols. (Paris, 1844–1903).

Peacham, Henry, *The Garden of Eloquence (1593)*, ed. Beate Maria Koll (Frankfurt am Main, 1996).

—— *The Garden of Eloquence Conteining the Most Excellent Ornaments, Exornations, Lightes, Flowers, and Formes of Speech, Commonly Called the Figures of Rhetorike*, 2nd edn. (1593).

Pererius, Benedictus, *Commentariorvm et Dispvtationvm in Genesim*, 4 vols. (Lyon, 1599).

—— *Dispvtationvm in Sacram Scriptvram, Continens super libro Exodi Centum Triginta Septem Dispvtationes* (Lyon, 1607).

Perkins, William, *The Arte of Prophecying* (Cambridge, 1609), in *The Workes of that Famous and Worthy Minister of Christ in the Vniuersitie of Cambridge*, 3 vols. (Cambridge, 1608–9).

—— *A commentarie or exposition, vpon the fiue first chapters of the Epistle to the Galatians* (Cambridge, 1604).

—— *HEPIEIKEIA, or a Treatise of Christian Equity or Moderation* (Cambridge, 1604).

—— *The Works of William Perkins*, ed. Ian Breward (Abingdon, 1970).

Petrarca, Francesco, *Le familiari*, ed. V. Rossi and U. Bosco, 4 vols. (Florence, 1933–42).

—— *Letters on Familiar Matters*, ed. Aldo S. Bernardo (Baltimore, 1985).

—— *Invective Contra Medicum*, ed. P. G. Ricci (Rome, 1950).

Petreus, Theodorus, *Confessio Tertulliana et Cypriana in Quatuor Digesta Libros* (Paris, 1603).

Piscator, Johann, *Omnium operum Diui Aurelii Augustini Episcopi . . . Epitome*, 3 vols. (Augsburg, 1537).

Pomerius, Julianus, *De Vita Contemplativa Libri Tres*, PL 59 (Paris, 1847).

Possidius, *Sancti Augustini Vita*, ed. and trans. Herbert T. Weiskotten (Princeton, 1919).

Prideaux, John, *Sacred Eloquence: or, the Art of Rhetorick, As It Is Layd Down in Scripture* (1659).

Prosper of Aquitaine, *Sententiae aliquot velut aphorismi, ex omnibus Augustini ac aliorum libris* (Cologne, 1531).

Quintilian, *Institutio Oratoria*, trans. H. E. Butler, 4 vols. (Cambridge, Mass., 1920–2; repr. 1993–6).

Reeves, Troy D., *Index to the Sermons of John Donne*, 3 vols. (Salzburg, 1981).

Ribadeneira, Pedro de, *Historia Ecclesiastica del Scisma del Reyno de Inglaterra* (Madrid, 1588–94).

Rivet, Andre, *Critici Sacri Specimen* (Heidelberg, 1612).

Roberts, Francis, *Clavis Bibliorum. The Key of the Bible, Unlocking the Richest Treasury of the Holy Scriptures* (1648).

Rupertus, *Commentariorum in Genesim, PL* 167 (Paris, 1854).

Saint German, Christopher, *Doctor and Student*, ed. T. F. T. Plucknett and J. L. Barton (1974).

Sarcerius, Erasmus, *Praecipui Sacrae Scripturae communes loci, a doctissimo et sanctissimo doctore Augustino tractati* (Frankfurt, 1539).

Schultingius, Cornelius, *Thesaurus Antiquitatem Ecclesiasticarum* (Cologne, 1601).

Scory, John, *Two bokes of the noble doctor and B.S. Augustine* (?Emden, 1556).

Scott, Thomas, *Christs politician, and Salomons puritan. Deliuered in two sermons preached before the Kings Maiestie* (1616).

Scultetus, Abraham, *Medullae Theologiae Patrum* (Heidelberg, 1598–1613).

Selden, John, *Table Talk of John Selden*, ed. Frederick Pollock and Edward Fry (1927).

Sidney, Philip, *Sidney's 'The Defence of Poesy', and Selected Renaissance Literary Criticism*, ed. Gavin Alexander (2004).

Simpson, W. Sparrow, *Registrum Statutorum et Consuetudinum Ecclesiae Cathedralis Sancti Pauli Londoniensis* (1873).

de Soto, Domingo, *Commentariorum Fratris Dominici . . . in Quatrum Sententiarum* (Salamanca, 1555–60).

Stanwood, P. G., and Asals, Heather R. (eds.), *John Donne and the Theology of Language* (Columbia, Mo., 1985).

Staupitz, Johann von, *Sämtliche Schriften. Abhandlungen, Predigten, Zeugnisse*, ed. Lothar Graf zu Dohna and Richard Wetzel, vol. 1: *Tübinger Predigten*, ed. Richard Wetzel (Berlin, 1987).

Stuart Royal Proclamations, ed. J. Larkin and P. Hughes (Oxford, 1973–83).

Tossanus, Daniel, *Synopsis de Patribus* (Heidelberg, 1603; English edn. 1635).

Traherne, Thomas, *Centuries, Poems and Thanksgivings*, ed. H. M. Margoliouth, 2 vols. (Oxford, 1972).

Tuke, Thomas, *A Very Christian, Learned and briefe Discourse, concering the true, ancient, and Catholicke Faith* (1611).

Urbino, Bartholomaeus de, *D. Aurelii Augustini Milleloquium Veritatis* (Lyon, 1555).

Vaughan, Edward, *A plaine and perfect Method, for the easie vnderstanding of the whole Bible*, 2nd edn. (1617).

Verzeichnis der im deutschen Sprachbereich erschienenen Drucke des XVI. Jahrhunderts, ed. Irmgard Bezzel et al., 25 vols. (Stuttgart, 1983–97).

Vignier, Nicolas, *Concerning the Excommunication of the Venetians. A Discourse against Caesar Baronius, Cardinall of the Church of Rome* (1607).

Walton, Izaak, *The Lives of John Donne, Sir Henry Wotton, Richard Hooker, George Herbert and Robert Sanderson*, ed. G. Saintsbury (1927).

Wheeler, G. W. (ed.), *Letters of Sir Thomas Bodley to Thomas James* (Oxford, 1926).

White, John, *A Defence of the Way to the True Church* (1614).

Whitgift, John, *Works*, ed. John Ayre, 3 vols. (Cambridge, 1851).

Wilson, Thomas, *Theologicall Rules for Guiding Us in the Understanding and Practise of Holy Scripture* (1615).

SECONDARY SOURCES

Achinstein, Sharon, *Milton and the Revolutionary Reader* (Princeton, 1994).

Adlington, Hugh, 'The Preacher's Plea: Juridical Influence in John Donne's Sermons, 1618–1623', *Prose Studies*, 26 (2003), 344–56.

—— 'Preaching the Holy Ghost: John Donne's Whitsunday Sermons', *John Donne Journal*, 22 (2003), 203–28.

Alcorn Baron, Sabrina (ed.), *The Reader Revealed* (Washington, 2001).

Alexander, Gavin, 'Prosopopoeia: The Speaking Figure', in *Renaissance Figures of Speech*, ed. Sylvia Adamson, Gavin Alexander, and Katrin Ettenhuber (Cambridge, 2007).

Allen, P. S., *Erasmus: Lectures and Wayfaring Sketches* (Oxford, 1934).

Almond, Philip, *Adam and Eve in the Seventeenth Century* (Cambridge, 1999).

Alter, Robert, *Art of Biblical Poetry* (New York, 1985).

Babcock, William S., '*Caritas* and Signification in *De Doctrina Christiana* 1–3', in *De Doctrina Christiana: A Classic of Western Culture*, ed. Duane W. Arnold and Pamela Bright (Notre Dame, 1995), 145–63.

Backus, Irena, 'The Early Church in the Renaissance and Reformation', in *Early Christianity: Origins and Evolution to AD 600: In Honour of W. H. C. Frend*, ed. Ian Hazlett (London, 1991), 291–303.

—— 'Erasmus and the Spirituality of the Early Church', in *Erasmus' Vision of the Church*, ed. Hilmar M. Pabel (Kirksville, 1995), 95–114.

—— 'The Fathers and Calvinist Orthodoxy: Patristic Scholarship. The Bible and the Fathers According to Abraham Scultetus (1566–1624) and André Rivet (1571/3–1651). The Case of Basil of Caesarea', in Backus (ed.), *Reception of the Church Fathers*, 2.839–65.

—— (ed.), *The Reception of the Church Fathers in the West: From the Carolingians to the Maurists*, 2 vols. (Leiden, 1997).

Baker, J. H., 'The Common Lawyers and Chancery', in *The Legal Profession and the Common Law: Historical Essays* (London, 1986), 205–29.

Bald, R. C., *John Donne: A Life* (Oxford, 1970).

Baldwin, T. W., *William Shakespere's Small Latine & Lesse Greeke*, 2 vols. (Urbana, 1944).

Barthes, Roland, *S/Z* (London, 1974).

Bawcutt, Nigel, and Kelliher, Hilton, 'Donne through Contemporary Eyes: New Light on his Participation in the Convocation of 1626', *Notes & Queries*, NS 42 (1995), 441–4.

Beal, Peter, *In Praise of Scribes: Manuscripts and their Makers in Seventeenth-Century England* (Oxford, 1998).

Beierwaltes, Werner, *Regio Beatudinis. Zu Augustins Begriff des glücklichen Lebens* (Heidelberg, 1981).

Béné, Charles, *Érasme et Saint Augustin, ou l'influence de Saint Augustin sur l'humanisme d'Érasme* (Geneva, 1969).

Bennett, Camille, 'The Conversion of Vergil: The *Aeneid* in Augustine's *Confessions*', *Revue des Études Augustiniennes*, 34 (1988), 47–69.

Bentley, Jerry H., *Humanists and Holy Writ: New Testament Scholarship in the Renaissance* (Princeton, 1983).

Bergvall, Åke, *Augustinian Perspectives in the Renaissance* (Uppsala, 2001).

Berman, Harold J., *Law and Revolution: The Formation of the Western Legal Tradition*, 2 vols. (Cambridge, 1983–2004).

Binns, J. W., *Intellectual Culture in Elizabethan and Jacobean England: The Latin Writings of the Age* (Leeds, 1990).

Bland, Mark, 'Jonson, *Biathanatos* and the Interpretation of Manuscript Evidence', *Studies in Bibliography*, 51 (1998), 154–82.

Blair, Ann, 'Note Taking as an Art of Transmission', *Critical Inquiry*, 31 (2004), 81–107.

—— 'Textbooks and Methods of Note-Taking in Early Modern Europe', in *Scholarly Knowledge: Textbooks in Early Modern Europe*, ed. Emidio Campi, Simone de Angelis, Anja-Silvia Goeing, and Anthony Grafton (Geneva, 2008), 39–73.

Blumenberg, Hans, 'Augustins Anteil an der Geschichte des Begriffs der theoretischen Neugierde', *Revue des Études Augustiniennes*, 7 (1961), 35–70.

Booty, John E., *John Jewel as Apologist of the Church of England* (London, 1963).

Bös, Gunther, *Curiositas. Die Rezeption eines antiken Begriffs durch christliche Autoren bis Thomas von Aquin* (Paderborn, 1995).

Bougerol, Jacques-Guy, 'The Church Fathers and the *Sentences* of Peter Lombard', in *The Reception of the Church Fathers in the West: From the Carolingians to the Maurists*, ed. Irena Backus, 2 vols. (Leiden, 1997), 1.113–64.

Bouwsma, William J., 'The Two Faces of Humanism: Stoicism and Augustinianism in Renaissance Thought', in *Itinerarium Italicum: The Profile of the Italian Renaissance in the Mirror of its European Transformations*, ed. Heiko Oberman and Thomas A. Brady, Jr. (Leiden, 1975), 3–60.

Braun, Harald E., and Vallance, Edward (eds.), *Contexts of Conscience in Early Modern Europe, 1500–1700* (Basingstoke, 2004).

—— and —— (eds.), *The Renaissance Conscience*, special issue of *Renaissance Studies*, 23 (2009).

Bray, Gerald L., *Biblical Interpretation Past and Present* (Downers Grove, Ill., 1996).

Brayman Hackel, Heidi, *Reading Material in Early Modern England: Print, Gender, and Literacy* (Cambridge, 2005).

Brown, Meg Lota, *Donne and the Politics of Conscience in Early Modern England* (Leiden, 1995).

Brown, Peter, *Augustine of Hippo* (Berkeley, 1967).

—— *Power and Persuasion in Late Antiquity: Towards a Christian Empire* (Madison, 1992).

Brown, Piers, '"Hac ex consilio meo via progredieris": Courtly Reading and Secretarial Mediation in Donne's *The Courtier's Library*', *Renaissance Quarterly*, 61 (2008), 833–66.

Brunner, Peter, 'Charismatische und methodische Schriftauslegung nach Augustins Prolog zu *De Doctrina Christiana*', *Kerygma und Dogma*, 1 (1955), 59–69; 85–103.

Bullough, Geoffrey, 'Donne the Man of Law', in *Just So Much Honor: Essays Commemorating the Four Hundredth Anniversary of the Birth of John Donne*, ed. Peter Amadeus Fiore (University Park, Pa., 1972), 57–94.

Burnaby, John, *Amor Dei: A Study of the Religion of St. Augustine*, 2nd edn. (Norwich, 1991).

Carpi, Daniela (ed.), *The Concept of Equity: An Interdisciplinary Assessment* (Heidelberg, 2007).

Carpi, Daniela (ed.), *Practising Equity, Addressing Law* (Heidelberg, 2008).

Carrafiello, Michael L., *Robert Parsons and English Catholicism* (London, 1998).

Carraud, Vincent, 'L'Anti-Augustinisme de Pascal', in *Augustin au XVIIe Siècle*, ed. Laurence Devillairs (Florence, 2007), 151–201.

Carruthers, Mary, *The Book of Memory* (Cambridge, 1990).

Cary, Phillip, *Augustine's Invention of the Inner Self: The Legacy of a Christian Platonist* (Oxford, 2000).

Cavallo, Guglielmo, and Chartier, Roger (eds.), *A History of Reading in the West* (Cambridge, 1999).

Cave, Terence, *The Cornucopian Text: Problems of Writing in the French Renaissance* (Oxford, 1979).

—— 'The Mimesis of Reading in the Renaissance', in *Mimesis: From Mirror to Method, Augustine to Descartes*, ed. John D. Lyons and Stephen G. Nichols, Jr. (Hanover and London, 1982), 149–65.

Ceyssens, Lucien, 'Le "Saint Augustin" du xviie siècle: l'édition de Louvain (1577)', *XVII Siècle*, 34 (1982), 103–20.

Chamberlin, John, *Increase and Multiply: Arts-of-Discourse Procedures in the Preaching of Donne* (Chapel Hill, 1976).

Chartier, Roger, 'Communities of Readers', in *The Order of Books: Readers, Authors, and Libraries in Europe between the Fourteenth and Eighteenth Centuries* (Stanford, 1994), 32–54.

Clark, Elizabeth A., *Reading Renunciation: Asceticism and Scripture in Early Christianity* (Princeton, 1999).

Clegg, Cyndia Susan, *Press Censorship in Caroline England* (Cambridge, 2008).

Colclough, David, *Freedom of Speech in Early Stuart England* (Cambridge, 2005).

—— 'Introduction', in *John Donne's Professional Lives*, ed. David Colclough (Cambridge, 2003), 1–16.

—— 'Upstairs, Downstairs: Doctrine and Decorum in Two Sermons by John Donne', *Huntington Library Quarterly*, 73 (2010), 163–91.

Compagnon, Antoine, *La Seconde Main, ou le travail de la citation* (Paris, 1979).

Courcelle, Pierre, *Les Confessions de S. Augustin dans la tradition littéraire* (Paris, 1963).

—— 'Le jeune Augustin, second Catilina', *Revue des Études Anciennes*, 73 (1971), 141–50.

Coward, Rosalind, and Ellis, John (eds.), *Language and Materialism: Developments in Semiology and the Theory of the Subject* (London, 1977).

Coyle, John Kevin, *Augustine's "De Moribus Ecclesiae Catholicae": A Study of the Work, its Composition, and its Sources* (Fribourg, 1978).

Crahay, Roland, 'Les censeurs louvanistes d'Érasme', in *Scrinium Erasmianum: mélanges historiques publiés sous le patronage de l'université de Louvain*, ed. Joseph Coppens (Leiden, 1969), 221–49.

Crane, Mary Thomas, *Framing Authority: Sayings, Self, and Society in Sixteenth-Century England* (Princeton, 1993).

Croatto, J. Severino, *Biblical Hermeneutics: Toward a Theory of Reading as the Production of Meaning* (Maryknoll, 1987).

Cromartie, Alan, *The Constitutionalist Revolution: An Essay on the History of England, 1450–1642* (Cambridge, 2006).

Cummings, Brian, 'Literally Speaking, or, the Literal Sense from Augustine to Lacan', *Paragraph*, 16 (1998), 200–26.

—— *The Literary Culture of the Reformation: Grammar and Grace* (Oxford, 2002).

Cushman, Robert E., 'Faith and Reason', in *A Companion to the Study of St. Augustine*, ed. Roy W. Battenhouse (Oxford, 1955), 87–314.

Daiches, David, *The King James Version of the English Bible* (Chicago, 1941).

D'Amico, John F., *Theory and Practice in Renaissance Textual Criticism* (Berkeley, 1988).

Dankbaar, W. F., 'De "Unio Dissidentium" van Hermannus Bodius', *Tijdschrift voor Geschiedenis*, 74 (1961), 367–81.

Davies, Julian, *The Caroline Captivity of the Church: Charles I and the Remoulding of Anglicanism, 1625–1641* (Oxford, 1992).

de Certeau, Michel, *The Practice of Everyday Life* (Berkeley, 1984).

de Ghellinck, Joseph, SJ, *Patristique en Moyen Age*, 3 vols. (Paris, 1948).

Dekkers, Eligius, 'Quelques notes sur les florilèges augustiniens anciens et médiévaux', *Augustiniana*, 40 (1990), 27–44.

Delius, Hans-Ulrich, *Augustin als Quelle Luthers* (Berlin, 1984).

Dideberg, Dany, 'Caritas', in *Augustinus-Lexikon*, ed. Cornelius Mayer et al., 5 vols. (Basel, 1986–), 1.730–43.

Diederich, M. D., *Virgil in the Works of Saint Ambrose* (Washington, 1934).

Di Giovanni, Alberto, *L'inquietudine dell'anima* (Rome, 1964).

Dihle, Albrecht, *The Theory of Will in Classical Antiquity* (Berkeley, 1982).

Dobranski, Stephen B., *Readers and Authorship in Early Modern England* (Cambridge, 2005).

Dodaro, Robert, 'The Secret Justice of God and the Gift of Humility', *Augustinian Studies*, 34 (2003), 83–96.

—— and Questier, Michael, 'Strategies in Jacobean Polemic: The Use and Abuse of Augustine in English Theological Controversy', *Journal of Ecclesiastical History*, 44 (1993), 432–49.

Eden, Kathy, *Hermeneutics and the Rhetorical Tradition: Chapters in the Ancient Legacy and its Humanist Reception* (New Haven, 1997).

—— 'The Rhetorical Tradition and Augustinian Hermeneutics in *De Doctrina Christiana*', *Rhetorica*, 8 (1990), 45–63.

Eisenstein, Elizabeth, *The Printing Revolution in Early Modern Europe* (Cambridge, 1983).

Empson, William, 'Donne in the New Edition', in *Studies in Renaissance Literature*, ed. John Haffenden, 2 vols. (Cambridge, 1993), 1: *Donne and the New Philosophy*, 129–58.

—— 'Rescuing Donne', in *Donne and the New Philosophy*, 159–99.

Ettenhuber, Katrin, 'Hyperbole', in *Renaissance Figures of Speech*, ed. Sylvia Adamson, Gavin Alexander, and Katrin Ettenhuber (Cambridge, 2007), 196–213.

Fallon, Stephen M., 'Intention and its Limits in *Paradise Lost*: The Case of Bellerophon', in *Literary Milton: Text, Pretext, Context*, ed. Diana Trevino Benet and Michael Lieb (Pittsburgh, 1994), 161–7.

Fatio, Olivier, 'Un florilège augustinien du XVIe siècle: l'*Omnium operum Divi Augustini Epitome* de Johannes Piscatorius (1537)', *Revue des Études Augustiniennes*, 18 (1972), 194–202.

Ferrell, Lori Anne, *Government by Polemic: James I, the King's Preachers, and the Rhetorics of Conformity, 1603–25* (Stanford, 1998).

—— and McCullough, Peter (eds.), *The English Sermon Revised: Religion, Literature and History, 1600–1750* (Manchester, 2000).

Festa, Thomas A., 'Donne's *Anniversaries* and his Anatomy of the Book', *John Donne Journal*, 17 (1998), 29–60.

Fiedrowicz, Michael, *Prinzipien der Schriftauslegung in der alten Kirche* (Bern, 1998).

Fincham, Kenneth, 'William Laud and the Exercise of Caroline Ecclesiastical Patronage', *Journal of Ecclesiastical History*, 51 (2000), 69–93.

—— and Lake, Peter, 'The Ecclesiastical Policies of James I and Charles I', in *The Early Stuart Church 1603–1642*, ed. Kenneth Fincham (Basingstoke, 1993), 23–50.

Finkelstein, David, and McCleery, Alistair (eds.), *The Book History Reader* (London, 2002).

Fiore, Peter A., *Milton and Augustine: Patterns of Augustinian Thought in Paradise Lost* (University Park, Pa, 1981).

Flasch, Kurt, *Was ist Zeit? Augustinus von Hippo: Das XI. Buch der Confessiones* (Frankfurt, 1993).

Forman, R. J., *Augustine and the Making of a Christian Literature* (Lewiston, NY, 1995).

Fortier, Mark, *The Culture of Equity in Early Modern England* (Aldershot, 2005).

—— 'Equity and Ideas: Coke, Ellesmere, and James I', *Renaissance Quarterly*, 51 (1998), 1255–81.

Foucault, Michel, *The Archaeology of Knowledge* (London, 1974).

Fox, Adam, *Oral and Literate Culture in England, 1500–1700* (Oxford, 2000).

—— and Woolf, Daniel (eds.), *The Spoken Word: Oral Culture in Britain, 1500–1850* (Manchester, 2002).

Fraenkel, Pierre, *Testimonia Patrum: The Function of Patristic Argument in the Theology of Philip Melanchthon* (Geneva, 1961).

Frend, William H. C., *The Donatist Church: A Movement of Protest in Roman North Africa* (Oxford, 1962).

—— 'Manicheism in the Struggle between Saint Augustine and Petilian of Constantine', *Augustinus Magister*, 2 (1954), 859–66.

Froehlich, Karlfried, *Biblical Interpretation in the Early Church* (Philadelphia, 1984).

Frost, Kate, *Holy Delight: Typology, Numerology, and Autobiography in Donne's Devotions upon Emergent Occasions* (Princeton, 1990).

Gadamer, Hans-Georg, *Wahrheit und Methode: Grundzüge einer philosophischen Hermeneutik*, 6th edn. (Tübingen, 1990).

Gallagher, Lowell, *Medusa's Gaze: Casuistry and Conscience in the Renaissance* (Stanford, 1991).

Galvão, Henrique de Noronha, 'Beatitudo', in *Augustinus-Lexikon*, ed. Cornelius Mayer et al., 5 vols. (Basel, 1986–), 1.624–38.

—— *Die existentielle Gotteserkenntnis bei Augustin. Eine hermeneutische Lektüre der Confessiones* (Einsiedeln, 1981).

Gardiner, Samuel, *History of England from the Accession of James I to the Outbreak of the Civil War 1603–1642*, 10 vols. (London, 1884).

Gilmont, Jean-Francois, *Jean Calvin and the Printed Book*, trans. Karen Maag (Kirksville, 2005).

Gilson, Etienne, *The Christian Philosophy of Saint Augustine*, trans. L. E. M. Lynch (London, 1961).

Ginzburg, Carlo, *The Cheese and the Worms: The Cosmos of a Sixteenth-Century Miller*, trans. John and Anne Tedeschi (London, 1992).

—— 'High and Low: The Theme of Forbidden Knowledge in the Sixteenth and Seventeenth Centuries', *Past and Present*, 73 (1976), 28–41.

Glowinski, Michal, 'Reading, Interpretation, Reception', trans. Wlad Godzich, *New Literary History*, 11 (1979–80), 75–82.

Goodblatt, Chanita, 'An Intertextual Discourse on Sin and Salvation: John Donne's Sermon on Psalm 51', *Renaissance and Reformation*, 20 (1996), 23–40.

Grabowski, Stanislaus J., 'Spiritus Dei in Gen. 1:2 According to St. Augustine', *Catholic Bibilical Quarterly*, 10 (1948), 13–28.

Grafton, Anthony, *Defenders of the Text: The Traditions of Scholarship in an Age of Science, 1450–1800* (Cambridge, Mass., 1991).

—— 'How Guillaume Budé Read his Homer', in *Commerce with the Classics: Ancient Books and Renaissance Readers*, Jerome Lecture Series (Ann Arbor, 1997).

—— *Joseph Scaliger: A Study in the History of Classical Scholarship*, 2 vols. (Oxford, 1983–93).

—— and Jardine, Lisa, '"Studied for Action": How Gabriel Harvey Read his Livy', *Past and Present*, 129 (1990), 30–78.

—— and Williams, Megan, *Christianity and the Transformation of the Book: Origen, Eusebius, and the Library of Caesarea* (Cambridge, Mass., 2006).

Grane, Leif, Schindler, Alfred, and Wriedt, Markus (eds.), *Auctoritas Patrum: Zur Rezeption der Kirchenväter im 15. und 16. Jh.* (Mainz, 1993).

——, ——, and —— (eds.), *Auctoritas Patrum II: Neue Beiträge zur Rezeption der Kirchenväter im 15. und 16. Jh.* (Mainz, 1998).

Greenslade, S. L., 'The Authority of the Tradition of the Early Church in Early Anglican Thought', *Oecumenica*, 3 (1971–2), 9–33.

—— (ed.), *The Cambridge History of the Bible: The West from the Reformation to the Present Day* (Cambridge, 1963).

—— *The English Reformers and the Fathers of the Church* (Oxford, 1960).

Griffiths, Richard (ed.), *The Bible in the Renaissance: Essays on Biblical Commentary and Translation in the Fifteenth and Sixteenth Centuries* (Aldershot, 2001).

Guibbory, Achsah, *Ceremony and Community from Herbert to Milton* (Cambridge, 1998).

—— 'Donne's Religion: Montagu, Arminianism and Donne's Sermons', *English Literary Renaissance*, 31 (2001), 412–39.

—— 'John Donne and Memory as "the *Art of Salvation*"', *Huntington Library Quarterly*, 63 (1980), 261–74.

Guite, Malcolm, 'The Art of Memory and the Art of Salvation: The Centrality of Memory in the Sermons of John Donne and Lancelot Andrewes', *The Seventeenth Century*, 4 (1989), 1–17.

Guy, John, *Christopher St German on Chancery and Statute* (London, 1985).

—— *Politics, Law and Counsel in Tudor and Early Stuart England* (Aldershot, 2000).

Halewood, William, *The Poetry of Grace* (New Haven, 1970).

Hall, Michael L., 'Searching and Not Finding: The Experience of Donne's *Essayes in Divinity*', *Genre*, 14 (1981), 423–40.

Hamm, Berndt, *Frömmigkeitstheologie am Anfang des 16. Jarhunderts* (Tübingen, 1982).

Hammond, Gerald, *The Making of the English Bible* (Manchester, 1982).

Harland, Paul W., 'Donne's Political Intervention in the Parliament of 1629', *John Donne Journal*, 11 (1992), 21–37.

Harrison, Simon, 'Do We Have a Will?: Augustine's Way in to the Will', in *The Augustinian Tradition*, ed. Gareth B. Matthews (London, 1999), 195–205.

Haugaard, William P., 'Renaissance Patristic Scholarship and Theology in Sixteenth-Century England', *Sixteenth Century Journal*, 10 (1979), 37–60.

Hessayon, Ariel, and Keene, Nicholas (eds.), *Scripture and Scholarship in Early Modern England* (Aldershot, 2005).

Hickey, Robert L., 'Donne's Art of Memory', *Tennessee Studies in Literature*, 3 (1958), 29–36.

Hill, Christopher, *The English Bible and the Seventeenth Century Revolution* (London, 1994).

Hill, Eugene D., 'John Donne's Moralized Grammar: A Study in Renaissance Christian Hebraica', in *Papers in the History of Linguistics*, ed. Hans Aarsleff, Louis G. Kelly, and Hans Josef Niederehe (Amsterdam, 1987), 189–98.

Hobbs, Mary, *Early Seventeenth-Century Verse Miscellany Manuscripts* (Aldershot, 1992).

—— '"To a Most Dear Friend"—Donne's Bellarmine', *The Review of English Studies*, NS 32 (1981), 435–8.

Holmes, P. J. (ed.), *Elizabethan Casuistry* (London, 1981).

Holte, Ragnar, *Béatitude et sagesse. Saint Augustin et le problème de la fin de l'homme dans la philosophie ancienne* (Paris, 1962).

Hull, Suzanne W., *Chaste, Silent, and Obedient: English Books for Women, 1475–1640* (San Marino, 1982).

Hurel, Daniel-Odon, 'The Benedictines of St.-Maur and the Church Fathers', in *The Reception of the Church Fathers in the West: From the Carolingians to the Maurists*, ed. Irena Backus, 2 vols. (Leiden, 1997), 2.1009–38.

Johns, Adrian, *The Nature of the Book: Print and Knowledge in the Making* (Chicago, 1998).

Johnson, Jeffrey, '"One, four, and infinite": John Donne, Thomas Harriot, and *Essayes in Divinity*', *John Donne Journal*, 22 (2003), 109–43.

—— *The Theology of John Donne* (Woodbridge, 1999).

Kahn, Victoria, and Hutson, Lorna (eds.), *Rhetoric and Law in Early Modern Europe* (New Haven, 2001).

Keeble, N. H., *The Literary Culture of Non-Conformity* (Leicester, 1987).

Keen, Ralph, 'The Fathers in Counter-Reformation Theology in the Pre-Tridentine Period', in *The Reception of the Church Fathers in the West: From the Caslingians to the Maurists*, ed. Irena Backus, 2 vols. (Leiden, 1997), 2.701–44.

Kendall, R. T., *Calvin and English Calvinism to 1649* (Oxford, 1979).

Kennedy, Robert K., 'Book 11: *The Confessions* as Eschatological Narrative', in *A Reader's Companion to the Confessions*, ed. Kim Paffenroth and Robert P. Kennedy (Louisville, Ky., 2003), 167–83.

Kiefer, Frederick, *Writing on the Renaissance Stage: Written Words, Printed Pages, Metaphoric Books* (Newark, 1996).

Klose, Thomas, 'Quaerere deum. Suche nach Gott und Verständnis Gottes in den Bekenntnissen Augustins', *Theologie und Philosophie*, 54 (1979), 183–218.

Knafla, Louis A., 'Mr Secretary Donne: The Years with Sir Thomas Egerton', in *John Donne's Professional Lives*, ed. David Colclough (Cambridge, 2003), 37–71.

Knauer, G. N., *Die Psalmenzitate in Augustins Konfessionen* (Göttingen, 1955).

Kneidel, Gregory, 'John Donne's *Via Pauli*', *Journal of English and Germanic Philology*, 100 (2001), 224–46.

—— *Rethinking the Turn to Religion in Early Modern English Literature: The Poetics of All Believers* (Basingstoke, 2008).

Koselleck, Reinhart, 'Perspective and Temporality: A Contribution to the Historiographical Exposure of the Historical World', in *Futures Past: On the Semantics of Historical Time*, trans. Keith Tribe (Cambridge, Mass., 1985), 130–55.

—— *The Practice of Conceptual History: Timing History, Spacing Concepts*, trans. Todd Samuel Presner et al. (Stanford, 2002).

Krey, Philip D. W., and Smith, Lesley (eds.), *Nicholas of Lyra: The Senses of Scripture* (Leiden, 2000).

Kristeva, Julia, *Desire in Language: A Semiotic Approach to Literature* (New York, 1980).

—— 'Word, Dialog and Novel', in *The Kristeva Reader*, ed. Toril Moi (New York, 1986), 34–61.

Lake, Peter, 'Joseph Hall, Robert Skinner and the Rhetoric of Moderation at the Early Stuart Court', in *The English Sermon Revised: Religion, Literature and History, 1600–1750*, ed. Lori Anne Ferrell and Peter McCullough (Manchester, 2000), 167–85.

—— 'Lancelot Andrewes, John Buckeridge, and Avant-Garde Conformity at the Court of James I', in *The Mental World of the Jacobean Court*, ed. Linda Levy Peck (Cambridge, 1991), 113–33.

—— 'The Moderate and Irenic Case for Religious War: Joseph Hall's *Via Media* in Context', in *Political Culture and Cultural Politics in Early Modern England*, ed. Susan Amussen and Mark Kishlansky (Manchester, 1995), 55–83.

—— with Questier, Michael, *The Anti-Christ's Lewd Hat: Protestants, Papists and Players in Post-Reformation England* (New Haven, 2002).

Lane, A. N. S., *John Calvin: Student of the Church Fathers* (Edinburgh, 1999).

—— 'Justification in Sixteenth-Century Patristic Anthologies', in *Auctoritas Patrum: Zur Rezeption der Kirchenväter im 15. und 16. Jahrhundert*, ed. Leif Grane, Alfred Schindler, and Markus Wriedt (Mainz, 1993), 69–95.

Latourette, Kenneth Scott, *A History of Christianity*, rev. edn. (New York, 1973).

Lawless, George, 'Interior Peace in the "Confessiones" of St. Augustine', *Revue des Études Augustiniennes*, 26 (1980), 45–61.

Lienhard, Joseph T., 'The Earliest Florilegia of Augustine', *Augustinian Studies*, 8 (1977), 21–31.

—— 'The Glue itself is Charity: Ps 62:9 in Augustine's Thought', in *Augustine: Presbyter Factus Sum*, ed. Joseph T. Lienhard, Earl C. Muller, and Roland J. Teske (New York, 1993), 375–84.

Lloyd, John G., *The Discovery of Hebrew in Tudor England: A Third Language* (Manchester, 1983).

Lorenz, Rudolf, 'Fruitio dei bei Augustin', *Zeitschrift für Kirchengeschichte*, 63 (1950/51), 75–132.

Lossky, Nicholas, *Lancelot Andrewes the Preacher (1555–1626): The Origins of the Mystical Theology of the Church of England*, trans. Andrew Louth (Oxford, 1991).

Lytle, Guy Fitch, 'The Church Fathers and Oxford Professors in the Late Middle Ages, Renaissance, and Reformation', in *Acta Conventus Neo-Latini Bononiensis*, ed. R. J. Schoeck (Binghamton, NY, 1985), 101–15.

MacCulloch, Diarmaid, *Reformation: Europe's House Divided 1490–1700* (London, 2003).

McCullough, Peter, 'Donne as Preacher', in *The Cambridge Companion to John Donne*, ed. Achsah Guibbory (Cambridge, 2006), 167–81.

—— 'Donne as Preacher at Court: Precarious "Inthronization"', in *John Donne's Professional Lives*, ed. David Colclough (Cambridge, 2003), 179–204.

—— 'Making Dead Men Speak: Laudianism, Print, and the Works of Lancelot Andrewes, 1626–1642', *Historical Journal*, 41 (1998), 401–24.

—— 'Preaching to a Court Papist? Donne's Sermon Before Queen Anne', *John Donne Journal*, 14 (1995), 59–82.

—— *Sermons at Court: Politics and Religion in Elizabethan and Jacobean Preaching* (Cambridge, 1998).

McGrath, Alister E., *The Intellectual Origins of the European Reformation*, 2nd edn. (Oxford, 2004).

Mack, Peter, 'Rhetoric, Ethics and Reading in the Renaissance', *Renaissance Studies*, 19 (2005), 1–21.

McKenzie, D. F., 'Speech-Manuscript-Print', *The Library Chronicle of the University of Texas at Austin*, 20 (1990), 87–109.

McKim, Donald (ed.), *Historical Handbook of Major Biblical Interpreters* (Leicester, 1998).

Maclean, Ian, *Interpretation and Meaning in the Renaissance: The Case of Law* (Cambridge, 1992).

McLeod, Randall, 'Obliterature: Reading a Censored Text of Donne's "To his Mistress Going to Bed"', *English Manuscript Studies 1100–1700*, 12 (2005), 83–138.

Madec, Goulven, 'Ascensio, ascensus', in *Augustinus-Lexikon*, ed. Cornelius Mayer et al., 5 vols. (Basel, 1986–), 1.465–75.

Mallard, William, *Language and Love: Introducing Augustine's Religious Thought through the Confessions Story* (University Park, Pa., 1994).

Malloch, A. E., 'The Definition of Sin in Donne's *Biathanatos*', *Modern Language Notes*, 72 (1957), 332–5.

—— 'John Donne and the Casuists', *Studies in English Literature 1500–1900*, 2 (1962), 57–76.

Manguel, Alberto, *A History of Reading* (London, 1996).

Markus, R. A., *Saeculum: History and Society in the Theology of St Augustine* (Cambridge, 1970).

Marotti, Arthur F., and Bristol, Michael D. (eds.), *Print, Manuscript, and Performance: The Changing Relations of the Media in Early Modern England* (Columbus, 2000).

Masselink, Noralyn, 'Donne's Epistemology and the Appeal to Memory', *John Donne Journal*, 8 (1989), 57–88.

—— 'Memory in John Donne's Sermons: "Readie"? Or Not?', *South Atlantic Review*, 63 (1998), 99–107.

Matthews, Gareth B. (ed.), *The Augustinian Tradition* (London, 1999).

Maule, Jeremy, 'Donne and the Words of the Law', in *John Donne's Professional Lives*, ed. David Colclough (Cambridge, 2003), 19–36.

Maxwell, Julie, 'How the Renaissance (Mis)Used Sources: The Art of Misquotation', in *How to Do Things with Shakespeare: New Approaches, New Essays*, ed. Laurie Maguire (Oxford, 2008), 54–76.

Mayer, Cornelius, 'Humilitas', in *Augustinus-Lexikon*, ed. Cornelius Mayer et al., 5 vols. (Basel, 1986–), 1.730–43.

Mazzeo, Carla, and Cormack, Bradin (eds.), *Book Use, Book Theory, 1500–1700* (University of Chicago Library, 2005).

Meijering, E. P., *Calvin wider die Neugierde. Ein Beitrag zum Vergleich zwischen reformatorischem und patristischem Denken* (Nieuwkoop, 1980).

Mellinghoff-Bourgerie, Viviane, 'Erasme éditeur et interprète de Saint Augustin', in *Augustinus in der Neuzeit*, ed. Kurt Flasch and Dominique de Courcelles (Turnhout, 1998), 53–81.

Menchi, Silvana Seidel, 'Whether to Remove Erasmus from the Index of Prohibited Books: Debates in the Roman Curia, 1570–1610', *Erasmus of Rotterdam Society Yearbook*, 20 (2000), 19–33.

Mette, Hans Joachim, 'Curiositas', in *Festschrift Bruno Snell zum 60. Geburtstag... von Freunden und Schülern überreicht* (Munich, 1956), 227–35.

Milton, Anthony, '"Anglicanism" by Stealth: The Career and Influence of John Overall', in *Religious Politics in Post-Reformation England*, ed. Peter Lake and Kenneth Fincham (Cambridge, 2006), 159–75.

—— *Catholic and Reformed: The Roman and Protestant Churches in English Protestant Thought, 1600–1640* (Cambridge, 1995).

Milward, Peter, *Religious Controversies of the Elizabethan Age: A Survey of Printed Sources* (London, 1977).

Milward, Peter, *Religious Controversies of the Jacobean Age* (London, 1978).

Moss, Ann, *Printed Commonplace-Books and the Structuring of Renaissance Thought* (Oxford, 1996).

Mueller, Janel M., 'The Exegesis of Experience: Dean Donne's Devotions upon Emergent Occasions', *Journal of English and Germanic Philology*, 67 (1968), 1–19.

Muller, Richard A., and Thompson, John L. (eds.), *Biblical Interpretation in the Era of the Renaissance: Essays Presented to David C. Steinmetz in Honor of his Sixtieth Birthday* (Grand Rapids, 1996).

Narveson, Kate, 'Donne the Layman Essaying Divinity', *John Donne Journal*, 28 (2009), 1–30.

Nelles, Paul, 'The Uses of Orthodoxy and Jacobean Erudition: Thomas James and the Bodleian Library', *History of Universities*, 22 (2007), 21–70.

Nelson, Brent, *Holy Ambition: Rhetoric, Courtship, and Devotion in the Sermons of John Donne* (Tempe, Ariz., 2005).

Norbrook, David, 'The Monarchy of Wit and the Republic of Letters: Donne's Politics', in *Soliciting Interpretation: Literary Theory and Seventeenth-Century English Poetry*, ed. Elizabeth D. Harvey and Katharine Eisaman Maus (Chicago, 1990), 3–36.

Norelli, Enrico, 'The Authority Attributed to the Early Church in the *Centuries of Magdeburg* and the *Ecclesiastical Annals* of Caesar Baronius', in *The Reception of the Church Fathers in the West: From the Carolingians to the Maurists*, ed. Irena Backus, 2 vols. (Leiden, 1997), 2.745–74.

Nussbaum, Martha, 'Augustine and Dante on the Ascent of Love', in *The Augustinian Tradition*, ed. Gareth B. Matthews (London, 1999), 61–90.

Oberman, Heiko A., 'Tuus sum, salvum me fac: Augustinréveil zwischen Renaissance und Reformation', in *Scientia Augustiniana: Studien über Augustin, den Augustinismus und den Augustinerorden*, ed. Cornelius Mayer and Willigis Eckermann (Würzburg, 1965), 350–94.

—— *Werden und Wertung der Reformation. Vom Wegestreit zum Glaubenskampf* (Tübingen, 1977; 2nd edn., Tübingen, 1979); published in English as *Masters of the Reformation: The Emergence of a New Intellectual Climate in Europe*, trans. Dennis Martin (Cambridge, 1981).

O'Daly, Gerald, *Augustine's City of God: A Reader's Guide* (Oxford, 1999).

O'Donnell, James J., *Augustine, Sinner and Saint* (London, 2005).

O'Donovan, Oliver, *The Problem of Self-Love in St. Augustine* (New Haven, 1980).

—— 'Usus and Fruitio in Augustine, *De Doctrina Christiana* I', *Journal of Theological Studies*, NS 33 (1982), 361–97.

Olin, John C., 'Erasmus and the Church Fathers', in *Six Essays on Erasmus* (New York, 1979), 33–47.

Oliver, P. M., *Donne's Religious Writing: A Discourse of Feigned Devotion* (London, 1997).

Olney, James, *Memory and Narrative* (Chicago, 1999).

O'Meara, J. J., 'Saint Augustine's Understanding of the Creation and Fall', *Studies in Augustine and Eriugena*, ed. Thomas Halton (Washington, DC, 1992), 233–43.

O'Toole, Christopher, *The Philosophy of Creation in the Writings of St. Augustine* (Washington, DC, 1944).

Pabel, Hilmar M., 'Reading Jerome in the Renaissance: Erasmus' Reception of the Adversus Jovinianum', *Renaissance Quarterly*, 55 (2002), 470–97.

—— and Vessey, Mark (eds.), *Holy Scripture Speaks: The Production and Reception of Erasmus' Paraphrases on the New Testament* (Toronto, 2002).

Papazian, Mary Arshagouni, 'The Augustinian Donne: How a "Second S. Augustine"?', in *John Donne and the Protestant Reformation: New Perspectives*, ed. Mary A. Papazian (Detroit, 2003), 66–89.

—— 'Literary "things indifferent": The Shared Augustinianism of Donne's Devotions and Bunyan's Grace Abounding', in *John Donne's Religious Imagination: Essays in Honour of John T. Shawcross*, ed. Raymond-Jean Frontain and Frances M. Malpezzi (Conway, Ariz., 1995), 324–49.

Patterson, Annabel, 'John Donne, Kingsman?', in *The Mental World of the Jacobean Court*, ed. Linda Levy Peck (Cambridge, 1991), 251–72.

Pearson, David, 'The Libraries of English Bishops, 1600–1640', *The Library*, 6th ser., 14 (1992), 221–57.

Pelikan, Jaroslav, *Reformation of Church and Dogma (1300–1700). The Christian Tradition: A History of the Development of Doctrine*, vol. 4 (Chicago, 1984).

Pellegrino, Michele, 'Via Christus Humilis (Sermone 142.2)', *Studium*, 55 (1960), 126–30.

Pender, Stephen, 'Essaying the Body: Donne, Affliction, and Medicine', in *John Donne's Professional Lives*, ed. David Colclough (Cambridge, 2003), 215–48.

Peters, Edward, 'What Was God Doing Before He Created the Heavens and the Earth?', *Augustiniana*, 34 (1984), 53–74.

Peters, Robert, 'Erasmus and the Church Fathers: Their Practical Value', *Church History*, 36 (1967), 254–61.

—— 'The Use of the Fathers in the Reformation Handbook *Unio Dissidentium*', *Studia Patristica*, 9 (1966), 570–7.

—— 'Who Compiled the Sixteenth-Century Patristic Handbook *Unio Dissidentium*?', in *Studies in Church History*, ed. G. J. Cuming, 2 vols. (London, 1965), 2.237–50.

Petitmengin, Pierre, 'A propos des éditions patristiques de la Contre-Réforme: le "saint Augustin" de la Typographie Vaticane', *Recherches Augustiniennes*, 4 (1966), 199–251.

—— 'Comment étudier l'activité d'Érasme éditeur de textes antiques?', in *Colloquia erasmiana turonensia*, ed. J. C. Margolin, 2 vols. (Toronto, 1972), 1.217–22.

—— 'Editions princeps et Opera omnia de saint Augustin', in *Augustinus in der Neuzeit*, ed. Kurt Flasch and Dominique de Courcelles (Turnhout, 1998), 33–51.

—— 'Les Patrologies avant Migne', in *Migne et le renouveau des études patristiques*, ed. André Mandouze and Joël Fouilheron (Paris, 1985), 15–38.

Pétré, Hélène, *Caritas: Étude sur le vocabulaire latin de la charité chrétienne* (Louvain, 1948).

Pigman, III, G. W., 'Versions of Imitation in the Renaissance', *Renaissance Quarterly*, 33 (1980), 1–32.

Pincherle, Alberto, 'Et inquietum est cor nostrum. Appunti per una lezione agostiniana', *Augustinus*, 13 (1968), 353–68.

Placher, William, *A History of Christian Theology: An Introduction* (Philadelphia, 1983).

Pollmann, Karla, 'Augustine's Hermeneutics as a Universal Discipline?', in *Augustine and the Disciplines: From Cassiacum to Confessions*, ed. Karla Pollmann and Mark Vessey (Oxford, 2005), 206–31.

—— *Doctrina Christiana: Untersuchungen zu den Anfängen der christlichen Hermeneutik unter besonderer Berücksichtigung von Augustinus, De Doctrina Christiana* (Fribourg, 1996).

Portalie, Eugene, *A Guide to the Thought of Saint Augustine*, trans. R. J. Bastian (London, 1960).

Prescott, Anne, 'Donne's Rabelais', *John Donne Journal*, 16 (1997), 37–58.

Quantin, Jean-Louis, 'L'Augustin du xviie siècle? Questions de corpus et de canon', in *Augustin au XVIIe Siècle*, ed. Laurence Devillairs (Florence, 2007), 3–77.

Quantin, Jean-Louis, *The Church of England and Christian Antiquity: The Construction of a Confessional Identity in the Seventeenth Century* (Oxford, 2009).

—— 'The Fathers in Seventeenth Century Anglican Theology', in *The Reception of the Church Fathers in the West: From the Carolingians to the Maurists*, ed. Irena Backus, 2 vols. (Leiden, 1997), 2.987–1008.

—— 'The Fathers in Seventeenth Century Roman Catholic Theology', in *The Reception of the Church Fathers in the West: From the Carolingians to the Maurists*, ed. Irena Backus, 2 vols. (Leiden, 1997), 2.951–86.

Quillen, Carol Everhart, *Rereading the Renaissance: Petrarch, Augustine, and the Language of Humanism* (Ann Arbor, 1998).

Quinn, Dennis, 'Donne's Christian Eloquence', *English Literary History*, 27 (1960), 276–97.

—— 'Donne's Principles of Exegesis', *Journal of English and Germanic Philology*, 61 (1962), 313–29.

Ramsay, Mary Paton, *Les Doctrines médiévales chez Donne*, 2nd edn. (Oxford, 1924).

Raven, James, Small, Helen, and Tadmor, Naomi (eds.), *The Practice and Representation of Reading in England* (Cambridge, 1996).

Reeve, L. J., *Charles I and the Road to Personal Rule* (Cambridge, 1989).

Rhatigan, Emma, 'John Donne's Lincoln's Inn Sermons' (unpublished D.Phil. dissertation, Oxford, 2006).

—— 'Knees and Elephants: John Donne Preaches Ceremonial Conformity', *John Donne Journal*, 23 (2004), 185–213.

Rice, Eugene F., 'The Renaissance Idea of Christian Antiquity: Humanistic Patristic Scholarship', in *Renaissance Humanism: Foundations, Forms, and Legacy*, ed. Albert J. Rabil, 3 vols. (Philadelphia, 1988), 1.17–28.

—— *Saint Jerome in the Renaissance* (Baltimore, 1985).

Ripanti, Graziano, *Agostino teoretico dell'interpretazione* (Brescia, 1980).

Robinson, Hastings (ed.), *Original Letters Relative to the English Reformation written during the Reigns of King Henry VIII, King Edward VI, and Queen Mary, Chiefly from the archives of Zurich*, 2 vols. (Cambridge, 1846–7).

Rosemann, Philipp W., *Peter Lombard* (Oxford, 2004).

Roth, Bartholomäus, 'Franz von Meyronnes und der Augustinismus seiner Zeit', *Franziskanische Studien*, 22 (1935), 44–75.

Saak, Eric-Leland, 'The Reception of Augustine in the Later Middle Ages', in *The Reception of the Church Fathers in the West: From the Carolingians to the Maurists*, ed. Irena Backus, 2 vols. (Leiden, 1997), 1.367–404.

Saunders, Benjamin, 'Circumcising Donne: The 1633 Poems and Readerly Desire', *Journal of Medieval and Early Modern Studies*, 30 (2000), 375–99.

Scarry, Elaine, 'Donne: "But Yet the Body is his Booke"', in *Literature and the Body: Essays on Populations and Persons*, ed. Elaine Scarry (London, 1986), 70–106.

Schaffner, Otto, *Christliche Demut. Des hl. Augustinus Lehre von der Humilitas* (Würzburg, 1959).

Schleiner, Winfried, *The Imagery of Donne's Sermons* (Providence, RI, 1970).

Schnaubelt, Joseph C., and van Fleteren, Joseph (eds.), *Augustine: Biblical Exegete* (New York, 2001).

Scholder, Klaus, *The Birth of Modern Critical Theology: Origins and Problems of Biblical Criticism in the Seventeenth Century*, trans. John Bowden (London, 1990).

Sellier, Philippe, *Pascal et Saint Augustin*, 2nd edn. (Paris, 1995).

Shami, Jeanne, 'Donne on Discretion', *English Literary History*, 47 (1980), 48–66.

Shami, Jeanne, 'Donne's Sermons and the Absolutist Politics of Quotation', in *John Donne's Religious Imagination: Essays in Honor of John T. Shawcross*, ed. Raymond-Jean Frontain and Frances M. Malpezzi (Conway, 1995), 380–412.

—— *John Donne and Conformity in Crisis in the Late Jacobean Pulpit* (Woodbridge, 2003).

—— 'Speaking Openly and Speaking First: John Donne, the Synod of Dort, and the Early Stuart Church', in *John Donne and the Protestant Reformation*, ed. Mary A. Papazian (Detroit, 2003), 35–65.

Sharpe, Kevin, *Reading Revolutions: The Politics of Reading in Early Modern England* (New Haven, 2000).

—— *Remapping Early Modern England: The Culture of Seventeenth-Century Politics* (Cambridge, 2000).

—— and Zwicker, Steven (eds.), *Reading, Society and Politics in Early Modern England* (Cambridge, 2003).

Shawcross, John T., 'All Attest his Writs Canonical: The Texts, Meaning and Evaluation of Donne's Satires', in *Just So Much Honour: Essays Commemorating the Five-Hundredth Anniversary of the Birth of John Donne*, ed. Peter A. Fiore (University Park, Pa., 1971), 245–72.

Sheen, Erica, and Hutson, Lorna (eds.), *Literature, Politics and Law in Renaissance England* (Basingstoke, 2005).

Sherman, William, *John Dee: The Politics of Reading and Writing in the English Renaissance* (Amherst, 1995).

—— *Used Books: Marking Readers in Early Modern England* (Philadelphia, 2008).

Sherwood, Terry, *Fulfilling the Circle: A Study of Donne's Thought* (Toronto, 1984).

Shuger, Debora, 'Literature and the Church', *The Cambridge History of Early Modern Literature*, ed. David Loewenstein and Janel M. Mueller (Cambridge, 2002), 512–43.

—— *Political Theologies in Shakespeare's England: The Sacred and the State in Measure for Measure* (Basingstoke, 2001).

—— *The Renaissance Bible: Scholarship, Sacrifice and Subjectivity* (Berkeley, 1994).

—— and McEachern, Claire (eds.), *Religion and Culture in Renaissance England* (Cambridge, 1997).

Sider, Robert, 'Erasmus and Ancient Christian Writers: The Search for Authenticity', in *Nova et Vetera: Patristic Studies in Honour of Patrick Halton*, ed. John Petruccione (Washington, 1998), 69–86.

Simpson, James, *Burning to Read: English Fundamentalism and its Reformation Opponents* (Cambridge, Mass., 2007).

Skinner, Quentin, 'Motives, Intentions and Interpretation', in *Visions of Politics*, 3 vols. (Cambridge, 2002), 1.90–102.

Slights, Camille Wells, *The Casuistical Tradition in Shakespeare, Donne, Herbert, and Milton* (Princeton, 1981).

Sluiter, Ineke, 'Metatexts and the Principle of Charity', in *Metahistoriography: Theoretical and Methodological Aspects in the Historiography of Linguistics*, ed. Peter Schmitter and M. J. van der Wal (Münster, 1998), 11–27.

Smalley, Beryl, *English Friars and Antiquity in the Early Fourteenth Century* (Oxford, 1960).

Smith, A. J. (ed.), *John Donne: The Critical Heritage* (London, 1996).

Smith, Bruce R., *The Acoustic World of Early Modern England: Attending to the O-Factor* (Chicago, 1999).

Snow, Vernon F., 'Francis Bacon's Advice to Fulke Greville on Research Techniques', *Huntington Library Quarterly*, 23 (1960), 369–78.

Solignac, Aimé, 'Exégèse et Métaphysique, Genèse I, 1–3 chez Augustin', in *In principio, Interprétations des premiers versets de la Genèse* (Paris, 1973), 153–71.

Sommerville, Johann P., 'John Donne the Controversialist: The Poet as Political Thinker', in *John Donne's Professional Lives*, ed. David Colclough (Cambridge, 2003), 73–96.

Spurr, John, '"A Special Kindness for Dead Bishops": The Church, History, and Testimony in Seventeenth-Century Protestantism', *Huntington Library Quarterly*, 68 (2005), 313–34.

Stachniewski, John, *The Persecutory Imagination: English Puritanism and the Literature of Religious Despair* (Oxford, 1991).

Stanwood, P. G., 'Donne's Art of Preaching and the Reconstruction of Tertullian', *John Donne Journal*, 15 (1996), 163–9.

—— 'Donne's Reinvention of the Fathers: Sacred Truths Suitably Expressed', in *Sacred and Profane: Secular and Devotional Interplay in Early Modern British Literature*, ed. Helen Wilcox, Richard Todd, and Alasdair MacDonald (Amsterdam, 1996), 195–201.

—— and Asals, Heather Ross (eds.), *Donne and the Theology of Language* (Columbia, 1986).

Steinmetz, David, *Luther and Staupitz: An Essay in the Intellectual Origins of the Protestant Reformation* (Durham, NC, 1980).

Stinger, Charles, *Humanism and the Church Fathers: Ambrogio Traversari (1386–1439) and Christian Antiquity in the Italian Renaissance* (Albany, 1976).

Stock, Brian, *Augustine the Reader: Meditation, Self-Knowledge, and the Ethics of Interpretation* (Cambridge, Mass., 1996).

Stubbs, John, *John Donne: The Reformed Soul* (London, 2006).

Studer, Basil, *Augustinus, De Trinitate: Eine Einführung* (Paderborn, 2005).

Sullivan, Ceri, *The Rhetoric of the Conscience in Donne, Herbert, and Vaughan* (Oxford, 2008).

Sullivan, Ernest W., 'The Genesis and Transmission of Donne's *Biathanatos*', *The Library*, 5 (1976), 52–72.

Targoff, Ramie, *John Donne, Body and Soul* (Chicago, 2008).

Tentler, Thomas N., *Sin and Confession on the Eve of the Reformation* (Princeton, 1977).

TeSelle, Eugene, *Augustine the Theologian* (New York, 1970).

Thiselton, Anthony C., *The Two Horizons: New Testament Hermeneutics and Philosophical Description with Special Reference to Bultmann, Gadamer, and Wittgenstein* (Exeter, 1980).

Towers, S. Mutchow, *Control of Religious Printing in Early Stuart England* (Woodbridge, 2003).

Trapp, Damasus, 'Augustinian Theology of the 14th Century. Notes on Editions, Marginalia, Opinions and Book-Lore', *Augustiniana*, 6 (1965), 146–274.

—— 'Hiltalinger's Augustinian Quotations', *Augustiniana*, 4 (1954), 412–49.

Trevor, Douglas, 'Donne and Scholarly Melancholy', *Studies in English Literature 1500–1900*, 40 (2000), 81–102.

Tutino, Stefania, *Law and Conscience: Catholicism in Early Modern England, 1570–1625* (Aldershot, 2007).

Tyacke, Nicholas, *Anti-Calvinists: The Rise of English Arminianism c.1590–1640* (Oxford, 1989).

Vessey, Mark, 'The *Citie of God* (1610) and the London Virginia Company', *Augustinian Studies*, 30 (1999), 257–81.

—— 'Consulting the Fathers: Invention and Meditation in Donne's Sermon on Psalm 51:7 ("Purge me with hyssope")', *John Donne Journal*, 11 (1992), 99–110.

Vessey, Mark, 'English Translations of the Latin Fathers, 1517–1611', in *The Reception of the Church Fathers in the West: From the Carolingians to the Maurists*, ed. Irena Backus, 2 vols. (Leiden, 1997), 2.775–835.

—— 'John Donne (1572–1631) in the Company of Augustine: Patristic Culture and Literary Profession in the English Renaissance', *Revue des Études Augustiniennes*, 39 (1993), 173–201.

Visser, Arnoud, 'Reading Augustine through Erasmus' Eyes: Humanist Scholarship and Paratextual Guidance in the Wake of the Reformation', *Erasmus Society of Rotterdam Yearbook*, 28 (2008), 67–90.

Walsham, Alexandra, *Charitable Hatred: Tolerance and Intolerance in England, 1500–1700* (Manchester, 2006).

Ware, Tracy, 'Donne and Augustine: A Qualification', *Notes and Queries*, NS 30 (1983), 425–7.

Warfield, B. B., *Calvin and Augustine* (Philadelphia, 1956).

Watt, Tessa, *Cheap Print and Popular Piety, 1550–1640* (Cambridge, 1991).

Weinrich, Harald, *Lethe: Kunst und Kritik des Vergessens* (Munich, 1997).

Wetzel, Richard, 'Staupitz Augustinianus: An Account of the Reception of Augustine in the Tübingen Sermons', in *Via Augustini: Augustine in the later Middle Ages, Renaissance, and Reformation: Essays in Honor of Damasus Trapp, O.S.A.*, ed. Heiko A. Oberman and Frank A. James, III, in co-operation with Eric Leland Saak (Leiden, 1991), 72–115.

White, Peter, *Predestination, Policy and Polemic: Conflict and Consensus in the English Church from the Reformation to the Civil War* (Cambridge, 1992).

Williams, Arnold, 'Commentaries on Genesis as a Basis of Hexaemeral Material in the Literature of the Late Renaissance', *Studies in Philology*, 34(1937), 191–208.

Wilson, Luke, *Theaters of Intention: Drama and the Law in Early Modern England* (Stanford, 2000).

Windsor, Graham, 'The Controversy between Roman Catholics and Anglicans from Elizabeth to the Revolution' (unpub. Ph.D. dissertation, University of Cambridge, 1967).

Wollman, Richard, '"The Press and the Fire": Print and Manuscript Culture in Donne's Circle', *Studies in English Literature, 1500–1900*, 33 (1993), 85–97.

Woods, Thomas, *English Casuistry of the Seventeenth Century and its Relations with Medieval and Jesuit Casuistry* (Leeds, 1947).

Wright, David F., 'Augustine: His Exegesis and Hermeneutics', in *Hebrew Bible/Old Testament: The History of Its Interpretation*, ed. Magne Saebø, 2 vols. (Göttingen, 1991), 1.67–89.

Yates, Frances, *The Art of Memory* (Chicago, 1966).

Young, R. V., 'Donne and Bellarmine', *John Donne Journal*, 19 (2000), 223–34.

Zumkeller, Adolar, 'Die Tugend der Demut nach der geistlichen Lehre des hl. Augustinus', *Cor Unum*, 40 (1982), 115–23.

Zwicker, Steven, 'Reading the Margins: Politics and the Habits of Appropriation', in *Refiguring Revolutions*, ed. Kevin Sharpe and Steven Zwicker (Berkeley, 1998), 101–15.

Index

accuracy 44, 103
Adlington, Hugh 191
Against Adimantus (Augustine) 228
Against Faustus the Manichee (Augustine) 101
Against Gaudentius, a Donatist Bishop
   (Augustine) 139, 143–4
Alain de Lille (Alanus de Insulis) 96
Alcuin 154
Alfonso, Archbishop of Toledo 42–3
Ambrose 33, 34, 73
   in Lombard's *Sentences* 95
Amerbach, Johann 32–3, 35–7
Ames, William 147, 166
analogy 163–4
Anatomie of Absurditie (Nashe) 47
Andrewes, Lancelot 58, 230
Annales Ecclesiastici (Baronius) 93
anthologies and intermediaries 61–2
anti-Calvinism and anti-Calvinists 58, 195
anti-Puritans 39
apathy 113, 114
Apello Caesarem (Montagu) 60
Apostolic Fathers *see* Fathers
Aquinas, Thomas 5–6, 22, 88–9, 124, 219, 220
   dismissed 101–3
   on divine ideas 84–5
   on divine mimesis 85–6
   as mediator 82, 84–6
Archaeology of Knowledge (Foucault) 4
Aristotle 61, 168, 172
Arminians and Arminianism 182–3, 185
Arnobius 34
Arte of Divine Meditation, The (Hall) 109, 131
Askew, Egeon 39
Athanasius 34
Athenagoras 35
Augustine *see also individual titles*
   Amerbach edition 41, 94, 104
   attacked by Donne 149, 159, 160–1
   available editions 32–3, 35
   biography 68–9
   in Candlemas 1627 sermon 220
   on cognition 210, 210, n. 11
   Donne's familiarity with 104, 107
   on Genesis 66, 198
   hermeneutics 16–17
   importance of 1–2, 8, 11–12
   and Jerome 210–11
   and Laud 188
   in Lombard's *Sentences* 95
   Louvain edition 39–40
   and Luther 173

   not quoted 207–8
   number of quotations from 3, 27–8, 189
   as polemicist 152–3
   as reader 9–10, 15–16
   recommended by Drexel 63
   self-quotation 73
   as source for other theologians 29
   textual allusions in 2
   on vision of God 207
Augustine the Reader (Stock) 15
Augustini et Chrysostomi theologia in communes
   locos digesta (Corvinus) 97
Augustinus, Archbishop of Tarragona 59–60, 61
authenticity 44

Babylonian Captivity (Luther) 30
Bacon, Francis 168–9
Backus, Irena 34
Baker, J. H. 179
Baldwin, T. W. 77
Baronius, Caesar 92–3
Barthes, Roland 8
Bartholomew of Urbino 61, 97–8
Basil 34, 42
Bastwick, John 58
beatific vision 205, 206–7, 223
Bellarmine, Robert 22, 27, 82, 87–8, 92, 100
Bellum Catilinae (Sallust) 2
Biathanatos (Donne) 57, 160–1, 225
   and Aquinas 103
   and Bellarmine 27
   casuistry in 138, 141, 226
   on charity 12, 22, 142–4, 148, 230
   on Lombard 52
   misquotation in 61
   misreading of Augustine 139–40, 153–4,
     156–7
   number of references to Augustine 28, 40
   patristic references in 87, 89, 90–1, 93, 98,
     100–1
   polemical targets 92
   on reading 47–8, 60
   textual protocols in 26, 49, 63–4
   on truth 181
Bible *see also* Vulgate 13, 64
   Donne's copy 89
biblical commentaries 89–92
biblical concordances 81
Bibliotheca Patrum 25
Bigne, Marguerin de la 35, 39
Blair, Ann 63
Bodius, Hermann 94, 97